Wissenschaftliche Untersuchungen
zum Neuen Testament · 2. Reihe

Herausgeber/Editor
Jörg Frey

Mitherausgeber / Associate Editors
Friedrich Avemarie · Judith Gundry-Volf
Martin Hengel · Otfried Hofius · Hans-Josef Klauck

 186

Willis Hedley Salier

The Rhetorical Impact of the Sēmeia in the Gospel of John

Mohr Siebeck

WILLIS HEDLEY SALIER, born 1959; 2003 Ph.D.; currently Lecturer in New Testament and Ministry at Moore Theological College, Sydney, Australia.

ISBN 3-16-148407-X
ISSN 0340-9570 (Wissenschaftliche Untersuchungen zum Neuen Testament 2. Reihe)

Die Deutsche Bibliothek lists this publication in the Deutsche Nationalbibliographie; detailed bibliographic data is available in the Internet at *http://dnb.ddb.de*.

The book was printed by Druckpartner Rübelmann GmbH in Hemsbach on non-aging paper and bound by Buchbinderei Schaumann in Darmstadt.

Printed in Germany.

Preface

This study seeks to provide a richer, more integrated perspective on the σημεῖα as they function within the final form of the Fourth Gospel. Previous research has discussed in detail an alleged 'signs source' and given less attention to the function of the σημεῖα within the Fourth Gospel's rhetorical purpose. In particular, little account has been taken of how the σημεῖα would have been received by the Gospel's early audience.

The investigation proceeds via two complementary angles of inquiry. The first angle moves outwards from the text to the early audience of the Gospel, asking how the text impacts upon the reader with respect to the general references to σημεῖα, and also the detail of the particular σημεῖα narratives. The second angle moves inwards from the early audience to the text. This is achieved via a socio-historical investigation that draws on vocabulary and situations presented in the Gospel and asks how an early audience, broadly conceived, might have received the σημεῖα language and narratives. It is hoped that this study will contribute to the Johannine conversation by illustrating further the narrative artistry of the Gospel, helping its modern readers to better appreciate its impact in its initial context, and highlighting further facets of the portrait of Jesus contained within its pages.

This book is a lightly revised version of a doctoral thesis submitted to Cambridge University in 2003. Gratitude must be expressed to Mohr Siebeck Publishing House for accepting this work and their efficiency in giving the guidance necessary to bring it to print. I would also like to thank Prof. Dr. Jörg Frey and Dr. Henning Ziebritzki for their valuable recommendations and advice during the process.

Over the course of the three or so years that it took to produce the initial work one accumulates an almost incalculable list of those who ought to be acknowledged and thanked. Sue and I are extremely grateful to the Lord for his abundant provision through so many people and in so many ways. Throughout the process of research and writing Prof. Graham Stanton provided wise supervision, skilfully blurring the lines between professional attention to task and personal care and interest. I am also thankful to the examiners of the thesis, Dr. Andrew Lincoln and Dr. James Carleton Paget, for their incisive evaluation of my work and their stimulating comments, which still provide cause for reflection on the issues that I have attempted to explore.

For the necessities of life (and some of the luxuries) we owe thanks to many people and organisations: the Moore College Council, the Joan Augusta

McKenzie Travelling Scholarship, the Sydney Diocese Educational and Book Committee, St Edmund's College Tutorial Committee, Cambridge University Faculty of Divinity (German Fund), St Martin's Church, Kensington NSW, St Edmund's College Commonwealth and Overseas Studentship provided scholarships and timely grants. I owe a special debt of gratitude to Vanda and Debbie Gould for their financial and spiritual support over many years. The Millard family also proved to be a 'home away from home away from home' on more than one occasion. Many other individuals, too numerous to name, have been generous to a fault.

We are grateful for the vast crowd of family, friends and colleagues who have prayed, read our interminable emails and letters, and encouraged us through visits and correspondence. My own family have always been enthusiastic in their support, even if at times they may have wondered about it all. Unfortunately my father will never get to read the finished product but he always thought that I could do it; and I think in the end he understood why I was doing it. His memory is dear.

The congregation at St Andrews the Great were a constant source of encouragement. The preaching and general ministry there kept our priorities where they ought to be. The girls were happy at school so that meant we were happy at home. The Janis provided transport for a year, incentives to both run and pray, while I am especially thankful to Fiona for taking on the arduous task of reading and attempting to correct my impoverished colonial expression! Sandra den Otter and Simon Moore were also extremely generous with both time and comments in this regard. The Waldocks also provided support and friendship in so many ways not the least being a family during the final Christmas. Our other 'congregation', the staff, and scholars (and their partners) at Tyndale House, under the wise leadership of Bruce Winter were a rich source of friendship and stimulation.

Much has happened (both good and bad) to my family, friends and country during the time it took to complete this dissertation. It was some great relief in the midst of all this to be studying the Fourth Gospel and be constantly reminded of the testimony to the Lord Jesus that John has recorded. He urges us to believe in Jesus, who is both able and willing to make good the most marvellous promises concerning eternal life. At times the grip on those promises was a little slippery but thankfully the Lord has a stronger grip than I do. To him be the glory.

During this time my wife, Sue, and daughters, Talitha and Anna, were my constant companions. They were unfailingly positive when it mattered. To them this work is finally dedicated for their patience and love in bearing with a husband and father who is always (it seems) 'just going to his desk for a while'.

Table of Contents

Preface V

Chapter 1: Reading the Signs

1.1 Previous Studies 1
1.2 The Present Study 5
    1.2.1 Three Issues 7
        1.2.1.1 Background and Foreground 8
        1.2.1.2 Implied Reader and Authorial Audience 9
        1.2.1.3 The Nature of the Audience 10
1.3 Moving Forward 15

Chapter 2: Speaking of σημεῖα

2.1 The Septuagint 18
    2.1.1 Overview 18
    2.1.2 Signs in Egypt 20
    2.1.3 Signs and the Prophets 23
2.2 Graeco-Roman Usage 25
    2.2.1 Introduction 25
    2.2.2 General Use 26
        2.2.2.1 Philo and Josephus 26
        2.2.2.2 Summary Remarks concerning General Use 27
    2.2.3 Religious Contexts 27
        2.2.3.1 Assessing Signs in the General Context 28
        2.2.3.2 Josephus 30
            2.2.3.2.1 Josephus: Summary 32
        2.2.3.3 Philo 33
        2.2.3.4 Summary: Religious Use 33
    2.2.4 The Vocabulary of Proof 34
        2.2.4.1 Aristotle 36
        2.2.4.2 Rhetorica ad Herrenium 37
        2.2.4.3 Cicero 38
        2.2.4.4 Quintilian 38
        2.2.4.5 The Vocabulary of Proof: Summary 38
2.3 Early Christianity 39
    2.3.1 General Observations 39
    2.3.2 The Synoptic Gospels 40
    2.3.3 Acts and Paul 43
2.4 Summary 43

Chapter 3: The Beginning of the Signs: σημεῖον in John 1–4

3.1 Overview of Chapters 1–4... 46
3.2 The Occurrences of σημεῖον.. 49
    3.2.1 The Occurrences of σημεῖον: Text to Reader 49
        3.2.1.1 The Beginning and the End of the Signs (Jn 2.1–11, 18)............... 49
        3.2.1.2 Requesting a Sign (Jn 2.23–25)...................................... 52
        3.2.1.3 Reading the Signs (Jn 3.2).. 54
        3.2.1.4 Unless You See Signs (Jn 4.48) 55
        3.2.1.5 The Second Sign (Jn 4.54).. 59
    3.2.2 The Occurrences of σημεῖον: Reader to Text 60
3.3. The Sign Narratives.. 61
        3.3.1.1 The Wedding at Cana (Jn 2.1–11): Writing the Sign 62
        3.3.1.2 The Wedding at Cana (Jn 2.1–11): Reading the Sign 64
        3.3.2.1 The Healing of an Official's Son (Jn 4.43–54): Writing the Sign 70
        3.3.2.2 The Healing of an Official's Son (Jn 4.43–54): Reading the Sign 72
3.4 Summary... 75

Chapter 4: Controversial Signs: σημεῖον in John 5–10

4.1 Overview of Chapters 5–10 77
4.2 The Occurrences of σημεῖον.. 79
    4.2.1 Occurrences of σημεῖον: Text to Reader...................................... 79
        4.2.1.1 Signs and Works (Jn 5.20, 36) 79
        4.2.1.2 Reading the Signs (Jn 6.2).. 82
        4.2.1.3 Signs of the Prophet? (Jn 6.14) 82
        4.2.1.4 Seeking Signs and Seeing Signs (Jn 6.30)........................ 84
        4.2.1.5 Signs of the Messiah? (Jn 7.31) 86
        4.2.1.6 A Man From God? (Jn 9.16) 89
        4.2.1.7 Messiah Again (Jn 10.24–38)....................................... 90
        4.2.1.8 John Did No Sign (Jn 10.41)... 91
        4.2.1.9 Text to Reader: Summary... 92
    4.2.2 The Occurrences of σημεῖον: Reader to Text 93
4.3 The Sign Narratives.. 96
        4.3.1.1 The Healing at the Pool (Jn 5.1–18): Writing the Sign 96
        4.3.1.2 The Healing at the Pool (Jn 5.1–18): Reading the Sign 99
        4.3.2.1 Feeding a Multitude (Jn 6.1–15): Writing the Sign........................ 102
        4.3.2.2 Feeding a Multitude (Jn 6.1–15): Reading the Sign........................ 104
        4.3.3.1 Walking on the Sea (Jn 6.16–21): Writing the Sign........................ 107
        4.3.3.2 Walking on the Sea (Jn 6.16–21): Reading the Sign........................ 109
        4.3.4.1 Healing a Man Born Blind (Jn 9.1–41): Writing the Sign 111
        4.3.4.2 Healing a Man Born Blind (Jn 9.1–41): Reading the Sign 114
4.4 Summary... 117

Chapter 5: Signs of Life: σημεῖον in John 11–12

5.1 Overview of Chapters 11–12 120
5.2 The Occurrences of σημεῖον 120
    5.2.1 Occurrences of σημεῖον: Text to Reader 120
        5.2.1.1 Seeing the Signs (Jn 11.45–47) 121
        5.2.1.2 Signs and the Hour (Jn 12.18) 122
        5.2.1.3 The Failure of the Signs? (Jn 12.37) 125
    5.2.2 The Occurrences of σημεῖον: Reader to Text 128
5.3 The Sign Narratives 129
        5.3.1.1 The Raising of Lazarus (Jn 11.1–44): Writing the Sign 129
        5.3.1.2 The Raising of Lazarus (Jn 11.1–44): Reading the Sign 135
5.4 Summary 139

Chapter 6: The 'Sign of Signs': σημεῖον in John 13–21

6.1 Overview of Chapters 13–21 142
6.2 The Occurrences of σημεῖον 143
    6.2.1 'Believe the Works' (Jn 14.10–12) 144
    6.2.2 Signs and Judgement (Jn 15.22–24) 146
    6.2.3 Signs and the Purpose of the Gospel (Jn 20.30–31) 147
        6.2.3.1 'These Signs are Written' 148
        6.2.3.2 Summary 154
    6.2.4 John 21.24–25 155
6.3 The Sign Narratives 155
        6.3.1.1 The Death and Resurrection of Jesus (Jn 18–20): Writing the Sign 155
        6.3.1.1a The Resurrection Account 161
        6.3.1.2 The Death and Resurrection of Jesus (Jn 18–20): Reading the Sign 163
6.4 Summary 169

Chapter 7: Conclusions

7.1 σημεῖα in the Fourth Gospel 172
7.2 σημεῖον and the Rhetorical Impact of the Fourth Gospel 173
7.3 Thinking Further 176
7.4 Jesus: The True Life-Giver 178

Bibliography 179
Index of Authors 207
Index of References 210
Index of Subjects 230

Chapter 1

Reading the Signs

This study examines the language of σημεῖον in the Fourth Gospel with special attention to its function in the Gospel's narrative and rhetorical strategy. The topic has a pivotal importance in Johannine studies. The prominence and importance of the term σημεῖον in the presentation of the Fourth Gospel is clear[1] and an understanding of the term is one of the keys to understanding the Gospel itself.[2] The reasons for this prominence in the Fourth Gospel remain elusive despite numerous studies devoted to various aspects of its use and meaning.

The approach adopted in this study integrates areas covered by previous examinations of the σημεῖον material with a view to elucidating the rhetorical impact of the term itself and the narratives it denotes. Examination of the biblical materials moves among the poles of author, text and reader. Most studies tend to focus on one or other of these poles. The question of the rhetorical strategy of the Fourth Gospel demands that a more even account be given. The quest is for the nature of the inter-relationships between the three, asking how the author connects with his audience via the text to achieve his stated purposes. In the light of this dynamic the questions are posed afresh: Why has this term σημεῖον been chosen? How does it operate within the rhetorical strategy of the Fourth Gospel?

1.1 Previous Studies

Much research on the signs has been conducted under the dominant paradigm of the search for the putative signs source of the Gospel. This was most famously promulgated by Rudolf Bultmann in his commentary.[3] Bultmann proposed that the source presented a popular Christology, in which Jesus is

---

[1] This is signalled by the presence of the term in two major summary statements in the Gospel: 12.37; 20.30.

[2] Nicol 1972: 1. Cf. Riga (1963: 402), 'Perhaps no single word can give such a profound insight into the whole theology of the Fourth Gospel as the word *sēmeion*.'

[3] Bultmann (1971: 113) noted the previous efforts of Faure, Wellhausen, Spitta and Meyer. For a detailed history of the development of thinking concerning the signs source as well as accompanying criticism see van Belle 1994.

regarded as a Hellenistic 'theios aner' because of his miracles. The author of the Gospel[4] deliberately sets this against his own deeper and more accurate Christology of Jesus as the Word of God who confronts mankind with the basic questions of existence. While the Hellenistic elements and possible gnostic influences of Bultmann's reconstruction have been all but repudiated, the search for the signs source has continued unabated to the present day. The work of Robert Fortna provides, arguably, the most complete account of the signs source.[5]

The most recent summary and critique of this thoroughly worked debate is to be found in a monograph by Gilbert van Belle.[6] Van Belle offers a comprehensive analysis of the major players in the debate and concludes with a detailed criticism. Differences in elaboration of the content of the source, overly subjective criteria for distinguishing between Johannine and non-Johannine elements, lack of unanimity as to date, origin, *Sitz im Leben* are a few of the areas covered. The most damaging evidence comes in an examination of the stylistic criteria employed to discern the signs source. Van Belle collates and compares the results of numerous studies of Johannine style and demonstrates clearly that Johannine style characteristics are 'nearly evenly distributed throughout the gospel and that they offer no evidence for source reconstructions'.[7] While there are still defenders of the signs source, the tide appears to be turning towards an appreciation of the difficulty of delineating its parameters, even if it is conceded to exist.[8] And, even if the source did exist, the question still remains as to why the *source* found σημεῖον to be a useful term and why John saw this as a useful term to adopt and use in his Gospel.

A small number of studies on the signs have approached the question from outside the perspective of the signs source. Four will be briefly mentioned. Sebald Hofbeck's concern was to explain the origin of the use of σημεῖον apart from source theories. [9] This origin was instead located in John's Jewish sensibility concerning the action of God in history, as expressed in the Hebrew Scriptures. Hofbeck suggested that the symbol-laden potential of the use of the expression by the prophets was creatively appropriated, and reflected upon in the light of the incarnation.[10] Hofbeck was chiefly interested

---

[4] Henceforth referred to as John. The precise identity of the author is not relevant to a study of his achievement in this text.

[5] Fortna 1988.

[6] Van Belle 1994.

[7] Van Belle 1994: 373. An appendix to his work on pp. 405–17 lists these characteristics.

[8] Cf. comments of Kysar (1999: 40), '(the) argument that source criticism is not a profitable enterprise in Johannine studies…is precisely right'.

[9] Hofbeck 1970.

[10] Hofbeck (1970: 205–12).

in the conceptual and theological origins of the term and took little account of relationships with the original audience of the text.

The search for the origins of the use of the term has been further pursued in the Hebrew Scriptures, in a series of shorter studies, with various combinations of exodus motifs, prophetic usage, wisdom motifs, and even the psalms mentioned.[11] The Hebrew Scriptures are the appropriate place to look for the origin of the usage in terms of its conceptual background.[12] However, it is suggested that the usage and impact of the term is better explained as a total function of the interaction between this conceptual background, the audience, and the fabric of the narrative in which the interaction takes place. This is to be explored in the course of this work.

Wolfgang Bittner explicitly critiqued signs source theories and pointed out, correctly, that a preoccupation with such theories had displaced the important question of the meaning and function of the term σημεῖον.[13] His study sought to redress this and set out to investigate the relationship between signs and faith in the Fourth Gospel as well as the testimony of the signs to the messianic status of Jesus. His persuasive presentation demonstrated a consistently positive relationship between signs and faith in the Gospel. That is, that the signs are recorded with the express intention of leading the reader to faith and that faith based on signs is not an inferior expression of faith. He further suggested that the roots of the terminology lay in the messianic thought of Isaiah.[14] While his study deals with the final form of the text and eschews any search for sources, it is more theological in its emphasis. No attention is paid to issues of audience reception. This study seeks to integrate the discussion of the sign language and narratives into the wider literary themes and thrust of the Gospel as well as take greater account of the rhetorical impact of the language and narratives on the early audience.

The move to a more literary approach to the biblical texts was taken up in Johannine studies with the publication of Culpepper's study in 1983.[15] This approach emphasises the final form of the texts and employs methods more at home in the literary world of narratology. Since 1983 there have been an increasing number of studies adopting this broad approach and focussing on various aspects of the Gospel's 'narrative art'. However, comparatively few

---

[11] See for example, Schnackenburg (1968: 515–28); Clark (1983); Kiley (1988); Johns and Miller (1994: 526–7); Köstenberger, (1995: 90–92).

[12] Especially with the increasing recognition of the importance of the Hebrew Scriptures generally for the Fourth Gospel. See, amongst others, Barrett (1947), R.H. Smith (1962); Brown (1968: lix-lxi); Hanson (1991). Hofbeck also effectively critiques other alternatives such as the thought of Philo and the Qumran community (pp. 199–202).

[13] Bittner 1987: 14–16

[14] Bittner 1987: 146–50, 245–8.

[15] Culpepper 1983.

have investigated the language of σημεῖον at any sort of length and depth.[16] Christian Welck's recent study of the signs is one that purports to do this.[17] He critiques previous attempts to isolate the sources of the Gospel and suggests that a narrative approach will avoid the problem of isolating the signs from their context, meaning that they can be seen as an integrated part of the Gospel's presentation.[18] He proposes that the evangelist has combined historical narrative with apocalyptic to create a new literary form in order to communicate the eschatological dimension of Jesus' miracles.[19] The miracle form found in the Gospel, designated as a σημεῖον, is the result. The signs are not merely miracles performed by Jesus during his earthly ministry but also literary entities designed to elicit faith in the Gospel's readers.[20] While Welck's study is a synchronic reading in that it focuses upon the final form of the text, it is not an entirely satisfactory literary reading in that little attention is paid to matters such as plot, character and theme. In effect, it is a form-critical study. The observation that this form was created to encompass both historical narrative and apocalyptic revelation is stimulating but the form itself is very general (person's need—narration of miracle—need has been met through the miracle—reactions to the miracle). Welck also concedes that the form is not consistently applied by the evangelist because of his desire to provoke his readers.[21] The nature of the audience of the Gospel and possible reception of the narrated signs is not discussed. His rigidly applied synchronic perspective also means that issues of Jewish messianic expectations and the understanding of the signs in the context of the Hebrew Scriptures are not explored. This is despite the fact that elements in the text would appear to invite this kind of examination. Such observations point to the limitations of a purely synchronic literary analysis. As helpful as such an analysis might prove to be, attention needs to be paid to the text, cotext and context for a complete analysis to be made of the rhetorical impact.[22] This inevitably leads to consideration of historical and background issues as well as a consideration of the cultural context into which the Gospel was originally communicated

Michael Labahn's concern is to provide an exhaustive account of the miracle narratives of the Gospel with a view to tracing the history of the traditions that lie behind the narratives as well as seeing how the redaction of

---

[16] Johns and Miller (1994: 520–21 n.6) remark on this apparent lack.

[17] Welck 1994.

[18] Welck 1994: 41-48.

[19] Welck: 1994: 236–9.

[20] Welck 1994: 289–93.

[21] Welck 1994: 253–4. Cf. criticisms by Labahn (1999b: 186) who points to the flexibility of form in the miracle stories.

[22] Cotterell and Turner (1986: 16) use these terms. The text is the actual words used; the cotext is the surrounding sentences, paragraphs and chapters; and the context is the sociological and historical setting of the text.

the narratives serves a new purpose within the context of the Gospel as it is received.[23] He points to the variety of different literary techniques that the evangelist uses in taking up the miracle traditions.[24] Different literary situations are created that serve different aims within the narrative as a whole. Various relationships with the formal structure of the tradition are discerned but overall Labahn suggests that the literary creativity serves a consistent hermeneutical strategy. This strategy is to bring the readers/hearers into contact with the narrated Jesus and therefore the life that he will bring according to the Father's will.[25] In the course of his excavation of the miracle traditions he broadens the discussion to consider the origins of features of the miracle narratives and in doing so begins to take in features of the broader cultural context. This thesis seeks to supplement his comprehensive analysis by locating the sign narratives within the more general context of the σημεῖον language used in the Gospel,[26] and considering the possible reception of this language and the narratives by the early audience of the Gospel.[27]

1.2 The Present Study

It is suggested, then, that there is room for a study of the signs in the Fourth Gospel that focuses on the rhetorical function and early reception of both the language of σημεῖον generally and, more specifically, the σημεῖα narratives in the Fourth Gospel. This study enters the continuing conversation in Johannine studies concerning the language of σημεῖον by focussing on the usage in the final form of the Gospel's narrative. The intention is to apply more thoroughly the insights of narrative criticism and also a 'conservative reader response'[28] approach to the sign language and narratives of the Fourth Gospel in a way that takes particular account of the possible early audience reception of the Gospel. In short, the focus will be on the story and the

---

[23] Labahn 1999a; 1999b.

[24] Labahn (1999b) provides a concise summary of some of the major findings of his more detailed work.

[25] Labahn 1999a: 501.

[26] Labahn's focus is on what he sees as the redaction of the miracle tradition and so he concentrates solely on the sign narratives.

[27] Labahn also works very much within the community model that is a dominant feature of Johannine scholarship (Cf 1999a: 466-72). This leads him to engage conflict models within the 'Johannine community' (30–33) and also, in an attenuated way, between the community and the synagogue (pp. 34–41). This study seeks to think about the issue of audience more broadly.

[28] Vanhoozer 1995: 306–7.

reader.[29] This will produce an account that better integrates the meaning of the sign language and the narratives this term designates into the wider themes and concerns of the Gospel itself as well as elucidating the rhetorical impact in its original cultural context.

In order to broach the interface between text and the early readers two complementary directions of inquiry will be undertaken.[30] The first direction moves outwards from the text to the reader. In examining this perspective on the sign language and narratives, the control of the reading experience is given to the text.[31] The analysis in this instance seeks to identify and explain the devices used in the text to produce the desired effect in the reader. The usual figure adduced at this point is that of the implied reader. This reader consists of 'the textual elements that invite the actual reader to respond to the text in certain ways'.[32] This reader is a textual construct who responds perfectly to every interpretative suggestion that the implied author (the textual counterpart of the implied reader) makes in the work. The implied reader adopts completely the assumptions and point of view of the work itself. In this part of the analysis, the meaning of the narrative will be elucidated by following the clues placed in the text by the author. These clues are 'perfectly' read by the implied reader and at the same time shape the creation of the implied reader in the narrative.[33] This analysis will be undertaken on the seventeen occurrences of σημεῖον in the text, and also with respect to the sign narratives. It must be admitted at once that the figure of the implied reader is an interpretational conceit. The reading offered under the guise of the implied reader is the provisional attempt of the 'real reader' who is writing these words at this point in time. This 'real reader' may well have missed many things or have 'over-read' as well, and is on the way to becoming the implied reader as with successive readings he too is being trained by the text to become its implied reader. Nonetheless, from the point of view of literary analysis, the figure of implied reader remains a useful construct.

The second direction of inquiry moves inwards from the reader to the text. Here the attempt is made to try and understand the persuasive impact of the Johannine presentation by asking what might the early audience bring to the

---

[29] This is the pithy summary of Moore (1989: *xxi*), though he would doubtless critique the conservative work done here in the name of both.

[30] I am indebted to Bolt (1997: 1–2) for this procedure.

[31] In a sense this means the author, though in narrative terms it is the control of the implied author, through a narrator, that is being examined. The terms narrator and John will be used interchangeably in this thesis.

[32] Van Iersel 1998: 17–18.

[33] Eco (1981: 7–8) speaks of a text presupposing a model of competence in the reader and working in the text to build that reader's competence.

text from their cultural background or repertoire as they hear the Gospel.[34] It is anticipated that the examination of the use of σημεῖον in the broader context of a variety of relevant ancient literary sources will help to see more clearly the reasons for the choice of the term as a centrepiece of the Fourth Gospel's presentation of Jesus, in the light of its potential early reception. Also, this investigation will elucidate further the impact that the selected sign narratives make within the persuasive purposes of the Gospel. By tapping into the broader cultural context of the early audience of the Gospel, the wider connotations of the material situations and occurrences presented in the sign narratives become clearer. This enables a better appreciation of their impact within the rhetorical purposes of the Gospel.

The convergence of these two directions of inquiry enables a more comprehensive description to be given of the function of the sign language and narratives in the Fourth Gospel. Such a description encompasses the function of the language and narratives within the Gospel's rhetorical strategy as well as an appreciation of the possible emotional impact of this language and especially the sign narratives. The sign narratives are occasionally regarded as simply providing a lead into the extended discourses that follow. This is based on the assumption that the 'word' is really where all the action of the Gospel takes place. While not denying the relationship that exists between sign and discourse in the Gospel, it is suggested that a little more time should be taken to pause and consider the effect and impact that the actual events recorded as signs might have on an audience. The events themselves, the dilemmas recorded, and their solutions also contribute to the portrait of Christ presented in the Gospel. They are more than just a lead into the discourse material.[35]

1.2.1 Three Issues

In terms of the investigation to follow, three issues need to be commented upon at greater length. The first concerns the relationship between what might be called the background and the foreground of the Gospel. The second concerns the legitimacy of an approach that attempts to bring into relationship

---

[34] The term repertoire is used by Bolt (2001: 5 n. 13) to refer to 'the prior understandings that already exist in the reader's mind before he or she reads a narrative'. Hawthorn (2000: 301) defines cultural repertoire a little more expansively as 'those cultural traits, objects, and practices to which a reader has expressive or participatory access'. Van Iersel (1998: 23–24) speaks of language, literary conventions, shared presuppositions, worldview, fund of general knowledge, and comparable experiences and ideas.

[35] Just (1997: 7) observes, with respect to studies on the healing of the blind in the Gospels, that 'since the focus of these studies is often on the "miraculous" activity of Jesus and the implications of his actions for such theological concerns as Christology or eschatology, the blind characters themselves quickly fade from view and little attention is paid to them as individuals'.

the implied reader and the early audience of the Gospel. The third concerns the composition of the Gospel's early audience.

1.2.1.1 Background and Foreground

There is a great deal of potential confusion that arises when discussing the difference, and also relationship, between the conceptual background of a work and its audience, the world behind the text and the world in front of the text.[36] Research on the Fourth Gospel has seen a considerable shift in focus concerning the sources of John's thought. In the early part of this century the search was conducted for the conceptual background of the Gospel mainly in the Hellenistic world until the discovery of the Dead Sea Scrolls. Since then the pendulum has swung markedly to seeing the conceptual background of the Fourth Gospel located within the world of Judaism. This is in fact the Gospel's own testimony (4.22). The question of conceptual background is different, though, to the question of audience and the world in front of the text. The repertoire of the audience in front of the text ought to be differentiated more clearly, as far as this might be possible, from the conceptual background of the text. It is not suggested that there is no relationship between the two, but that it is a matter of emphasis and orientation. It is a question of conceptual origins and communication strategy. The same story or concept may be communicated to different communities and groups in different ways and in fact may need to be in order to communicate it effectively.[37] Moloney's comments on this matter are appropriate,

> The Gospel of John told the old story of Jesus in a radically different fashion without betraying the roots of the original Christian tradition: the life, teaching, death and resurrection of Jesus of Nazareth. One of the reasons for these remarkable differences, might I suggest, was an awareness of the new world into which Jesus' story had to be announced...The Gospel of John builds bridges from one socio-cultural and religious world... into another... and in doing so serves as a paradigm for all who seek to tell and re-tell the story of Jesus.[38]

There is little doubt that the audience to whom the particular piece of communication is addressed will colour and shape the presentation but this is different to saying that the origins of the conceptual content of the communication are to be found there as well. The difference may be fine but it is real. Such a distinction acknowledges that a skilled communicator is in command of her material and couches it in terms that accurately communicate

---

[36] The terms can be found in Moloney (1998: 13).

[37] G. Ebeling (1971: 265) suggests that 'in some cases the same word can be said to another time only by being said differently'.

[38] Moloney 2002: 649.

across a cultural or conceptual divide without the essential message being necessarily contaminated in the process. All of this is to say that the nature of the audience may go some way to accounting for the form and emphasis of a work but not necessarily the conceptual content and origins of the material. The reader is important but so is the author. Authors are important but so also will be an examination of the social context, as far as it can be established, of the situation into which their writing is released. Both examining how an author communicates and asking what might be heard in this communication by a real flesh-and-blood audience are relevant and complementary perspectives for investigation.

1.2.1.2 Implied Reader and Authorial Audience

Literary studies focus on the final form of the text and use the figure of the implied reader in their analysis. The implied reader is normally seen to be a purely textual construct and therefore not to be confused with any real reader, past or present.[39] There are three good reasons, however, for attempting to broach the relationship of this textual construct to the world of the early, or authorial, audience of the Gospel.[40]

First, from a historical perspective, there is a relationship between the authorial audience and the implied reader. The point is that while the implied reader may very well be a textual construct, it remains the creation of a real author communicating via a specific language at a specific place and time. Unavoidably features from this wider context will influence the portrait of the implied reader and make the move to examine the relationship between the intended audience/early readers of the text and the implied reader a necessary one for comprehension of the text. This would appear to be especially so for a work that is seeking to persuade.

Secondly, an ethical reason proceeds from this observation. The original addressees of the text have some sort of right or priority when it comes to the interpretative task. With respect to the Fourth Gospel, this is based on the 'you' (plural) address in 20.31. Motyer makes the point that here is a group, which is definable by historical investigation, to whom this text is addressed.[41] A relationship is clearly established at this point between the

---

[39] Vorster (1989: 35–36) warns that the 'reader in the text' cannot be used to go directly to the 'flesh-and-blood original readers'.

[40] What follows is indebted to the discussion of Rabinowitz (1977: 121–41), Culpepper (1983: 205–227) and Moloney (1993: 9–22). Culpepper (1983: 206) defines the authorial audience as the 'real' audience for whom the author is writing, about whom certain assumptions have to be made. He suggests that most authors try and keep the distance between the real audience and the authorial audience to a minimum. Moloney's term 'the intended reader' appears to cover the same ground.

[41] Motyer 1997a: 115–6.

implied reader and the intended audience.[42] Motyer suggests further that the members of this group are the natural 'owners' of the text. 'They' have the right to describe the precise force of the arguments presented in the text that are intended to move them to a particular response.[43]

Thirdly, from the hermeneutical perspective of later appropriation of the text, van Iersel points out the necessity of this interpretative move. He states that 'one of the principal means of bridging or at least diminishing the distance between later readers and the text is examination of the presumed effect of the story on its original audience'.[44] While he concedes the problematic and speculative nature of this enterprise, the necessity remains. There is some justification, then, for probing the text for indications of the authorial audience and bringing these observations into relationship with the figure of the implied reader.

1.2.1.3 The Nature of the Audience

Finally, how broadly or narrowly ought the authorial audience of the Gospel be conceived? This is an important issue for a topic such as signs, which are 'read' or 'heard' in a cultural context and will draw their meaning and significance from their location in that context. What might be the reasonably expected components of the cultural repertoire of the early audience of the Gospel? This will depend upon how the early audience is conceived.

The authorial audience of the Fourth Gospel can be conceived of in quite broad terms. This breadth is posited in terms of both ethnic makeup and Christian experience and would apply whether one adheres to a view that sees the Gospel written for a narrowly conceived Christian community or the more expansive view of recent critics of Gospel community hypotheses.[45] This is suggested on the basis of the likely provenance of the Gospel and hints within the narrative of the Gospel itself. It is also in line with the observation that exegetes appear increasingly more prepared to acknowledge the possibility of diversity in John's audience.[46]

When it comes to the provenance of the Gospel, most scholars are hesitant about being too dogmatic. Ephesus is the traditional favourite, though usually tentatively supported. The other two principal candidates are Alexandria and

---

[42] Cf. Moloney (1993: 20), 'The intended reader both *is* and *is not* the implied reader'. There is also a sense in which the generality of this address creates a relationship with all subsequent (real) readers but this does not deny the original circumstance of address.

[43] Motyer 1997a: 116; cf. Motyer 1997b.

[44] Van Iersel 1998: 24.

[45] For the more expansive view see Bauckham (1998b). The most extensive critique of his position, and therefore restatement of the Gospel communities hypothesis, is by Sim (2001).

[46] C.R.Koester (1996), Moloney (2002: 35, esp. n.69) and Edwards (2003: 45) are amongst those who have recently commented to this effect.

Syrian Antioch.[47] The scholarly equivocation in this matter is ultimately pointed to by the suggestion of Beasley-Murray, following Manson, that the Fourth Gospel originated in traditions based in Jerusalem, then taken to Antioch and then to Ephesus where the final literary form was achieved.[48] The point about any of these suggested locations is that they are large and cosmopolitan cities situated in the Roman Empire. This observation encourages an examination of the broader context of the empire in order to ascertain relevant features of the cultural foreground. It also needs to be acknowledged that with increasing recognition of the process of Hellenisation throughout the Roman Empire, including Palestine,[49] it is difficult to divide off into watertight compartments the worlds of Judaism and Hellenism. The interpenetration is at depth. Even if the audience of the Gospel were to be identified as a Jewish Christian community or even Jews, with an eye to evangelism,[50] it is an audience located in a broadly Hellenistic milieu, in the midst of the Roman Empire. There are many shared cultural realities in such a broad context. These include a social context where the threat of death, disease and want is constant,[51] a religious context that is 'full of gods',[52] and a political context that is dominated by the reality of Roman imperial power and the imperial cult associated with it.[53] The sign narratives may be profitably read in the light of these realities for their rhetorical impact.

While these realities are generally applicable, attempts to delineate the more specific historical, social, political, economic and religious context of

---

[47] See the discussions in Barrett (1978: 128–34) and Brown (1966–70: ciii-civ) for reasons for and against these alternatives.

[48] Beasley-Murray 1987: lxxxi. This construction implies nothing about the identity of the bearer of the tradition or even its form but is simply an attempt to account for the evidence and the possible influences on the 'Johannine tradition'. See originally Manson (1946–7).

[49] The work of Martin Hengel is important to this observation. With specific reference to the Fourth Gospel see Hengel (1987).

[50] See Van Unnik (1959); Robinson (1959–60); Carson (1991: 90–95); Motyer (1997a: 215, tentatively).

[51] Cf. the sober assessment of Stark (1992: 154), 'Not only was the Greco-Roman world struck by deadly epidemics, but illness and physical affliction were probably dominant features of life in this era'. His entire discussion paints a grim picture of life in a Graeco-Roman city (cf. pp. 152–6).

[52] This is the expressive title of Hopkins (1999). The New Testament writers acknowledge the polytheistic context in which they lived, cf. Acts 17.16; 1 Cor 8.4–6; 1 Jn 5.21. See also the richly imaginative account in Hopkins (1999: 12–43) that records the adventures of two time travellers in the first century world. Cf. also his comments on how strange the Christian faith would have appeared in this environment (p. 78) and his description of Ephesus (pp. 202–3). For further material on the polytheistic context of Ephesus, see Knibbe (1978), Oster (1990), and Aurenhammer, in H. Koester (1995: 251-80).

[53] Cf. the assessment of Mitchell (1993: 100) 'The diffusion of the cult of Augustus and of other members of his family in Asia Minor and throughout the Greek east from the beginning of the empire was rapid, almost instantaneous'. See also the survey by Winter (1994).

the origin of the document may yet prove valuable in the investigation of the way in which the Gospel may have been heard by its early audience. The question is one of how homogeneous the ancient world was and the degree of regional variation that may have been in existence. This may apply to very widespread phenomena such as the practice of the Imperial cult.[54] For this reason, it will be assumed (where necessary) that Ephesus is the likely provenance of the 'production' of the final form of the Gospel. This also accords with the ancient traditions making this connection.

There are indications in the text of the Fourth Gospel that a diverse audience is in view. The references to the Samaritans in John 4, the Greeks in John 7 and 12, the other sheep in John 10, and the multi-language proclamation of Jesus as King in John 19 all suggest an interest, if not an audience, that encompasses Gentiles.[55] Other indications include the notes of explanation scattered throughout the narrative and the detailed geographical information presented. These appear to assume, on the part of some readers, little knowledge of the geography of Palestine and Jerusalem (5.2; 11.1, 18) and some ignorance of Jewish religious customs (2.13; 7.2; 10.22). This has led some exegetes to suggest that the audience is Gentile.[56] The prevalence of the term 'Jews' in the Gospel probably indicates that a largely Gentile audience is in view. This appears to be the practice of both Jewish and non-Jewish writers when writing with either Gentile audiences in mind or else when the material they are writing about concerns a speech situation involving Gentiles or interaction with Gentiles.[57]

At a more general level the broad perspective introduced by the prologue into the Gospel is to be noted. The prologue is important because it sets the

---

[54] With respect to this point see the summary comments of Price in Horsley (ed.) (2004: 175-83). Price notes the necessity of such a step as well as suggesting that the resources to do this kind of local analysis are increasingly available from historians.

[55] Frey 1994a: 262–3.

[56] This is Culpepper's cautious conclusion (1983: 224–5); cf. also Witherington (1995: 34–35). Robinson (1959-60) and Carson favour a Jewish audience (1991: 90–91), while Brown (1966: lxxviii) suggests a mix. Admittedly these observations are ambiguous. There are also many terms left unexplained that would appear to beg for similar definition and explanation. Culpepper's survey (pp. 212-23) highlights the ambiguities well.

[57] Kuhn (1971: 360–79; esp. 377) makes this observation. According to Casey (1999: 286) his work should be used very carefully due to Kuhn's anti–Semitic views. The more recent study by Tomson (2001) is important. Tomson restates some of Kuhn's position following a fresh analysis of the evidence. Tomson particularly stresses the 'speech situation' (p. 181) where 'Jew' is used in situations that include non-Jewish listeners. He also focuses on situations of dual usage where a predominant use of Israel is interrupted by the use of Jew and vice versa to demonstrate the point. In another study Tomson (2001: 192) speaks of a 'non-Jewish setting'. It needs to be noted that his work appears in a volume discussing the anti-Judaism of the Gospel. He does not see this observation as in any sense alleviating what he sees as the anti-Judaic nature of the Fourth Gospel, which has developed over time.

scene for the rest of the Gospel. Two sections contained within verses 1–13 (1–5, 6–13) speak of the coming of the λόγος from two related perspectives. The opening verses (1.1–5) establish a cosmological, almost mythical, perspective in eternity within which everything that follows is to be read.[58] They focus attention on the identity of the λόγος (1–4) and hint at a story of opposition and conflict (1.5). The second section (1.6–13) focuses more specifically on the 'coming' of the λόγος and the implications of this event.[59] The final section (1. 14–18) records the reflections of the author speaking as a representative of the Christian community—those who, by the will of God, have become the children of God. This reflection is upon the event of the incarnation of Jesus and its implications. The narrative of the prologue tells these three stories with echoes amongst all three.[60] The cosmological story of the encounter of the λόγος and the κόσμος in verses 1–5 is recapitulated in the story of the historic people of Israel (vss. 6–13)[61] and then in the participants in the Gospel narrative (vss. 14–18).[62] The issue of the historical referent of verses 6–13, whether to the time before or after the incarnation, dissolves in the light of this recapitulatory mode. As Dodd puts it

> The life of Jesus therefore *is* the history of the Logos, as incarnate, and this must be, upon the stage of limited time, the same thing as the history of the Logos in perpetual relations with man and the world. Thus not only verses 11–13, but the whole passage from verse 4 is *at once* an account of the relations of the Logos with the world, *and* an account of the ministry of Jesus Christ, which in every essential particular reproduces those relations.[63]

While the detail of the story that follows in the body of the Gospel is located very much in the specific story of the encounter of Jesus with his people, the universal implications arc never far away as a result of this expansive opening.

This is reinforced by the pervasive presence of κόσμος language throughout the Gospel, which sets the mission of Jesus within a wider context than simply the history and life of Israel. The disciple's mission is presented in John 13–17 as finally being to the κόσμος, the content of the κόσμος being defined in the narrative as both Jews, in the bulk of the Gospel, and the

---

[58] Barrett (1978: 149) describes these verses as a cosmological statement.

[59] This is suggested by van der Watt (1995: 329). The above analysis is similar to that of van der Watt except that he suggests two main sections and differs over the interpretation of the significance of John in verse 6 that is suggested above.

[60] This construction is partially indebted to the analysis of Reinhartz (1992: 17–25) concerning these tales.

[61] The testimony of John epitomises the prophetic witness to the word. Barth (1986: 49–50) hints at this possibility.

[62] This is explored in Salier (1998: 116–7).

[63] Dodd 1970: 284.

wider world, especially the Roman government via the trial narratives. This establishes a universal feel to the Gospel and its message. Finally, as will be suggested in a subsequent chapter, the language of σημεῖον itself has universal implications in its usage in the Hebrew Scriptures. This applies especially in Isaiah, which appears to be a special point of reference for the Fourth Gospel.[64]

There are grounds for thinking of a diverse audience for the Fourth Gospel and therefore looking to a wide context in the examination of the language and narratives of the Fourth Gospel involving σημεῖον. In fact it is suggested that the language of σημεῖον is chosen as one of the strategies employed with a view to enabling access to the Gospel for such a broad readership. The term itself and the narrative events to which this term refers are a point of identification and potential impact for a wide variety of readers living in the context of the Graeco-Roman world. This language and the narratives to which it is applied provide an entry point for this spectrum of readers.

This is not to deny that the theological perspective of the Gospel is deeply rooted in a Jewish framework immersed in the Hebrew Scriptures. The reader is to acknowledge that Jesus is the Jewish Messiah in order to enjoy the gift of life offered in the Gospel. The member of the early audience familiar with, or even steeped in, this thought world has a dramatic head start on the reader otherwise uninitiated into this world and is, therefore, further down the track to becoming the ideal or realised implied reader of the Gospel in terms of belief. In order to 'become' the implied reader, the reader will have to take on a deep appreciation of this framework as expressed in the Gospel through its many allusions and specific references to the Scriptures of Israel. However, access is not denied on this account.

The Gospel educates the reader into this perspective and prepares the ground for growth to maturity through repeated reading and contemplation. The signs are integral to both processes—that of coming to faith and of growing in faith.[65] The Gospel bridges the culture presupposed by the conceptual background of the Gospel and the broad world in front of the text. In the terms of the Gospel itself, 'salvation is from the Jews' (4.22) and Jesus is 'the saviour of the world' (4.42). The Gospel is sufficiently open so as to allow a person with little knowledge of this story access to the purpose of the Gospel, that is, faith in Christ as the divine Messiah of Israel, with an inkling of what this actually means, at least in functional terms. The signs provide one point of identification such that the real reader can join the implied readership and grow, with the aid of the implied author, to become the implied reader in the fullest possible sense. The signs will play their part in

---

[64] See, for example, Young (1955).

[65] The view concerning the purpose of the Gospel that is implied by this statement will be explored at greater length in the discussion of 20.30–31 below.

this ongoing process as they continue to present Jesus in ever increasing depth. This process will be ongoing as the reader returns to the text time and again.

1.3 Moving Forward

This study proposes to investigate the function of the language of σημεῖον and the σημεῖον narratives within the literary and rhetorical framework of the Gospel by pursuing the two directions of investigation outlined above. In chapter two the language of σημεῖον will be surveyed in a variety of ancient literary and cultural contexts in an attempt to establish the range of denotation and connotation that might be part of the early audience's repertoire. In chapters three to six, the language of σημεῖον and the sign narratives will be examined in the Gospel, following the narrative sequence.

While a narrative can be read and re-read in both part and whole, it is suggested that following the linear development of the Gospel narrative is a method that is faithful to the narrative style of the presentation. It is also anticipated that this will approximate the early reading/listening experience.[66] No matter what familiarity with the text is assumed through repeated re-readings, the experience of a narrative text is always, in some sense, a linear one. Even if a reader encounters the text at a later point on a subsequent reading, there is still a sense in which, due to familiarity with the whole, the particular section encountered contains a narrative trace of what has preceded it. The narrative will be read in part and re-read, with knowledge of the whole in mind. Connections may be more readily established between parts of the story but the narrative form always retains a sense of plot and forward movement. Having said this, at times some liberty will be taken in anticipating developments within the narrative by a look ahead to subsequent uses and contexts. The Gospel itself invites this move with its occasional mention of events that are ahead in the narrative as providing a perspective on a particular matter at hand (e.g. 2.22; 6.71; 7.39; 12.16).[67] While the main route of exploration will be via the narrative sequence, at times the perspective of the narrative whole will need to be taken into account. This approach gives an opportunity to note, where appropriate, significant interaction with other theological themes in the Gospel.

Chapters three to six will be presented as follows. Following a brief contextual overview of the portion of the Gospel under consideration, the first main section will examine the occurrences of σημεῖον in the order in which

---

[66] It is assumed that most early 'readers' were 'hearers' but the terms 'reader' and 'audience' will be used.

[67] Crouch 1996: 121.

they occur in the narrative. The second major section will then examine the sign narratives that occur in the portion of the Gospel being investigated. This might appear to violate the principle of narrative progression that has just been discussed but the following justification is offered. First, it is suggested that the sign narratives are located within the broader context of the σημεῖον language generally and that treating them in this separate fashion will enable the interrelationships between the general language and the sign narratives to be better elucidated. The reader responds to the presence of the language of σημεῖον as it appears through the narrative and also to the materiality of the sign narratives. Together the rhetorical impact is made. It is suggested that the structure adopted here will better facilitate the explication of this impact. Secondly, this separation will allow the two directions of approach, text-to-reader and reader-to-text, to be more clearly applied.[68]

In each chapter, the *individual occurrences* of σημεῖον will be considered firstly from the perspective of text-to-reader. This examination will seek to understand the developing sense of σημεῖον communicated in the text to the reader, especially as the term is used in relationship with other significant terms, phrases, and more general literary and theological motifs.[69] There will then follow a brief reflection on this material from the perspective of reader-to-text. Brief comments will be made on the reception of the language of σημεῖον by readers with some familiarity with the Hebrew Scriptures with more extensive comments directed to exploring the reception of the language in a more general Graeco-Roman context. A particular focus will be on the reception of the language of σημεῖον embedded in the context of a legal trial as one of the Gospel's major literary themes.

The investigation of the specific *sign narratives* will follow along similar lines. In the investigation of these narratives the text-to-reader perspective will look for clues that help the readers to make sense of these narratives within the structure of the Gospel as a whole, particularly noting keywords and concepts in the course of the narratives. Particular attention will be paid to the efforts made to help the readers to identify with various characters and situations presented in the sign narratives. From the perspective of reader-to-text, the sign narratives will be probed for their possible cultural resonance.

---

[68] It may appear to the reader that there will be the potential for replication of material between the two sections that could become tedious. This will be avoided as far as possible and in practice is more illusory than real as a concern. The broader investigation will focus specifically on the occurrences of σημεῖον, while the more specific examination will focus on the material of the sign narratives. While there is obviously overlap and relationship, as already conceded, this approach will provide opportunity for a mutually enriching synthesis rather than tedious repetition.

[69] This will avoid the problem highlighted by Barr (1961: 209–216) of confusing word and concept.

This investigation will take its starting point from the vocabulary and material nature of the narratives. Each chapter will conclude with a summary.

The outcome of the text-to-reader examination will demonstrate the integral nature of the sign language and narratives to the rhetorical purposes of the Gospel. It will be suggested that, together, the σημεῖον references and the σημεῖα narratives make their impact by being embedded, at a literary level, in a forensic motif that forms 'arguably the most distinctive, persuasive, and comprehensive motif'[70] in the Gospel, and, at a theological level, in a context that locates the story of Jesus, and the signs he works, firmly within the prior story of God's dealings with his covenant people. At either one or both of these levels the language of σημεῖον has cultural resonance enabling a variety of readers to gain access to the narrative and to embark on its depths of meaning.

In terms of the sign narratives, it will be seen that each narrative portrays Jesus as a life-giver in ways that would be intelligible to a variety of readers in the ancient world.[71] While pointing to the identity of Jesus, these narratives also provide an opportunity for engagement at a more emotional level and allow the readers to see the practical consequences of the elevated Christology presented in the Gospel. At the same time there is also a subtle critique being mounted against other would be life-givers in the ancient world, culminating in a critique through the Gospel, as a whole, targeted towards the claims of the imperial cult. These aspects emerge in dialogue with various aspects of the audience's cultural background. This is an audience that lives in a world 'full of gods' promising life, but is riddled with disease and circumstances that conspire to bring death.

The σημεῖα are related in the Fourth Gospel to persuade the reader of the claims of Jesus. They do this by identifying him as the divine Messiah of Israel, illustrating his mission as the true life-giver, and providing a point of comparison and contrast with potential rivals.

---

[70] Lincoln 2000: 12.

[71] Labahn (1999a: 501 and throughout) emphasises that the presentation of Jesus as a life-giver is a key part of the Gospel's presentation.

Chapter 2

Speaking of σημεῖα

This survey of the use of the term σημεῖον will begin with the Hebrew Scriptures in their Greek translation, before moving to consider the wider usage in the Graeco-Roman world. The survey begins with the Septuagint because it is assumed that the major conceptual background for the thinking of the Fourth Gospel is to be found in the Hebrew Scriptures. The use of the term in the Greek translation will therefore help to inform the perspective of the text-to-reader analysis. The story of Jesus is explicitly set against the background of the work of God with the people of Israel. This is acknowledged to be implicit throughout the Gospel as well as explicit in the occasional quotations from Scripture.[1] This background will also form part of the cultural repertoire for many amongst the early audience of the Gospel, through their contact with these Scriptures and traditions. The use of the term in the wider Graeco-Roman literature will then be examined for both comparison and contrast. Finally the occurrences of σημεῖον that occur in the rest of the writings that came to be known as the New Testament will be briefly assessed for points of contact and distinction in relation to the other two areas of investigation.

2.1 The Septuagint

2.1.1 Overview

In the Septuagint translation the term σημεῖον occurs some 125 times.[2] The majority of occurrences are in the Pentateuch and the prophetic literature, with a few instances in the historical, poetic, and wisdom literature.

In approximately 80% of the cases σημεῖον translates the Hebrew אות. There are a number of other Hebrew terms that are also rendered by σημεῖον.

---

[1] Barrett (1978: 29) comments to this effect. See also Barrett (1947). Barrett (1978: 28-29) also notes that John 'regularly used the LXX in making his Old Testament quotations, but that he was capable of going direct to the Hebrew…He may have used other traditional versions and interpretations'. Freed (1965: 130) concludes similarly. Menken (1996: 205–9) stresses the use of the LXX, with 'occasional recourse to the Hebrew text' (205).

[2] All references to verses in the LXX in this chapter are cited with reference to Rahlf's edition (1952) unless otherwise stated.

In Ezekiel 9.4–6 the population of Jerusalem is be marked on the forehead with a Tau. The Tau is designated as a σημεῖον to give an indication of the function of the marking. Similarly, in Joshua 2.18 σημεῖον denotes the cord (תִּקְוָה) that Rahab uses to alert the Jewish spies to her family's house. On a number of occasions σημεῖον renders the Hebrew נֵס (Num 21.8, 9; 26.10; Isa 11.12; 13.2; 18.3; Jer 28 [MT51]. 12,27). Often this refers simply to an object or signal that is easily seen such as a marker flag or standard. However there are a few instances where a more metaphorical use of נֵס is rendered by σημεῖον (Num 26.10; Isa 11.12). Occasionally σημεῖον is used to render the Hebrew מוֹפֵת (cf. Exod 7.9; 11.9, 10; 2 Chron 32.24), but τέρας is more usually used.

At the most general level σημεῖον suggests a visible phenomenon that conveys information of some kind. In more overtly theological contexts σημεῖον denotes 'an object, an occurrence, an event through which a person is to recognize, learn, remember, or perceive the credibility of something',[3] through the activity of God. Such activity is not necessarily miraculous and can include natural phenomena as well as the activity of individuals. A response is generally anticipated as the signs mediate understandings of various kinds and motivate behaviours in response.

Such signs can simply be given by Yahweh or requested of him (cf. 1 Kgdms 10.1; Judg 6.17, cf. 36–40). They can be worked directly by Yahweh or they can be worked through authorised representatives. Signs can occur in a number of different settings including creation (Gen 1.14; 9.12; Isa 37.30; Jer 10.2), history (Exod 4.7–8; 7.3; Num 26.10) and the cult (Gen 17.11; Exod 31.13). These are not discrete categories with overlap amongst them often occurring.

Signs fulfil a number of purposes. These include providing knowledge (Gen 1.14), indicating refuge or protection (Gen 4.15), arousing belief (Num 14.11), prompting remembrance of an event or commandment (Gen 17.11; Exod 13.9; Num 17.3; Deut 6.8), and confirming a promise or prophetic word (Exod 3.11; 4.31; 1 Sam 14.10).[4] Yahweh grants and works signs that warn, accompany his word, and vouch for its reliability. Other signs reinforce the promise of his saving presence (Exod 3.12; Judg 6.16–24, 36; 3 Kgdms 10.1–16 and Isa 7.10–17). Yahweh's messengers can authenticate their mission and message by signs which either performed (Exod 4.1–9) or predicted (1 Kgdms 10.1–16; 3 Kgdms 13.1–6; 4 Kgdms 19.29). Signs can operate as acts of judgement as in the exodus account and in the prophetic sign acts of Isaiah, Jeremiah and Ezekiel. The term is also used in an

---

[3] Helfmeyer 1974: 170.
[4] Bittner (1987: 24) suggests these categories.

argumentative or forensic context in Job 21.29.[5] The context surrounding the references in Wis 5.12–13; 2 Macc 6.13; 3 Macc 6.32 may suggest a similar nuance is in view in these occurrences as well.

2.1.2 Signs in Egypt

A major and distinctive use of σημεῖον in the writings of the LXX occurs where it indicates an event that attests or confirms the authority of a prophetic word or the status of the prophet himself. This use can best be seen in an examination of the two prominent clusters of occurrence of the language of σημεῖον around the exodus account and in the prophetic books. The exodus account may be considered foundational to the later development and understanding of this conception of sign in the Old Testament material.[6]

The term is prominent in the narrative relating the call of Moses by Yahweh to be the agent whereby the people of Israel will be rescued and released from their time of slavery in Egypt. In response to Moses's concern regarding his worthiness for the task (Exod 3.11), Yahweh responds by affirming his presence with Moses and then promising a σημεῖον to confirm his choice (Exod 3.12). As unusual as this might appear,[7] the most straightforward interpretation is that the sign that Moses is chosen by God will be the successful completion of the mission when Israel arrives at the mountain of God. There is a call to trust and faith based on the promise of God's assured presence. Moses has to move forward.[8] The future nature of the sign goes part of the way to explaining Moses's continued objections through the rest of the passage.

As the narrative ensues, Moses questions whether the Israelites will listen to him or not. In response, Yahweh gives Moses three actions to perform—the changing of his staff into a snake, causing his hand alternatively to become diseased and then healed and, finally, transforming some water from the Nile into blood. These signs function initially for two audiences; first, to Moses himself and, second, to the elders and people of Israel. The signs confirm the presence of Yahweh with Moses and the assurance is given to Moses that the Israelites will believe on the basis of these signs, as indeed they do (Exod 4.30–1).

---

[5] Job points to the prosperity of the wicked as observed by travellers. This is to show that the doctrine of retribution, presently on the table for discussion, does not measure up and needs to be revised. While this might be seen as an example of a confirmatory use, the argumentative context creates a slightly different nuance that is more akin to proof offered in the course of an argument.

[6] Bittner 1987: 24–26.

[7] See the discussion in Childs (1974: 56–9), Propp (1998: 203) considers a number of other alternatives.

[8] Cf. the comments of Cole (1973: 68) and Fretheim (1991: 62). 1 Kgdms 2.34 and Isa 37.30 are similarly future orientated signs.

There are few indications as to why these particular events should have been chosen to be signs. Houtman points to the connotations of the ancient art of snake charming and its prominence in Egypt. The one who can control snakes was assumed to have some sort of special relationship with the deity.[9] While there is a difference in that Moses transforms a staff into a snake – a different class of snake-charming feat – this appears to be an excellent means, in an Egyptian context, to demonstrate that the deity was with him. Sarna suggests a hint of judgement in the skin disease sign,[10] while Propp suggests that both the snake and hand signs indicate the ability of Yahweh to send disease and healing (cf. Deut 32.39)[11]. While these connections are only tentatively suggested, it may be observed that in these cases, at least, the nature of the sign may not be completely arbitrary and unconnected from the social and cultural context in which the particular sign is given. To a certain extent, part of the impact of these signs may derive from some intelligible connection with the cultural repertoire of the audience so that it 'makes sense'.

The connection between sign and belief is clearly established in the narrative. The language of belief (πιστεύω) is prominent in the section (Exod 4.1, 5, 8, 9, 31; cf. Gen 9.15, Num 14.11; Deut 7.18–19 where the recollection of an event may produce faith as well). On a number of occasions the language of belief is paralleled with the language of hearing (Exod 4.1, 8, 9). The hearing language is a departure from the more normal visual associations of signs but, while idiomatic rather than literal, serves to reinforce the communicative nature of the signs that are given.

In Exod 4 a connection may also be discerned between the signs and the theme of sonship. After the encounter at the burning bush Moses is sent back to Pharaoh, having been told what to say and do. He is to tell Pharaoh that Israel is the first born son of Yahweh (4.22, υἱὸς πρωτότοκός μου) and that Pharaoh will forfeit his first born son for disobeying the word brought by Moses. In the ensuing conflict not only is the issue at stake who is the legitimate god or power but also who is the true son of the true God. This aspect tends to be lost amongst the other legitimating functions of signs.

As the confrontation with Pharaoh proceeds, a preview is given to Moses of the future course of events (Exod 7.1–7). The narratives of the ensuing plagues, denoted as τὰ σημεῖα μου καὶ τὰ τέρατα, follow. Several features of these narratives are of particular interest. First, there is a threefold intended audience for the signs. The first audience mentioned is the people of Israel. As a result of the whole process of rescue brought about by the sign-acts of judgement on Egypt, rescue for them, the people of Israel will know

---

[9] Houtman 1993: 391.

[10] Sarna 1987: 60. Cf. also Durham (1987: 45).

[11] Propp 1998: 209.

that Yahweh is the Lord God who rescues them (Exod 6.7; 10.2). The second audience is the Egyptians (Exod 7.5; cf. 8.22; 9.14). In the course of the narrative, Pharaoh represents the Egyptians. Nonetheless, as they experience the judgement of God they too will know that Yahweh is God, as Pharaoh himself will be forced to acknowledge. The third audience mentioned is the whole earth (Exod 9.16). The signs are connected with the revelation of the identity and the glory of Yahweh.

The final action in the sequence of judgements is also described as an act of judgement on the gods of Egypt (Exod 12.12; cf. Num 33.4). In its position, this seems to stand as a comment over the rest of the sign-acts of judgement as well (cf. 9.14 and the note of supremacy struck there). There is some dispute as to what extent the signs may be said to be directly attacking the gods of Egypt,[12] but the statement in Exod 12.12 seems clear enough as to their overall intent. There is a polemical edge to the account in theological terms. Not only do the signs positively identify the true God and his authorised representative but they also attack and lay bare other erstwhile divine pretenders. This is clearly Pharaoh in the context. These pretenders are rendered impotent in the face of the power of the one true God. The signs are contentious in this respect and this needs to be emphasised. This observation remains valid whether the sign judgements are read as attacking specific gods in the Egyptian pantheon or simply the role of the divine Pharaoh as protector of his people and guarantor of the prosperity of his land and people.[13] All and any pretenders to the place of the God of Israel are dethroned through the account and the signs performed are intrinsic to this occurrence. Some of the subsequent references to signs and wonders in the biblical account will further emphasise the transcendence of Yahweh, often with specific gods and figures in the foreground as foils.[14] The same polemic is seen at various points in the Hebrew Scriptures in narrative form (e.g. 1 Kgdms 5.1–5; 6.4–6; 3 Kgdms 18.20–40). This polemic applies to all concerned. The signs performed in Egypt are intended to draw forth a confession to the effect that the God of Israel is the true God of all the earth (Exod 7.3; 8.18–9). Israel is to embrace this God and eschew all potential rivals.

There is no simple acceptance of signs and wonders as indicating the work of Yahweh. It is plainly acknowledged that the Egyptian magicians had power to perform miracles by their secret magical arts, albeit that they were inferior acts to the miracles wrought by Yahweh's representative. This cautious

---

[12] The literature here is voluminous. See, for example, Sarna (1987: 57–60; 78–80); Zevit (1990). Houtman (1996: 21) 'fails to see' any specific references to gods in the individual plagues.

[13] Sarna 1987: 65.

[14] Formesyn 1962: 876–7. See Deut 4.34–5; 9.2–3; Josh 24.2–5; Ps 134.5–13; Dan 4.1–3 (θ); 6.25–8; Sir 36.3–6.

perspective is also expressed in the warnings in Deuteronomy 13 concerning false prophets who will delude Israel. Signs and wonders alone are not enough to authenticate a prophet sent from Yahweh. The teaching of the prophet must also be assessed. A tight correlation between a sign and the interpretative word is suggested here and by the fact that most signs are accompanied by an interpretative word. The word and the work of the prophet combine to authenticate their commission.

As the language and themes of these accounts are picked up and repeated in the traditions of Israel, a cluster of themes is associated with their mention. The signs are regularly referred to as pointers to Yahweh himself. They reveal his might and glory. In them Israel, indeed all the nations of the world are to encounter Yahweh and to recognise that he is God alone (Deut 4.35; 3 Kgdms 18.36–40; Ps 85.8–9). Unbelief and disobedience in the face of the signs are regarded as the expression of an utterly incomprehensible hardness of heart (Num 14.11, 22–24; Ps 77. 32–57).

With respect to the Fourth Gospel, one other reference to σημεῖον in connection with Moses needs to be mentioned. In an incident recorded in Num 21. 4–9, Israel rebels and Yahweh punishes the people by sending poisonous snakes. The people cry out for mercy and Yahweh commands Moses to fashion a bronze snake and set it on a pole so that everyone who gazes upon the snake might be preserved from death if they are bitten. The imagery will be used by Jesus in the Fourth Gospel as an illustration of his mission (Jn 3.14–15). It remains to be seen how the reference to the pole as a σημεῖον might be used in the Gospel.

2.1.3 Signs and the Prophets

The second cluster of usage in the prophets contains a number of innovative prophetic sign actions. It is the actions of Isaiah (e.g. Isa 20. 1–4), Jeremiah (e.g. Jer 13.1–11) and Ezekiel (e.g. Ezek 4–5) that are usually in focus with this term although there are a number of similar actions in the earlier prophetic material (3 Kgdms 11.29–31; 3 Kgdms 22.11; 4 Kgdms 13.14–19). The innovation in these 'sign actions' is the apparently overt symbolic dimension they contain. In delineating the general features of what he terms 'prophetic dramas' Stacey points out that they were performed by prophets at the behest of Yahweh and were deliberate, artificial actions. An oracle usually accompanies them or an explanation is supplied. The prophetic act had a specific and finite meaning.[15] It might be added that the presence of eyewitnesses is usually mentioned, or assumed, though there may be instances where this is not the case, depending on what is included as a prophetic

---

[15]Stacey 1990: 60–62.

drama/sign action.[16] Stacey suggests that these actions have an intrinsic quality of proclamation and must not be regarded as merely divine visual aids.[17] Nor are they to be conceived of as instrumental with respect to the events they symbolise.[18] In themselves they present the truth of God that the prophet feels compelled by Yahweh to speak/perform; a truth that is already in existence in the will of God himself.[19] Stacey's discussion is stimulating but his metaphysical perspective on these actions needs to be supplemented by an acknowledgement of the rhetorical and communicative function of the sign acts.[20] The aim of many of the sign acts is to proclaim judgement and hope and to elicit the recognition that Yahweh is the true and living God (cf. Ezek. 12.15, 16, 20; 14.8; Jer. 51.29).

A final point of interest in the prophetic material comes from the use of sign in the metaphorical sense and in an eschatological context. This is especially to be seen in the prophet Isaiah. The final appearance of the word σημεῖον in Isaiah occurs at Isa 66.19. Here a rescued people from the wreckage of Israel are spoken of. They will bear signs upon them as they are sent to the nations. [21] Their role will be to declare the glory of Yahweh amongst the Gentiles. The culmination of this process includes the naming of those from the nations as brothers, from amongst whom will be taken priests and Levites. The stunning universalism of this picture is connected with the language of σημεῖον. This reference culminates previous references to a sign raised before the nations in Isaiah, most notably the important verse Isa 11.12. Here, the root of Jesse is said to lift a σημεῖον to gather the lost of Israel and Judah from the ends of the earth,[22] placing the language of σημεῖον in close connection with a significant messianic passage. Other references to the related term σύσσημον performing a similar function are present (cf. Isa 5.26; 49.22; 62.10). This theme culminates in the σημεῖα of 66.19. In this

---

[16] One of the problems of this discussion is the question of defining what is and is not a prophetic drama. Stacey (1990: 62–66) has a discussion.

[17] Stacey 1990: 260–82, esp. 264–6. However Friebel (1999: 466), focuses specifically on the communicative and rhetorical function of the sign acts in Ezekiel and Jeremiah and stresses 'the ability of the non-verbal behaviors to communicate graphically specifiable message-contents'.

[18] Cf. also the discussion in Friebel (1999: 41–51) on this point.

[19] Stacey 1990: 278–82. Cf. also the brief summary in Hooker (1997: 4).

[20] Friebel 1999: 47, n.96. His monograph explores these dimensions with the help of rhetorical and nonverbal communications theory.

[21] The reading in both Rahlfs and Ziegler is the plural σημεῖα, while Brenton records σημεῖον. The underlying Hebrew is the singular אות. The plural reading is found in Alexandrinus and also as a correction in Sinaiticus.

[22] The connection with the 'root of Jesse' is made even more explicit in the Hebrew text of Isaiah 11.10 where this figure is explicitly identified as the sign raised. It appears that the translator(s?) wished to stress the rule of the Messiah over the Gentiles and removed the language of sign/banner in doing so.

context the language of σημεῖον is connected with the final fulfilment of God's purposes regarding the gathering of his scattered people, be they Jew or Gentile, as well as displaying the glory of God to the nations.[23]

2.2 Graeco-Roman Usage

2.2.1 Introduction

The following section will survey the use of σημεῖον in the wider Graeco-Roman cultural context. This wider background is often examined in perfunctory fashion because the background and origin of the term has been sought solely from the author's conceptual perspective. The attempt to 'hear' the word in its wider cultural setting requires a more extensive examination.

The following survey will range over a variety of Greek and Roman writers and also the work of Philo and Josephus, who together provide a perspective that bridges the 'worlds' of Hellenism and Judaism. The writers and material discussed below have been chosen with a view to providing an overview of usage both antedating the Fourth Gospel by up to two hundred years and immediately following.[24] Occasionally older works will be mentioned where this is appropriate.

This material will be presented under three broad headings: general use, uses in religious contexts, and use in rhetorical or forensic contexts. The general category is by far the most diverse and least interesting from the perspective of this investigation. The religious uses will include those instances where the connection is made with the will of the gods expressed through omens and phenomena of various kinds. The rhetorical or forensic uses are those where σημεῖον is used in a more argumentative or evidential sense to make a particular point. It obviously derives from the more general use in terms of signification but appears to be used on a number of occasions in a more rhetorical fashion.[25] This last use has been differentiated from the earlier general category because of its interesting links with the rhetorical tradition. While this link has been occasionally acknowledged in examinations of John's usage,[26] it has not been given the weight that its

---

[23] Barrett (1978: 76) is working from the Hebrew text. See n. 22 above.

[24] This assumes a dating of the final 'published' edition of the Gospel within the latter quarter of the first century.

[25] Rhetorical is used in the sense of a general level of persuasive communication. For a discussion of the ambiguity and complexity involved in the use and definition of the term rhetorical as well as an attempt to schematise its usage see Kern (1998: 7). The meaning here is akin to Kern's level 1: 'strategic communication'.

[26] Barrett 1978: 75.

prominence in the wider context and also its connection with the Johannine usage suggests it merits.

2.2.2 General Use

At the most general level σημεῖον has retained a stability of meaning in that it denotes things or processes that lead to insight or knowledge by way of perception, usually visual.[27] This is evident from the earliest strata of usage. In Homer σῆμα is used for a series of phenomena that bring knowledge through some kind of visual phenomena. It can be the mark by which something or someone is recognised (*Od.* 24.329–332, Odysseus's scar), a monument (*Il.* 7.86); the turning point in a race (*Il.* 23.326) or a mark of individual achievement (*Il.* 23.843; *Od.* 8.192, 195). A σῆμα is generally seen (cf. *Il.* 23.326–8 and *Od.* 8.192–198), although it can also be connected with an audible phenomenon (*Od.* 20.111).

Such diversity is illustrated by works closer to the time of the Fourth Gospel. For Strabo a σημεῖον can denote a mathematical or geographic point (e.g. *Geog.* 1.1.6; 1.4.1; 2.1.17), a signal beacon (*Geog.* 3.1.9), or the marks that record the least, greatest, and mean rises of the Nile (*Geog.* 17.1.48).

The writings of Dio Chrysostom provide a good coverage of the range of possibility. The location of a city as low lying and facing to the south is indicated by the fact that ships could not enter its harbour except with a southerly wind (*Or.* 6.3). The presence of pain in a treated part of the body is often an indication of healing (*Or.* 31.35.8) while sores that shrink from the touch show their bad condition (*Or.* 32.17.4). A standard or flag is also described by way of the use of σημεῖον (*Or.* 36.16.2). A more metaphorical use is also present when he describes snorting as signifying a number of attitudes (*Or.* 33.50.8). The σημεῖον of a true king is that all good men can praise him without compunction during and after his life (*Or.* 1.33.2 cf. 4.61.1; 63.1). The well-born nature of families of ancient wealth and high repute is attested by a whole series of signs (*Or.* 15.30.1). This variety is reproduced in many other writers.[28]

2.2.2.1 Philo and Josephus

A similar breadth is found in Josephus and Philo. At the most prosaic level, the verb is employed to indicate the meaning of a name in the Hebrew language (*A.J.* 1.34, 36; 2.13; 3.252). The meaning or interpretation of a dream is also the context for the appearance of the noun or verbal form (*A.J.* 2.11; 2.63). It can denote the blowing of a trumpet to signal an attack (*A.J.* 7.242, 279), pre-arranged signals to enact an attack or ambush (*A.J.* 5.46;

---

[27] The conclusion of Rengstorf (1971: 202) is sound at this point.

[28] Other writers examined include Flavius Arrianus and Diodorus Siculus.

5.161), a conspiracy (*A.J.* 19.101), or the passwords used to communicate amongst soldiers (*A.J.* 19.29, 31, 53).

In Philo there are a number of occasions where σημεῖον is used to denote a point in the mathematical sense (e.g. *Opif.* 49; *Decal.* 24, 25, 26). Laughter is described as a sign of joy (*Praem.* 31.4), while the sign that gold has been tested is its solidity (*Sacr.* 80).

2.2.2.2 Summary Remarks concerning General Use

Three brief observations can be made. First, though the word was also used to denote communication from the gods, it did not automatically denote religious revelation; it is an ordinary word and does not have an exclusively religious meaning or provenance.[29] Secondly, a sign is, generally speaking, some tangible phenomenon that communicates insight or knowledge. Thirdly, the meaning of a particular sign is a matter of interpretation and context. A sign cannot mean anything but conveys specific insight or information within a context established by an explanation, arrangement, or precedent. Varying degrees of possibility and accuracy are therefore possible in the reading of a particular sign, depending on one's position with respect to the context that establishes its meaning. This distinction will become more important in the next category to be described.

2.2.3 Religious Contexts

The range of use of σημεῖον in 'religious' contexts varies. Dionysius of Halicarnassus, who is enthusiastic about religious matters, especially Roman religion,[30] makes extensive use of the word in such contexts while Strabo is derisive concerning popular religion and has almost no such references.[31]

Dionysius frequently refers to divine providence and speaks scornfully of atheistic philosophers who deny that the gods intervene in human affairs (*Antiq. Rom.* 2.68.2; 8.56.1). Dionysius says that the gods do intervene and have particularly favoured the Romans, manifesting their will through the various phenomena that he records in his work. Amongst a variety of terms used for omens and portents, σημεῖον is encountered. In *Antiq. Rom.* 1.59.4 a number of σημεῖα are recounted as occurring during the building of Lavinium. Aeneas interprets these to the effect that the good fortune of heaven was more powerful than the envy of men who opposed the city that was being built. Dionysius also recounts the story of Romulus and Remus as they look for a σημεῖον from the gods as to who should give their name to the colony and lead it (*Antiq. Rom.* 1.86.3).

---

[29] This observation by Rengstorf (1971: 203–4) remains valid over a wider range of material than he surveyed and is confirmed also in the light of more recent discussion.

[30] Cary 1933: I.xxiv–v.

[31] Jones 1917: I.xix.

There are conventions and procedures in place for interpreting signs. In *Antiq. Rom.* 2.5.1–5 there is an extensive discussion based around the request for a sign from Jupiter and the other gods by Romulus. Lightning flashes from left to right and this is interpreted as a good omen because of instruction by the Tyrrhenians and their ancestors. Signs that appear from the east, in the heavens and in mid air, are said to be the best. In *Antiq. Rom.* 12.11.3 Dionysius records a Roman asking a Tyrrhenian to interpret σημείων τινῶν καὶ τεράτων that had recently appeared. In *Antiq. Rom.* 4.6 he speaks of augurs who know, by certain signs, that they have refused a god-sent blessing. An incident, where an eagle takes and replaces a cap (*Antiq. Rom.* 3.47.4), is seen as a wonderful and extraordinary sign and is 'read' by a woman, named Tanaquil, whose ancestry from the Tyrrhenians meant that she could interpret these things.

Signs from heaven confirm the results of elections (*Antiq. Rom* 3.46.1; 9.41.3) and are required as part of the process of recognising sovereignty (*Antiq. Rom.* 4.80.2). Signs can portend good news (*Antiq. Rom* 5.46.1) and ill (*Antiq. Rom.* 2.67.5). In *Antiq. Rom.* 9.40.1, Dionysius records the city being gripped with fear from the beginning of the year. This is due to τεράτων τε καὶ σημείων πολλῶν. All the augurs and pontiffs declared the anger of the gods because certain rites were not being performed in a holy manner.

The range observed in Dionysius can also be observed in other ancient writers and their testimony to the prevalence and fear of various portentous omens.[32] Generally, the sense of σημεῖον and the various phenomena to which the term refers is best seen as a communication from the gods. This communication requires interpretation. There are exceptions but these are rare. The message from the gods was in the sign itself and a subsidiary function for the sign was rarely conceived.[33]

2.2.3.1 Assessing Signs in the General Context

While Plutarch also records numerous signs from Rome's history, his writings also, on occasion, pursue a valuable discussion concerning signs and their genuineness. He is questioning, equivocal, and at times, sceptical. In *Them.* 10.1.3–4 he recounts how Themistocles seeks to convince a multitude of his views, by contriving a series of signs and oracles. The ambiguity of signs is illustrated in *Nic.* 23. Here a discussion ensues on the eclipse of the moon as a sign. Plutarch describes the terror of the armies, questions their superstition,

---

[32] Cf. here also Plutarch *Num.* 6.4.2; *Publ.* 13.1-3; *Cam.* 3.3.8; 35.5.12; *Per.* 6.2.7; *Fab.* 2.2.4. Dio Chrysostom: *Or.* 11.85.1; 11.98.4. In *Or.* 38.18.1 Dio laments the fact that his audience does not take notice of the signs sent by the gods; by which they mean to teach people to live on good terms with one another. Appian, *Bell. civ.* 2.5.36; 2.16.116; 4.1.4.

[33] Formesyn 1962: 865–6. Formesyn is particularly interested in showing that the origins of the Johannine usage cannot be found in the Graeco-Roman milieu.

and then discusses the causes of eclipses. He comments that men could not abide the natural philosophers and visionaries reducing everything to natural explanations.[34] Nicias is left to interpret this sign without a soothsayer. However, the same sign is also interpreted, by Philochorus, as being advantageous. It provides an opportunity to attack under the cover of darkness. Nicias does not read it this way and waits.[35] In *Alex.* 75.1.4 Plutarch recounts that Alexander had become so sensitive to indications of the divine will that he turned every unusual and strange occurrence into a prodigy and portent (τέρας; σημεῖον). It is in this context that Plutarch then goes on to discuss the dire consequences of both ignoring the divine will and being overly superstitious. His verdict in this case is that Alexander was becoming prey to his fears.

The same caution can be seen in the work of the later Roman historian Tacitus. Tacitus relates his history within the Roman understanding of punishment and reward from their gods. When he focuses on Vespasian's accession to power, Tacitus attributes this in terms of *fortuna* and notes that there are numerous prodigies and prophecies in operation to demonstrate this working for Vespasian.[36] This understanding of the events comes close to the legitimating function noted previously in the context of the Hebrew Scriptures.[37] However Tacitus, too, is at times sceptical or at least evaluative in assessing prodigies and omens, and provides some indication of how to make such an evaluation. In his account of Vespasian's healing miracles at Alexandria, Tacitus stresses the presence of witnesses for whom falsehood would be no reward (*Hist.* 4.81). Tacitus recounts a further incident involving Vespasian. Vespasian has a vision of man who was, at the moment of the incident, some 80 miles away (*Hist.*4.82). Apparently, both ignorance of the matters at hand as well as a lack of opportunity for personal gain on the part of the witnesses are suitable criteria when it comes to evaluating the credibility of an eyewitness to an extraordinary occurrence. In this account, as before, Tacitus also stresses the accumulation of eyewitnesses and careful investigation.[38]

---

[34] Cf. also his discussion of the interpretation of a one-horned ram in *Per.* 6.4.2. The cause of the phenomenon is explained but Plutarch does not therefore discount the possibility of it being a portent as well. He adds further that the logic of the position would mean that artificial signs such as the ringing of gongs and shadows on a sundial would also have to be discounted; each of them being made, through some causal adaptation, to have a meaning.

[35] Cf. also the incidents in *Tim.* 26.3.1, *Alex.* 14.8.2

[36] Lattimore (1934: 443) has a comparison with other emperors. Both Augustus and Vespasian are reported as accompanied by a significant number of portents and prophecies.

[37] Contra Formesyn (1962: 865-6) who denies this understanding in the wider context.

[38] For further discussion see R.T. Scott (1968) who points out that Tacitus can distinguish genuine omens and those that are a result of the anxieties of the times (p. 73).

2.2.3.2 Josephus

Josephus's more prosaic use of σημεῖον has already been noted. However, in his recounting of the history of the Jews he regularly speaks of signs in an overtly religious context. Josephus knows the use of the term in the context of communication from the gods that has been described above. In his description of the events surrounding the fall of Jerusalem he records a variety of portents and phenomena, including a sword shaped star, a comet, the birth of a lamb to a cow and the spontaneous opening of a gate (*B.J.* 6.288–294). These are possibly a concession to a stylised feature of Graeco-Roman historiography.[39]

However, it is also clear that in many places Josephus's use of σημεῖον reflects the understanding of the Scriptures that are his source. The cloud above the camp signifies the fact that God is present (*A.J.* 3.310). Rahab speaks of the signs given her by God that indicate to her the future of her city (*A.J.* 5.12). God signifies to Samuel that Saul is his chosen King (*A.J.* 6.50). Hezekiah asks for, and receives, a sign to help him believe the prophetic word of Isaiah (*A.J.* 10.28). The use in this case reflects a sense that differs from the wider Graeco Roman understanding of the sign as a portent or omen, and moves in the direction of a demonstrative or legitimating sign.[40]

Arguably the most significant use of the terminology comes in Josephus's recounting of the events at the exodus. Josephus uses the term in describing the activities centred on the time of Moses and the deliverance of the people of Israel from Egypt. The three miraculous works given to Moses to convince his fellow Israelites that he has been sent by God for the task of liberation are described as signs (*A.J.* 2.274) to convince (τὸ πιστεύεσθαι) all men (πᾶσι) that he has been sent by God and does everything at the command of the Lord. These signs then operate to convince his fellow Israelites (*A.J.* 2.279–80) and also serve to bolster his own confidence in the oracle he had received and the saving power of his God (*A.J.* 2.276). When the signs are performed before the Egyptian king, however, they are not 'read' correctly (*A.J.* 2.284–288) and the recounting of the ensuing plagues follows. At a later point, Josephus describes the plagues as signs of liberation (τὴν εθλευθερίαν....σημείων *A.J.* 2.327). This phrase will prove to be significant in Josephus's later tales of the so-called sign prophets. This instance is the (ambiguous) exception to the general 'rule', noted by Gray,[41] that Josephus only uses σημεῖον to refer to the first three signs given Moses to authenticate his role as the one God has sent to liberate Israel.

---

[39] 'The seven portents which Josephus lists sounds like a page from almost anyone of a half a dozen of his contemporaries in the Graeco-Roman world', McCasland (1932: 329). Appian, *Bell. civ.* 2.36 has one such list.

[40] Formesyn (1962: 869) particularly stresses this.

[41] Gray 1993: 126–7.

The signs confirm the identity and mission of Moses as the true prophet of God and therefore his representative. They point to the activity of God through him. Further, there is a relationship established between signs and faith. They are intended to invoke and confirm faith in the fact that God is at work through his chosen representative (*A.J.* 2.274, 276, 283; 8.327, 343, 350). This sense obviously draws from the presentation of these events in the Hebrew Scriptures.

Moses's activity is specifically said to compare with that of the magicians around him. Their activities proceed from magic (μαγείας) and witchcraft (γοητείαν) and deception of true judgement (πλάνην τῆς δόχης τάμα) while Moses's signs proceed from God's providence and power (*A.J.* 2.286). Josephus appears to eschew the language of signs and wonders in his account of Moses's activity, preferring the language of sign alone. Josephus deliberately tries to avoid the works of Moses being seen in a magical light and emphasises the 'significant' aspect of the actions.

Josephus also countenances the necessity for interpretation and the possibility of misreading of signs. With respect to signs given through dreams, Josephus's understanding is that a correct interpretation or reading can be given by a certified representative or inspired individual. This is the case for Josephus (*A.J.* 2.11, 14, 72) and Daniel (*A.J.* 10.214, 239). Occasionally an individual provides his or her own interpretation (Jacob, *A.J.* 2.15). The possibility for misreading a sign is also therefore alive. A dream can be misinterpreted or misunderstood and omens can be read the wrong way (*B.J.* 6.295). Occasionally they can be deliberately misread (to please oneself, *B.J.* 6.315). In the account of the fall of Jerusalem, Josephus relates how the people were deluded by charlatans (οἱ ἀπατεῶες) who had urged the crowds to gather in the temple courts with the promise of tokens of deliverance (τὰ σημεῖα τῆς σωτηρίας, *B.J.* 6.286). They had actually ignored the plain warnings of God. One of the signs he records, the spontaneous opening of a gate (*B.J.* 6.288–294) is misinterpreted as an indication that God is opening the gates of blessing. However, the learned (οἱ λόγιοι), as opposed to the inexperienced (ἀπείροις; *B.J.* 6.291), according to Josephus, read it as a σημεῖον of coming desolation (*B.J.* 6.296).

Josephus also describes the 'careers' of a number of figures designated as 'sign prophets' who gather followings of various magnitude and generally meet a disastrous end. [42] His account is interesting for the light that the presence of these figures, and Josephus's account of them, sheds on the historical context for the ministry of Jesus.[43] Josephus mentions a Samaritan

---

[42] 'Sign prophets' is not Josephus's term, but was coined by Barnett (1981: 679).

[43] Hill (1979), Barnett (1981) and Gibson (1995: 290–93) all discuss the implications of the 'sign prophets' for the study of the Gospels. Barnett's tentative suggestion that the sign

(*A.J.* 18.85–87), the brief career of Theudas (*A.J.* 20.97–99), an unidentified number of γόητες καὶ ἀπατεῶνες who call upon the people to follow them into the desert (*B.J.* 2.258–60; *A.J.* 20.167–8), and others as well.[44]

Throughout these accounts language echoing the exodus accounts is prominent, including that of (promised) signs and wonders. The accounts of the sign prophets suggest a volatile context of prophetic speculation in the times that Josephus describes. The importance of the Mosaic traditions in both the populist movements that Josephus describes and his criticisms of them is clear. The promise of signs of freedom or salvation and the symbolism of withdrawing to the desert draw on the patterns established in the Scriptural record. The sign prophets appear to have regarded their activities as heralding the coming of God's salvation and even, as Barnett suggests, in some sense forcing this salvation to come about.[45] Certainly their claims or promises were convincing and evocative enough to attract a crowd. On the other hand, Josephus uses the same Mosaic traditions to criticise the sign prophets. They are consistently described in terms that evoke the magicians of Egypt, who are the opponents of God and his true prophet. The Mosaic traditions remain central for Josephus and perhaps the only genuine signs in the sense of miraculous acts.[46]

2.2.3.2.1 Josephus: Summary

While there is evidence in Josephus of the full range of meaning connected with the use of the word σημεῖον, his portrayal of signs as confirming the activity of God or attesting God's chosen representatives is indebted to the Hebrew Scriptures. This is distinct from the sense of a sign as an omen portending the future. Josephus's understanding is most clearly seen (and shaped) by the use in connection with Moses. There are strong connections established between the perception of signs and the stimulating of faith present as well. This connection, while established in the Mosaic accounts, needs to be qualified by Josephus's awareness of the possibility of misreading signs and the disastrous consequences for those who do so. His general attitude to the followers of the sign prophets is one of incredulity for their gullibility. While the possibility exists for genuine faith based upon the genuine signs of God, signs can also be ignored, misread and rejected.

---

prophets were inspired by the activities of Jesus is the most radical suggestion. For a critique of his position see Bittner (1987: 71–4).

[44] Josephus also refers to an anonymous Egyptian (*B.J.* 2.261), an unnamed γόης (*A.J.* 20.187), a weaver named Jonathan (*B.J.* 7.438). Judas the Galilean is also mentioned as a potential figure amongst this gallery (*B.J.* 2.118; *A.J.* 18.23) but see Hill (1979: 146–7).

[45] Barnett 1981: 688.

[46] MacRae (1965) suggests that Josephus is the 'victim of tensions between Judaism and Hellenism', accepting miracles as the work of God but also offering pseudo-scientific or pseudo-philosophical explanations if they come to mind (p. 142).

2.2.3.3 Philo

Like Josephus, Philo knows of the sense of σημεῖον as both omen and accrediting sign. In *Aet.* 2, the knowledge of heavenly things is said to be possible through dreams, oracles, signs and wonders. He also points out that God has refused to impart knowledge of heavenly things due to injustice and folly (cf. also *Somn.* 2.1; *Opif.* 58).

Philo also draws at length on the Hebrew Bible's presentation of signs, especially the Mosaic accounts (*Mos.* 1.76–83; 210). Again, signs attest to the authority of God's messenger. For Philo signs are a significant part of God's revelation to man (*Det.* 177; *Mos.* 1.71, 1.76, 1.199). They are given for the purpose of persuasion (*Mos.* 1.76, 1.82, 1.90) and belief and obedience are expected in response (*Mos.* 1.95–165; cf. *Migr.* 68). From Philo's perspective, God does not chastise the righteous for asking for signs (*QG* 3.2; *Aet.* 2). Rather, signs both reveal God's will and substantiate the authority of his messenger; they are given to persuade the recipient to belief and as such are an integral part of Israel's history and are to be remembered and celebrated as such (*Spec.* 2.189; *Contempl.* 85–89).

The meaning of a particular sign is generally clear although the precise nature of a particular sign may be unknown. This is the case for example in Philo's discussion of the mark placed on Cain (*Det.* 177.1). However, a particular sign can also be ambiguous. This is illustrated by a discussion concerning the placement of the law, in a phylactery, on one's hand. Philo admits that the meaning of this particular placement is indeterminate because it is a sign of many things (*Spec.* 4.138). Philo also acknowledges that the meaning of signs can be resisted. Despite a demonstration before the Egyptian magicians of the superiority of Moses's sign, Philo records that they resisted the will of God indicated with 'the proofs of signs and wonders, which are clearer than oracles' (*Mos.* 1.95, trans. F.H. Colson).

2.2.3.4 Summary: Religious Use

Both Philo and Josephus distinguish the attesting sense of σημεῖον from the omen sense and acknowledge that their readers might not be entirely familiar with the former use. This is seen in passages where the function of a sign is clarified. Philo does this through the addition of ἀποδείξεσι in his discussion of the Mosaic signs (*Mos.* 1.95), while Josephus seems to go to some lengths as well to show that the signs he speaks of with respect to Moses have this more demonstrative role (*A.J.* 2.274, 276, 280). Both writers affirm the ultimate origin of the sign as residing with Yahweh, although the sign itself might be performed by an authorised representative and accompanied by an interpretative word. This stands in contrast to the

Graeco–Roman understanding of the omen as being the direct work of the gods and the sign as an omen having to be interpreted for its content.[47]

The significance of this distinction between σημεῖον as an omen and σημεῖον as an attesting sign is twofold. In the first instance, when it comes to assessing the background of John's use, it is more likely that he has taken it in the sense of attesting sign via the Hebrew Scriptures than from the Hellenistic use. Second, clarifying the use of the term, in a manner similar to that attempted by both Philo and Josephus, is necessary in order to establish its precise nuance in the Gospel. There is potential for confusion, especially if the word is to be used in an overtly religious context.

2.2.4 The Vocabulary of Proof

It was observed above that at least one of the many possible nuances in usage afforded by σημεῖον was in the realm of proof or evidence. Most of the writers surveyed also use σημεῖον in this sense. This aspect of usage remains to be explored for its implications concerning the use of σημεῖον in the Fourth Gospel.

Strabo uses σημεῖον regularly in this sense (cf. the phrase σημεῖον δέ, in *Geog.* 1.1.18; 8.3.30; 8.4.1; 17.1.53). Such evidences consist of names indicating the beginning of the alps (*Geog.* 4.6.1) and the production of fine grain as the proof of the fruitfulness of a country (*Geog.* 5.4.3). Strabo can also qualify the word to give various nuances (οὐ μικρὰ σημεῖα, *Geog.* 8.6.22; and more negatively μοχθηρίω σημείω, *Geog.* 12.3.27). This is a feature of other writers as well as they seek to communicate the relative weight of the proofs they are presenting.

Dionysius also uses σημεῖον with some frequency in this evidential sense (*Antiq. Rom.* 4.13.4; 7.46.4). Dionysius can also qualify his use of sign to indicate a greater degree of certainty (cf. *Antiq. Rom.* 7.52.2, μέγα δὲ τούτου σημεῖόν ἐστιν). Varying degrees of certainty with respect to evidences and proofs are indicated in other passages. In *Antiq. Rom.* 3.72.4, some opponents of King Tarquinius attempt to lay the blame for certain calamities at his feet. Dionysius says that there was neither proof nor evidence (τεκμήριον οὔτε σημεῖον) for this action (cf. *Is.* 15.22 and *Dem.* 12.73 for the same combination). While Dionysius seems to be almost using these terms as equivalents for rhetorical effect, there is in fact a distinction between these two terms that goes back to, at least, Aristotle. In another work when he is discussing the rhetorical abilities of Lysias (*Lys.*19.8), Dionysius comments that Lysias is very good at distinguishing the evidences (σημεῖα) that actions leave behind them and elevating them to the status of positive proof (τεκμηρίων).

---

[47] Formesyn 1962: 868–9.

Plutarch also uses σημεῖον with the sense of proof. In *Comp.Lys.Sull* 1.3-4. he suggest that Sulla's coming to power cannot be regarded as a σημεῖον that Sulla was the best man for the job, as his later dictatorial actions willl demonstrate. It is also used of other incidents that indicate or prove various personal qualities e.g. *Comp. Nic. Crass.* 3.5.6; *Arist* 25.7.2; *Dem* 8.3.3; 8.7.2. In his moral writings the stock phrase σημεῖον οὐ φαῦλόν ἐστιν in various combinations occurs with some regularity (cf. *Virt. Prof.* 76F; 78B; 82A; 84A).

Philo consistently uses σημεῖον in a sense that moves in the realm of proof, indication or argument. What appears to be a stock phrase, σημεῖον δέ, occurs in numerous places during the course of a discussion (e.g. *Det.* 1; *Prob.* 39, 89; *Aet.* 23, *Prov.* 2.26). It can also be qualified, occurring in combinations that stress the more certain nature of the point being made (e.g. σημεῖον ἐναργές, *Mos.* 2.263; σημεῖον δ ἐναργέστατον *Spec.* 1.90; σημεῖον δὲ μέγιστον, *Det.* 3).

In addition to these literary texts, there is also some evidence that the sense of σημεῖον as a proof was also known at a popular level. This surfaces in a series of letters where the use of σημεῖον appears to possess this nuance. In a letter written demanding the settling of accounts, Anthestianus mentions to Psois that he records the details of their affairs 'so that you may know the proof' (ἵν᾽ εἰ[ῆ]c τὸ cημεῖον).[48] There are several other letters where similar references are made apparently with a view to indicating that the letter has originated with the person from whom it purports to have been sent. The indications are of two kinds. Either the details of a conversation are alluded to that can only be known to the participants or else a conversation or incident is described at which the writer was not present and yet he is able to reveal intimate knowledge of its details.[49]

An analogous usage in the New Testament occurs at 2 Thess 3.17 (cf. Gal 6.11) where Paul appears to add a greeting in his own distinctive handwriting to attest the genuineness of his letter. While the usage appears to be particular to the epistolary context these references suggest the use of σημεῖον in ordinary contexts with a sense of proof was perhaps relatively widely known and practiced

---

[48] *P.Oxy* 2996, l. 34.

[49] See Youtie (1970) for further details. The other texts are *P.Petaus* 28, 2nd century A.D., ἄλλο σημίόν σοι γράφω περὶ αὐτοῦ ὅτε ἡ γυνὴ σου ἐξελθοῦσα ἠγόρακε ὀβολῶν ἀρτύματα τῷ ναυτικῷ..., *Sammelbuch* V.8005, 2nd century B.C. (Text in *Aegyptus* 15 [1935]), [Π]άντως οὖν ἀπαρε[ν]όχλητον αὐτὸν [π]οίησον ἐμοὶ χαριζόμενος σημεῖον ὅτι ἡ προθεσμία σου ἐνέστηκεν;, *Sammelbuch* V.7574, 2nd century B.C. (*Aegyptus* 13 [1933]) Σημεῖον ὅτε εἰπά σοι λυτρῶσαι τὸν καινὸν χιτῶνα...; *P.Oxy* 1683 'σημίου δὲ χάριν, ὅπου ἠπάντηκά σου...' and P. Cair.Zen. II 59192 (*Select Papyri* I § 92 [255 B.C.]), σημεῖον δὲ ὅτι σοι ἀπέστειλα παρὰ Σώσου ἐρεβίνθου κριοῦ ἀρ(τάβας) β..

This particular nuance of the use of σημεῖον reflects a discussion that is also to be found at a more technical level in Aristotle and as a basic category in the rhetorical handbooks of various Roman writers.

2.2.4.1 Aristotle

Aristotle's discussion begins by defining the nature of a sign as opposed to a probability (εἰκός) in *An. pr.* 2.27

> A probability is a generally accepted premiss (sic); a sign, however, means a demonstrative premiss which is necessary or generally accepted. That which co-exists with something else, or before or after whose happening something else has happened, is a sign of that something's having happened or being (trans. H. Tredennick).

From this general distinction he then goes on to nuance the discussion further in *Rhet.* 1.2.15–18. He distinguishes between necessary signs (τεκμήριον) upon which demonstrative syllogisms can be built that cannot be refuted and 'non-necessary' signs that are capable of refutation. While these are not specifically labelled, σημεῖον seems to be included as a 'non-necessary' sign.

He distinguishes between the two by way of example. If one says that a woman has had a child because she has milk then this is a necessary sign. If the fact is true then the argument is irrefutable. If, however, one were to say that it is the sign of a fever that a man breathes hard then, although the fact be true (the man breathes hard), this is not a necessary sign as there may well be a number of other explanations. In a later passage he states that 'no sign can furnish a logical conclusion' (*Rhet.* 2.25.8), due to this more tentative nature.

As noted above, many of the writers surveyed appeared to know and employ this distinction between what might be called an unassailable evidence or strong proof and a 'softer' evidence or indication which appears more tentative and is better seen as part of a cumulative case.[50] Aristotle's basic distinction appears with minor variations in the rhetorical works of the later Roman period.

---

[50] Τεκμήριον occurs three times in the LXX—Wis 5.11; 19.13; 3 Macc 3.24. The distinction mentioned above is not so marked in the two instances from Wisdom, but is suggested in the third reference. Luke uses the word in Acts 1.3 with respect to the appearances of Jesus following the resurrection, its only New Testament occurrence. It is also found in Philo, Josephus and the other writers mentioned above with the basic distinction in meaning between the two terms more or less preserved.

2.2.4.2 Rhetorica ad Herrenium

While most likely from the pen of neither Cicero nor Cornifice, an anonymous writing provides another example of Roman rhetoric from early in the first century B.C. As such it sheds further light on the evidential value of signs; it also locates the terminology within the context of legal trials.

The author speaks of the rhetorical task of the public speaker in a judicial cause under six headings, one of which is proof. It is under this heading that the most expansive discussion of signs takes place. In the context of a criminal trial it is stated that it is 'By Signs (*signum*) one shows that the accused sought an opportunity favourable to success' (*Rhet. ad Her.* 2.4.6–7). These signs include the following six divisions: the place, point of time, duration of time, occasion, hope of success and the hope of escaping detection. Then follows a discussion of the dimensions of each sign. This use of sign differs from the presentation of Aristotle and Quintilian (see below) but the principle remains the same, that of cumulative proof.[51]

> When there is a concurrence of many circumstantial indications and signs that agree with one another, the result ought to appear as clear fact, not surmise. Again, signs and presumptive proof deserve more credence than witnesses, for these first are presented precisely as they occurred in reality, whereas witnesses can be corrupted... (*Rhet. ad Her.* 2.7.11; trans. H. Caplan).

On the other hand, the author also speaks of how to argue against signs and presumptive proofs:

> we shall show that nothing is safe from attack by suspicion, and then we shall weaken each and every reason for suspicion and try to show that it applies to us no more than anyone else; it is a shameful outrage to consider suspicion and conjecture, in the absence of witnesses, as sufficiently corroborative (*Rhet. ad Her.* 2.7.11, trans. H. Caplan).

Later, when speaking of style, the author will speak of 'Accumulation' under the heading of figures of thought. There are two types of 'Accumulation'. The first aims at impressiveness, sharpness, or incrimination. The second aims at proof and is described as,

> very useful in conjectural cases, when the implications, which were petty and weak because expressed separately, are collated in one place and so seem to make the subject evident and not dubious, as follows: "Do not, therefore, men of the jury, do not consider singly the things I have said, but join them all together and combine them in to one". (*Rhet. ad Her.* 4. 40.53, trans. H. Caplan).

---

[51] For an examination of the language of sign, the connections and correspondences amongst the various terms used see Crapis (1988) and Manetti (1993).

2.2.4.3 Cicero

In a passage from *De Inventione*, Cicero speaks about what it would take to disprove a sign in the rhetorical/legal context (*Inv.* 1.43.81). According to Cicero, a sign must be shown to be true, a proper sign of the thing under discussion. It is to be an indication that something has been done which ought not to have been done or something not done which ought to have been done. The person concerned must be shown to have known the law and custom with respect to the matter at hand. In refuting a sign each of these areas can be used to show that the matter under discussion is either not a sign, that it is not an important sign or that it, in fact, favours one's own side and not the opponent's.

2.2.4.4 Quintilian

In his *Institutio Oratoria*, Quintilian outlines the basics of Aristotle's division of artificial and inartificial proofs and discusses the uses and ways of counteracting them in legal speeches.

In 4.9.8–11, Quintilian speaks of other indications (εἰκότα) which do not involve a necessary conclusion. Such probabilities may not be sufficient in themselves to remove doubt but may be of great value if taken in conjunction with other indications. He then mentions the Greek term σημεῖον, its Latin equivalent, *signum* and other possible synonyms (*indicium* or *vestigium*). Such signs enable one to infer that something else has happened. The example he uses is that of a bloodstained garment which may enable one to infer that a murder has taken place. Such a sign is ambiguous. The blood may be the result of a sacrifice or a nosebleed. People who have blood on their garments are not necessarily murderers. Such an indication on its own may not amount to a proof yet it may be useful in evidence along with other indications. A cumulative case may be adduced. Quintilian notes that as result of this process what was previously only a suspicion may become a certainty. Such indications may serve either party in a case; their ultimate force depends upon the extraneous support that they receive.

2.2.4.5 The Vocabulary of Proof: Summary

Aristotle, Cicero, Quintilian and the author of Rhetorica ad Herrenium demonstrate an awareness and analysis of differing levels of proof with particular respect to judicial rhetoric. They offer a more extensive elaboration and discussion of the use found casually amongst the other writers.

There are two points of interest. The first is the use of σημεῖον in this context and its denotation of a kind of proof that is not conclusive. The term τεκμήριον appears to be reserved for this. Signs can form part of a cumulative case, as all the writers agree, but there is an ambiguity, a 'softness' about the evidence they provide which makes the cumulative case and other corroboration necessary. This softness is also indicated by the numerous expressions which attach a qualifier to the use of σημεῖον.

Second, the location of this discussion is the area of judicial rhetoric. The handbooks provide guidelines and instruction for those making legal defences before magistrates or perhaps in the Senate itself. While not all were obviously privy to training in classical rhetoric, it seems that the law courts were an arena with which the language of σημεῖον was connected and, perhaps, widely known. This is suggested by the extensive use of σημεῖον in the rhetorical/legal speeches of Demosthenes. The stock phrase σημεῖον δέ appears (*Or.* 19.58; 21.35) as well as σημεῖον with various qualifiers (*Or.* 19.61; 42.24). The distinction between a τεκμήριον and a σημεῖον is also in evidence (*Or.* 36.12; 54.9).

2.3 Early Christianity

While the interests of this study are in the broader cultural associations that might comprise the repertoire of the early auditors of the text, the possibility must also be acknowledged that many of the early auditors of the Fourth Gospel could well have come to its contents with some familiarity of the writings that comprise what is now known as the New Testament. It will be necessary then to briefly consider some of both the broad and specific features of the usage of σημεῖον in the New Testament writings, with a particular focus on the Synoptic Gospels. The discussion will begin with some general observations before moving to a more specific examination of the clusters of usage in the Synoptic Gospels. Some brief comments will then follow with respect to occurrences in Acts and Paul.

2.3.1 General Observations

In general, it may be observed that the wide range of usage observed above is in evidence with respect to the use of σημεῖον in the New Testament. A σημεῖον can simply be a mark or signal indicating some kind of information. The archetypal usage in this case is the kiss that Judas offers as the pre-arranged sign at the arrest of Jesus (Matt 26.28; cf. Josephus *A.J.* 12.404). A similar sense is implicit is the disciples' question as to what signs ought to be expected as indicating the coming of all that Jesus has spoken of in the temple discourse in the Synoptic Gospels (Matt 24.3. Mk 13.4; Lk 21.7). The sense is that of indicators with the question being left open as to possible miraculous nature or otherwise of these indicators. A more overtly miraculous sense is present in verses where σημεῖον is coupled with τέρας, especially in the book of Acts where σημεῖον on its own is also connected with a specific act of healing (Acts 4.22). Signs and wonders in the instances in Acts are actions performed in the name of Jesus by his appointed apostles and they have an attesting function in that they verify the authorised representatives of Jesus. This is similar to the signs that accompanied and attested the chosen prophet of God in the Old Testament, and verified the truth of their message. The performing of signs and wonders is also said to have attested the identity of Jesus to the crowds who heard Peter's sermon a Pentecost (Acts 2.22; cf. Heb 2.4). An occurrence, early in Luke, has a sense akin to proof and uses the expression, καὶ τοῦτο ὑμῖν τὸ σημεῖον, familiar from the Old Testament Scriptures (Ex 3.12; 1Sam 2.34; 2Kings 19.29; Isa 37.30). The shepherds are told that the sign of the great news of the birth of the Son of David is the presence of a baby in manger (Lk 2.12). While the occurrence in mind is unique there is no indication that there is anything special to be observed about the child. It is the circumstances of the occurrence that will confirm to the shepherds that what is being spoken about is true (cf Luke 2.16, 20). The sense of σημεῖον as a proof also occurs in the New Testament in an epistolary context. At the end of 2 Thessalonians Paul writes a greeting in his own hand as a sign of the letter's veracity (2 Thess 3.17).

2.3.2 The Synoptic Gospels

When speaking of the Synoptic Gospels the first point to note is their avoidance of the use of the term σημεῖον when describing the miracles of Jesus. The preferred term is δύναμις. This is generally accounted for by the greater concentration in the Synoptic gospels on the inbreaking of the Kingdom of God. In the powerful deeds of Jesus, God's rule is anticipated and begins to have its effect.[52]

The Synoptic usage of σημεῖον clusters in two main areas. The first concerns the rejection, by Jesus, of requests for a sign (Matt. 12.39; 16.1,3,4; cf. Mk. 8.11, 12; Lk 11.16). This statement is generally seen as evidence of a negative attitude on the part of the Synoptic authors to the category of σημεῖα.[53] The request is described in the various accounts as a test or temptation (πειράζω Matt. 16.4; Mk. 8.11). Jesus refuses the request with the accompanying statement (in Matt. 12.39; 16.4; Lk. 11.29) that no sign shall be given except for the sign of Jonah.

Rengstorf observes that the way that the request is reported suggests that the miracles in the Synoptic perspective are not considered signs but, rather, that the performance of miracles gives rise to the request for a sign.[54] What

---

[52] Betz 1976: 603.

[53] Eg. Hooker 1997: 17.

[54] Rengstorf, 1971: 235; cf. Hooker 1997: 18

appears to be requested is an authenticating miracle demonstrating that Jesus' authority comes from God and not Beelzebul.[55]

In the accounts in Matthew and Luke Jesus does offer a sign in response to the crowd's request: the enigmatic τὸ σημεῖον 'Ιωνᾶ (Matt 12.39; 16.4; Lk 11.29–32). This is an enigmatic reference and appears to be intended in both Matt 12 and Luke 11 as a genitive of apposition in the sense that term σημεῖον is clarified by the following term Jonah.[56] Beyond this there is much debate amongst scholars as to the precise meaning of the sign offered.[57] In Matt. 12 Jesus appears to be using the sign reference to point to his resurrection, while in Luke the comparison is between Jonah as a sign to the Ninevites and Jesus as a sign to this generation. While this appears to put the focus on the relative preaching ministries of the two figures, it is more likely also to be a reference to the resurrection as Jesus' miraculous escape from death.[58] Whatever the specific interpretation of the passage the implication is clear at least that an individual can 'be' a sign in some sense (cf. Isa. 8.18; 20.3; Ezek. 12.6)

The second cluster of occurrences concerns the eschatological signs requested by the disciples with respect to discerning the destruction of the temple and the end of the age (Matt 24.3; Mk 13.4; Lk. 21.7, 11, 25). In this context Jesus mentions that false prophets and false Christs will also perform signs (Matt 24.24; Mk 13.22). Here a cautionary note is certainly introduced concerning thinking about signs. If false Christs and prophets can perform such signs and lead astray the elect then dependence upon them is implicitly questioned. There is at least some reserve expressed in these statements as to

---

[55] Hooker 1997:18. Gibson (1995: 299) suggests that this is not a refusal of a request for signs per se but for a certain type of sign, one that is ἀπὸ τοῦ οὐρανοῦ (Matt 16.4; Mk 8.11). He suggests that most likely background for understanding this request is the presence of the Jewish sign prophets (see above pp.). In this context, what Jesus was being requested to perform was a sign of deliverance similar to that promised by this group; a sign that would be considered as a 'triumphalistic, imperious' activity that Jesus eschews throughout the Gospels. Hence, Jesus' refusal. Gibson (pp. 276-9) further points to the 'sign like' quality of a number of Jesus' actions; especially the linking of the healing of the paralytic in Mark 2 with the assertion that he is able to forgive sins. For Gibson this demonstrates that the Markan Jesus is not averse to giving of signs. Hooker (1997: 34) notes the resemblance but suggests that what is occurring in this instance is not an authenticating sign but a prophetic sign demonstrating 'the much more significant thing the Son of man has *already* done' (p. 34). While both these observations are of interest and worthy of further thought it remains true that the vocabulary of σημεῖον is not connected with the performing of the miracles in the Synoptics, which are designated by the term δύναμις.

[56] Hooker 1997: 18-20; Rengstorf 1971: 233. Wallace (1996: 94-100) differentiates simple apposition and the genitive of apposition.

[57] Hooker (1997: 18-31) has a summary of the discussion and the various interpretative options.

[58] Marshall 1978: 485.

the use of σημεῖον. It is also to be noted that this note is repeated in many of the references to signs in Revelation (cf. Rev. 13.13, 14; 16.14; 19.20).

Finally, two references may be considered where the language of σημεῖον is applied to the person of Jesus. First, in the context of the apocalyptic discourse as recorded by Matthew, there stands a reference to τὸ σημεῖον τοῦ υἱοῦ τοῦ ἀνθρώπου (Matt 24.30). Davies and Allison's discussion of this verse is illuminating.[59] Drawing on the work of Higgins and Glasson[60] they suggest that the most plausible background for this statement is the use of the Hebrew נס as sign or ensign. The Davidic connections with this usage (cf Isa. 11.10) also make plausible the suggestion that the phrase be read as a genitive of apposition. The complex idea being expressed is that the sign of the Son of Man is the Son of Man himself coming on the cross as a rallying sign for the ingathering of the people of God.[61] While Davies and Allison, with most commentators see this as an eschatological sign connected with the parousia the possibility is also open that this is a reference to the eschatological coming of the Son of Man on the cross.[62]

Second, Luke 2.34 records the words of Simeon, prophesying that Jesus will be a sign that is opposed (ἀντιλέγω)[63] and that will divide the people of Israel. Once again Jesus himself is referred to as a sign. While most commentators agree that the imagery of the stone that causes stumbling is behind the saying[64] (despite the fact that there is no verbal link), Nolland pushes further and suggests that the idea of the banner or נס may also lie behind this statement as well.[65] Here at least is some verbal correspondence. If this is so then there are two references in the Gospels that refer to Jesus as a sign, employing language that refers to the eschatological ensign raised in passages such as Isaiah 11.10-12; 49.22; 62.10; 66.19). The possibility of further Davidic connections via Isa 11.10-12 are also suggestive.

While it is likely that the Synoptic Gospels (or at least the traditions recorded in them) were known to John and many in his audience, the relationship between the Synoptics and John is an area of investigation that

---

[59] Davies and Allison, 1997: 358-60.

[60] Higgins 1962-3: 380-2; Glasson 1964: 299-300.

[61] Gundry 1994: 488

[62] This suggestion is based on an extrapolation from the suggestive work on Mark 13 completed by Bolt (1991; 1995). Bolt's conclusions on the relationship of the apocalyptic discourse in Mark of the narrative of the Gospel and its climax in the death of Jesus at least invites another look at the narratives in Matthew and Luke to see whether the apocalyptic discourses in these Gospels might also be read in similar fashion.

[63] Rengstorf (1971: 238) suggests contested to indicate the twofold nature of the response to Jesus.

[64] See for example Bock (1994: 249) and Green (1997: 149).

[65] Nolland, 1989: 121.

lies outside of the remit of this particular study.[66] The reader familiar with the usage in the rest of the documents that comprise the New Testament would, however, be most likely struck by the prominence of the term in the Fourth Gospel, the apparent freedom with which John applies σημεῖον to miraculous activity, and its positive connections with faith in the narrative.

2.3.3 Acts and Paul

The further evidence of Acts and Paul may be dealt with briefly. Of note is the concentrated use of the phrase signs and wonders in Acts (Acts 2.22, 43; 4.30; 5.12; 6.8; 7.36; 14.3; 15.12); cf 8.6, 13 where σημεῖον is used alone), and also the fact that it is the apostles who perform these signs and wonders in the name of Jesus as his accredited representatives. A similar attesting function is in evidence in Paul's writings (cf. 2 Cor 12.12). A further interesting feature of the Acts references is the apparent implied equivalence of δύναμις and σημεῖον in a couple of references (Acts 8.13; cf. 19.11). In Acts 4 the miracle performed is referred to as a γνωστὸν σημεῖον (4.16) and the hearing of the report of the action leads to faith (4.4).

2.4 Summary

It is clear that σημεῖον is an ordinary word, in common use, and capable of a considerable variety of denotation. In the most general sense, it denotes some perceptible phenomenon, possibly extraordinary, that communicates information or an understanding of some kind that will invite a response. It seems reasonable to suggest that a reader coming across the word will pay some attention to the context in which it is found to limit the possible range of meaning. It has a considerable history of use in religious contexts, thereby denoting communication from the gods and, allied to this use, can carry evidentiary connotations with respect to either the bearer of the divine communication or the content of the divine communication. For a reader with some knowledge of the Hebrew Scriptures the expression could not fail to conjure images of the acts of God, through Moses, in the exodus: actions that attest his chosen representative and 'son', judge the gods of Egypt and bring about the release of his people. The expression may also recall the language used in the prophetic books, again attesting to the chosen status of God's

---

[66] Though the discussions on Matt 24.30 and Luke 2.34 below are suggestive for their possible implications re the relationships amongst the Gospels. It could be argued that there is a narrative appropriation and expansion of one or both of the concepts suggested in these two texts in the Fourth Gospel. The interpretations of both verses involve numerous difficulties and further speculation along the lines suggested is best left for further research.

appointed representatives, guaranteeing the veracity of their message and in some situations 'embodying' the message itself. Those familiar with the content and vocabulary of the Synoptic gospels will also come with an understanding of the use of the term with respect to the ministry of Jesus recorded there.

While it is doubtful whether readers unfamiliar with this background would initially grasp this particular nuance, σημεῖον is eminently suited to a piece of writing that presses the claims of an individual to be an attested representative of God. This is true both from the perspective of a Jewish or Graeco–Roman audience. The patently religious context of the Gospel according to John immediately limits the potential understanding of the term, although the apparently different understandings of a σημεῖον as an omen or as an attesting or legitimating sign remain to be explored and perhaps negotiated in the text of the Gospel. However, enough of a connection is established in the term itself and the surrounding context for resonance to be established.

For all readers the expectation of some sort of context for the interpretation of the sign would also seem to be a realistic possibility. This might be in advance of the sign, accompanying the sign or, as in the case of 'future signs', seeing the fulfilment of the prophetically predicted events as the sign itself. Finally, the term raises the dilemma of authenticity. How may it be discerned that this sign is genuine communication from the gods/God? This question was posed in both Jewish and Graeco–Roman writings.[67] Steps would need to be taken to establish a frame of reference that would enable the reader to come to the conviction that these signs are indeed genuine.

The forensic setting of much of the Fourth Gospel's narrative brings into play the evidential connotations as well. The idea of 'non-necessary signs' or soft proof is a useful connotation to explore. The necessity of a cumulative case with respect to such signs is suggestive in the light of the numerous signs contained in the Gospel. This accumulation might add up to an impressive case in the absence of conclusive or irrefutable proof. The use of σημεῖον may, in itself, suggest the kind of case being argued or proved is of a certain kind, which admits of ambiguity and room for doubt and disbelief.

This is not to suggest, however, that the use of the term σημεῖον is a direct borrowing from the law and senatorial defence world – only that the word would have this weight/connotation for the hearer in the wider Graeco-Roman context. This is suggestive in a Gospel where the presence of legal language and an extensive forensic theme has been frequently noted.[68] It is

---

[67] Betz (1974: 23–30) has a discussion of this point with respect to Josephus and the Rabbis.

[68] Most recently Lincoln (2000).

not suggested that John uses formal rhetorical categories and strategies.[69] The suggestion is, rather, that at least one of the contexts outside of the Gospel where a term like σημεῖον might be regularly associated is the rhetorical tradition as expressed in a legal situation.

This examination has opened up the range of possible connotation for an early reader of the Fourth Gospel. Just what associations might be triggered in the light of the use of the term in the Gospel can only be assessed subsequent to an examination of the use of σημεῖον in the Gospel itself. Such an examination will now be undertaken. This will enable a view to be gained of the way in which the term is used, the context within which it is embedded and the way in which an understanding of the term accrues for the reader throughout the course of the narrative. The results of this investigation can then be correlated with the observations recorded above to yield an integrated view of the function of σημεῖον in the rhetorical strategy of the Gospel; a view that takes account of both directions of approach: text-to-reader and reader-to-text.

---

[69] For the difficulties of establishing such a connection see Stamps (1997: 619–20).

Chapter 3

The Beginning of the Signs: σημεῖον in John 1–4

The next four chapters of this thesis will examine the occurrences of σημεῖον, and the narratives that are designated as σημεῖα, in the major sections of the Gospel. The procedure for each chapter will be as follows. After a brief overview of the section under consideration (Part A), the main analysis will fall into two parts. The first part (B) will look at the specific occurrences of σημεῖον, while the second part (C) will examine the narratives designated as σημεῖα. Each part will first examine the material contained within it from the direction of text-to-reader and then, secondly, from reader-to-text. The reader-to-text comments will briefly comment on the reception of the material by readers familiar with the Hebrew Scriptures before considering, at greater length, reception in the broader Graeco-Roman context. A final summary (D) will complete the investigation in each chapter.

3.1 Overview of Chapters 1–4

John 1–4 comprises the first major section of the Gospel. The first eighteen verses of the Gospel are a prologue that plays a foundational role for the rest of the Gospel in its introduction of main themes and even the pattern of the structure of the Gospel itself.[1] The prologue provides a fundamental perspective to accompany the reader into the rest of the Gospel that is centred on the divine origin and person of Jesus Christ and his place within the flow of salvation history.[2]

1.19–4.54 is delineated as a unit by the presence of the prologue on the one hand and the spatial and numerical markers between incidents in chapters 2 and 4 (2:1 and 4:46; 2:11 and 4:54) on the other. While it is possible to section off 1:19–51, connections exist between 1:19–51 and 2:1–4:54 via the sequence of days established through chapter 1 (1:29, 35, 43, 2:1). It is also possible to argue that 2.1–11 concludes the section from 1.19 as an extended introduction because of the sequence of days. However, the inclusio established with 2.1–11 by 4.54 suggests that 2.1–11 might be better

---

[1] The division of the Gospel into two halves 1–12 and 13–21 is based in part on the division implied in 1.11–13.

[2] Barrett 1972: 45.

considered as a hinge between the two sections 1.19–51 and 2.12–4.54, in effect unifying them.[3]

The section, John 1.19–4.54, presents the credentials of Jesus to the reader in a very positive manner.[4] He is acclaimed with a series of titles (1.45–51, 4.42), performs two miracles, sees many in a village come to believe in him (4.39) and encounters no significant opposition. While there is a subsidiary examination of responses to Jesus, the focus of the presentation is on the person and work of Christ.[5] The identity of Jesus is announced in the prologue (1.1–18), testified to by John (1.19–34) and then corroborated by a series of witnesses (1:35–51).

His story is firmly situated within the context of God's dealings with his people. This is indicated by the structure of the prologue generally,[6] and especially where Jesus' relationship to Moses is presented as one of fulfilment and replacement in the plan of God (1.17). The testimony of John is introduced with a quotation from the prophet Isaiah promising a second exodus for the people of God with the coming of the Lord. The eschatological expectations aroused by this statement are confirmed when John denies his identity as one of three expected figures (1.24–28) and testifies to a future coming one. The focus is on his messianic identity (1.34[7], 1.41, 45, 49; 4.25) and the new order he will bring within the Jewish religion as the fulfilment of the plan of God. The importance of these perspectives is summed up in Jesus' statement to the Samaritan woman that 'salvation is from the Jews' (4.22). At the same time, the focus is broadened from purely national interests via the introduction of κόσμος language (1.29; 3.16) and the recording of narratives dealing with Samaritans and possibly a Gentile (4.46–54). The positive portrayal of Jesus is completed with the acclamation by the Samaritans of Jesus as the 'saviour of the world' (4.42), bringing the section to a climax.

In these early accounts the basis is laid for one of the major thematic elements of the Gospel: a forensic or trial motif.[8] This motif is present

---

[3] Pryor (1992: 98) calls 1:19–51 a 'bridge passage'.

[4] Culpepper (1983: 91), points out the powerful 'primacy effect' that this creates. The identity and mission of Jesus are firmly established in the reader's mind.

[5] Contra Moloney (1980) who over-emphasises the anthropological issues of correct and incorrect faith in his treatment of the whole section.

[6] See the comments above concerning this: pp. 11–12.

[7] This is based on reading ὁ ἐκλεκτός with its messianic connections (cf. Isa 42.1, LXX), rather than ὁ υἱός. It is attested in ℵ b e ff²* syrˢ ᶜ and more recently 𝔓¹⁰⁶ (*P.Oxy* 4445; cf. Head 2000:11). It is far more likely that ὁ ἐκλεκτός was changed to the more familiar ὁ υἱός, while the title itself is coherent in the context of the variety on show in John 1.

[8] The presence of this theme is increasingly recognised in Johannine studies. The studies of Preiss (1954), Dahl (1962), Harvey (1976) and Trites (1977) are important. The most recent and comprehensive examination of this theme in the Fourth Gospel is by Lincoln (2000).

throughout the Gospel and centres on the presentation of the career of Jesus as a 'giant juridical contest'.[9] The confrontation between God and the world is played out in the encounter between Jesus and the Jews in the Gospel. The point at issue in this trial is the recognition and worship of the true God. Jesus is sent to testify to the identity and purposes of God, to take away the sin of the world, and therefore to bring life. His testimony is questioned, accepted by some and rejected by others. In their response to Jesus, people either receive life or remain under condemnation.

The motif draws on the extensive use of legal motifs in the Hebrew Scriptures, especially Isaiah 40–55 where a controversy is presented between Yahweh and the false gods of the nations.[10] The debate is over the claims of Yahweh as creator, the only true God and Lord of history. Yahweh is the presiding judge as well as one of the parties in dispute. The silence of the opposing gods is evidence of their falsehood and they are condemned. In the midst of this trial Israel is called to be a witness and servant (43:10,12). Jesus takes the role of the chief witness in the application of this motif in the Fourth Gospel (3.11, 32). He will also cite a number of other witnesses to aid his testimony in the disputes between himself and his opponents (cf. 5.30–47). His testimony is heatedly examined in disputes with the Jews. A further nuance is observed when Harvey notes the fluidity of role between accused and accuser in Jewish trials. The accused could become the accuser and judge in the course of the trial, as, he suggests, happens in the Gospel's trials.[11]

---

[9] Preiss 1954: 17.

[10] Trites (1977: 84–88) and Lincoln (2000: 38–51) explore this link.

[11] Harvey 1976: 46–66. A recent study by Asiedu–Peprah (2001) challenges the way in which this motif is conceived. He contends that previous work in this area has traded on a faulty understanding of the Old Testament rîb pattern of controversy. The rîb is not a trial or judicial process, as been previously understood, but rather a juridical controversy which is essentially bilateral. In this fresh understanding the two disputants deal with the problem themselves, with each party attempting to convince the other of the justice of their position. The dispute goes to a third party for a final judgement when agreement cannot be reached (pp. 14–16). Asiedu-Peprah claims that this understanding more accurately reflects the Gospel's approach. It describes a juridical process between Jesus and the Jews and not a trial as such. This avoids the 'legal monstrosity' that is created when it appears that a judge is involved in a case where he has a vested interest as Harvey (1976: 55, 103) suggests occurs in the 'trials' of the Fourth Gospel. However Asiedu-Peprah's position fails to appreciate the use of the motif in the narrative of the Fourth Gospel and take account of the places where it is clear that Jesus (and the Jews) are prepared to pronounce judgement, as indeed Yahweh appears to be doing so as well in the Old Testament material. In the background narratives of the rîb pattern in Isaiah it is difficult to identify the third party to whom a dispute between Yahweh and the nations or Yahweh and Israel can be referred; Yahweh is after all the judge of all the earth. Harvey (2002: 224) speaks of the need to distinguish between civil and criminal cases as well as take account of the fact that the dispute is about divine law, where those who witness the offence may be best qualified to accuse, prosecute and *execute* the penalty.

The trial theme also carries on beyond the frame of the Gospel narrative. The Paraclete, with the help of the disciples, will continue to press the substantial issues of the trial conducted in the Gospel, beyond the time of Jesus, as the disciples testify to the world (cf. 15.26–27; 16.8–11).

The motif is carried initially by the use of vocabulary in chapters 1–4 and then also by the setting in chapters 5–12. It is established initially by the solemn pronouncements made by John, which introduce the declaration concerning his μαρτυρία (1:19). The testifying function of John is important throughout the section (cf. 1.7; 1.19–35; 3.27–30). Jesus also refers to himself as a witness in the conversation with Nicodemus (3.11–13) and then his ministry is spoken of in terms of judgement (3.19), hinting at this role that will be filled out in the course of the Gospel's presentation. The language of testimony also occurs in the section of the Gospel dealing with the testimony of the Samaritan woman to her compatriots (4.39).

These opening chapters introduce the main characters in the trial to be conducted through the Gospel and present the claims and credentials of the chief witness in the trial, Jesus. Readers are therefore encouraged to align themselves with the perspective on Jesus presented in these opening chapters. This perspective is then tested in the controversy narratives of chapters 5–10.

3.2 The Occurrences of σημεῖον

3.2.1 The Occurrences of σημεῖον: Text to Reader

There are six occurrences of σημεῖον in this opening section of the Gospel. Three are mentioned in asides by the narrator (2.11, 2.23, 4.54), two occur on the lips of characters in the narrative (2.18, 3.2) and one occurs on the lips of Jesus (4.48). In each case, the verbs associated with the occurrence indicate the visual nature of the actions referred to (ποιέω, δείκνυμι, ὁράω). Two incidents are clearly designated as signs. They are the transforming of water into wine at the wedding at Cana in chapter 2 (2.11) and the healing of a court official's son in chapter 4 (4.54). The term σημεῖον and the sign narratives are prominent and immediately marked as a significant part of the Gospel's discourse.

3.2.1.1 The Beginning and the End of the Signs (Jn 2.1–11, 18)

The term is first introduced in the Gospel at the conclusion of the narrative describing the transforming of water into wine at the wedding at Cana (2.11). This statement labels the account the ἀρχή sign, Jesus is said to manifest his glory and his disciples are said to believe in him. As well as designating this particular incident as a σημεῖον, the three parts of this statement provide a powerful initial orientation for the audience to the meaning and function of the term and also the incidents that are subsequently designated as signs in the Gospel.

2.11 states that this was the ἀρχὴν τῶν σημείων that Jesus did.Ἀρχή is often translated as 'first', understandably so considering the later use of δεύτερος at 4.54 and the expectation of a sequence implied by the plural σημείων. However, more seems to be intended by ἀρχή and it is better rendered 'beginning'. This preserves the idea of a sequence but also exploits the potential of the foundational or paradigmatic sense that 'beginning' can have.[12] This seems to have been the understanding of some additions in the manuscript tradition. Both 𝔓⁶⁶* and ℵ* have the additional word πρῶτον in the verse. The addition in both cases seems be either an attempt to specify the meaning of ἀρχή further or to bring it into line with 4.54. In either case the meaning of ἀρχή seems to have been taken as other than purely temporal and certainly not read as wholly synonymous with πρῶτος.[13] The implication is that this sign is not only the first in a series but the 'opening act of a much larger work, the foundation and pattern for everything that follows'.[14] The statement also suggests that other signs are anticipated in the narrative and that they are also to be read within the framework of understanding that is established in this inaugural sign.

An essential part of this framework of understanding is that Jesus manifests his δόξα in the sign. With the mention of glory the reader is taken back to the prologue of the Gospel where the reader was informed that glory beheld in the person of Jesus is that of the μονογενοῦς παρά πατρός (1.14). The explicit connection forged between the signs and glory in the statement of 2.11 tells the reader how to interpret the sign at Cana and the further signs that are anticipated. The signs will function to display the glory that marks out the Son as the unique divine representative of the Father. Moreover, it is the glory of one who shares in the divine nature of the Father, as both the opening and closing verses of the prologue assert. 'His glory' (2.11) is that of the Father and therefore divine glory. This is confirmed when it is stated in 1.14 that the glory of 'the unique one' is full of grace and truth.[15] The combination of grace and truth in the prologue most likely reflects the description of Yahweh in the Hebrew Scriptures, as expressed in the Hebrew phrase חֶסֶד וֶאֱמֶת. The particular background for this expression is the

---

[12] BDAG: 'ἀρχή', 137–8; see also Barrett (1978: 193).

[13] Olsson 1974: 64.

[14] Ridderbos 1997: 113. See also R.F. Collins (1990).

[15] The indeclinable πλήρης most likely refers to μονογενοῦς. It could refer to either λόγος, μονογενοῦς or πατρός. πατρός is unlikely in the light of the fact that the ongoing discussion concerns the λόγος. The closest antecedent is μονογενοῦς, though the distinction from λόγος is negligible.

revelation of Yahweh to Moses in Exod 34.[16] In this context, the terms together refer to the character of Yahweh expressed in his covenantal faithfulness as evidenced in the fulfilment of his promises. The reference at 2.11 establishes for the reader an understanding of the signs as indicating a divine manifestation which is to be understood within the framework of the history of Israel (1.16) and the relationship between the only Son and the Father. Ultimately the signs designate Jesus as one who shares in the divine identity.[17]

The third part of the statement demonstrates that believing is the appropriate response to such a manifestation of glory. However, only the response of the disciples is recorded. It appears to be important for the reader to know that they were present as witnesses to the event and responded to what they saw. According to the prologue, this belief entitles them to become children of God (1.12). The situating of this reaction in this final comment indicates the paradigmatic response to a sign—see Jesus' glory and believe. The reader is implicitly invited to join the disciples and draw the same conclusions.

The next reference to σημεῖον occurs in the context of the account of Jesus cleansing the temple (2.18). The 'Jews', as a group are introduced here for the first time in the Gospel and they answer (ἀπεκρίθησαν) Jesus' actions with a request for a σημεῖον. On their lips, the term has a different nuance to that suggested in the previous occurrence at 2.11. While the σημεῖον there was a visible manifestation of the glory of Jesus, here it is a demand for an authenticating or legitimating action in the light of Jesus' actions and statements in the temple.

The reader may be confused at this point. The statement at 2.11 has led to the expectation of more significant actions from Jesus. The drama of the activity of the temple cleansing, his strong words of denunciation and implicit identification with God as his Father suggest that this event might also be viewed as a σημεῖον. The Scripture that is recalled by the disciples adds further significance to the event (2.17). On the other hand, the Jews then request a sign. This suggests that they, at least, do not see this action as a sign. Is the point, then, that this incident is not a sign or rather that, from John's

---

[16] Both Brown (1970: 14) and Gese (1971: 204–9) have extensive discussions. חֶסֶד is never rendered by χάρις except in Esther 2.9, though as Gese points out, in later writings this identification was made. The translation of the Hebrew Text by Symmachus attests to the identification as well (Gese 1971: 205). Barrett (1978: 167) notes much of the above and points to the christological appropriation of terms that have currency in both the Hebrew and Hellenistic conceptual worlds. Moloney (1998: 45) demurs on this point in favour of a hendiadys that focuses on the gift of truth. However, the allusion to the exodus material remains likely in view of the multiple allusions in the context of vss. 14–18.

[17] Bauckham (1998a: 7–9, 40–41) suggests the term divine identity in his study of monotheism and Christology.

perspective, the obtuseness of the Jews is being highlighted in that they are asking for a sign having just seen one?[18] It is difficult to decide. The initial impression is that what occurs here is a significant action that is not designated as a sign by either its observers in the narrative or the narrator of the Gospel. The offering of a sign by Jesus, that would certainly have a spectacular element about it, if taken up, and the narrator's comment clarifying the referent of Jesus' statement (2.19–22), together point in this direction. Later references to σημεῖον in the Gospel suggest that powerful, extraordinary actions are denoted by the term.[19]

Regardless of the decision made concerning the status of the temple cleansing, it is clear that one complex incident is designated as a sign: the destruction and rebuilding of the temple. While this is interpreted on the literal level, with some incredulity, by the hearers (and no doubt also the reader), John intervenes at this point to suggest a symbolic interpretation by pointing out that the statement refers to Jesus' own body (2.21). The destruction and rebuilding of the temple refers to the complex event that is the death and resurrection of Jesus.[20] This is offered as a sign to the audience of the Gospel in an explanatory aside (2.21–22). This statement places the concluding events of the story in the mind of the audience from the very beginning and suggests that those later events are to be read in σημεῖον terms. Jesus' dramatic and controversial action in the temple will receive its ultimate justification in his death and resurrection. The disciples are also said to have recalled and understood Jesus' saying and the Scripture following Jesus' resurrection from the dead. This points to a time beyond the resurrection when a final understanding of Jesus (including the significance of all his actions, sign or otherwise) will be possible.

The combination of the opening two references to σημεῖον has led the reader from the 'beginning of the signs' to contemplate the 'end' of the signs in the death and resurrection of Jesus. Already subtle linkages are established to help the reader to understand that the death and resurrection of Jesus are a sign that manifests divine glory.

3.2.1.2 Requesting a Sign (Jn 2.23–25)

A jarring note is introduced into the presentation with the next reference to σημεῖον (2.23–25). The initial reading of this passage suggests that it falls into line with the pattern already established by John's comments at 2.11. Many in the crowd see τὰ σημεῖα ἃ ἐποίει and ἐπίστευσαν εἰς τὸ

---

[18] Carson (1991: 181) suggests this.

[19] For an extended argument for considering the temple cleansing as a sign see Köstenberger (1995).

[20] This is perhaps indicated by the unusual phrase ἐν τρισὶν ἡμέραις which Wilkens (1969: 63–4) suggests encompasses the entire complex of the death and resurrection of Jesus.

ὄνομα αὐτοῦ. This appears to be true belief in the prologue's terms (cf. 1.12; 2.11). Again, signs lead to belief. The mention of the plural σημεῖα is significant in that a quantity of signs is suggested although none are specifically mentioned. This implies that a process of selection has taken place. Σημεῖα is not a special term for a few incidents. Rather, the relatively few incidents recorded are a selection from a much wider possible array. Jesus' ministry is, by implication, full of σημεῖα.

In the light of the connection apparently established between signs and belief it comes as a surprise when Jesus refuses to entrust himself to those who would come to him (2.23). The reason given is that Jesus knows all about people. This whole sequence may appear to call into question the relationship between signs and faith in the Fourth Gospel. It is often suggested that John views with suspicion such signs-based faith and favours a higher faith based on the word of Jesus.[21] At best, however, this is an open question at this stage of the Gospel. The explanation is given in terms of Jesus' knowledge of humanity and not in terms of the inadequacy of faith based on signs. Admittedly, this occurs in the context of the relationship between signs and belief. However, John raises the larger issue of what it means to believe, as much as the relationship between faith and signs. In the course of the Gospel narrative a similar problem occurs with people who come to believe in Jesus on the basis of his word (cf. 8.31). The two imperfect verb forms, ἐπίστευσεν and ἐγίνωσκεν hint at the ongoing nature of both Jesus' knowledge and response to humanity. There is a gap, already hinted at in the prologue (1.5, 10, 11), that will need to be crossed in order for the promise of the prologue (1.12–13) to be finally achieved. This gap is stressed by the repetition of αὐτός in vv. 24–25 that emphasises the contrast between Jesus and the rest of humanity.[22] The Gospel hints at a fundamental instability in humanity when it comes to the knowledge of God so that Jesus will not entrust himself to the many who believe in his signs. While Jesus is presented as drawing followers, he deliberately does not entrust himself to others who believe. The initiative in any kind of relationship remains with Jesus.[23] There is a fundamental flaw in the simple equation of signs and faith but that flaw does not reside in the signs, rather it resides in the perceiver of the sign.

---

[21] The classical statement of this position is that of Bultmann (1971: 207–9), who describes the Gospel's position as acknowledging faith based upon miracles but anticipating that people will move beyond this. There are a number of variations that follow this basic line, e.g. Schnackenburg (1968: 571). Becker (1970), Nicol (1972: 99–103), C. R. Koester (1989: 332).

[22] Wallace 1996: 349.

[23] Bonney (2002: 68) suggests that this is an example of the presentation of Jesus throughout the Gospel acting independently and directing his own affairs.

3.2.1.3 Reading the Signs (Jn 3.2)

This point is illustrated and expanded upon almost immediately in the discussion between Jesus and Nicodemus. The repetition of ἄνθρωπος (2.25; 3.1) connects the two sections. Here is a man whom Jesus 'knows'. The introduction of Nicodemus as both Pharisee and a leader of the Jews characterises him as a religious expert. His plural address (οἴδαμεν) of Jesus suggests that the assessment that he makes concerning Jesus is authoritative and probably reflects the consensus of a group for whom he speaks.[24] Nicodemus greets Jesus as ἀπὸ Θεοῦ ἐλήλυθας διδάσκαλος on the basis of the signs that he has performed. The plural σημεῖα again emphasises the multitudinous nature of Jesus' actions while Nicodemus's assessment connects the observation of these actions with perception concerning divine matters. In this comment the audience is instructed on how to both read and misread the signs. They are read correctly in that they attract attention to Jesus and provide some intimation of his identity and relationship to God. They are misread in that the reader sees that the acknowledgement made by Nicodemus is true but unsatisfactory, falling well short of the assessment revealed already in the opening chapter of the Gospel. Nicodemus' statement will be challenged and shown to be totally inadequate as the conversation ensues.[25]

In his response to Nicodemus's christological assessment, Jesus replies, referring to himself, that no-one can see the Kingdom of God unless he is born from above. Jesus' signs indicate that he is ἀπὸ Θεοῦ ἐλήλυθας διδάσκαλος but they do so in a far more profound sense than Nicodemus suggests. Nicodemus's misunderstanding of Jesus' term ἄνωθεν (from above, cf. 3.31) demonstrates his earthly understanding. It also gives the opportunity for Jesus to speak of entry to the kingdom in terms of spiritual rebirth, drawing on the paradigm established in Ezekiel 36. While not the primary intent of the exchange, the discussion with Nicodemus hints at the 'solution' to the problem implicitly posed concerning signs and the recognition of Jesus. One must be born from above. Nicodemus, and the group he represents, have seen the signs but missed the point concerning Jesus' origin, despite moving in the right direction. They need to be born from above and the way to experiencing this is tied to receiving the testimony to both earthly and heavenly matters from the one who has been born from above (3.11–12; cf. 3.31–33[26]).

---

[24] Bittner 1987: 106–7. For the authoritative sense of first person plurals see the discussion by Jackson (1999: 12–22).

[25] Neyrey (1981: 118–122) shows how clearly this is portrayed.

[26] The plurals in 3.11 are often thought to reflect the background of the Johannine community, e.g. Moloney (1983: 115–6). This is unnecessary. The plural is an authoritative plural, used when a solemn pronouncement is made. For details see Jackson (1999: 12-22). It is clear that it is Jesus who speaks and bears witness (Jn 3.31–34; cf. 3.11).

A tension is therefore introduced into the Gospel's presentation of signs. The signs may be seen by all, and will present the glory of the Son, but will only be rightly perceived by 'insiders' who have been born from above.

Readers may also be intended to pick up a further subtle reference to signs in the conversation with Nicodemus. Jesus uses a story from Israel's past to illustrate the manner and benefits of his exaltation as the Son of Man (3.14). The story concerns poisonous snakes, sent as a judgement of God upon Israel in the wilderness (Num 21.6–9). Moses lifts up a bronze snake that allowed any of the Israelites, who looked to the snake, to be saved from the judgement (21.8). The pole on which the snake is lifted up is described in the LXX as a σημεῖον (Num 21.9). The future lifting up of the Son of Man is a reference to the cross of Jesus (cf. 8.28; 12.32, 34). The explicit comparison between this incident and Jesus' future activity on the cross is made in terms of being lifted up (ὑψόω), not in terms of σημεῖον. However this does not deny that, on an implicit level, the cross of Jesus is linked with the language of σημεῖον.[27]

3.2.1.4 Unless You See Signs (Jn 4.48)

The final two references to σημεῖον occur in the context of the narration of the healing of the nobleman's son (4.46–54). Jesus' remark in v. 48 is often held to be critical concerning the faith of the Galileans (and other readers) who rely on signs and therefore critical of the positive connection that signs lead to faith that has been displayed in the narrative so far.[28] However, it may also be possible to read this statement as further affirming the relationship.

The juxtaposition of the transitional passage 4.43–45 with the sign passage and the double repetition of Galilee in v. 46 and v. 47 (that echoes the reference to the Galileans in v. 45) suggest that the remarks of vv. 43–45 are to be taken into account in interpreting v. 48.[29] The Galileans are said to have welcomed Jesus because they saw all that he had done at the feast in Jerusalem (v. 45). The reading ὅσα ἐποίησεν clearly alludes to the mention of signs in the earlier passage (2.23) and emphasises again the quantity of signs observed in Jerusalem.[30] However, the reference also recalls the

---

[27] This is a connection made explicit by some later Christian writers; see *Barn.* 12.5–7; Justin Martyr, *Dial.* 94.112. Brown (1966:133) wonders whether this reference might not be one of the factors that precipitated the choice of σημεῖον for the miracles. Cf. also Glasson (1963: 33–9).

[28] See for example Haenchen (1984: 234).

[29] Contra Labahn (1999: 171–2).

[30] The reading ὅσα is the most likely original here. While some manuscripts have ἅ (א* D), John's usage appears to be that, when referring more generally to the actions or words of Jesus, he prefers either a qualifier stressing the quantity of actions performed or information given or else the use of ὅσα which carries this nuance without the use of such qualifiers. There is a certain amount of variation in the textual tradition based around the usage of these two pronouns (cf. 4.29, 4.39, 11.45, 11.46, 14.26, 21.25).

statement made there concerning Jesus' unwillingness to entrust himself to the response made to his signs. The allusion to this earlier statement in chapter 2 extends the assessment of 2.24-5 to the Galileans as well as the Judeans.

The suspicion cast over the nature of the Galileans' welcome is enhanced by the insertion of v. 44. On any account this is a difficult verse. Its meaning, taken as an isolated axiom,[31] is clear but its positioning in the sequence and its ambiguity are puzzling. Where is Jesus' homeland? This has been variously seen as Judea, Galilee and other more specific places within these two locations. It is clear in the context of this Gospel that Galilee is the homeland of Jesus (1.46; 7.1; 7.42) and the rejection of Jesus in Jerusalem is not so clear cut as interpretations favouring Judea as the homeland suggest.[32] The more immediate context of the statement is the move by Jesus to Galilee from Samaria, where he has been acclaimed as the saviour of the world (4.42) in a land that is patently not his own (4.9). This broader context and the comparison with the response in Samaria suggests that Galilee might stand for Israel as a whole or, 'Jewish turf',[33] an understanding that also reflects the broad reference of the statement in the prologue (1.11).[34] As Jesus continues his journey to Galilee, following his itinerary to order to come to his own people, the statement of v. 44 is an expression of his own testimony.[35] The statement recalls 2.24 and operates in a similar fashion in another summary passage. An element of tension or dissonance is created for the reader in the midst of what is apparently a positive response to the ministry of Jesus. The mention of Jesus' πατρίς recalls the words of the prologue (1.9–11) and places the statement in that context as well. Jesus testifies concerning the reception of a prophet and he foreshadows the ultimate rejection of his ministry in his homeland. The reference back to the statement in 2.23 implies that there is some measure of belief in this group of Galileans but the combination of references raises the question once again as to what it means to believe in, and welcome Jesus.

---

[31] The sentiment of the statement is reflected in both the Synoptic tradition (Matt 13.57) and wider Graeco-Roman sentiment; BDAG: 'πατρίς', 788–9 has some examples.

[32] E.g. Moloney (1998: 152), Barrett (1978: 246). Both appeal to the rejection of Jesus in Jerusalem in 2.13–22, which is questionable. If anything, it is Jesus who rejects those in Jerusalem. Moloney's further suggestion that an impression is given of Jesus' regular presence in Judea is barely applicable at this point in the Gospel. Moloney also discounts the clear reference in 1.45 as a misunderstanding spoken by Philip who is an unreliable source.

[33] This is Carson's expression (1991: 236).

[34] See also Pryor (1987).

[35] The γάρ of v. 44 is not strictly causal but rather introduces a statement that is intended to illuminate or support the context in which it occurs. Cf. BDAG: 'γάρ', 189, sense 2, 'marker of clarification'. This use of γάρ is found elsewhere in John (3.16; 4.8).

With these tensions raised, the reader comes to the remarks made by Jesus in response to the request of the nobleman in v. 48. This is a surprising statement for a number of reasons. Jesus does not directly address the substance of the man's request. The official has not requested a sign; he has asked for help. The issue of signs is also not taken up in the official's reply or in Jesus' later remarks. The plural address (ἴδητε) is also surprising in an encounter that initially seems to be private. The use of the phrase σημεῖα καὶ τέρατα stands out in the context of the Gospel as this is the only time this particular phrase is used.

Commentators have often read the statement as a rebuke of a faith based on signs and wonders.[36] However, this often appears to be assumed rather than proved, perhaps because of prior judgements about the relationship of signs and faith. A number of considerations, however, suggest that the statement be read as a positive expression of the relationship between belief and signs.

First, this is the only occurrence of the phrase σημεῖα καὶ τέρατα in the Gospel. This phrase, with the addition of τέρατα, makes an explicit connection with the traditions mentioned in the Hebrew Scriptures. It is clear that in the Hebrew Scriptures there is an expectation that seeing signs and wonders will enable the truth that Yahweh is the Lord to be grasped (e.g. Deut 4.34–5). At times Yahweh expresses his frustration that belief has not followed the impressive array of signs and wonders that his people have seen (cf. Num 14.11). The other occurrences of the phrase in the New Testament do not appear to be supportive of the phrase being judgmental to any great degree.[37] These observations are not sure indicators of the absence of a rebuke in Jesus' statement, as traditions may be inverted or used ironically. However, there are grounds for at least attempting a reading of the statement as expressing a true observation rather than jumping too quickly to a negative conclusion.

Secondly, the grammatical construction of a conditional clause followed by an emphatic negative does not immediately suggest anything other than a statement of fact, especially when compared with similar constructions in the Gospel. Thomas echoes the precise construction when he asks to see the hands, feet, and side of Jesus before he will believe (20.25). There is no hint of irony in this usage and Jesus grants his request. There are a series of statements made using ἐὰν μή and οὐ (3.3,5; 13.8; with οὐ preceding ἐὰν μή 3.27; 5.19; 15.4) and in each case a solemn statement or pronouncement is made. Similarly this is seen with statements containing οὐ μή (4.14; 6.35;

---

[36] Dodd (1954: 141) and Schnackenburg (1968: 466) exemplify what would appear to be a sizeable consensus.

[37] The more negative uses of the phrase seems to be connected with the perpetrators rather than the signs and wonders themselves (cf. Matt 24.24; Mk 13.22; 2 Thess 2.9).

6.37; 8.12; 8.51,52; 10.5; 10.28; 11.26; 11.56; 13.38; 18.11). The evidence from the New Testament more generally together with occurrences in the LXX (cf. Gen 44.23; Num 19.12; Eccl 11.10; 12.15) also supports the same conclusion.[38] While 4.48 may well be an exception to this pattern, in view of the context, it would stand out as an unusual usage.

A final consideration comes from observing the conclusion of the account where the response of the household to the sign echoes that of the disciples at 2.11. If 4.48 is intended to critique the connection of signs and faith, then it is strange that the following story immediately appears to endorse the connection that is criticised.

The clues to a reading of v. 48 that affirms and does not critique the relationship between signs and faith are found in the context indicated by the statement at 4.44 and in the explicit connection that is established between this whole incident and the incident at Cana by the statement in v. 46. The structure of the recounting of the two incidents is very similar. Each begins with a request, followed by a 'rebuke', the performance of the requested action, and then a conclusion emphasising a response of faith. This pattern is repeated in several other places in the Gospel and appears to be intended as an assertion of the absolute independence of Jesus. He acts according to his own programme (or better, his Father's) and not in response to the urgings of others.[39] The recall of 2.23–5 that occurs in 4.43–44 sets up a context in which the actions of the next character are to be read. A man comes to Jesus and seeks healing for his son based on what he has seen himself, or heard about, happening in Jerusalem. He 'believes' in Jesus to this extent. Jesus' comment in 4.48 appears straightforward rather than ironic or expressing frustration when he says that unless signs and wonders are seen belief will not follow. The man is challenged as to whether he has 'seen' the signs in Jerusalem. From his experience he has glimpsed something of the truth concerning the identity of Jesus. The question is: Is he willing to place his trust in Jesus? The statement operates in a similar way to the challenge to Jesus' mother in chapter 2.[40] It is not a rebuke of a request to see signs. It is a rebuff that causes the man to re-evaluate his relationship with Jesus and, in this instance, to question whether he has actually seen.

The plural ἴδητε addresses the group that the reader assumes to be travelling with the official. The plural form also has the effect of generalising the statement into a principle and addressing the audience of the Gospel. This is similar to the effect of similar addresses in the second person plural at other

---

[38] Both Bittner (1987: 130–131) and Johns and Miller (1994: 530) have further details.

[39] Giblin (1980) outlines this pattern in four incidents in the Gospel. For his conclusions see pp. 210–11.

[40] Thompson (1988: 72–3) also sees this connection with the earlier incident but assesses the significance differently.

places in the Gospel (e.g. 3.12; 20.30-31). The repetition of the request implies that the man has seen the sign clearly and knows that here is the one who can heal his son. The man persists with Jesus by asking again. This mirrors the trust expressed in Jesus by the statement of Jesus' mother to the servants at Cana (2.5). When he receives the assurance that his son lives and the command to depart, his response demonstrates that he has seen truly and believes that his request is granted on the basis of his perception of Jesus. Parties independent of the exchange confirm the occurrence of the sign and belief is extended to his household on the basis of the sign.

The sign is not portrayed as unimportant to the expressed belief and neither are the signs in Jerusalem, alluded to in 4.45. Rather, the narrative has admirably communicated the complementary unity of the signs and word of Jesus. These words and works are the words and works of Jesus—his identity is expressed in both. Jesus being the object of belief means that to respond to him is to respond to both his word and deeds. Rather than critiquing faith based on signs, the statement in 4.48 suggests that there will be no belief in Jesus without 'seeing' his signs. The issue is in what sense the signs are seen.[41]

3.2.1.5 The Second Sign (Jn 4.54)

A second narrative incident is labelled as a sign at 4.54. The numbering (δεύτερον σημεῖον) appears awkward. It apparently carries on a numbering begun at 2.11, but which abruptly stops at this point in the Gospel. The numbering also seems to ignore the reference to multiple signs performed at Jerusalem (2.23). The most obvious function of the numbering is a literary one. The reference forges an explicit connection with the earlier sign recorded at 2.11 and creates an inclusio with the Cana sign that marks a completion of a narrative sequence.[42] This, in turn, invites both comparison between the two incidents and reflection on the connections between the two signs and the material that lies between them. In both of the signs Jesus' glory is revealed as they demonstrate his power and the essence of his mission. Jesus has come to reveal God by manifesting his glory in signs. Together these signs bracket a section where the audience is encouraged to align themselves totally with the Gospel's perspective on his divine identity. The 'numbering' references delineate this section and the reference in 4.54 creates a pause before moving

---

[41] This reading depends in part on the sense of perceiving for the verb of sight ἰδεῖν and the suggestion is that in this case it moves beyond physical perception. Attempts to correlate different dimensions of sight/perception to specific lexical items in the Gospel have proved unsuccessful as Brown (1966: 501–3) demonstrates. The nuance described is a function of context more than a specific word.

[42] This is observed by many exegetes; e.g. Barrett (1978: 248).

into a new section of the Gospel where the general claims made concerning Jesus will be expanded and tested.

The numbering also reminds the reader that Jesus has performed more than one narrated sign and that there may be more to come in such a sequence. A pattern is established whereby the reader is expecting similar lengthy narrated incidents.[43] This reinforces the general impression created by the other plural references to signs that occur in the narrative. The reader is constantly reminded in these asides that the signs and incidents chosen are only a selection from a vastly more numerous range of incidents.

3.2.2 The Occurrences of σημεῖον: Reader to Text

The language of σημεῖον engages the repertoire of a wide range of early readers. First, the context of Jewish expectation means that readers cognisant of the Hebrew Scriptures would immediately recognise the language as significant within that matrix. The function of signs as attesting the representatives of God in these Scriptures, as well as functioning to promote the knowledge of God, would resonate richly with those familiar with these Scriptures. Such resonance would extend from the intimation that Jesus is an accredited representative of God through to the anticipation that these signs may presage a movement of salvation similar to that which occurred in Egypt. This sense is reinforced by the mention of Moses in 1.17 and allusions to various themes connected with him (1.25, 3.15).

The use of the language within the context of an emerging forensic motif draws on the rhetorical/proof aspects noted in the previous chapter's investigation and provides a point of entry for the less well informed reader. The general emphasis on the plurality of signs characterising the ministry of Jesus and the specific numbering of the signs contributes to this motif. The suggestion of an accumulation of proofs concerning the claims of Jesus is given. This is in line with the cumulative nature of signs in the legal/rhetorical context. Over the course of the Gospel this will draw the reader into participation in the trial conducted through the Gospel. The signs recorded in the Gospel provide the basis on which the reader must also make a decision regarding the claims made concerning Jesus.

At the same time, the interaction of these two motifs might aid the understanding of those who approach the Gospel with a vastly different view

---

[43] Though this does not place the emphasis on the specific form of the narrative as Welck (1994: 146–8) suggests. Welck attempts to describe a specific literary form that is a vehicle of revelation. For him, the sign narratives are signs themselves (pp. 54–5; 305–7). While his emphasis on the revelatory function of the narratives is correct, the narratives are not σημεῖα. The sign narratives are vehicles of revelation only insofar as they recount the signs that Jesus performed. Welck's position underestimates the importance of testimony as a theme in the Gospel.

of signs as omens or direct communication from the gods. The embedding of the language within the forensic motif draws on the resonance with rhetorical/proof usage. This helps to form a bridge from the pagan understanding of signs as portentous omens requiring interpretation to the more Jewish notion of signs as actions attesting the designated representatives of the true and living God. The forensic motif and resonance help the signs to be read in this way with respect to Jesus.

The forensic context may provide a further nuance for interpreting the numbering of the signs. The first involves the legal requirement in Jewish law for matters to be established on the basis of two witnesses (Deut 19: 15–21). The two signs constitute two 'witnesses' to the person of Jesus. They 'testify' to the reader his identity and will provide the basis for claims concerning both this and the nature of his mission, which will both be explored and challenged through the rest of the Gospel. This reading will be even more plausible if there is some specific connection established between the signs and the notion of witnesses at a later point in the Gospel (cf. 5.30–38). The enumeration of the signs indicates to the reader aware of the 'soft' nature of σημεῖον as a proof that there are more signs to come. There is no need to enumerate any more. The sense is clearly given here that there are more signs to be seen and that a cumulative case concerning the identity and mission of Jesus is being presented to the reader.

3.3 The Sign Narratives

Within the broad framework established by the use of the language of σημεῖον occur two specific incidents designated as signs. It is now time to turn to these two narratives and examine them from the two directions that form the framework of this investigation. Each narrative will be examined under two headings. The first, entitled 'Writing the Signs' will examine the movement from text to reader. In this section particular attention will be paid to the way that the readers are encouraged, in varying degrees, to sympathetically align themselves with the characters and situations in the various narratives.[44] This is a function of such matters as the proportion of 'telling' or 'showing' in the text,[45] the way in which a scene is focalised

---

[44] Bolt (2003: 19) notes that the term align is a more appropriate descriptor than a term like identification because it focuses on the movement from text to reader.

[45] The distinction between 'telling' and 'showing' goes back to Plato's distinction between narration (διήγησις) and imitation (μίμησις) (*Rep.* 3.392–394). The greater the proportion of 'showing' that is present the greater the encouragement to be identified with the action. See also S.H. Smith (1996: 173).

through certain characters,[46] and the use of devices such as naming, explanation of weaknesses or failings, emotion and inside views.[47] Various details in each narrative that help the reader to grasp their significance in the wider context of the Gospel's story will also be discussed.

The second section, entitled 'Reading the Sign', will examine the movement from reader to text. This section will investigate the possible resonance the narratives have for the Gospel's audience, living in the wider context of the Roman Empire in the late first century.

3.3.1.1 The Wedding at Cana (Jn 2.1–11): Writing the Sign

Jesus, his mother and his disciples are depicted attending a wedding. The reader is aligned with the situation when the failing of the wine supply is signalled both by the narrator and the statement of Jesus' mother (2.3). This double reference emphasises the dilemma and invites the reader to ponder the awkwardness for those concerned.[48] The reader senses her discomfort, moves with her to speak with Jesus and feels his rebuff (2.4). Her request clearly expects a response, though what this might be is not hinted at. The mother's charge to the servants (2.5) expresses confidence that he will in fact act and is trusting in the sense that it is an open ended charge to the servants to do whatever they are told by Jesus.

The reader is forced to wait for the word from Jesus as attention is drawn to a number of water jars. The statement that they are for Jewish cleansing purposes at least explains the presence of so many jars with such capacity, apart from whatever other significance might eventually be accorded to them. Jesus commands the servants to fill the jars and take some of the water in them to the chief steward. The fact that the water has become wine is revealed by the narrator (2.9) and affirmed in the comment of the steward to the bridegroom responsible for the provision at the feast (2.10). His 'joke' about the practice of serving poor wine when no-one will notice testifies to the quality of the wine that Jesus has produced. The reader now knows that an enormous quantity of wine of excellent quality has been produced. An impartial witness, who knew nothing of the behind-the-scenes manoeuvres of Jesus and the servants, attests to the transformation.

---

[46] Focalisation concerns the position or perspective through which a story is told answering the question: in whose 'shoes' is the reader is invited to stand during the narrative? The story can be focalised on a particular character but focalised through another. The concept of focalisation is discussed in Bal (1983: 100–114) and Rimmon-Kenan (1983: 71–85).

[47] See Berlin (1983: 59–82) for an analysis of such factors.

[48] See the account of ancient weddings in terms of honour and shame in Malina & Rohrbaugh (1998: 70). Derrett (1963) has a wealth of information concerning the wedding customs and the possible financial implications of the event.

The account has moved the reader from involvement in the potentially embarrassing situation through to its joyful resolution and he is even invited to share in the joy by laughing with the steward at the observation about the wine's quality. The anticipated social catastrophe is averted through the kind intervention of Jesus. His ability and willingness to do this creates an immediate impression of both power and generosity in response to need. The reader may sigh with relief, smile, and thank God that Jesus was there.

The final comment on the incident at 2.11 points to the significance of the incident and shows the appropriate response to a manifestation of glory. A response has been drawn from the disciples to the action of Jesus. It is less clear in what way the incident is significant, how the glory of Jesus is revealed and what this implies. Certainly the incident concerns a generous provision in order to alleviate a potentially embarrassing situation. It concerns a powerful and creative action. Various details in the account help the reader to discern its significance.

First, the opening time phrase (2.1) connects the narrative to the sequence of days established already throughout chapter one (1.29, 35, 43). The exact number of days is disputed with exegetes suggesting allusions to the six or seven days of creation. The ambiguity over the precise number of days makes certainty difficult to establish but, on either count, the sequence is suggestive of creation. The mention of the days also ties the accounts together so that the wedding account forms part of the sequence of the initial revelation of Jesus. This is further reinforced by the placing of the account immediately after the statement, made by Jesus, that the disciples will see μείζω τούτων (1.50). This statement, made in response to Nathanael's ringing endorsement of Jesus, entices the reader on to see what greater things might be in store. Jesus also alludes to the account of Jacob's revelation at Bethel, where he intimates that the Son of Man will be the locus of divine communication. This initially puzzling reference is reasonably inferred from the context as a self-reference. It will later become clear that the Son of Man references refer to Jesus generally and more specifically to his fate on the cross.[49] 'Greater things' do not seem to be immediately in prospect as the account of a wedding begins. However, the final remark of 2.11, especially with the mention of glory and the connections that are established with the prologue, suggests that this incident is to be seen as a part of the unfolding of the greater things. The sign is to be seen in this immediate context of promised revelation from God.

---

[49] So Loader (1991: 255, 274) who argues that 'the greater things' refer exclusively to the cross and resurrection in line with the other Son of Man statements. His point is correct but overstated. There is a sense in which everything leads to the cross in this Gospel. The signs form an integral part of the preparatory testimony to the event of the cross and as such are included amongst the greater things.

Secondly, the mention of ἡ ὥρα in Jesus' conversation with his mother, while enigmatic, introduces a further significant detail. The hour referred to by Jesus is his hour (μοῦ v. 4, note the emphatic position) and it is clear that Jesus perceives that he is being asked to act in way that pre-empts some kind of action for which he feels the weight of a personal timetable. Jesus' statement puts some distance between himself and her request. It establishes the independence of whatever he will do next and implies that he will not act, as it is not his time to do so.[50] Furthermore, Jesus' mother is not referred to here by name but rather defined by her relationship to her son. Already Jesus has been described as related to the Father on two occasions (1.14,18). Perhaps the implication is that Jesus is subject to the will and hour of his Father alone. The reference to the hour will be built upon as the narrative progresses (cf. 7.30; 8.20; 12.23). As this happens the reader becomes aware that the hour is specifically referring to the hour of Jesus' death and resurrection, conceived of as the hour of his glorification. The incident at Cana may be seen, retrospectively, as subtly introducing the idea of Jesus' death as part of the understanding of the signs.

Thirdly, scholars have interpreted the comment concerning the use of the water pots for Jewish purification rites (2.6) as contributing to a general theme of replacement of the institutions of Judaism in the person and work of Jesus.[51] Such a symbolic reading is not immediately obvious but is later encouraged by the important clue given in 2.21 that suggests the potential for symbolic readings of various aspects of the narrative.[52] Such reading is further encouraged by the proximity of the narrative to the narrative of the temple cleansing which more overtly contains this replacement motif. This, in turn, fits into a general pattern of narratives that focus very much on the 'newness' associated with the mission of Jesus.[53] The comparison between Jesus and Moses in the prologue has already struck a note of fulfilment and replacement. This note is reinforced by the collection of titles that accrue to Jesus throughout chapter 1. The narrative as a whole then adds further to this theme. The signs also explicate the fulfilment of God's programme.

3.3.1.2 The Wedding at Cana (Jn 2.1–11): Reading the Sign

The most prominent feature of the account is the prodigious quantity and fine quality of wine that was produced. The mention of wine, in both quantity and quality could not fail to evoke several connotations in the minds of readers. Wine had been a feature of the Mediterranean diet since Mycenean times

---

[50] This the conclusion reached by Giblin (1980: 210) following his exposition of this pattern.

[51] See, amongst many others, Dodd (1954: 299).

[52] Staley (1988: 90–91) makes this observation.

[53] As Dodd (1954: 297) pointed out.

forming part of the staple trio along with bread and olives (oil).[54] There is a vast array of references to wine, its pleasures and its abuse, scattered throughout ancient literature.[55] Wine was the everyday drink of all classes in Greek and Roman society and its virtues are extolled for medicinal purposes as well.[56] The wealthy enjoyed fine wines from various regions of both Greece and Rome while the poor drank *deuterias* or after-wines. These were 'seconds' made up from wine skins soaked in water, which Pliny suggests cannot be rightly styled wines 'but nevertheless they are counted among the wines of the working classes'.[57] The general tenor of remarks, the establishment of the symposium or the drinking party amongst the wealthy of Greek and Roman culture, and the festive associations of wine and the celebrations conducted in the name of the god Dionysus combine to suggest an element of joy and celebration associated with the production of the wine that is reflected in the Cana account.[58] This is even 'shared' with the reader in the chief steward's 'joke' at the conclusion of the account. One can imagine both rich, with their knowledge of vintages and regions, and poor, with the harsh taste of the *deuterias* on their palate, speculating with some relish about the 'good wine' produced by Jesus and how it might compare to their favoured or desired Falernian or Lesbian wine.[59]

Aside from the more general connotations of wine and joy, Johannine scholars have also speculated about connections with both Jewish and pagan traditions.

---

[54] Younger (1966: 79–165) has an extensive history. See also Unwin (1991: 94–131).

[55] Hagenow (1982: 42–98) and Weeber (1993: 99–117) both have extensive surveys. For a very positive view see Horace, *Carm.* 3.21.13–20; Athenaeus, *Deipn.* 1.2.37a-b. The negative side of abuse is readily observed as well but this does not take away from the positive note that is generally struck

[56] Aretaeus, *Cur. acut.* 1.1.28 2.3; *Cur. acut* 2.3.10, 12 (μοῦνος γὰρ οἶνός ἐλπὶς ἐς ζωὴν ψυχροῖσι) mentions the medicinal benefits of wine. He also acknowledges the dark side of abuse. Over-consumption of wine plays a role in conditions such as madness, paralysis and liver disease (*Sign. diut.* 1.7; *Sign. acut.* 1.7).

[57] Pliny, *Nat.* 4.12.86. See also the discussion of Younger (1966: 114–5, 221–2) of what could be afforded in Greece and Rome. His figures for Greece are drawn from material found in Delos around 250 B.C. and Athens c. 400 B.C. but give some idea of the general breadline existence of much of the population as well as the relative inaccessibility of many of the fine wines of the past. The comparable examination of Roman lifestyle is situated in the mid first century and he estimates that a half litre of wine would have cost the Roman labourer half a sesterce of his daily wage of 3–4 sesterces. This was most likely drunk diluted. The data the figures are based upon are scant for too many solid judgements.

[58] Cf. Philo, *Legat.* 88 where he asks the emperor Gaius to emulate the character of the gods he desires to imitate, 'Did you imitate Dionysus?…Did you fill the inhabited world with joyfulness?' (trans. F.H. Colson).

[59] Pliny, *Nat.* 4.14 and Athenaeus, *Deipn.* 1.2.36–37 contain discussions of various varieties of wine.

Just as wine generally has connotations of joy and life so it also has these connotations within the specifically Jewish framework expressed in the Hebrew Scriptures. Wine is a symbol of God's blessing (Deut 32.14) and prayed for as such in the blessing bestowed upon a child (Gen 27.28). Its presence expressed the richness of the land promised to Moses and the people of Israel (Num 13.23,26) and it was viewed as a gift from God and as part of the familiar triad of staples (Deut 7.13; 11.14). Wine was to be used in sacrifices to celebrate the goodness of God (Num 15.5,7). God provides the wine that gladdens the heart (Ps 104.15), and drinking wine and eating bread were signs of prosperity and peace (2 Kgs 18.31; Prov 3.10). At the same time wine and its drinking and removal were also considered to be signs of the judgement of God (Deut 28.39; Hos 2.9 (LXX); Joel 1.9; Isa 16.10, 24.7; Jer 28 (51).7). There are indications that wine and its supply was to be a part of the end times celebration of the people of God. The renewed abundance of wine was considered as a blessing of the restoration of all things in the promised kingdom (Gen 49.11–2; Isa 25.6; 27.2–6; Jer 31.12; Hos 2.22; 14.7; Joel 2.19, 24; 3.18; Amos 9.13–14; Zech 9.15–17; 10.7). This is further reflected in the late first century A.D. Jewish tradition that associates wine with the coming of the messianic kingdom (2 Bar 29.5). The presence of wine cups, pitchers, grape leafs and grapes that appear on the coins of the Jewish uprisings of 66–73 A.D. and 132–5 A.D. are most likely motivated by messianic-eschatological considerations.[60] Certainly the supply of an abundance of wine could connote the advent of the messianic kingdom.

However, scholars have also noted parallels between the motif of changing water into wine and incidents recounted in connection with the Greek god Dionysus. There is no doubt that Dionysus is strongly associated with wine. This is attested as early as Plato (*Leg.* 2.672B) and is a consistent feature of accounts of this god throughout Graeco-Roman literature.[61] His name can even be used as a metonym for wine (Achilles Tatius, *Leuc.Clit* 4.18.5; 8.4.2). A note of abundance, joy and celebration is struck throughout many of the references to Dionysus and his gift of wine (See for example Philo, *Legat.* 82–3, 88, Horace, *Carm.* 2.19, Euripides, *Bacch.* 706–711).[62] However, references to Dionysus in connection with the account of the wedding at Cana are disputed in Johannine studies. There are strong opinions on both sides as to the extent of Dionysian influence in the recounting of the event. Bultmann states: 'There can be no doubt that the story has been taken over from

---

[60] Hengel 1987: 101.

[61] See for example the extensive recounting of the various legends concerning the birth of Dionysus in Diodorus Siculus *Hist.* 3.62–63.

[62] For a number of accounts concerning the presence of Dionysus and his many connections with wine see Younger (1966: 117–126).

heathen legend and ascribed to Jesus'.[63] Commentators are equally trenchant in the opposite direction.[64] The work of Noetzel is frequently cited as being decisive in the dismissal of any possibility of Johannine dependence upon Dionysian legends for the construction of this incident.[65] However, the attraction of Dionysus has proved strong.[66] This is not least due to the fact that attempts to derive the motifs and themes suggested from OT passages prove to be at least as tenuous in their application to the Cana story as any of the Dionysian motifs. This is particularly so when it comes to the precise motif of changing water into wine.[67]

Scepticism about connections with the Dionysus stories arises for several reasons. These include the inherent implausibility of John choosing to base a story on the Dionysian legends and problems concerning the level of knowledge of the Dionysian legends throughout the ancient world. In addition the absence of Dionysus at the occurrences attributed to his influence and the observation that he does not change water into wine are mentioned.[68]

In response, the following observations are pertinent. The question of plausibility has often been raised concerning the possibility that the account in John is dependent upon the Dionysian legends for its artistic creation. A slightly lesser standard of plausibility is required if the question shifts to audience reception and the possibilities of potential subtle polemic. Secondly, Dionysus' presence is reported widely throughout the Graeco-Roman world. There is evidence of his presence in Palestine, Asia Minor and Italy. Dionysus appears to have been one of the most widely known and popular of the gods.[69] Thirdly, with respect to the Cana account there are stories of Dionysus which are similar to the focal point of the miracle, the changing of water into wine. These include rivers that taste of wine (Lucian, *Ver. hist.* 1.7; cf. Plutarch, *Lys.* 28.4), ceremonies that involve the miraculous production of wine in jars

---

[63] Bultmann 1971: 118–20.

[64] See for example Ridderbos (1997: 111).

[65] Noetzel 1960.

[66] See for example, Lindars (1981: 127); Grayston (1990: 29); C.R. Koester (1995: 80–81); even more extensively, though improbably, the account of Stibbe paralleling Euripides' Bacchae with the passion narrative, Stibbe (1992: 139–147).

[67] See for example the discussion of Linnemann (1974) and Labahn (1999a: 146–60). Parallels are also occasionally sought in the Elijah/Elisha stories (e.g. Betz (1974: 38-41) but these appear even more tenuous. Granted there is a generous supply given but the liquid is oil and there is no transformation. Attempts to locate backgrounds in the Mosaic sign of changing water into blood (R. H. Smith: 1962: 334–5; Betz: 1974: 41) are similarly tenuous. The general connection with the Mosaic signs as accrediting signs is more tenable.

[68] Noetzel 1960: 26–38.

[69] See M. Smith (1974), Hengel (1987), Broer (1983), Younger (1966: 90). Tacitus, *Hist* 5.5 and Plutarch, *Q.Conviv.* 671C-D speculate on links between Jews and Dionysus. Aurenhammer (1995: 267–269), Oster (1990: 1673–76), and Van Tilborg (1996: 95–8) all provide evidence of extensive Dionysian presence at Ephesus.

left locked up overnight in a temple (Pausanias, *Descr.* 2.26), and springs and fountains that produce wine on days celebrating the appearance of the god (Pliny, *Nat.* 2.231; Diodorus Siculus, *Hist.* 3.66.2). Most of these accounts are ambiguous and more likely to indicate the production of wine rather than the transformation of water. However, at times the tenor of the story seems very close to a transformation and is certainly closer to this central feature of the Cana account than any adduced Old Testament parallel.[70] Two accounts seem to more definitely describe such a transformation. Achilles Tatius (*Leuc. Clit. 2.2*) recounts the story of Dionysus visiting a hospitable herdsman who gives him a meal. The only drink they have however, is 'the same as that of the oxen' (2.2.3). Dionysus gives the man a drink but it turns out to be wine. Nonnus (*Dion.* 14.411–8) recounts a tale whereby Dionysus pours wine into a stream to cleanse it of blood from a battle. The river changes colour and turns to wine.[71] While the transformation aspect might be ambiguous, testimony to both quantity and quality of wine is not. Intriguingly, and coincidentally, one account of Dionysus includes also the language of σημεῖον where Diodorus Siculus comments that the god has left σημεῖα of his presence ἐν πολλοῖς τόποις (*Hist.* 3.66.3).

One of the problems in deciding the question of influence has been that scholars have tended to look for the origin of the story and have not considered as fully the possible impact on the audience. Attempts to trace dependence on either pagan or Jewish parallels for the creation of the Cana story to illustrate a spiritual truth about Jesus have proved unconvincing. A better explanation is that this account has been chosen from the traditions available because it would resonate with its diverse audience. There are obviously hints that point to the identity of Jesus in the Jewish context but there are also enough associations present to evoke wider connections with pagan religion. This does not mean that a Dionysian sect was the intended audience of the Gospel as Linnemann suggests.[72] Rather, the suggestion is that a skilled writer and evangelist like John takes the opportunity to testify to Jesus and at the same time provide a point of comparison and contrast with a rival claimant for the allegiance of his audience. Both aspects of this use of sign take their cue from the Old Testament usage where a sign positively attests a representative of God but can also test or judge a rival god (Exod 12.12; Num 33.4; Isa 19.1). The point of the miracle is to draw attention to

---

[70] In fact the clearest reference to the transformation of water into wine comes in Philostratus, *Vit. Apoll.* 6.10, in a passage where the virtues of the god Apollos are expounded. It is said that Apollos answers questions at Delphi with no miraculous display, although he could easily convulse the mountains of Parnassus or alter the waters of the Casalian fountain so that they might run with wine.

[71] Nonnus's work appears much later than the Gospel (fifth century A.D.). It is difficult to know, however, how old the legend behind the tale might be.

[72] Linnemann 1974: 417–8

Christ. If, while doing this, a popular rival in the surrounding religious context might be implicitly trumped then all the better. Such an implicit comparison contributes to another theme that develops through the Gospel. In a mass of details and incidental references it is clear that the teaching of the Gospel is that Jesus is the only true representative of God and is the only one who can truly reveal God and bring his benefits to the world. This occurs in explicit statements (1.18; 3.13[73], 31) and also implicitly in statements that emphasise the uniqueness of his position and the exclusiveness of the offer of life that he makes (cf. 3.16–21, 36).[74] These details create the context in which the supremacy of Jesus is portrayed and in which implicit comparisons such as those observed in 2.1–11 are situated.

There is a sufficient basis to consider the impact that the account in John 2 might have made on readers familiar with the Dionysian stories and to conclude that there may have been many such readers. The hearing of the text in a mixed environment suggests that the story could communicate the significance of Jesus to a wide spectrum of readers at least at the basic level of association of the production of wine and the indication of a god.[75] Once a foothold has been gained, the possibility of deeper understanding of Jesus is possible through the ongoing reflection/tutelage by the Spirit. It is a miracle of Jesus and thus reveals his glory as the one who is instrumental in bringing the joy of the end times salvation of God. John is able to discern these elements in the narrative. The incident is also chosen because of the polemical possibilities with respect to a popular cult. Faith can be both created and sustained by this story, in the midst of competing rivals.

One further possibility is that the action is reminiscent of the actions of various benefactors of the first century. An inscription from Kyme celebrates the various benefactions of Kleanax who amongst other actions distributed 'sweet wine' to everyone in the city.[76] There is also some evidence of the distribution of wine and pastries at banquets that could sometimes extend to the citizens of a town.[77] Such benefactions were part of the life of the empire

---

[73] The polemical edge to this statement with respect to mystical figures and Roman emperors who ascended to heaven after their death are noted by Segal (1981: 255).

[74] Though this exclusiveness is understood with respect to Jesus himself. The offer of life is inclusive in that anyone may come. It is exclusive in that it only comes through Jesus.

[75] C.R. Koester 1995: 81.

[76] Text and translation from *NewDocs* VII §10 l. 32. The inscription is dated in the late first century B.C. to early first century A.D. Kyme is located in Asia Minor.

[77] See Ehrenberg & Jones (1976) §101.15–16. Cf. also Unwin (1991: 132), 'A second way in which the Roman elite used wine to maintain its status and authority during the Empire, was through the regular distribution of *mulsum*, sweetened wine, to the urban poor'.

at a local and imperial level.[78] While the Emperors seemed to be mainly concerned with the grain supply, part of the imperial largesse also included wine until Augustus stopped this when he declared that his son-in-law had provided a fresh supply of water via aqueducts.[79] The possibilities of such a connection are reinforced by similar connections with the account of the feeding of the five thousand (6.1-14). Such subtle Imperial connections may be traced through the sign narratives and further established in this particular instance where there is evidence of various rulers and emperors being lauded as 'the new Dionysus'.[80]

3.3.2.1 The Healing of an Official's Son (Jn 4.43–54): Writing the Sign

This concise account concludes the first major section of the Gospel. It is the first mention of healing in the Gospel. A (possibly Gentile?) royal official[81] is described as coming to Jesus and entreating him to come to Capernaum and heal his son, who is ill and about to die (4.47). The reader is immediately aligned with the man and his dilemma through the accumulation of detail. The pause created by Jesus' statement concerning signs and wonders and belief increases both the tension of the account and sympathy for the man. At the same time the challenge is issued as to whether the man has actually 'seen' the reality expressed in the signs that he has either seen himself or heard about in Jerusalem. The reader is also addressed with the same question by the second person plural (ἴδητε). The official's repeated request, directly spoken and not related by the narrator; the hint of desperation in the repeated request; and affection conveyed for his son in the request (τὸ παιδίον; cf. τὸν υἱόν v. 47) serve to increase audience sympathy and identification with his plight.

---

[78] M.S. Collins (1995: 105–6) points out how unusual Jesus' action is if read in the context of such benefactions. He is apparently content to allow another to take the credit for the generous abundance and quality of the wine served at the wedding.

[79] Suet. *Aug.* 42. Hagenow (1982: 126–8) makes this suggestion.

[80] Magie (1950: I.214, 616-7; II. 1102, n. 31; 1477–8, n. 24) mentions figures including Mithradates and the later rulers Trajan, Hadrian and Commodus. Antony (Cassius Dio, *Hist.* 48.39.2; 50.25.3-4; Plutarch, *Ant.* 24.3) is also identified as such. Martial describes Domitian as surpassing Bacchus (*Epig.* 8.26). The frequency of occurrence and longevity of the tradition suggests that it might have been a relatively common and even sought association. Oster (1990: 1675) notes that an inscription that mentions the Emperor Commodus as the 'new Dionysus' reflects, in his view, 'the long history of association between the god and the contemporary ruler'. Philo (*Legat.* 75-81) speaks of Gaius dressing himself as Dionysus, amongst other gods, in his desire to be seen as divine.

[81] BDAG: 'βασιλεύς', 169–170. The ethnic identity of the man is unclear. Mead (1985) argues that it is likely that he is a Gentile. This is not explicit. The Gentile nature of the man is most plausibly suggested by the progression of characters from chapter 3 forwards as Moloney (1993: 183) suggests. This would fit in also with a major focus of the section as summarised in the exclamation of the Samaritans in 4.42. However it would need to be more explicit in the text before much could be based on the possibility.

At this point it is still a matter of conjecture as to what Jesus could do. He has been previously shown to be able to turn water into wine. The reader has been deliberately reminded of that. What can he do in this instance?

Jesus' command to the man to depart (v. 50) comes as a shock in view of the situation. The expectation would most likely have been for some kind of physical contact to effect the healing requested but the man is simply given the assurance that his son lives. The reader remains with the man's perspective as his belief is reported and he sets out on his way. The reader is faced with a choice at this moment. Having been drawn in to identify with the man's plight, can the reader now share his confidence and if so, on what basis? Is the word of Jesus sufficient for the reader, as it has been for the man in the narrative? The man apparently believes; he has seen enough. Will the reader?

The reader travels with the man for the rest of the narrative, shares his (unreported but imagined) joy and relief at the news that his son lives and realises with him the truth expressed in the servant's report of the timing of the fever leaving the boy. The statement by the narrator concerning his belief and that of his household challenges the reader who has shared the man's journey to reach the same conclusion as them. Again there is a transition from unbelief to belief mentioned and again there is impartial testimony to the occurrence of the sign.

Jesus is clearly presented as a life-giver in this account. This is emphasised by the twofold reference to the son's dying (vss. 47,49) and the threefold reference to the son's subsequent living (vss. 50, 51, 53). This presentation anticipates further statements concerning this. In terms of the connection with the first sign, it is now clear that a more literal kind of life is on offer through the ministry of Jesus. Jesus has supplied wine that brings life in a metaphorical sense; he now shows himself to be able to prevent the death of this boy in a more literal sense.

The presentation of Jesus as a life giver in this incident comes in the context of the declaration by the Samaritans that Jesus is the saviour of the world (4.42). This incident illustrates how the recognition of Jesus as saviour is manifest in a very basic sense. A young boy is saved from death. The fact that there is no precise clarification of the official's ethnic identity precludes any further suggestions concerning the scope of this salvation for the world beyond Israel, although this trajectory has already been established in the encounter with the Samaritans.

The incident demonstrates Jesus' ability to heal without physical contact and is therefore a testimony to his power and divine nature. The account leads to a deepening understanding of the relationship between signs and faith, which has already been established in the narrative. Unless people see the signs they will not believe. The signs are an essential part of the ministry of

Jesus for John. As such, they testify to the identity of Jesus and point to his power to bring life. However, for many they may only be accessible through the testimony of others, a testimony that must be examined and trusted. The signs can still be 'seen', but it will be through the testimony of others.

3.3.2.2 The Healing of an Official's Son (Jn 4.43–54): Reading the Sign

The boy's condition is revealed to be a fever when the servants report to the official. While for the modern reader this presents no particularly significant alarm, there were different connotations in the ancient world. Fever was common in the ancient world as evidenced by the continuous discussion of it throughout various medical writings, as well as casual references in other writings. In these writings it tends to be treated as a condition in itself, rather than as a symptom of another condition, as might be considered in modern medicine. The ancients had developed a taxonomy of fevers and used a number of terms denoting type, duration and severity.[82]

Fever was known to be a serious and painful state. Philo attests to its severity, likening torture under the emperor's rack and wheel to its effects (*Legat.* 206). It affected the whole body (*Sobr.* 45) and its symptoms were dramatic and terrible.[83] Fever was a killer and known to have taken leaders in the ancient world including the emperor Vespasian (Cassius Dio, *Hist.* 66.17), Alexander the Great and Herod the Great (Josephus, *B.J.* 1.106, 656). Fever would also have been associated with a number of epidemics that ravaged various populations (cf. Thucydides, *Hist.* 2.47–52 and the plague that devastated Athens). Epictetus reflects the association with death in his comment, 'What do the swords of the tyrants do? They kill. And what does fever do? Nothing else (πυρετὸς δὲ τί ποιεῖ; ἄλλο οὐδέν)', Epictetus *Diatr.* 4.7.26–27; cf. Lucian, *Peregr.* 44).[84] Fever was also associated with the gods (Seneca *Apol.* 6; Pliny *Nat.* 2.16) and demons (Philostratus, *Vita Apol.* 4.10).

Philo reports the received wisdom that the seventh day of a fever was significant in the matter of survival (*Opif.* 125). This appears to be an incidental reporting of a widely held view, although the Hippocratic case studies vary widely and report deaths prior to this moment as well as both deaths and recoveries some days beyond this (up to 120 days). The Hippocratic case studies tend to suggest the onset of a death-threatening fever which progressed to a point of a 'crisis' that would either see the patient die or would signal the point of recovery. The step of a patient taking to bed

---

[82] See Hippocrates, *Epid.* 1,3.

[83] See for example the description of the suffering of the wife of Dromeades (Hippocrates, *Epid.* 1, 11).

[84] The threat of fever seemed to have been so prevalent that to survive was almost to consider oneself immortal; cf. Thucydides, *Hist.* 2.51.6.

seems to be significant in a number of cases and seems to signal almost certain death (though note *Epid.* 3, Case 9).[85]

The pathos of the account is compounded by the fact that the threat was to a child. Death was a constant reality for all in the ancient world, but the child was amongst the most vulnerable.[86] Evidence from literature, grave inscriptions, and comparisons with other pre-industrial societies combine to suggest that the infant mortality rate was 35 per cent, 49 per cent of children saw their fifth birthday and just 40 per cent of the population survived to the age of 20.[87] It has been difficult to gather hard data on children because there is no way of knowing how many died under the age of 40 days and were therefore buried using different customs.[88] There is also no account taken of infanticide. However, these assessments are broadly consonant with most studies of the subject.[89]

The death of a child had other connotations as well. Classical Romans saw their children primarily as an investment for future security. Children would look after their parents in old age in return for the sustenance provided for them as infants and the child (normally the son) would bury his parents just as his parents had brought him to life. In Greek literature these themes also recur as well as the thought that premature death meant that the child itself had failed to get anything worthwhile out of life.[90] Despite the prevalence of death in childhood, there is contemporary evidence for the despair felt by parents at the loss of a child more generally. Plutarch comments on the behaviour of most mothers, who at the death of their children 'give themselves up to an unwarranted and ungrateful grief' (*Cons. ux.* 609E). Garland concludes his examination by stating that 'all the evidence suggests that the death of a Greek child was a painful and disturbing event'.[91]

The combination of the threat of the death of a child from fever would have evoked powerful sympathy amongst the early readers of the Gospel. The references to the expected death of the boy in the narrative are not simply

---

[85] Bolt (1997: 69–70) notes the significance of this step of taking to bed with respect to several curses and a magic formula used to predict death for a fever sufferer. The time of death could be calculated by a formula based on the day that the sick person took to bed.

[86] Wiedemann 1989: 17–18. *Infirmitas* was the characteristic associated with children by Cicero, *Sen.* 10.33.

[87] Wiedemann 1989: 16.

[88] They were buried near the wall of the house; cf. Wiedemann (1989: 179).

[89] Cf. for example the narrow study of van der Horst (1991) who looks specifically at Jewish grave inscriptions. While commenting on the methodological problems involved, he does observe that of the epitaphs that indicate the age of death the average turns out to be men 29; women 27 (p. 79).

[90] See the discussion in Wiedemann (1989: 39–43) and the many examples of Greek and Latin epitaphs lamenting a premature death in Lattimore (1962: 184–198). *NewDocs* IV §114 also speaks of a father's infinite grief at the loss of his daughter.

[91] Garland 1985: 86. See also the epitaphs in Lattimore 1962: 179–80.

hyperbole but would reflect the normal expectation as events progressed. The father knew the young boy was on the brink of death, no doubt due to the significant length of his illness, or perhaps to his having taken to bed. As John emphasises in his narrative, the young boy is rescued from death and given life. Jesus' power is clearly demonstrated in his ability to banish this fever with a word. The boy is given life with no more than a word, and with no clinical examination or therapy such as the doctors of the day might have done. Jesus is presented in John's narrative as the life giver. The realistic situation that he recounts could only have vividly reinforced this impression in the minds of the early readers.

A final possible nuance to be mentioned arises from the observation that this incident is related very much in the shadow of the climactic statement made by the Samaritans that Jesus is ἀληθῶς ὁ σωτὴρ τοῦ κόσμου (4.42).[92] This statement occurs in the context of a presentation of Jesus that continually stresses his uniqueness as previously noted.[93]   Jesus is demonstrated to be a saviour in that he gives life to the young boy and there is the sharpening of the polemical edge that may be detected in this earlier statement.

The title 'saviour' had a wide currency in the Graeco-Roman world where it was used of a variety of gods and the Roman Emperor.[94] The presence of the adverb ἀληθῶς suggests an implicit polemic in the narrative directed at the claims made for the Roman Emperor and any other would-be saviours. The Augustan ideology that lay behind the Imperial cult promised life and salvation for the world in the new beginning offered under Augustus and his successors.[95] Here Jesus, the one acclaimed to be truly the saviour of the world, offers life with a word thereby demonstrating the truth of this acclamation

---

[92] Labahn (1999a: 212) emphasises this point.

[93] See above, p. 61.

[94] The title 'saviour' was also used in the ancient world for gods like Zeus, Asclepius, Isis and Serapis and for philosophers and leaders of various ranks; cf. Barrett (1978: 244) for details. C.R. Koester (1990) also has an extensive discussion. A list of examples of similar formulations describing a variety of emperors can be found in Magie (1905: 67-8). Deissmann (1927: 364–5) points to the significant use of analogous terms describing Nero.

[95] This is famously expressed in the letter of proconsuls and decrees of the province of Asia, around 9 B.C. Augustus' birthday is proclaimed as the ἀρχὴν τοῦ βίου καὶ τῆς ζωῆς (Ehrenberg & Jones (1976) § 98.10). The possible resonance with the Fourth Gospel in terms of both the beginning (cf. 1.1) and life (1.4) are suggestive. This point will be returned to in chapter 6.

3.4. Summary

The narrator has skilfully woven the sign language and narratives into his persuasive presentation of Jesus. The sign narratives nestle within the framework created by the more general references. They provide a focal point in the larger context of the many signs alluded to that, for the narrator, form a significant portion of the ministry of Jesus.

From the point of view of text to reader, the narrative has given the reader a clear perspective on the signs as the manifestation of the glory of the one who truly reveals God. The signs, Jesus' powerful actions, are significant as indicators of his person and work. They point to his identity as the divine Son who manifests the glory of the Father and attest to his role as the giver of life and saviour from death. The relationship between signs and faith has been presented in positive terms. The signs are presented in order to facilitate faith. Having said this there is a question mark raised over the response of some to the revelation of Jesus' identity in the signs. The 'resolution' of this issue has been hinted at in terms of the supernatural working of the Spirit of God. This too will continue to be worked out in the Gospel as the question of faith and its exercise towards Jesus is revisited. The hint has also been given that this 'beginning of the signs' will find its 'end' in the sign towards which the whole Gospel moves—the death and resurrection of Jesus. The veiled reference to the hour (2.4), the more explicit reference of 2.18 and the subtle connection forged for the informed reader with knowledge of the LXX version of Num 21.9 (3.14) have indicated a move in this direction.

The signs are embedded in a narrative that draws extensively on the Hebrew Scriptures for its presentation of Jesus. The associations with the person of Moses lead the implied reader to begin to associate the signs Jesus is performing with the key salvific events of the time of Moses that the mention of σημεῖον recalls. As well as these Mosaic connotations the narrative has also endorsed the role of Jesus in messianic terms, which has suggested the possibility of a broader reference for the signs in view of the Messianic kingdom including gentiles as well as Jews (cf. Isa 11.12; 49.3; 66.19–20). The response of the Samaritans has hinted in this direction as well. The relationship between the signs and presentation of Jesus drawing on Mosaic and messianic themes will have to be considered further. However, the glory motif, introduced at 1.14 and connected to the σημεῖα by the reference at 2.11, suggests that any understanding of Jesus in either Mosaic or Messianic terms will be surpassed in the revelation of him as the divine Son.

The signs are also embedded in a narrative that has begun to employ forensic language that will contribute to the construction of an elaborate and pervasive motif that informs the presentation in the Gospel. It has been suggested that the references to the plurality of signs and perhaps the numbering of the first two have contributed to the construction of this motif. This forensic motif poses the question as to who is the true God and who is the true representative of this God. The signs point to the answer to both these questions by attesting Jesus as the divine representative of the true God and pointing even beyond this to his own identity as divine.

The two sign narratives have been characterised by a number of common features. In each narrative steps have been taken to lead the reader to identify with the situations presented. Both narratives have featured a conversation with Jesus and a rebuff that causes an evaluation of the relationship between the inquirer and Jesus to be made. The accounts have also featured impartial witnesses to the miraculous event they describe. They have also featured a believing resolution that suggests to the reader the required response.

The sign narratives have drawn the audience in by aligning them with the characters and situations involved. The impact of Jesus' ability to give life in the widest sense has been felt. The substance of the signs is such that the life giving connotations would be perceived by a very wide range of readers given the linkages that prominent motifs in each of the narrated episodes would make within the wider cultural context. It has also been suggested that, in the first sign at least, an implicit comparison would be made with another acclaimed life-giver in the form of the god Dionysus. It was also suggested that there might also be a subtle presentation of Jesus as a benefactor along the lines of the Roman emperor. This would contribute to a subtle critique suggested in other places in the narrative (e.g. 4.42) and is part of a general presentation of Jesus that asserts his uniqueness with respect to divine revelation and activity.

Already the sign language and narratives have, together, attested to the identity of Jesus, illustrated and manifested the life that he offers,[96] and mounted a subtle critique of potential rivals in the surrounding religious milieu.

The section ends with the language of σημεῖον prominent in the Gospel. Clues have been given as to how to interpret and respond to the various narratives that relate incidents designated as σημεῖα. The audience is led to anticipate more signs to be presented through the Gospel narrative and encouraged to wait and see how they too might reveal the glory of the unique Son, who has been sent from the Father.

---

[96] Manifested is the term used by Thompson (1991: 105). This emphasises the fact that the signs do more than illustrate a distant spiritual reality. They enact or manifest the very reality they illustrate as they are the works of God performed in the material realm.

Chapter 4

Controversial Signs: σημεῖον in John 5–10

As in the previous chapter, the analysis of John 5–10 will begin with an overview of the narrative and themes of the section. Then the occurrences of σημεῖον will be discussed firstly from the point of view of text-to-reader and then reader-to-text. The four σημεῖα narratives will then be dealt with from the same two perspectives.

4.1 Overview of Chapters 5–10

The whole section from chapter 5 through to chapter 12 shifts the focus of action from the general introduction of Jesus and his mission to the κόσμος in chapters 1–4 to a more agonistic account of his interaction with the Jews. The dispute with the Jews dominates the discourse right through until the end of chapter 12 and culminates with an extended and final comment on the mission of Jesus to the Jews in 12.37–50.[1] This final address is the climax to the extended trial motif that is prominent in these chapters and marks a point of transition to the events of chapters 13–17. The final speech of chapter 12 concludes the story of the light coming to 'his own' and being rejected (cf. 1.10–11).

Chapters 11 and 12 can be seen either as an independent unit or connected with the following chapters. The verses at the end of chapter 10 concerning the testimony of John create an inclusio with John's testimony from chapter 1 and form a narrative 'semi-colon', if not full stop.[2] The event described in chapter 11, the raising of Lazarus, also is linked in to the arrest and trial of Jesus recorded in chapters 18–19, and anticipates Jesus' death and

---

[1] The dispute is conducted in general terms with the Jews, although there are various elements within this general category that are distinguished as having varying responses and levels of hostility towards Jesus (ὁ ὄχλος, οἱ Φαρισαῖοι, οἱ ἀρχιερεῖς).

[2] Though as with so many decisions that can be made with respect to the structure of the Gospel, it is not as simple as it might look. Frey (2000: 409-11) makes a good case for also seeing 10.40-42 as forming an inclusio with 11.47-54 and providing the account of Lazarus's raising from the tomb with a narrative as well as theological framework. He also goes on (411-16) to point out a number of other narrative links between the Lazarus story and the remainder of the Gospel. In view of the 'seamless' quality of much of the narrative of the Fourth Gospel, most decisions re structure and sections are best tentatively held.

resurrection. However, the trial motif that is prominent throughout the section continues through to the end of chapter 12, as does the general presentation of the public ministry of Jesus. A definite break is signalled with the prologue-like statements of 13.1–3[3] as well as the move to the setting of a meal with the disciples. Chapters 11 and 12 are best seen as forming a bridge or hinge passage that simultaneously concludes one section and introduces another in much the same way as the account of the wedding at Cana. They will be treated separately in the following chapter.

Following the generally positive tone of the opening four chapters of the Gospel, there is a distinct shift as this next section proceeds. The debate becomes sharper and conflict rises throughout the section as Jesus engages with the Jews in both the synagogue and temple (cf. 18.20). The focus of the debates between Jesus and the Jews is the identity of Jesus and the claims that he makes in both word and deed.

The section from chapter 5 to chapter 10 is clearly organised around a series of Jewish festivals (5.1; 6.4; 7.2; 10.22). While the Passover has already been mentioned (cf. 2.12), the festivals are a far more explicit feature of these chapters. It is clear in these chapters that Jesus has come to 'his own' in the context of a series of prominent Jewish festivals and is decisively rejected, as the prologue has anticipated (1.10–11). Jesus teaches in both temple (5.14; 7.14) and synagogue (6.59) and presents major statements about his identity (5.19–47) and his mission (6.35–58). It is in this explicitly Jewish context that the sign narratives of chapters 5–12 are recorded as Jesus comes to his own people, both teaching and performing signs. The speculation of various audiences of the signs is recorded and this reflects expectations concerning a variety of figures connected with the expectations of the Hebrew Scriptures, notably ὁ προφήτης (6.14; 7.40) and ὁ χριστός (7.31; 7.40; 10.24). The seeing of the σημεῖα by the various audiences is fundamental to this speculation. The sign language and narratives continue to be embedded in the context of expectations arising from the Hebrew Scriptures.

This section is also marked by the development of the forensic motif. In John 1–4, this motif was carried in the narrative mainly by the presence of distinctive vocabulary (μαρτυρία, κρίσις). In John 5–10 (and to a lesser extent 11–12) this vocabulary continues to appear but the shape of the narrative itself also suggests the prominence of the motif as Jesus engages in continuous and contentious dialogue with his interlocutors. These exchanges involve accusation, counter-accusation, and an intense examination of Jesus' claims within a framework of Jewish legal principles.[4] As well as being located in the context of this developing motif, the language of σημεῖον and the σημεῖα narratives also contribute to the structure and substance of the

---

[3] Dumbrell (1994: 254) notes the recurrence of themes from 1.1–18.

[4] See Harvey (1976: 46–102) for a detailed account.

forensic examination in which Jesus is involved. The disputes that arise between Jesus and 'the Jews' are usually precipitated by the performing of a sign and the signs form an important part of the 'evidence' in the dispute between the two parties.

4.2 The Occurrences of σημεῖον

4.2.1 The Occurrences of σημεῖον: Text to Reader

Of the seven specific references to σημεῖον in this section three are found in comments by John (6.2, 14; 10.42). Jesus uses the term once (6.26), two are found in either requests or comments from various crowds that are speaking with Jesus, and one is uttered by a group of Pharisees in dialogue with another group of Pharisees (9.16). The verbs associated with σημεῖον are again verbs of sight and action (ποιέω, ὁράω, θεωρέω, ἐργάζομαι). In two of the general references to the signs that Jesus is performing there are adjectives stressing the quantity (πολύς, 9.16) and quality (τοιοῦτος, 7.31) of his actions. Two incidents are clearly designated as signs, the feeding of the crowd in John 6 (6.14) and the healing of the blind man in John 9 (9.16). A further two incidents are implied to be signs; the healing at the pool in John 5 and the walking on the water in John 6. Finally, in this section, the language of 'works' (ἔργον) is prominent and has an impact on the reader's understanding of the use of σημεῖον. The relationship that develops between these two terms requires exploration.

4.2.1.1 Signs and Works (Jn 5.20, 36)

The first reference to σημεῖον does not occur until 6.2. However in chapter 5 the significant term ἔργον occurs several times and this will have an impact on the reader's further understanding and interpretation of the σημεῖον language. This cluster of occurrences will be discussed first. These occur in an extended speech by Jesus defending himself against the Jews' accusations that he was making himself equal with God (5.16–18). This accusation arises when he claims his healing of the man at the pool on the Sabbath is legitimate because he is working in a similar manner to his Father. This is the first of a number of trial-like sequences where an accusation is made and Jesus is given the opportunity to defend himself. As he does this, the 'tables are turned' and Jesus accuses his accusers.[5] In his speech (5.19–47), Jesus first explains the

---

[5] Harvey (1976: 57) notes this phenomenon and places it in the context of the informal process of the Jewish legal system. This will be a recurring feature of the dialogues of Jesus with accusers throughout the section. Asiedu–Peprah (2001: 23) strongly objects to this construction. See below, p. 48, n. 11.

nature of the relationship that exists between himself and the Father (5.19–30) and then turns to the matter of witnesses that support his claims (5.31–47).

The language of works (ἔργον) occurs in this speech firstly at v 20.[6] Jesus has spoken of his inability to do anything other than that which the Father has shown him (5.19). He then goes on to state that the Father has shown him all the things that he does and will in fact show him greater works than these (τούτων). In the context of his defence against charges arising from his healing of the man at the pool, τούτων and therefore ἔργα, at least in part, must refer to the healing performed by Jesus and by implication to his other extraordinary actions. A connection is established between the two terms, given that the healing of the man is also to be seen as a sign within the narrative of the Gospel (cf. 7.21, 23).[7] The mention of greater works also suggests that the actions which are surpassed are also most likely to be the events John chooses to call signs but which Jesus will refer to as works.

Given this connection, the whole speech (5.19–30) makes two important contributions to the understanding of signs presented in the Gospel. First, Jesus states that he can do nothing by himself but only does what he sees the Father doing. Given that the works encompass the signs, the signs are therefore the works of the Father. This confirms the observations arising from 2.11. The works testify to Jesus' relationship with the Father. Onlookers are to acknowledge this relationship and 'marvel' (5.20). The works, and therefore signs, are intrinsic to the identity of the Son in his relationship to the Father.

Secondly, it soon transpires that the greater works will include the giving of life and the pronouncing of judgement (5.21–30), indicating that the referent of ἔργα is broader than the σημεῖα recorded in the Gospel. However, it is hinted that the signs/works foreshadow the greater works of giving life and executing judgement, despite the comparison, and therefore contrast, suggested between the present works and the greater works (5.20). This is suggested by the general unity posited between the works of the Father and the Son and the subsequent reference in 5.36 that appears to embrace the totality of the works mentioned in 5.20, especially with the addition of the verb τελειόω (cf. 4.34; 17.4). Jesus' ministry, referred to by John as marked by signs, points to his future role as the judge who has the power to preside over the resurrection to both life and judgement.[8] The signs also demonstrate the reality of that future ministry as it breaks into the present time in the person of Jesus. The previous two signs/healings, in the narrative, are vivid

---

[6] The word has already been introduced into the Gospel at 4.34 where it is used by Jesus to refer to the whole of his mission or task given to him as the sent Son. An inclusio is created with this reference by the use of ἔργον at 17.4.

[7] See further, p. 82.

[8] As suggested by Nicol (1972: 117–9).

manifestations of this reality. Jesus has given life to a boy on the brink of death (4.43–54) and brought healing and wholeness to a man who has been ill for a lifetime (5.1–18; see pp. 96–99). The positive side of this judgement role is specifically reflected in the life giving judgement Jesus pronounces to the royal official concerning his son (4.50). The negative aspect of this future judging role is intimated when he tells the man at the pool to stop sinning so that nothing worse should happen to him (5.14).

In the second 'half' of the discourse (5.31–47), Jesus anticipates the legal objection that he is testifying on his own behalf. This objection reflects the teaching in Deuteronomy 19.15 concerning the necessity of a plurality of witnesses. Jesus cites a number of witnesses concerning himself, and amongst these is a prime focus on the witness of the works that he performs.[9] The works that Jesus accomplishes are evidence of his credentials as the sent one of God (5.36; cf. the Jews' statement in 2.18). They are a greater witness than that of John (5.33–36) and they comprise the testimony of the ἄλλὸ (v. 32) who is clearly the Father (5.37). The καί at the beginning of v.37 does not add a new testimony to the list but completes, in emphatic fashion, the introduction of the Father's testimony begun at v. 32.[10] The testimony of the Father consists in the works that Jesus does (v. 36). While the works may well be broader than the signs, in this statement they are closely identified. Consequently, the signs are brought into close connection with the forensic theme of the Gospel. They are witnesses in the trial.

The relationship between σημεῖα and ἔργα will have to be monitored as it occurs through the Gospel. For the moment, it is observed that Jesus uses ἔργα in the context of speaking of his relationship to the Father, though it has appeared in more general contexts prior to this (3.18). The narrator and other characters have used σημεῖον; Jesus occasionally uses this language (4.48; 6.26), though not in reference to his own activity. In this Gospel, Jesus refers to his activity using the terminology of works while the narrator uses the term signs. There is significant overlap but not total identity in the terms. The σημεῖα are included in the ἔργα, and comprise their focal point, but do not exhaust their referent. With suitable caution, the subsequent references to works may be examined for the implications they hold for the Gospel's presentation of signs.[11] The reader is certainly encouraged by these connections to read the terms into one another.

---

[9] The connection between signs and works established here and their witnessing function lends support to the idea earlier expressed with regard to the witnessing function hinted at in the numbering of the first two signs (p. 61)

[10] The καί is consecutive, rendered 'and so'. See BDF: 227 § 442.2 and also Asiedu-Peprah (2001: 105).

[11] Welck (1994: 56–7) briefly discusses the relationship and suggests that the signs are specific works of Jesus. Neither Bittner (1987) nor Labahn (1999) appear to consider the relationship germane to their interests.

4.2.1.2 Reading the Signs (Jn 6.2)

The first occurrence of σημεῖον is at 6.2. This occurs in the context of the introductory remarks by the narrator as the scene is set for the feeding miracle that is to follow. The shift in locale is dramatic, moving from the events related in Jerusalem on to the Sea of Galilee in the north. It is reported that Jesus is being followed by large crowds drawn by the fact that they have seen the signs ἃ ἐποίει ἐπὶ τῶν ἀσθενούντων. Jesus' ministry is again generally characterised as marked by signs in an aside (cf. 2.23). This reference points, in particular, to his ongoing (imperfect ἐποίει) healing ministry as included amongst those signs.

While the σημεῖα in 6.2 cannot be specifically referring to the incident at the beginning of Jn 5 due to the geographical reference, the proximity and shape of the comment suggests that the healing of the lame man in Jerusalem also falls under the ambit of the term σημεῖον. This is especially so when the man healed in chapter 5 is recorded as being amongst the ἀσθενούντων by the pool (5.4). A further indication that the incident is to be identified as a sign occurs in chapter 7 when the healing of the man is referred to as a work in the midst of the disputes in which Jesus finds himself embroiled during the Feast of Tabernacles. This incident is also included in the general reference to signs at 7.31, when this verse is read in combination with the statement at 7.23.

The mention of a great crowd recalls the response of the many in Jerusalem who believed in him (2.23) and the evaluative judgement of Jesus in that instance, but there is no explicit judgement concerning the response of the crowd stated in the passage.[12] The observation simply reminds the reader of the numerous signs performed by Jesus and the attractive power of these actions. The stage is set for a further examination of their response. What do they see in the signs?

4.2.1.3 Signs of the Prophet? (Jn 6.14)

The presence of the great crowd precipitates the next powerful action of Jesus as he takes a few loaves and fish and feeds the multitude before him. The incident is specifically labelled amongst the σημεῖα at 6.14 when the crowd's response is recorded by the narrator. While the majority of manuscripts record the singular σημεῖον, a small but powerful combination of manuscripts (𝔓[75] B 091 a) differ and record the plural σημεῖα. This combination is strong

---

[12] Despite the suggestions of commentators, e.g. Schnackenburg (1980: 13–4), all the previous uses of the verb ἀκολουθέω have been positive in the sense that they describe the actions of disciples (cf. Jn 1.37–43). This will remain generally true though there are enough exceptions to guard against building too much on the use.

enough to force the question to be considered as to which is the original. In terms of possible reasons for the reading, the shift from singular to plural is as explicable as the shift from plural to singular. The shift to the singular from the plural would be explained on the grounds of context with the reference immediately following the single action of the feeding of the crowd. The shift from singular to plural would be explicable on the grounds of accommodation to, or recollection of, the plural in 6.2 and conformity to other plurals throughout the Gospel. In such narratorial asides the pattern generally appears to be that the plural is used (e.g. 2.11, 23; 4.54, 6.2; 12.37, 20.31). Arguably in the present context, the plural reading is the more difficult of the two readings, though the tendency just noted in the wider context of the Gospel makes the decision a finely balanced one. It is suggested, against NA27, that the plural reading be adopted for a combination of internal considerations. The relative consistency of plurals in similar summary statements by the narrator suggests that a similar reading is likely to have been adopted here, while the change to the singular is marginally more explicable in view of the immediate context. The plural is in line with the general emphasis on the accumulated weight of signs leading to various conclusions being drawn concerning Jesus. At the same time, the possibility is not precluded that the sign just seen is also a final confirmation of the conclusion that the crowd draws.

On the basis of the signs, the crowds acclaim Jesus as ὁ προφήτης ὁ ἐρχόμενος εἰς τὸν κόσμον. This figure has already been referred to when John denied any identification of himself in these terms in chapter 1 (1.21). Already in the narrative Jesus has been recognised in prophetic terms (4.19) but this statement is an advance in that a specific figure is referred to, drawing on the expectation of the 'prophet like Moses' promised in Deuteronomy 18.15–22. Jesus' actions are reported as being interpreted within the broad framework of Jewish eschatological expectation. The surprise in 6.15 is that the figure of the prophet is apparently associated with a royal function as the crowd is then reported as attempting to make him king. The connection has led to speculation concerning the relationship between the figures of 'the prophet' and king in both the expectations of the crowd and the presentation by the narrator, especially the possible connections with traditions that consider Moses in royal terms.[13] This will be considered at greater length below. Jesus' reaction suggests that the conclusion drawn is not an adequate one and that he will not entrust himself to this crowd and their attempts to make him their leader.[14] For the moment, it is enough to observe that the

---

[13] Meeks (1967) has the most thorough investigation.

[14] Meeks (1967: 99) suggests that this is a postponement of the taking up of the title of Mosaic king. Bittner (1987: 152–164) suggests that it is a rejection and that the kingship taken up by Jesus at a later point in the Gospel will be Davidic in flavour. See below on 7.31.

positive relationship between sign and response is preserved. The signs are 'read' by the crowd as indicating something about the identity of Jesus that calls for a response. In the light of Jesus' withdrawal, the question remains, as to whether the signs have been correctly understood. One option for 'reading' the signs has been presented and apparently rejected as Jesus separates himself from the crowd and their demand.

4.2.1.4 Seeking Signs and Seeing Signs (Jn 6.30)

On the day following the feeding of the crowd, Jesus again finds himself confronted by a crowd (6.25). He is reported as having walked across the sea to join his disciples in the boat heading for this new location. The awkward transitional verses 6.22–25 establish the sea walking as actually having occurred. The formal and precise detail of the crowd's knowledge of the locations of Jesus, the disciples and their boat is outlined in detailed terms in v. 22 and their observations are confirmed in v. 24. This account has the effect, at least for the reader, of confirming the occurrence of the sea walking and suggests that it is to be read amongst Jesus' signs.[15] The reported confusion of the crowds in the passage suggests that the narrator is hinting that they, also, should have realised that something unusual had occurred.[16] The plural σημεῖα in 6.26 may also provide a hint that the sea walking is to be seen as a sign but this can be no more than the barest of hints in view of the other, general, plural uses.[17]

Jesus responds to the crowd's question as to how he arrived by declaring that they have been searching for him, not because they saw signs but because they ate bread and were filled (6.26). The crowd is criticised not for following him because of signs but rather because they did see a sign and did not perceive its significance. They have come to Jesus for food rather than for what he really has to offer. Again, the question is raised of what it means to see a sign. This time it is raised in an overtly figurative sense. Far from criticising a believing response to the signs, the statement instead criticises the misreading of a sign intended to bring knowledge and belief. The crowd should have come to Jesus because they saw the signs in the sense of perceiving the deeper meaning implied in them concerning his identity. The audience of the Gospel is implicitly challenged as to how they also see the signs.

Following a brief exchange, the crowd is then reported as requesting a sign from Jesus (6.30). Jesus has just challenged the crowd to work for the food that lasts forever (6.27) and clarified that the work that God requires is to

---

[15] As Welck (1994: 164) suggests. Labahn (1999a: 298) comments on the attempt to legally establish the facts of the incident with a view to showing that it actually occurred.

[16] Calvin (1994: 152) notes this.

[17] Both Welck (1994: 164) and Labahn (1999a. 300) are more confident.

believe in the one whom he has sent. The crowd's request picks up on the references to work. The language of σημεῖον is then brought alongside the language of work (τί ἐργάζη;, 6.30), reinforcing the connection forged between σημεῖον and ἔργον that was established in chapter 5.

The request is reminiscent of that made in 2.18. In this instance it seems an absurd request in view of the event that they have recently witnessed and demonstrates that they have not 'seen' the previous sign(s).[18] This is further accentuated in v. 36 when Jesus tells the crowd that they have seen him and yet do not believe.[19] The connections of this verse, with its reference to seeing (ὁράω), back to 6.26; 6.30 (εἶδον) and forward to 6.40 (θεωρέω) confirm the play on the idea of seeing that is occurring.[20] The crowd have seen Jesus in that they have seen his signs. If they see him in the signs as the Son of the Father and believe, they will have life.

The crowd suggests a suitable sign would be the provision of manna. The reference to Moses recalls their previous acclamation of Jesus in Mosaic terms (6.14). Jesus doesn't answer this request, reinforcing that he performs signs entirely at his own initiative (cf. 2.18–19). Instead he picks up on the second half of the crowd's statement referring to Moses and his provision of manna and proceeds to apply the substance of the request to himself.[21] Jesus' promise that the Father will give them true bread from heaven is an oblique answer to their request for a sign and draws attention to himself as this true bread (6.35). As the dialogue continues with the crowd, the comparison quickly moves beyond one with Moses as the giver of bread to a comparison between the manna and Jesus (6.33). This, in turn, leads to the graphic imagery of eating his body and drinking his blood that depicts the identification required with Jesus if the benefits of his ministry are to be received (6.53–58). Again, a request for a sign leads to an oblique reference to the death of Jesus (cf. 2.18–20).

---

[18] This would be so even if, with Borgen (1997: 103–4), this request be seen as a request for a legitimating sign in the light of the apparently new claim made by Jesus that he is the one sent into the world (6.29).

[19] Some important manuscripts omit μέ (ℵ B) but the early 𝔓66.75vid and much of the manuscript tradition include it. The omission may mean that the link to v. 26 is clearer (Barrett 1978: 293), though the addition does not overly affect this (Beasley-Murray 1987: 85). Leaving μέ reinforces the sense that if the signs are truly seen then Jesus is truly seen and conceptual links are maintained through to v. 40.

[20] The context is determinative rather than any specific lexical items. Cf. Brown (1966: 500-503).

[21] Borgen (1965: 61–98) has pointed out the following discourse is structured around the three elements of the verse cited in 6.31 along the lines of a synagogue exposition. This analysis is a useful structuring device for the ensuing dialogue but misses the connection in the broader narrative context with the initial sign recorded at 6.1–15. The dialogical exposition is of the sign itself, as Anderson (1996: 17) points out.

This is a significant moment for the interpretation of the signs. Whatever evidential functions might be attributed to the σημεῖα are now supplemented by a symbolic application at some considerable depth. This carries on a trajectory of symbolic significance established in the extensive monologue following the healing of the man at the pool. In the dialogue in John 6 an explicit identification is made that suggests that, for this sign at least, one level of interpretation sees it as referring directly to Jesus. This is a deeper level of identification from that proposed for the previous signs, which have indicated in some sense the identity of Jesus as a life-giver. This sign does this but in a more profound sense as the material substance of the sign is picked up and directly applied by Jesus to himself. There is a sense in which Jesus himself is the sign.[22] This is reinforced by the first of a series of 'I am' sayings, with predicate, that punctuate the narrative from this point (6.35, 48, 51; 8.12; 10.9,11; 11.25; 14.6; 15.1). Not only is there a profound unity of event and proclamation in the signs, but the unity now encompasses the person of Jesus as he not only offers a sign or explains a sign but *is* the sign.

The identification of Jesus as the bread of life takes place in the context of the Festival of Passover (6.4). The connections that Jesus draws between the significance of the sign and his own death intersect with the Passover setting and contribute to the overall impact that the place of the Passover has in the narrative of the Gospel.[23] Jesus has already implicitly referred to his death at a previous Passover (2.19) and has been declared the Lamb of God who takes away the sin of the world (1.29). Now as the referent of the sign that is the feeding miracle, he explains that he must be lifted up and that his flesh must be eaten if anyone would have life in him (6.53–58). This chain of associations forges an understanding, with the help of the sign and its exposition in chapter 6, of the importance of the death of Jesus in the overall programme of the Son in bringing life. The reader is being led to understand the cross as a σημεῖον, when it occurs at the final Passover in the Gospel.

4.2.1.5 Signs of the Messiah? (Jn 7.31)

The next explicit reference to signs occurs in the midst of a series of disputes with crowds at the Feast of Tabernacles in Jerusalem. Immediately prior to this, there are two more references to ἔργα to consider briefly. Jesus' brothers urge him to go to Jerusalem so that his disciples may see the ἔργα he is doing (7.3). While a little surprising on the lips of Jesus' brothers, ἔργα in this instance refers to the actions described as σημεῖα elsewhere in the Gospel. This same equation is also implied in Jesus' statement in 7.21 where he refers

---

[22] Menken 1987: 146.

[23] Porter (1994) writes of the relative neglect of the theme of the Passover in the Gospel. There is however an extended reflection on this theme in the Gospel in Lightfoot (1956: 349–56).

to ἓν ἔργον performed on the Sabbath. The healing at the pool in chapter 5 is clearly being referred to in the reference to the Sabbath and the echo of ὑγιής(v. 23). In both 7.3 and 7.21 ἔργα and σημεῖα appear synonymous, reinforcing the connection established in chapter 5 between σημεῖα and ἔργα.

7.31 occurs in the midst of a section that lies close to the heart of the exposition of the Gospel's narrative in terms of the forensic motif. The claims of Jesus have been presented in chapters 5 and 6 and are then heatedly examined in chapters 7 and 8. The presentation in chapters 7 and 8 has been observed to have affinities with both Jewish and Roman legal procedures.[24] Jesus' identity is the issue as a number of options are canvassed and objections raised. Important in the midst of these debates is the issue of the reliability of the witnesses adduced by either side.[25] The signs continue to play an integral part in the presentation of these chapters, having been identified as witnesses by their previous association with works in chapter 5. The extended forensic examination is flanked by the presentation of signs performed on the Sabbath (5.1–11; 9.1–14), while the thesis presented in the signs, that Jesus is the divine messiah of Israel, is challenged most overtly in this section. In the midst of this debate, the healing in chapter 5 is specifically referred to (7.21–2), while the signs of Jesus are mentioned as an important testimony to his messianic identity (7.31), and then alluded to in chapter 8. The σημεῖα are well integrated into the legal motif.

The discussion concerning Jesus' messianic credentials is explicitly connected with the topic of signs in Jn 7.31, where the question is posed as to whether the Christ would do more signs when he came. The expectation is clearly expressed that signs are associated with the figure of the Messiah. The quantity of signs performed is emphasised in the statement (πλείονα). The rhetorical question that is posed by those in the crowd who believe in Jesus points to an abundance of evidence that is compelling by its volume. This verse fits in with the pattern of discussion concerning the signs seen so far. The sheer number of σημεῖα leads to the conclusion that Jesus is the Messiah. The appropriate response of belief is also mentioned.

A little later, in response to Jesus' words, the speculation concerning his identity as Messiah is continued (7.41). This is juxtaposed with speculation concerning his identity as the prophet (7.40). This oscillation and the earlier reference to the prophet (6.14) has led to discussion concerning whether John presents Jesus as the prophet or Messiah. Meeks has argued that the figure of Moses was seen as both a king and a prophet and that John specifically

---

[24] Harvey (1976) emphasises the various elements of Jewish legal process present while Neyrey (1987: 510, 1995a: 109–110) points to Roman elements in the presentation.

[25] As stressed by Harvey (1976: 20). According to Crook (1995: 18–30) this was also a feature of Greek and Roman settings.

endorses a Mosaic-prophetic Christology against a Davidic-messianic Christology.[26] On the other hand, Bittner sees an explicit rejection by Jesus, and the narrator, of a prophetic role in favour of a Davidic understanding expressed through the Gospel. He suggests that this is because of the dangerous political connotations attached to the more prophetic figure.[27] Both overstate their case. On the one hand, there is material linking Jesus with the figure of the 'prophet like Moses'. According to Deuteronomy 18 this prophet will be sent from God and speak the words that God puts in his mouth. Jesus is frequently referred to as having been sent (e.g. 7.16, 28; 8.26) and refers to his words as the ones that God has given him to speak (cf. 7.16; 8.26, 28). Explicit connection and comparison with the figure of Moses has also been a feature of the narrative and will continue to remain so (1.17; 3.15, 5.47, 6.3–33).[28] However, it is clear that the overall perspective of the Gospel is that Jesus is the Christ in Davidic terms (20.30–31). This is also clear from the accumulation of titles in the first chapter that reflect royal expectations.[29] The entry into Jerusalem as a king and the prominence of the theme of kingship in the trial before Pilate also point in this direction.[30]

Some have suggested that there is a blurring or blending of the various figures in the Gospel but this is unnecessary.[31] John carefully distinguishes the various figures of Jewish eschatological expectation (cf. 1.21) and especially between the expectations concerning the prophet and the Messiah (7.31, 40, 41). The discussions concerning the identity of Jesus as either the Messiah or 'the prophet' do overlap one another in that the signs lead to the identification of Jesus as both figures. Consequently, tests applying to the validity of signs as affirmed in the Hebrew Scriptures are also applied to the

---

[26] Meeks 1967: 17–31.

[27] Bittner 1987: 285–9.

[28] Anderson (1996: 174–5) has an extended listing. Bittner's insistence on the complete rejection of this role in his presentation of Jesus (cf. Bittner [1987: 285–8]) is puzzling, especially as this then means he has to posit that John has chosen the word σημεῖον as a central feature of John's presentation of Jesus as Messiah and then continually deny the straightforward connection between σημεῖον and the role of prophet throughout his Gospel. One wonders if it was such a good choice after all. His case for the messianic connections of σημεῖον is plausible but perhaps he ought to concede that there are a variety of figures from the tradition of the Hebrew Scriptures in his portrayal of Jesus and Jesus surpasses them all.

[29] This includes 1.45, which is occasionally seen as referring to the prophetic figure in Deut 18 (Brown 1968: 86). There are two significant references to the Davidic Messiah present in Gen 49.10 and Num 24.17. The combination law and prophets suggests a Davidic figure.

[30] The detailed study by Daly-Denton (2000) locates much material concerning the figure of David alluded to throughout the Gospel in the references to the Psalms through the Gospel, and in a variety of other allusions (for a concise summary see pp. 319–20).

[31] This is tentatively suggested by Hooker (1997: 65). Martyn (1979: 114) suggests an 'easy modulation from the Mosaic Prophet to the Mosaic Prophet-Messiah'.

examination of the claims that Jesus is making. While, strictly speaking, the warning of Deut 13.1-6 applies to a prophetic claim, the application of it as a test to the claim of Messiah seems to be a natural one.[32]

There are prophetic elements to the Johannine presentation of Jesus but he is presented, ultimately, as more than a prophet. 'Messiah' emerges as the main category out of the two for understanding his identity and mission. However, even the recognition of Jesus as Messiah appears to be finally understood in terms of the relationship between Father and Son (cf. 20.31).[33]

Chapter 8 continues the forensic examination of Jesus by his opponents, developing issues already raised in the extended sequence from 7.14–39.[34] Jesus' absolute claim to be the light of the world (8.12) is immediately objected to because it is a self-testimony and unsupported (8.13). Jesus responds by pointing to the extraordinary nature of his testimony that makes it valid and then declares that the Father testifies concerning him as well. If the law demands two witnesses then Jesus will cite himself and the Father (8.18). He does not say what the witness of the Father is but this has already been established in Jn 5 as including the works that he does (5.36–37). The signs are again an integral component of the debate concerning Jesus' identity; in this instance at an implicit level through their connection with the works as testimony from the Father. In fact works are integral to any individual's identity as Jesus goes on to suggest that the works of his opponents indicate their true origins (8.41).[35] It is implied that his own works and words (8.28–9) testify to his origin.

4.2.1.6 A Man from God? (Jn 9.16)

The forensic examination of Jesus' claims is continued in chapter 9, in his absence, as the Pharisees interrogate a man healed by Jesus of congenital blindness. The point at dispute is the identity of Jesus and the conflicting evidence presented concerns his healing of the man. The discussion is internal to the group interrogating the man who has been healed. The argument oscillates between two points in 9.16. On the one hand, some of their number object that Jesus cannot be from God because he does not keep the Sabbath.[36]

---

[32] Hooker (1997: 65) suggests that this expectation would not have been surprising.

[33] de Jonge 1977: 69.

[34] Lincoln 2000: 82.

[35] This connection would be familiar in the wider culture and has a long history. Aristotle states that achievements (ἔργα) are signs of moral habits (*Rhet.* 1.9.33). See Heiligenthal (1983: 8–25) for details.

[36] Despite only being mentioned in vss. 14 and 16, the fact that the healing took place on the Sabbath is a key feature of the incident. Just (1997: 253–6) downplays this aspect claiming that the setting and the Pool of Siloam are more significant. This ignores the ensuing debate over whether Jesus is a man from God or a sinner. This debate can only arise because of the Sabbath setting.

This is the main piece of evidence against the claim that Jesus is from God and reflects the warning of Deuteronomy 13. On the other hand, an alternative group replies that the evidence of Jesus' signs is such that he cannot be a sinful man.

Again the plurality of signs is mentioned but it is also qualified such that the quality of the signs is also emphasised (τοιαῦτα). This is entirely appropriate in view of the unprecedented nature of the healing (cf. 9.32). The resolution of the Sabbath issue is one that the reader must supply on the basis of Jesus' claim that he is able to do what he does because he is doing his Father's work (5.18). His 'breaking' of the Sabbath is testimony to his identity in this Gospel. This 'resolution' is in turn reinforced by the unprecedented nature of the sign in question.

The unprecedented nature of the quality and quantity of signs that Jesus is performing is emphasised in this statement. All other rivals are implicitly dismissed from the scene. The outstanding nature of this occurrence is reflected again in the statement that concludes the extended dialogue that proceeds from the incident of the healing of the man born blind. Jesus is accused of having a demon (10.20), an accusation that has recurred at various points during his 'cross-examination' in chapters 7–8 (7.20; 8.48, 52). In reply, the evidence of his words and works is offered (10.21, recalling 9.16, 30, 32). The work in this case is the healing of the man born blind. Demons produce distress and death (*Sib. Or.* 3.331) and the restoration of a good thing like sight would not fall within their ambit. This is more likely to be the work of a god, as the reference to ἐκ τοῦ αἰῶνος (9.32) might suggest. The signs, through their association with the works, continue to play their part in the Gospel's presentation of Jesus' claims.

4.2.1.7 Messiah Again (Jn 10.24-38)

In the final discussion of Jesus' claims set within the context of the Jewish feasts (10.22), the possibility of Jesus' messianic identity is again raised. He is asked to state plainly whether he is the Christ (10.24). Jesus replies that his works testify to his identity (10.25). The immediate context suggests that the healing of the blind man is in view and that the primary referent of ἔργα on the lips of Jesus is the events designated as σημεῖα. This is reinforced by the presence of the verbs ποιέω (10.25, 37, 38) and δείκνυμι (10.32). While these verbs are not exclusively restricted to the mention of signs, they recall the language generally used in connection with σημεῖα in the Gospel. The connection between the signs and the Messiah is again implicitly drawn. When his accusers seek to stone him, Jesus again refers to many good works that he has shown them from the Father and asks for which of these works they oppose him (10.32). The reply of his accusers shows that they have divorced the evidence of the works of Jesus from the testimony of his words and are accusing and condemning him on the basis of his words. They have failed to see clearly. They apparently concede the 'good' nature of the works that Jesus is doing but do not penetrate to the conclusion to which these works ought to lead. The signs/works continue to be used as witnesses in the trial conducted in the narrative.

The final point of this particular conversation is reached when Jesus asks the Jews to believe his claim to have come from the Father on the basis of the works that he does (10.37–8). The evidential line of thought that is presupposed in 10.37 further reinforces the presentation of the signs as testimony in a trial. The appeal is firstly expressed negatively—'if I am not doing the works of my Father, then do not believe me'. The connection between Jesus' works and the works of his Father is reinforced as Jesus stakes the recognition of his mission and person on them. The thought of 2.11 and 5.20 lies close at hand. The works are the works of the Father, through the Son, and in them the glory of the only begotten Son is seen. They, therefore, testify to the divine identity of the Son.[37]

The second part of the statement (10.38) presents the appeal in positive fashion. Jesus suggests that although the Jews might not believe him,[38] they should believe the works. Presumably this means that if they will not accept his verbal testimony then they ought at least to consider the evidence of the works/signs presented to them and draw their own conclusions. These will, if believed, lead them to the conclusion that Jesus has been speaking about. At this point, with the relationship between signs and works established, the testifying power of the signs is again implicitly established at the level of the story and at the level of the dialogue with the reader. The signs are consistently portrayed as leading to faith or at least providing the basis on which faith might be based.

4.2.1.8 John Did No Sign (Jn 10.41)

In this final reference to σημεῖα in the section under consideration, the testimony of John is affirmed as true in the light of Jesus' activity. The use of σημεῖον at this point reminds the reader of the significance of this term for describing the ministry of Jesus, especially after the extensive use of ἔργον in the dialogues of chapter 10. In hearing that John did no sign, the audience is reminded of the various references to the signs of Jesus that have emphasised both their quantity and quality. Jesus' ministry, in contrast to that of John, is full of signs.

---

[37] See the discussion in Ensor (1996: 278–90).

[38] The use of πιστεύω with the dative suggests that this is more an intellectual sense of 'believe' in contrast to the more personal tones of πιστεύω εἰς. This is more of a tendency than a clear distinction (e.g., 5.24, 38).

The truth of John's testimony is not attested to by signs that he himself performs, as might be expected.[39] Rather the ministry of Jesus' signs attests to the accuracy of John's testimony. Jesus is the sign who authenticates John's ministry in that his ministry of signs has amply demonstrated that he is the one to whom John accurately bore testimony. John had no need of other signs to demonstrate the veracity of his message—the unity between his testimony and the one to whom he bore testimony is sufficient.

The placement of this passage is significant, coming as it does after an explicit rejection of Jesus and his ministry by the Jews in chapter 10 (cf. 10.39). The geographical note recorded in 10.39–40 takes the reader back to the beginning of the Gospel, to the testimony of John the Baptist. This statement reminds the reader that the signs are explicitly linked with Jesus and his identity as testified to by John. John testified to one who comes after him and yet ranks before him (1.16; 27); the Lamb of God who takes away the sins of the world (1.29,36); the one upon whom the Spirit descended and remained (1.32–33); and who is also the elect one of God (1.34). The endorsement of John's testimony in the prologue (1.6–7) suggests that after the various options have been canvassed in these chapters that here the position of the narrator is given as to how the signs ought to be read. The signs mark Jesus out in messianic terms. It remains to be seen how the Lamb of God will take away the sin of the world.

The testimony of πολλοί demonstrates that, despite opposition and rejection, Jesus' ministry is also being recognised. The σημεῖα continue to do their work. The testimony of John at the beginning of the Gospel is affirmed to be true when the response of the leaders of Israel might in fact lead one to conclude that it has been mistaken.[40]

4.2.1.9 Text to Reader: Summary

The general references to σημεῖα throughout this section have stressed both the quantity and quality of the signs that Jesus has performed. They have been a key feature of the trial that is ensuing over the claims of Jesus. Their evidence is ambiguous and is able to form part of the case both for and against the claims that are made on Jesus' behalf, especially his healings on the Sabbath. The issue throughout has been seeing the signs correctly. Several alternative (mis)readings have been presented throughout the section, continually reminding the reader of the correct reading through references back to the seminal information given in the prologue and testimony of John. The forensic metaphor has been prominent throughout the section both in terms of vocabulary and narrative setting. The language of σημεῖα has

---

[39] As Bammel (1965: 181, 188) notes.
[40] Lightfoot 1956: 218.

participated in this metaphor, in its own right, as well as in conjunction with the use of ἔργα. In terms of the dialogue with the reader, this language operates within this metaphor to attest the identity of Jesus and suggest that there are many incidents that prove the claims made concerning him. The use of σημεῖα has also taken on more overtly symbolic dimensions in this section, and accompanying discourses/dialogues have been recorded that draw out these dimensions.

4.2.2 The Occurrences of σημεῖον: Reader to Text

The language of σημεῖον continues to engage the repertoire of a wide range of early hearers. As for the previous section, a brief examination of the reception by those familiar with the Hebrew Scriptures will be followed by a more extensive reflection from the perspective of a broader Graeco-Roman audience.

The overall context of the Jewish feasts and the sustained dialogue concerning the identity of Jesus in terms reflecting two figures of Jewish eschatological expectation locates the significance of the references to σημεῖα within the context of the Hebrew Scriptures for the reader familiar with these Scriptures. The designation of Jesus as a prophet like Moses echoes with the Hebrew Scriptures as well as with popular expectation.[41]

The messianic connection is also important in terms of passages in the Hebrew Scriptures that suggest the messianic era will be marked by signs (Mic 7.15; Isa 26.19; 29.18; 35.5–6; 48.20–21; 53.4; 61.1). Despite the lack of a clear statement outside of the Gospel that the Messiah himself would perform signs,[42] it is plausibly suggested that such an expectation is raised by the depiction of the messianic figure found in Isaiah.[43] Isaiah 11 refers to a ruler from the line of David who will be anointed with the Spirit of power (Isa 11.2) and will reign over a kingdom of righteousness and peace in which the earth will be full of the knowledge of God (Isa 11.9). A similar Spirit-endowed figure is referred to at later points in Isaiah (Isa 42, 61). Links could also be established with the depiction of the events of the messianic times in

---

[41] Schnackenburg (1980: 19) suggests there is not a great deal of evidence for the expectation of a prophet like Moses in popular Jewish consciousness, but does point to the reports of the 'prophets' in Josephus and the hints in the Dead Sea Scrolls (1QS 9.10–11; cf. 4QTest 5–8) of the expectation of a prophet attached to the expectations expressed in Deut 18.18. 1QS 9.10–11 is the clearest but some scholars suggest that the collection of texts in 4QTest 5–8 refer to the three eschatological figures mentioned in 1QS 9. If this connection is made, then Deut 18 clearly lies behind the expectation and the three figures are distinguished.

[42] So Klausner (1956: 506). Both de Jonge (1977: 92) and Schnackenburg (1980: 149) suggest the statement in 7.31 is Christian messianic dogma.

[43] Bittner 1987: 136–50. Bauckham (2002: 21) suggests that 'Jewish messianism was not so much a tradition of ideas as a tradition of exegesis' that depended upon recognising links between passages. Bittner follows a similar approach in establishing the connections.

passages such as Isa 26.19; 29.18–19; 35.5. Accordingly, this Spirit-endowed figure will be empowered to perform various works, including opening the eyes of the blind (Isa 35.5; 42.7), healing the lame (Isa 35.5), and bringing out prisoners from their captivity (42.7; 61.1).[44]

As noted above, a link is more strongly forged between the σημεῖα and the forensic theme that constitutes a major element of the Johannine presentation. The signs of Jesus are the testimony of the Father to his identity and mission and are therefore an integral part of the mission of the Son. Jesus appeals to the works he does in unity with the Father as an obvious witness that should have allowed his opponents to believe that the Father had sent him. They also show the Jews that they have no grounds for controversy against him on the specific charge of Sabbath violation. In the Jewish context, where the character of witnesses and their trustworthiness and reliability is of paramount importance,[45] the signs are reliable witnesses. The Jews have already asked for a sign in response to Jesus' action in the temple and Nicodemus has drawn the conclusion that Jesus is a teacher come from God on the basis of his signs. Such testimony then appears to be acceptable in a dispute of this nature.[46]

The legal language neatly dovetails with the forensic/rhetorical usage noted in the wider cultural context (Chapter 2, below) as the signs are presented as witnesses in the trial that is presented in the Gospel. They are testimony to the participants in the narrative and they are testimony in the trial being conducted with respect to the reader through the Gospel as a whole. The progressive accumulation of signs through the narrative is building a case for the reader as the (many) signs presented in the earthly ministry of Jesus did the same for his onlookers. The tentative and apparently inconclusive nature of the evidence of any single sign is alleviated by the presentation of multiple signs. This accords well with the usage in the wider rhetorical and legal context where σημεῖον indicated a proof, but one that required some

---

[44] Further possible evidence concerning such a connection appeared in 1992 with the publishing of the Qumran document 4Q521, which speaks of the anointed one or messiah and goes on to say that God will release captives, give sight to the blind, and raise the dead as well as preach good news (lines 11–12). The surprise is that it appears to be God who is described as preaching good news, a work that is normally the work of an agent or messenger (cf. 11Q13 l. 18). The passage in 4Q521 appears to be based on Psalm 146 and to draw in Scriptures from other places including Isa 61.1. The clearest allusion to Isa 61.1 comes with the mention of preaching to the poor and there is the phrase added concerning the raising of the dead (reflecting perhaps Isa 29.18). In view of the unusual description of God as the one proclaiming good news, Collins suggests that God is acting through an agent in 4Q521 and that this would explain the introduction of messiah in the first line. This discussion is found in John J. Collins (1998: 112–115). Fitzmyer (2000: 95) demurs and suggests that the Lord is the subject. However see Evans (1997: 97) for further support of Collins.

[45] Harvey 1976: 20–21.

[46] Asiedu-Peprah 2001: 104–5.

accumulation. In the dialogue maintained with the reader through the occurrences of σημεῖα the quantity and quality of Jesus' actions has been continually reinforced. The general references to the quality and quantity of Jesus' actions are, in turn, illustrated by the σημεῖα narratives. The cumulative case presented is powerful and leads the reader both to, and deeper into, the identity of Jesus.[47]

At the same time, the forensic motif has provided opportunity for a variety of objections to the claims made concerning Jesus to be raised and either dealt with or dismissed. This has occurred throughout Chapters 7 and 8. While the precise details of the discussion might elude many readers, the impression is given that the claims concerning Jesus have been well aired. The general tone of evaluation and assessment is reinforced by the details in the individual sign narratives that appear to be related in order to help the reader see that the events occurred and that impartial witnesses can attest to these occurrences. Such details are important in view of the evaluation of signs that was noted in some ancient authors. The forensic context reinforces the sober nature of this process. All of this combines to provide the persuasive thrust of the overall case being presented to the reader as the trial of Jesus before his contemporaries is related.

The sustained focus on the person of Jesus continues to educate the reader more familiar with the notion of a sign as an omen or direct communication from the gods. The embedding of the language within the trial motif continues to facilitate this as well. The development in this section, whereby the sign narratives are accompanied by either extended monologues or dialogues also provides an extra layer of interpretation for the reader who is drawn to Jesus through the presentation of his σημεῖα in the narrative of the Gospel.[48]

The general references to σημεῖον, situated within the matrix of thought informed by the Hebrew Scriptures and embedded within the forensic motif, continue to provide the context within which the σημεῖα narratives are to be

---

[47] The failure to appreciate fully this dimension of the sign language in the Fourth Gospel mars the presentation of Welck (1994), who purports to be presenting a literary study but fails to explore fully the implications of the material in terms of this major literary theme of the Gospel's presentation. This arises partly because of a focus on the sign narratives and a relative neglect of the wider narrative context in which they are embedded. Similarly, the studies of Bittner (1987) and Labahn (1999) do not explore this connection. Further exploration along these lines might also have enhanced the presentation of Lincoln (2000) on the forensic theme of the Fourth Gospel.

[48] Bittner (1987: 283, 287–8) argues that signs need a context or framework in which to be understood and that for the signs this context is the Hebrew Scripture. This is mainly true. The requirement of a context to establish the meaning of a sign is correct (cf. p. 25). However, there is also provided through the discourses and dialogues attached to the signs a further framework or context in which the signs are located. This would enable the reader unfamiliar with the Scriptural context of the signs to begin to appropriate their meaning apart from the general connotations of the σημεῖα narratives.

located. It is time then to turn to a more detailed examination of the four σημεῖα narratives found in this section. For each of the narratives to be considered the two angles of approach, text to reader (*Writing the sign*) and reader to text (*Reading the sign*), will be considered in turn.

4.3 The Sign Narratives

4.3.1.1 The Healing at the Pool (Jn 5.1–18): Writing the Sign

While it is not specifically labelled a sign, there are enough connections made for the reader to recognise the healing at the pool as such.[49] The scene moves from the general to the particular as the reader is taken to Jerusalem at the time of an unnamed feast (5.1), then to a precisely identified pool (5.2), through some more specific descriptions of the variety of ill people (5.3) and finally to a specific individual (5.5). The excessive detail has the effect of slowing the action and vividly establishing the scene in the reader's mind as well as sympathetically aligning the reader with the plight of the individual concerned. The man is described as having been ill for 38 years, a length of time that arouses further sympathy for his plight as well as accentuating the reader's appreciation of the magnitude of its resolution. While the details of his illness are not recounted he is initially numbered amongst the blind, lame and paralysed. Throughout the account he will continue to be referred to in very general terms as simply 'the man', 'the sick one' (5.7) or 'the one who had been made well' (5.10, 13). While there are hints as to his actual condition through the passage, the general setting and general nature of his affliction lend an air of universality to the account. This healing is a paradigmatic one in that Jesus is shown to be dealing with an illness in a place that is full of illness.

After this lengthy introduction, the audience is given a view from Jesus' perspective. They are told that Jesus knew of the man's illness and the length of time that he has been there. This view reinforces the desperate state that the man is in through an implied repetition of the details of his illness. It also reinforces in the reader's mind the powers of Jesus (the knowledge is probably meant to be inferred as supernatural[50]) as well as heightening the expectations that Jesus is about to act.[51] Such a perspective might normally be expected to align the reader with the one perceiving (i.e. Jesus),[52] but the nature of the view offered here instead reinforces the reader's sympathy with

---

[49] See above, p.p. 73–74.

[50] Especially when other instances of Jesus' apparently extraordinary knowledge are taken into account (1.49; 2.23; 4.18).

[51] Asiedu-Peprah 2001: 63.

[52] Berlin 1983: 90–91.

the man at the pool. This process is furthered when the man's reply to Jesus' question as to whether he wants to be healed, emphasises his helplessness further (5.7). The reply also draws further attention to the presence of the pool and its apparently miraculous healing powers as well as to his desire to be healed.

The healing itself is narrated simply and emphasises the powerful word of Jesus. He simply commands that the man rise, take up his bed and walk. Immediately the man is made whole and obeys the word of Jesus. The key word employed to describe his healing is ὑγιής, which receives emphasis through repetition (5.6, 9, 11, 14, 15).

The reader's sympathy is further maintained as the Jews question the man and accuse him of breaking the Sabbath. The mention of the Sabbath (5.9) is another turning point in the story and sets the scene for the extended discourse to follow. It appears that Jesus has deliberately precipitated this development in that he has been in total control throughout.

In the light of what has just happened to the man this rebuke of his activity by the Jews is harsh and disengages the reader from the interlocutors immediately. The ignorance of the man who has been healed concerning the identity of Jesus (5.13) demonstrates the gratuitous nature of the healing. Jesus apparently requires neither request, recognition, nor relationship in order to be able to heal. He can perceive a need and take the initiative.

There is a pause for a moment as Jesus speaks again with the man. The action has moved from the pool to the temple and this move prepares the scene for Jesus' extended speech to the Jews concerning himself. His statement to the man in 5.14 emphasises the permanent effects of the healing by partially echoing his previous question to the man (cf. 5.6; ὑγιής, γίνομαι). Jesus' deliberate action of finding the man and warning him to stop sinning so that nothing worse will happen to him serves the purpose of disclosing his identity to the man and therefore the authorities but the warning itself is difficult to interpret. Connections between physical illness and sin are probably hinted at in this statement,[53] and it seems reasonable to infer with many exegetes that the suggestion is of either physical death, eternal consequence or perhaps both.[54] The suspicion is raised that the life on offer is more than simply physical wholeness.[55] The ominous nature of this pronouncement hints at the role that Jesus exercises as both life-giver and

---

[53] Thomas 1995: 16–17. This connection is not the only way of viewing the relationship in the Gospel (cf. 9.3).

[54] Carson (1991: 245–6) sees the threat of physical illness; Beasley-Murray (1987: 74) reads eternal consequences. Thomas (1995: 17) rightly cautions against too dogmatic a distinction here in view of the Johannine interplay between present and future realities.

[55] Moloney (1996: 6) suggests that the reader accepts the association of the healing with the greater offer of eternal life based on earlier passages in the Gospel.

judge (cf. 5. 21–24). The details of the sign demonstrate how the action itself points to the truths that it proclaims.

The final report of the man's action in identifying Jesus to the authorities clearly facilitates the Gospel narrative by bringing Jesus and the authorities together but is enigmatic in terms of how the reader is being invited to view the man's action. Is it a cowardly attempt to shift blame on to Jesus or is it an action that gives glory to the one who has healed him? His actions are often viewed negatively by exegetes,[56] but this may be hasty. The verb ἀναγγέλλειν is used positively elsewhere in the Gospel (cf. 4.25; 16.13, 14, 15) and the man's report to the Pharisees emphasises the fact that Jesus made him whole rather then commanded him to take up his mat.[57] In its own way it is a testimony to the power of Jesus and indicates the movement to faith that has been a feature of the two previous sign narratives.

The exchange may leave the reader ambivalent regarding the man and his response but it certainly causes the Jews to be seen in a worse light. They seem to ignore the possibility of any sort of healing and continue to focus their attention on the identity of the one who has apparently broken the Sabbath. This also has the effect of continuing to maintain the focus of the narrative on Jesus.[58]

The broader significance of Jesus' actions is hinted at in the combination of the repeated ὑγιής, the command to rise and the ominous tone of his warning to the man concerning the possibility of worse things happening. Together these point to a restoration of life that moves beyond a simple healing and links into the themes of life and judgement that will be the focus of the extended discourse that follows (5.21–4). The most significant detail is the timing of the healing of the Sabbath (5.9). This leads into the more extended discussion of the rest of the chapter. The whole account exhibits a unity.[59] The Jews' accusations flow from the healing incident and Jesus' defence of his activity on the Sabbath. Jesus' response to the allegations provides the platform for an extensive exposition of his personal claims, which serves to justify his activity. The healing takes on a deeper christological focus. At the heart of the controversy is Jesus' justification for his action by claiming to be doing the Father's work in performing the healing on the Sabbath. The fact that this statement connects with a long established discussion concerning the activity of God on the Sabbath is well known.[60] His

---

[56] Morris (1995: 272–3) describes the man as an 'unpleasant creature' who 'betrays' Jesus. Witherington (1995: 139) suggests he 'passes the buck', while Brown (1968:209) simply accuses him of 'persistent naïveté'.

[57] John Chrysostom, *Hom. Jo.* 38.2.

[58] Asiedu-Peprah 2001: 69–70.

[59] See Asiedu-Peprah (2001: 58); cf. Labahn (1999a: 215) sees an agglomeration of traditions.

[60] See for example the discussion in Brown (1966: 216–7).

interlocutors would have accepted the premise expressed in v. 17 but not his conclusion. This is construed as blasphemy as Jesus appears to be usurping God's divine prerogative in claiming to be able to work on the Sabbath in the same sense as God does, thereby making himself equal with God (5.18).

Jesus' defence draws out the further significance of the incident in terms of his relationship with the Father. The healing of a man suggests his power and compassion but, because of its timing, ultimately points to his divine identity with the Father. The contribution of this speech to the understanding of the function of the signs has been noted previously.[61] This monologue also establishes a pattern of signs and discourse that will recur through the rest of the Gospel.

4.3.1.2 The Healing at the Pool (Jn 5.1–18): Reading the Sign

When it comes to assessing what wider connotations this account may have held for the early audience, a number of details are important. While the man's condition is initially described in the most general terms, the reader is also given some clues as to what his specific problem might be. He is placed amongst the ἀσθενούντων, τυφλῶν, χωλῶν, ξηρῶν (5.4). The term ἀσθενής denotes general illness and sickness but the following terms are more specific. Χωλός designates the lame or crippled of the hand and, outside of John, the plural form is almost always found with τυφλός and often in association with other infirmities (cf. Matt 15.30; 21.14; Lk 14.21). Ξηρός can be used of either hands or feet and suggests that these limbs are shrunken, withered or paralysed. The implication of the man's comment, that he has no one to place him into the pool (5.7) is that his problem is a mobility one. This is further emphasised by the fact that Jesus commands him to rise and walk. He is almost certainly lame in some severe sense, possibly even a paralytic.[62] The man is also placed amongst the ill near a pool, awaiting a miraculous disturbance of the waters that promise healing. This grouping of the ill in this context is reminiscent of healing sanctuaries described in ancient writings.[63] Connections can be established with the audience's cultural repertoire in terms of both the locale and the posited nature of the man's disease.

From the perspective of the Hebrew Scriptures, the messianic implications of the incident would be readily apparent in that the healing of the lame is one of the blessings associated with the messianic kingdom (Isa 35.5). The more general task of giving life is of course acknowledged as the preserve of Yahweh (Gen 2.7; Deut 32.39; Job 33.4).

---

[61] See pp. 71–73.

[62] The addition of παραλυτικός (5.3) in D suggests that this was an early supposition.

[63] Examples of such descriptions can be found in Aristophanes, *Plut.* 653–80; Strabo, *Geog.* 14.1.44.

If he is a paralytic, or even lame, then a connection with the idea of death may be implicit in this description. A paralysed man or even a lame man would have been seen as in some sense under the grip of death. Hippocrates regarded a paralysed leg as if it were a corpse's leg (the remark is recorded by Aretaeus, *Sign. diut.* 1.7.2). Bolt explains that this thought arises from beliefs regarding the anatomical/physiological role of the sinews.[64] In the first century, a variety of diseases could be classified as diseases of the sinews.[65] Prior to the time when Galen clarified matters in terms of the nervous system, paralysis was also thought to have resulted from the loosening of the sinews. These views were held on the basis of an ancient understanding of the body, whereby the soul is located in the bones which were held together by the sinews, which, in turn, occupied a position just short of the marrow. The marrow contains the soul and the sinews nurture the marrow. To loosen the sinews in a paralysis was a step towards death.[66]

Another interesting connection occurs with respect to the ξηρῶν. In ancient medicine the balance between moistness and dryness was critical. Moisture nourishes the marrow but too much dryness leads to death (Plato, *Tim* 77C, 88D). When a limb has dried up there is something seriously wrong and such a limb may be considered as dead already (Aretaeus, *Sign. diut.* 1.7.2). This draws further on Plato's theory, expressed in the Timaeus, concerning the balance of elements in the body and the importance of this balance for health. In this schema, moistness and dryness were important in relation to the soul as well. Plutarch notes that the moister the soul, the more fitting it is for the body, while the dry soul is prepared for above (*Sera* 566A). An Aramaic curse bowl inflicts dryness upon its victim's legs prior to requesting his death.[67]

Once the man was recognised by the reader as being a victim of some sort of paralysis, he would have been seen as living under threat of death for what amounts to more than a lifetime for many.[68] If this is the case then Jesus' command to rise is even more evocative, especially in view of the fact that he will go on to imply that he has the authority to raise the dead as does his Father (5.21). The connotations of the man's illness and his place amongst those afflicted in these ways reinforce the connections made between health,

---

[64] Bolt 1997: 95–7.

[65] Dioscorides *Mat. med.* 3.78. According to Homer, Odysseus' mother speaks of the dead as those whose sinews no longer hold together the flesh and bones (Homer, *Od.* 11.218–222).

[66] The Platonic ideas behind this analysis were influential throughout the first century particularly through the Timaeus (69D–84C). See Runia (1986: 38–57) for an assessment of the influence of Plato and the *Timaeus*.

[67] Bowl 9 in Naveh & Shaked (1985: 175–9).

[68] This comment is based on the estimated life expectancy of a person living in the first century. See Chapter 3, n. 86.

life and power over death that are established between the narrative of the incident and its subsequent discourse.

The healing occurs at a pool surrounded by the lame, sick and blind. This description evokes descriptions of similar healing places throughout the ancient world, connected with healing deities (cf. Pausanias, *Descr.* 2.27.2; 10.32.12; Aristophanes, *Plut.* 410, 653–680; *Vesp.* 122; Strabo, *Geog.* 14.1.44; Plautus, *Curc.* 1.1.61; 2.1.18-21). While other gods were thought to heal, the principal god of healing was Asclepius.[69] He was the son of Apollo and upon his death was made first a hero and then a god.[70] His daughter was Hygeia, the personification of health and well being. Asclepius was a widely known god, introduced to Athens in 420 B.C. and Rome in 292/1 B.C.[71] In imperial times it was the Asklepieon of Pergamum that took precedence over all others, while important centres are also recorded as existing at Kos and Epidaurus. Asclepius's presence is also recorded in Palestine.[72] Boring comments that 'Alongside Hercules, Isis, and Mithras, Asclepius was the Hellenistic deity with which Christianity was most in the situation of entering into competition'.[73] The connections with the Asclepius phenomenon are strengthened when it is considered that in this account the repetition of ὑγιής is prominent. This is a component of a phrase that appears regularly in the accounts of Asclepius' s healings. These accounts were inscribed on the steles outside of the healing sanctuary at Epidaurus.[74] While ὑγιής is a common word and its repetition is not enough in itself to prompt this connection, it is the combination with the pool and the general setting that is most suggestive.[75]

A further intriguing connection with this type of miracle is observed in connection with the Emperor Vespasian. During his visit to Alexandria,

---

[69] Cf. Diodorus Siculus, *Hist.* 1.25.2–7 on Isis. Hercules is also acclaimed as a healer; cf. Aelius Aristides, *Herc.* 40.12. Cotter (1999: 11) comments that in principle any deity or powerful hero in the Graeco-Roman period could be claimed to have healed but that in practice only a few are regularly described as doing so.

[70] Pindar, *Pyth.* 3.47–56 has an account of the history.

[71] See Klauck (2000: 155–160) for details.

[72] McCasland 1939; Duprez 1970: 64–72. There is evidence also for the presence of Asclepius in Ephesus in early Hellenistic times and during Nero's reign; cf. Oster (1990: 1669–70); Aurenhammer (1995: 266).

[73] Boring 1995: 267.

[74] See Wells (1998: 31–3) for further details.

[75] Duprez (1970: 57–127), on the basis of archaeological work near St Anne's monastery in Jerusalem, has suggested that there were pagan healing pools in existence in the vicinity of Jerusalem (outside the walls) during the first century. The site certainly appears to have been associated with Serapis from 135 A.D. Murphy-O'Connor (1992: 31) seems to accept that the incident describes Jesus healing a client of a pagan healing pool. Davies (1974: 312–13) speculates on the audacity of Jesus in healing at a pagan cult centre if this is correct but leaves the question open. Hengel (1999: 313) suggests that the presence of such a pool is impossible.

Vespasian is reported to be involved with two healings. There are three reports of this incident, with the most extensive being that of Tacitus (*Hist.* 4.81), The other two are found in the works of Suetonius (*Vesp.* 7) and Cassius Dio (*Hist.* 65.8.1). All three agree that one of the healings was a blind man while Suetonius describes the healing of a lame man as opposed to the account of a man with a withered hand in the other two writers. The discrepancy might be explained via the transmission of a verbal account using a term like withered that could be applied to any limb. The account of the healings is interesting in itself, especially in connection with Dio's statement that 'Heaven was thus magnifying him'. Suetonius introduces the account by saying that it helped Vespasian with an image problem. Apparently he 'as yet lacked prestige and a certain divinity'. These miracles appear to add legitimacy to the divine credentials of Vespasian. While this appears to be an acknowledgement of healings in a legitimating role, the more explicit connection with a lame man in the account of Suetonius is also intriguing.

Jesus' action in this instance contrasts with all would-be healers and sources of healing in the ancient world. There is no formal request by the man. There is no approach to a temple, pool, or sacred places of healing. There is no elaborate ceremony to perform; no nights spent sleeping in a sanatorium and no dreams to decipher.[76] For much of the narrative, the man is oblivious to the identity of his benefactor. He does not have to do anything regarding his healing and the healing is instantaneous. The external connections reinforce the emphasis of the narrative. The man is restored to health and life as he is raised from a state of living death. Jesus is again portrayed as the life-giver. In a world riddled by death and disease this could not help but be an action that indicated divine power. The identity and mission of Jesus are again revealed to all in a sign recorded in the Fourth Gospel. At the same time, a comparison is implicit with potential rivals.

4.3.2.1 Feeding a Multitude (Jn 6.1–15): Writing the Sign

The next sign narrated involves the feeding of a large multitude. Jesus is beside the Sea of Galilee, followed by a crowd attracted by his signs. The fact that he is on a mountain and the time is Passover immediately places him in a setting reminiscent of the exodus and Moses.

The account of the feeding then follows. The narration shifts from a general scene setting account (vv. 1–4) to a view from Jesus' perspective as he views the crowds gathered around him (6.5). The narrator then informs the reader of Jesus' motive in asking Philip his question. The reader is also told that Jesus knows exactly what he is about to do. This has a number of effects. First, the control of Jesus over circumstances is again asserted as a part of the

---

[76] These are three features of the accounts of cures effected by Asclepius; cf. Burkert (1985: 215).

general picture of such sovereignty that is presented through the Gospel. Secondly, the anticipation of the reader is raised that something extraordinary is about to happen (cf. Jn. 5.6). Thirdly, there is no doubt that Jesus deliberately and self-consciously performs the σημεῖα. They are not accidental products of his being but a deliberate exercise of power with specific goals in mind. In fact, in this instance the sign itself is portrayed as specific testing of the disciples (6.6). The more 'aggressive' nature of this sign that is suggested by this reference suits the general trajectory of the signs as portrayed in this section of the Gospel.[77] The previous sign (5.1–11) is deliberately performed on the Sabbath and provokes a confrontation with the leaders of Israel. The feeding and its dialogical aftermath test people other than the disciples.

The reader's interest is now focussed on the disciples, wondering how they will respond to this challenge. Perhaps also some sympathy with their predicament is aroused as Jesus raises the problem of how to feed these people with the meagre resources they have. The magnitude of what is about to happen is emphasised as the cost of feeding the crowd is emphatically stated in 6.7. A small boy is mentioned as providing some few resources but again the comparison serves to counterpoint the task and its subsequent achievement.

The details of the rest of the event are sparingly but evocatively related. The crowd is divided and placed on the grass. The magnitude of the event is further accentuated with the numbering of the group (6.10). Jesus gives thanks and is portrayed as the sole provider as he distributes the bread and the fish to the crowds (6.11). The abundance of the provision is emphasised when it is related that everyone ate as much as they wished and the detail of the collection of a large quantity of leftovers is recounted. The incident is counted amongst the signs (6.14),[78] and the spontaneous reaction of the crowd is described as Jesus is acclaimed as the prophet come into the world and an attempt is made to make him king. At this point yet another impressive incident in the life of Jesus has been narrated. On any account the feeding of such a great crowd with such scarce resources is an amazing feat and as such is duly acknowledged by the crowd. The further significance of the narrative is elucidated in the dialogue between Jesus and the crowds that follows the next recorded sign (6.16–25).

The theme of Jesus as a life-giver was a prominent part of the discourse that arose from the sign recorded at the beginning of chapter 5. This was intimately connected with his person as Jesus spoke of his relationship with the Father. The theme of life is no less prominent in the dialogue that arises

---

[77] Anderson (1996: 173, 193) highlights this 'testing' motif. He sees the theme of testing continuing on through the dialogue of chapter 6.

[78] The variant σημεῖα is discussed on p.74.

from the feeding sign. The references move from the general discussion of the possibility of life (6.27, 33) through the close association of the concept of life with Jesus himself (6.35, 40, 48, 51) to the final and most intimate association of the believer with Jesus (6.53–58) in his death, as a means to accessing the life that Jesus promises. The profound nature of the life on offer is emphasised by being portrayed in a dialogue that is punctuated with the promise of resurrection at the last day (6.39, 40, 44, 54). The shift from the materiality of the sign to its exposition has resulted in an extended reflection on the life giving ability of Jesus. Other elements indicating the significance of the account have been discussed above.

The dialogue ends in mixed fashion with many of Jesus' disciples no longer able to stay with him (6.60–71). The divisive function of his words and works together produce this crisis. At the same time the twelve stay and demonstrate what faith in Jesus might mean at this moment. Although confusion and even offence have been caused there are no other alternatives but to remain with the one who has the words of life (6.68). The brief discussion anticipates the further crisis and division brought about by the person and ministry of Jesus that will be the subject of the following two chapters as his claims are debated ever more vociferously.

4.3.2.2 Feeding a Multitude (Jn 6.1–15): Reading the Sign

The associations triggered by the feeding account are strong in the Jewish milieu. Echoes of the Elijah/Elisha narratives in the mention of barley and the presence of παιδάριον (cf. 2 Kgs 4.42–44) make this connection. The connections with the Mosaic provision in the wilderness and the figure of 'the prophet' are clear as the crowd acknowledge. These echoes continue to establish the context for reading the signs within the history of God's dealings with Israel. The connections with Moses recall the deliverance of Israel, as does the Passover context. John helps the reader to see that Jesus is characterised by features of previous of God's servants.[79] Certainly the picture of Jesus presiding over a large meal picks up images of plenty as a sign of the messianic era from the prophetic witness (e.g. Isa 25.6; 55.1–2).

In terms of the wider cultural context, there is resonance to be considered with regard to the abundant and generous gift of food. That this food was supplied in a society that suffered from chronic malnutrition is not to be quickly glossed over. Garnsey notes that there were no divisions in the ancient world when it came to an obsession with food. Greek and Roman, rich and poor, alike lived in a world that involved a 'perpetual struggle for survival'.[80] There were regular food shortages and the spectre of endemic

---

[79] Köstenberger 1999: 99.
[80] Garnsey 1999: xi.

undernourishment or chronic malnutrition underlay the periodic shortages.[81] Anxiety over food was manifested in the many religious rituals and celebrations conducted over food as well as the veneration of deities such as the grain goddess Demeter in Greece. Her popularity attests to the immense importance of grains for the population. Bread was her gift (Epictetus, *Diatr.* 2.20.32). Grains formed one of the essential triad of grain, wine and oil and barley was the grain of choice in the more arid climes of Greece and Asia Minor. Cereals were central to the ancient diet, comprising in some estimates 70–75% of the daily dietary intake.[82]

It is therefore understandable that the abundant and effortless supply of food was a common feature of utopian literature, whether in a Graeco-Roman or Jewish apocalyptic context.[83] Texts from the Hebrew Scriptures (Isa 25.6; 55.1) join ancient Greek texts (Homer, *Od.* 9.108–11; Lucian, *Ver. hist.* 2.11–13 [ironically]) and apocalyptic visions (*Sib. Or.* 7.774–746; *2 Bar* 29.5–8) in picturing the abundance of food as a key feature of an anticipated utopian order.

The adequate provision of food was a matter of societal stability and public order where anxiety over the food supply could threaten both.[84] Most food consumed was grown locally and all but the largest cities produced their own basic food supplies; imported grain was expensive and most of that was already spoken for.[85] The fluctuating price of grain was a cause of urban suffering and a potential incentive for urban unrest.[86] Every city had to establish an office or a board to ensure a reasonable supply of grain and oil at reasonable prices. This was more often than not achieved through private citizens exercising benefaction. The wealthy spent their own money to buy grain, sold it at lower prices, and earned the title benefactor (εὐεργέτης). The practice of euergetism was one of the important mechanisms for maintaining the food supply and the supply of free bread was one of the best known institutions of the Hellenistic cities.[87] Such benefactions could take a variety of forms from the offering of a feast to whole population on the first day of

---

[81] Garnsey 1999: 2.

[82] Garnsey (1999: 18), suggests this. He draws on evidence from Galen and records of food given out to soldiers and slaves.

[83] Pervo 1994: 177–182.

[84] Garnsey 1999: 2–3.

[85] Garnsey (1988: 16) concludes that 'the vast majority of communities of the Mediterranean…were endemically vulnerable to food crisis through a combination of human and natural causes'.

[86] See Lewis and Reinhold (1955) §§ 138–42, 336–40.

[87] According to Veyne (1990: 99). Strabo, *Geog.* 14.2.5 on the Rhodians provides an example.

one's assumption of office,[88] through to the creation of a bank offering loans from which the interest earned would purchase corn to be distributed monthly.[89] Such acts of generosity were the standard and accepted response to the food supply problem.[90] The system worked to everyone's advantage with the benefactor looking for both financial profit and public gratitude and the restless populace placated by the provision of life's necessities. Garnsey comments that

> the local elites showed just enough concern for the welfare of the masses to keep the peace. They worked the rudimentary food supply system…and ensured through their periodic acts of euergetism that food crises did not degenerate into famines. In antiquity, food was power.[91]

It was power because it was life.[92] Such benefactions, especially the distribution of grain, was also expected of the emperor.[93] In the *Res Gestae*, Augustus speaks of his maintenance of the grain supply on several occasions as well as his general generosity in welfare matters (*Res gest. divi Aug.* 5.2, 15.1–3, 18.1).[94]

The scenes in John 6 are also reminiscent of reports that describe holidays as occasions for public banquets. The picture that emerges of such banquets is of a crowd eating communally outdoors, perhaps arranged in groups of 50 or 100, recently bathed with oil, garlanded with flowers and preparing to enjoy a banquet.[95] The leftovers testify to the generosity of the host.

These are not strictly speaking parallels to the incident described in John 6. However, they do provide some context for their possible understanding as an act of generous benefaction. While the duties and benefactions of the εὐεργέτης were wider than bread, this action of Jesus would have been seen as the action of a generous and wealthy benefactor, if not a god. Perhaps the

---

[88] See for example *IPriene* 108.42, 57, 68, 253–5. On the first day of his tenure in the position of στεφανηφόρος Moschion of Priene offered the whole population a feast.

[89] This happened in Samos in the second century A.D; see *SIG* 976; Cf. also the multiple benefactions of Kleanax (*NewDocs*. VII §10). The inscription is dated between 2 B.C. and A.D. 2. He organises feasts in honour of Dionysius, fed crowds on his daughter's wedding day, distributed sweet wine to the populace of the city one New Year's day and also provided porridge and milk for all the freemen and slaves of the city.

[90] Garnsey 1999: 33.

[91] Garnsey 1999: 33.

[92] So much so that philosophers were reported to be able to live on bread and water alone (Diogenes Laertius, *Vita* 7.27; 10.11, 131). One philosopher is reputed to have been able to live for three days simply on the smell of fresh bread (Diogenes Laertius, *Vita* 9.43)

[93] Grimm 1996: 38.

[94] Other references to the practice by Roman rulers may be found in Cicero, *Sest.* 48.103; Juvenal, *Sat.* 7.174; 8.118; 10.44–46; 10.81 and Dio Chrysostom, *Or.* 32.31; 66.26.

[95] Pervo 1994: 183. See *SIG* 976.54–8; Athenaeus, *Deipn.* 4.153B; Virgil, *Aen.* 5.101–2; Apollonius Rhodius, *Argon.* 1.450–60 for descriptions of feasts.

more so as he is depicted in the narrative as personally distributing the materials and also supplying fish which would have been seen in some areas of the empire as a generous and luxurious addition.[96] The sign forms a pair with the wedding at Cana where again Jesus has been presented in terms reminiscent of a benefactor. He has now shown himself willing and able to supply an abundance of two of the three staples of the Mediterranean diet, two of the three products that signify the blessing of God (Deut. 7.13; 11.14; Ps. 4.8(LXX); Joel 2.19).

Finally, a subtle polemic against one of the more popular deities of the day is hinted at in that the provision of grain was the special provenance of the goddess Demeter. The Eleusian mysteries, with which the name of Demeter was intimately connected was amongst the more popular of the cults that proliferated.[97] While there remains little clear detail regarding the practices of this cult there are indications that the promise of life was on offer through participation in a manner similar to that in the Dionysiac mysteries.[98] Certainly the name of Demeter was synonymous with grain and its production (Diodorus Siculus, *Hist.* 2.36.2; Epictetus, *Diatr.* 2.20.32).[99] Jesus feeds a massive crowd through the multiplication of loaves and fish. The correspondence is not exact and the polemic not sharp but in view of the pattern of subtle polemic observed thus far perhaps the incident might make this connection as well for many in the audience.

The materiality of the sign creates a wider cultural resonance that reinforces the point made concerning the sign in the narrative of the Gospel. The feeding is a generous benefaction of the very basic material of life. It is little wonder that the crowd is described as attempting to make Jesus their leader.

4.3.3.1 Walking on the Sea (Jn 6.16–21): Writing the Sign

The next sign is narrated as the aftermath of the events of the feeding. Jesus has escaped the crowd by withdrawing again to the mountain mentioned at the beginning of the chapter. The disciples meanwhile have gone to the lake,

---

[96] Fish lends its name to the ὀψάριον, the relish that accompanied the staple bread. Purcell (1995: 136) comments that 'A taste for fish was something only affordable by the seriously well-to-do; the very wealthy went even further than eating them and reared them'. See also Wilkins (1993).

[97] Meyer (1987: 17-18) discusses the popularity and details of the mysteries of Demeter at Eleusis.

[98] Many details of the Mystery religions are obscure. (Meyer 1987) has details and texts for Demeter (pp. 18–45) and Dionysus (pp. 63–108).

[99] Though admittedly this is chiefly corn and not barley; Burkert (1985: 159). However, Demeter's connection to the Eleusian mysteries makes her a well known deity; cf. Tripolitis (2002: 17–21). Demeter's presence is also attested in Ephesus; Knibbe (1978: 32–3), Tilborg (1996: 95).

embarked onto a boat and are making their way across the lake towards Capernaum. The account is narrated from the disciples' point of view. Darkness and distance separate them from Jesus, whose absence is unexplained. The obstacles between Jesus and the disciples mount further when the details of a strong wind and disturbed sea are added in 6.18. A hint of danger for the disciples might be inferred from the details that multiply but this is not emphasised in the account.[100] The chief effect is to set the scene for the impossibility of what is about to happen next.[101] This is even further accentuated with the mention of the distance they had travelled when they saw Jesus coming to them (6.19).

The focus is now firmly on the disciples' view of the scene with all these details and the apparently effortless walking of Jesus (6.19). The disciples' reaction of fear is recorded, drawing the reader further into the scene with this inside view. Jesus is recorded as meeting their reaction by simply identifying himself and exhorting them not to fear. His entry into the boat is also related from their perspective, keeping the focal point of the story on the disciples and their perceptions. The statement that they were then on the other shore, may indicate another miracle but may also suggest that the rest of the journey proceeded without incident.[102] This incident reminds the reader of the importance of the disciples as the audience for the signs. By providing the view of the disciples in each of the incidents, the reader is asked to see things through their eyes, share their wonder and fear and to imagine perhaps their relief (or terror?) at hearing the words 'I am'. The incident may not have been totally private either. The accumulation of detail and inquiry recorded in 6.22–25 suggests that the crowd were at least bordering on a realisation of the event before turning to more mundane matters. The 'innocence' of the crowd's line of inquiry further attests to the event in a manner seen in the sign narratives previously.

The incident provides a powerful and dramatic counterpoint to the high but inadequate response of the crowds to Jesus' previous action. It may be honourable to acclaim Jesus as a king but as this incident demonstrates there is even more to the story as the disciples and the reader are privileged to see. The crowds stand in the vicinity of this realisation but Jesus' penetrating comment in v.26 exposes their curiosity and the true motives for their enquiries.

The exact nature of Jesus' identity and his kingship is revealed in this incident. His words, 'I am', are more than a simple self-identification in that they echo the self-revelation of God. This is further indicated by the

---

[100] Contra Heil (1981: 77-78).

[101] Ridderbos 1994: 217.

[102] Barrett (1978: 281) thinks a second miracle is recorded; Ridderbos (1997: 218) is dismissive, and Brown (1966: 252) leaves the question open.

exhortation not to fear that is often connected with such revelations (e.g. Gen 15.1; 26.24; 46.3; Isa 44.1–5; 43.1). The disciples' response is to take Jesus on board. This may be a way of demonstrating the movement to belief that has become a regular feature of the sign narratives. This movement is more explicit at the end of the chapter as the disciples affirm their belief in Jesus. This incident on the sea provides part of the context that ought to be taken into account when reading the final discussion with the twelve (6.70–71). Their confession of Jesus as the one with the words of eternal life, and his person as the holy one of God,[103] ought to be seen, at least partly, as a function of the revelation of Jesus' identity that they received on the sea.

The revelation of the true identity of Jesus implied in this incident also provides an added depth to the ensuing dialogue with the crowds as Jesus goes on to expound the meaning of the feeding for the crowds. The reader realises that all the references subsequently made by Jesus concerning himself as the bread of life are made by the one who has revealed himself as divine in this action on the sea. The crowd is exhorted to eat the flesh and drink the blood of the divine Son.

Again details of the narrative and its position with respect to ensuing events and dialogue work together to help the reader to grasp the meaning of the incident. The sign takes its place amongst those events that attest to the identity of Jesus and forms part of the cumulative case advanced before the reader.

4.3.3.2 Walking on the Sea (Jn 6.16–21): Reading the Sign

In terms of the mastery of the sea expressed in the incident, the primary background against which the disciples and a Jewish audience would no doubt have viewed the incident would have been the OT. The unique authority of Yahweh over the sea is emphasised in a number of places.[104] This is reinforced by the use of the phrase 'I am' in the midst of the story. While this doubtless operates as a statement of self-identification, the combination of the phrase without context, the situation in which it is uttered and the disciples' reaction of fear all suggest that more is meant and that this is in fact a statement of divine self-identification. The admonition by Jesus, 'do not fear', also accompanies divine manifestations (cf. Gen 15.1; 26.24; Judg 6.23; Isa 43.1).

The divine connotations of the incident would also have been suggested to a wider audience. There is also a tradition in pagan accounts of the gods testifying to similar abilities. There are both Greek and Roman accounts of

---

[103] This reading has strong and widespread support ($\mathfrak{P}^{66}$ $\mathfrak{P}^{75}$ ℵ B C* L W D) while other alternatives are explained as assimilations to various other formulas (1.49, 11.27)

[104] For example Exod 14–15; Job 9.8, 38.16; Pss 29.3; 65.7; Isa 43.1–5; 51.10.

the god Poseidon/Neptune exercising such mastery. Homer describes Poseidon's journey across the sea (*Il.* 13.26–30) and Virgil describes the Roman God Neptune (Virgil, *Aen.* 5.1057–9, 1081–85).[105] There are also several traditions where the god Poseidon grants to several of his sons the gift of travel over the sea unharmed (Apollonius Rhodius, *Argon.* 1. 179–84; Asclepiades in Schol. ad Pind. *Pyth* 4.61; Apollodorus. *Bib.* 1.4.2–3). Seneca preserves a tradition that suggests Heracles crossed over the seas on foot (*Herc. fur.* 322–4).

By the fifth century B.C., power over the sea had begun to be associated with rulers and kings. This was the case for Xerxes and his crossing of the Hellespont, which, while a technical feat, came to be spoken of in mythical terms (Herodotus *Hist.* 7.33–37; Dio Chrysostom *Or.* 3.30–31).[106] Alexander is also referred to in these terms (Menander, *Frg.* 924). There is also an imperial connection with the emperor Caligula reproducing and outdoing Xerxes's feat by assembling a raft of boats to create a roadway so that he could ride from Baiae to Puteoli, a distance of three and half miles (Suetonius, *Cal.* 19.2–3; Josephus, *A.J.* 19.1). 'Walking' on water was associated with both what was humanly impossible and with the arrogance and power of those aspiring to empire (2 Macc 5.21).[107] Dio Chrysostom dreams of walking on water (*Or.* 1.29). The activity is not only represented as humanly impossible but also so wild and unrealistic as to be the stuff of dreams. Artemidorus (*Oneir.* 3.16) even provides interpretations of dreams of walking on water. Such dreams can have a variety of meanings depending on the gender or status of the dreamer, but if a ruler dreams of walking on water it signifies gain and great fame because the sea represents a crowd because of its instability. This reinforces the link between walking on water and rule.[108]

The incident has resonance in the wider cultural context. This is not an argument for dependence in the sense that the Gospel narrative was created based on older Graeco-Roman stories. The parallels are far too incomplete for this. However, there is enough evidence to show the potential divine connotations of the incident in the wider cultural context.[109] It is a truly extraordinary feat that demonstrates mastery over the sea in a way that can only be attributed to the divine operating in some sense. The context in which the story is told precludes Jesus being presented as a divine man or hero of ancient times however. His revelation of himself to his disciples with the

---

[105] There is an extensive discussion of this point in A. Y. Collins (1994: 214–23). Cf. also Cotter (1999: 131–163).

[106] Dio Chrysostom rejects the point of view but the fact that he has to reject it is an indication of a view worthy of attention.

[107] A.Y. Collins 1994: 220.

[108] Cf. A.Y. Collins (1994: 223).

[109] Cotter 1991: 321.

words, 'I am' suggests that this is a divine epiphany to be read and understood in the Jewish context of the Gospel generally.

Again an incident is recounted that draws its ultimate significance from the Jewish religious context but is told in such a way that connections and resonance are suggested that enable its significance to be accessed by a variety of readers. The ease with which Jesus is presented as performing this again provides a contrast to all other claims to divinity and power based on similar performances. It certainly puts to shame and ridicule the attempts of various human emperors and leaders who might assert their power through ostentatious attempts to walk on water.

The phrase 'I am' that Jesus speaks to the disciples may well be a simple statement of self-identification but it too has potential wider resonance as a divine title. Perhaps in this phrase a further implied contrast is made with another rival. In a series of well-known inscriptions lauding the Egyptian goddess, Isis, a series of 'I am' sayings are recorded.[110] The connection is only tentatively suggested but may be one more example of a detail in the Gospel contributing to the portrayal of the supremacy of Jesus in a world full of gods.

4.3.4.1 Healing a Man Born Blind (Jn 9.1–41): Writing the Sign

While the actual account of the action here in chapter 9 takes only a few verses, the whole narrative includes an extended discourse that is an integral part of the presentation. This narrative is marked by the prolonged absence of Jesus from the scene, though there is a sense in which he remains as the focal point of the conversation and action. It is through the dialogue between the Pharisees and the healed man and other witnesses that the significance of the action is conveyed.

The narrative begins with the encounter between Jesus and his disciples and a man blind from birth. Apparently, the disciples and Jesus have knowledge of the duration of his blindness in that the question is asked concerning the cause of this calamity. Jesus' response that he is blind in order that the works of God might be manifest in him provides an alternative perspective on the connection between sin and illness suggested in chapter 5. From the reader's point of view, the use of ἔργα and its close connection

---

[110] See C.R. Koester (1995: 94). The inscriptions appear in translation in F. C. Grant (1953: 128–33). They date from the early second century. Two more recently discovered aretalogies of Isis, dated in the first or second century appear in *NewDocs* I § 2. The plethora of 'I am' statements is remarked upon (p. 20). Isis is also claimed to be able to heal eye diseases (l. 6) and called a saviour (l. 11). There is also some evidence connecting Isis with Ephesus until the demise of Antony in 31 B.C and then again in the reign of Antoninus Pius (A.D. 137–61); Walters (1995: 286–93). For a more general survey of the presence and appeal of the Egyptian cults of Isis and Sarapis see Tinh (1982).

established with σημεῖον earlier in the narrative, set the scene for another action by Jesus. When the healing is identified as a σημεῖον (9.16), the close relationship between the two word groups is further confirmed. The expectations of the reader are raised further when Jesus speaks of doing the works of the one who sent him 'while it is still day' (9.4). The imagery of night and day contributes further to the imagery of light and darkness that is contrasted and this reaches its fullest expression in the reiteration of Jesus' claim to be the light of the world (9.5; cf. 8.12). These statements lay the ground for the appropriation of the symbolic meaning of the action by the reader.

The event of the healing action itself is described as Jesus spits, makes some mud and smears it on the man's eyes and then commands him to go and wash in the Pool of Siloam (9.6–7). Siloam is the only named place in the account and is a surprise. The reader might have expected Jesus to send the man to Bethesda because of the earlier incident. The pool at Siloam has no known healing properties and is in fact quite a distance and a difficult walk for the man to undertake.[111] The point concerning the name of the pool is laboured for the audience so that they understand that the healing of the man's blindness is connected with him going to the pool called Sent. This obviously ties in with the fact that by now in the Gospel Jesus is known, amongst other titles, as the one who has been sent by the Father. The man must go to the sent 'one' for washing and healing.[112]

Upon washing in the pool, the man sees. The miracle is confirmed through the discussion of his neighbours and those who knew that he was a beggar (9.8). The momentary confusion over his identity, probably stressing the unbelievable nature of what has happened, is clarified with the man's own confession (9.9). The man speaks for the first time in the incident. His first words echo the 'I am' confession of Jesus and, in a sense, align him with Jesus, although this is clearly a statement of self-identification.[113] The division amongst his friends concerning his identity, which echoes the similar divisions that have been reported concerning Jesus, further reinforces his alignment with Jesus. While Jesus has disappeared from the scene, these echoes help the reader to see that the trial of Jesus is continuing in the questioning of this man. When asked how his eyes were opened he recounts precisely the details of his healing (9.11). The reader observes that the man can name Jesus and this has the effect of suggesting that the previous

---

[111] This of course would only be noticed by readers familiar with the topography of Jerusalem. See Just (1997: 253) for details.

[112] Grigsby (1985) develops the understanding of this incident as a prefiguring of the cross.

[113] This shows the use of the phrase as a statement of self-identification and so urges caution in interpreting the other absolute ἐγώ εἰμι statements on Jesus' lips.

exchanges between Jesus and the disciples were conducted in his earshot, helping the reader to be aligned a little more closely with his plight and its solution.

The man is then led to the Pharisees (9.13). Initially the reader might assume that this is for some sort of confirmation of the healing, but the next verse introduces information that changes the complexion of the discussion. The narrator informs the reader that this was a Sabbath (9.14). In a move similar to that made in John 5, this information has been withheld until a strategic moment. Again, a straightforward healing story becomes the catalyst for a more extended discussion of the claims of Jesus. This appears to be another 'testing' sign, deliberately timed to provoke controversy.[114]

The sense of Jesus being on trial in the situation of the man is maintained as the Pharisees begin their questioning. At the same time, the audience is aligned more closely with the man as he comes under attack and answers in the first person (v. 15). The issue of the Sabbath is an important one for the incident in view of the connections established with chapter 5 and the charge laid against Jesus. Verse 16 is a key verse as the Pharisees divide amongst themselves and pose the question raised by Jesus' apparently contradictory actions.[115] The action is plainly recognised as a sign and a connection is again made in the narrative between the works of God and σημεῖον. The blind man's own assessment confirms that he reads what has happened to him in sign terms when he acknowledges that Jesus is a prophet.

The interrogation of the man's parents pursues the question as to whether the man was actually blind (9.18–22). They confirm this fact. The man is asked for a second time and this time his interrogators use the phrase 'Give glory to God' (9.24). The man does so by not fearing his interlocutors and simply recalling the events that have happened to him. As he relates the sign, God is given the glory as Jesus' significant actions are announced (9.25). The connection between signs and glory is implicitly reinforced.

The objection that Jesus is a sinner is met by the testimony of the previously blind man (9.31–33). He begins from the known fact that God does not listen to sinners, which is common ground between himself and the Pharisees, through the extraordinary nature of the miracle, to the conclusion that Jesus is from God (παρὰ θεοῦ, echoing Jn. 1.1; cf. 6.46; 8.40). This chain of reasoning could be aimed at the reader seeking to persuade or provide the reader with a chain of reasoning to use himself. The final riposte of the Pharisees, that the man was 'born in sin' (9.34) is ironic in that it echoes the position explicitly rejected by Jesus at the beginning of the account. The man was said to be blind by Jesus for the sake of the revelation

---

[114] This is an extension of Anderson's observations concerning Jn 6.6; see Anderson (1996: 173, 193).

[115] See pp. 80–1 for a discussion of this verse.

of the glory of God; the Pharisees have rejected this display of the glory of God, reverted to a false premise and demonstrated their absolute miscomprehension of the whole incident.

The man's own movement from blindness to sight is completed with his final acknowledgement of who Jesus is in word and action (9.37). Jesus' reference to the man seeing reflects the healing and invites the deeper level of perception to which the man responds with confession and worship.

The reader is increasingly aligned with the blind man throughout the narrative. The horror of his condition would create immediate connection but then the pettifogging reaction of the Pharisees to his healing and his own courage under questioning create even greater empathy, encouraging the reader to join him in his own movement of understanding of the person of Jesus.[116]

Jesus then speaks reflecting upon the meaning of the event. The whole incident has become a parable of Jesus' own ministry in the division that it has caused amongst those who observe him. A remarkable physical healing is expounded for its symbolic meaning. He has made the blind to literally see, while those who thought they could see have been revealed as blind. The chilling connection between sin and the Pharisees 'seeing' (9.41) recalls the previous words spoken by Jesus concerning those who will die in their sins (8.21). The giving of sight has become conceptually linked to the remission of sins and to life. To 'see' Jesus is to be forgiven and to have life. The irony of the statement is that in order to 'see' one must apparently first confess one's blindness (10.41).

4.3.4.2 Healing a Man Born Blind (Jn 9.1–41): Reading the Sign

The outstanding feature of this account is the blindness of the man who is healed by Jesus. Blindness and eye conditions generally appear to have been a feature of the ancient world. The vocabulary for various eye conditions is quite extensive but the Greek τυφλός is generally reserved for total loss of vision.[117] The normal expectation of conditions described with this term is that blindness is a permanent and irreversible condition.

There are many blind people referred to in Graeco-Roman literature from Homer onwards.[118] Infants born without eyes (Livy, *Ad Urb. Con.* 34.45.7) or deformed (Pliny, *Nat.* 7.12.51; 11.55.149) were considered monstrous or portentous (Aelian, *Nat. an.* 4.34; 10.45; Cicero, *Fin.* 4.64; Pliny *Nat.* 8.54.126, 8.62.151) and often babies with deformities were killed (Pliny *Nat.* 11.113.272; Livy, *Ad Urb. Con.* 34.45.7).[119] This practice suggests that a

---

[116] Lee 1994: 185; cf. Resseguie (1982: 303).
[117] Just 1997: 21.
[118] See Esser (1961: 121–81) for a comprehensive account.
[119] See Garland (1995: 13–18; 59–72).

person blind from birth would be a relatively rare occurrence, although Pausanias does record an encounter with a man blind from birth (*Descr.* 4.10.6). There is also some philosophical discussion on whether a man blind from birth could see colour (Sextus Empiricus, *Pyr.* 3.264; *Math.* 1.34; 11.238). There are a number of cases of blind people in the Hebrew Scriptures but there are no cases of congenital blindness recorded. Blindness because of old age appears to be the most common occurrence.

The lot of the blind was not a happy one. It was often seen as a divine punishment or an unmerited affliction. Blindness is listed as one of the curses for covenant breach in the Hebrew Scriptures (Lev 26.26; Deut 28.28–9; 28.65; Zeph 1.17; Zech 12.4; Job 11.20; 17.5; 21.17; Ps 69.23; Prov 13.9; 20.20; 24.19–20; 30.17) though this appears to be metaphorical on many occasions (except Lev 26.16; Deut 28.28–9; Prov 30.17). Occasionally blindness is seen in a positive light for the special perception it might bring and there are a number of examples of blind people leading productive and socially successful lives. Cicero (*Tusc. Disp.* 38–39) produces a list of the blind who have thrived but the necessity of producing such a list probably testifies to the rarity of the occurrence. The presence of special laws concerning the treatment of the blind (e.g. Lev 19.14; Deut 27.18) testifies to the weakness, generally, of their situation. The blind were usually considered to be unfortunate, helpless and worthless (Philo, *Ebr.* 155–6; *Fug.* 123; *Mos.* 1.123–26). They could go nowhere without a guide (Sophocles, *Ant.* 989; Apuleius, *Metam.* 8.12) and required the protection of others (Job 29.15). The blind and lame were almost proverbially related to ineffectual weakness and dependency (2 Sam 5.6; Jer 31.8). They are likely to be beggars (Diogenes Laertius, *Vita* 6.56), as good as corpses (Philo, *Spec.* 4.202), driven to despair and suicide (Philo, *Sobr.* 4; *Virt.* 11.1).[120]

In some texts, the blind are even more closely associated with the dead. Isa 59.9–10 and Lam 3.1–2, 6 hint in this direction. Tobit regards his blindness as a living death (Tob. 5.10). According to the chorus in Oedipus 'thou wert better dead than living blind' (Sophocles, *Oed. tyr.* 1367; cf. also Seneca, *Oed.* 949; *Phoen.* 179). Instead of seeing the light, the blind dwelt in perpetual darkness, the gloom of the underworld (Apuleius, *Metam.* 8.12).[121] A particularly striking saying is found in the later Rabbinic writing *Gen. Rab.* 71.6 where four groups are considered to be as good as dead—lepers, the blind, the childless and the impoverished.

---

[120] Philo does have some positive comments as well. He suggests that fevers and certain other diseases are worse than blindness (*Praem.* 143) and that people who lose their sight will develop other senses more keenly (*Cher.* 58). For Philo the blindness of paganism or polytheism is also worse than physical blindness (*Decal.* 67–8).

[121] Bolt 1997: 201.

In terms of the medical literature, there are numerous attestations to eye salves, magical cures and other materials associated with eye conditions. Spittle is also prominent in accounts of the healing of eye diseases (Pliny, *Nat.* 28.7.36–39; 28.22.76; Columella, *Rust.* 6.33.1; see also Pliny *Nat.* 7.2.13). However, while there is a great deal of attention given to eye diseases and their treatment nowhere is the claim made to be able to heal total blindness.[122] A person went to the gods for this kind of miracle. Of the seventy inscriptions recorded at Epidaurus, ten relate to eye problems and their cure.[123] Other references to the healing of eye problems tend to be related to the gods (Plutarch, *Mor.* 373e; Isis is reported to heal the blind in Horsley, *NewDocs* I § 2, 1. 6).

Occasionally an emperor might give some assistance, as Vespasian does at the Temple of Serapis in Alexandria (Suetonius, *Vesp.*7; Tacitus, *Hist 4.81*). Vespasian is told that the eye condition is curable and even if it did not work the failure would look worse for the man than for the emperor. Vespasian moistens the man's eyes with spittle and when the man is healed, Vespasian is lauded. This is the second miracle he performed there at a time when such things were very useful to his attempts to consolidate power. The Emperor Hadrian is also reputed to have healed a blind man (Aelius Spartianus, *Script. Hist. August.* 9.32) though the account is questioned in a work that is itself prone to exaggeration. The giving of sight to the congenitally blind is almost without precedent.[124] Pausanias does record an incident where a man born blind receives his sight after suffering a sharp pain in the head (*Descr.* 4.12.10). This incident occurs without warning and is recorded as an omen. Certainly it is presented as a work of the gods and there is no human action or intervention recorded. The ability to heal is within the power of the gods, whether they are the traditional healing gods or the new pretenders.

As far as reversing blindness is concerned, the expectation in the Hebrew Scriptures is that Yahweh can open the eyes of the blind as well as cause blindness (Exod 4.11). Occasionally the imagery of light and darkness is used in connection with expectations concerning the advent of the Messiah. In Isa 42.6–7, for example, the servant of the Lord will be a light to the Gentiles and open eyes that are blind. While the reference to opening the eyes of the blind is likely to be primarily metaphorical (in line with numerous examples of metaphorical blindness in the Hebrew Scriptures: Deut 28.65; Zeph 1.17; Zech 12.4; Job 11.20; 17.5; 21.17; Ps 69.23; Prov 13.9; 20.20; 24.19–20), the literal opening of the eyes of a blind person could easily be seen to fulfil the

---

[122] Just 1997: 134.

[123] The references are from LiDonnici (1995: A4, A9, A11, A18, A20, B22, B32, B40 [This involved a spear wound that affected the person's eyesight], C55 [A badly damaged inscription makes this uncertain], C65, D690).

[124] Just 1997: 153.

metaphorical sense of the statement in Isa 42. A sign of the restoration of Israel in the second exodus as described in Isaiah will be the opening of the eyes of the blind (Isa. 29.18; 35.5). The healing of the blind man, in John 9, is to be seen in this context together with the other signs. The prerogative of opening the eyes of the blind is a divine one (Isa 35.5; 29.18; 42.7; Ps 146.8; cf. Ep Jer 37 where it is asserted that idols cannot restore sight, this being the prerogative of Yahweh alone). The action of Jesus would lead to speculation in those terms, especially with the emphatic statements contained in the narrative concerning the unprecedented nature of the action. Within the Jewish context, this action has significant connotations.

A final connection between the narrative and the wider discussion concerning blindness might be discerned with respect to the 'metaphorical' use of blindness in the discussion at the end of the account between Jesus and the Pharisees. This has resonance with the old story of Oedipus who accuses Teiresias of being blind but who is in fact shown to be blind himself (Sophocles, *Oed. tyr.* 371, 412) and in the comments of philosophers (Epictetus, *Diatr.* 1.20.12).

Another incident has been well chosen and exploited. The incident obviously fits well into the symbolic scheme of the Fourth Gospel with the obvious connections established with light, darkness, life, and judgement. However, the incident itself is an example of an action that falls within the remit of the gods and has divine connotations for the wide spectrum of the early audience of the Gospel.

This is another piece of evidence declaring Jesus to be the divine Messiah. It builds on, and adds to, the previous sign accounts. Connections are established with the expectations connected with the advent of the messianic king foreshadowed in the Hebrew Scriptures. At the same time, the unprecedented nature of this action and its potential reading as a rescue from death and giving of life creates a further comparison and contrast with other would–be life givers of the ancient world.

4.4 Summary

In chapters 5–10 the language of σημεῖον remains prominent. The signs continue to be referred to in terms of both quantity and quality. They continue to attest to the identity of Jesus as the divine Son sent from the Father. The importance of seeing the signs correctly has been emphasised and Jesus himself has been presented as the substance of at least one of the signs. The introduction of lengthy discourses and several 'I am' sayings, picking up features of the sign narratives, has added depth to their meaning and added symbolic depth to their attesting function. These features have supplied the interpretative element that would be most likely looked for by the ancient observer of a σημεῖον. The accent has remained on the positive relationship intended between signs and faith. The important thing appears to be to read the signs correctly and respond to the fullness of the person offered in them. A more aggressive posture has been noted in the performance of many of the signs in this section. They are portrayed as deliberately provoking discussion concerning the claims of Jesus, testing and dividing his audience.

The possibility that Jesus is the divine Messiah of Israel is presented to the reader through the signs. This has been facilitated through the embedding of the signs in a forensic narrative where the claims of Jesus have been examined in depth and with great heat. The forensic examination has been embedded within the framework of the signs themselves such that the two interpenetrate. The forensic connotations of the sign language mentioned earlier would help the audience to see that, through the signs, a cumulative case is being made with respect to the Gospel's claims concerning Jesus. A number of different facets of Jesus' person and work have been addressed through the signs as well as a gradual escalation in the magnitude of the sign performed. The cumulative effect leads to a rounded appreciation of the glory said to be presented in the signs under the paradigm presented in the ἀρχή sign of 2.1–11. The embedding in the forensic motif also enables a number of objections against the claims made for Jesus to be canvassed.

Jesus has been presented as a generous provider of the staples of life in the feeding miracles. He has shown that his word alone is powerful and effective and can save a child from the brink of death. He has shown himself to be a powerful healer at a pool where those who live a life full of the death of disease gather. He has generously fed a crowd with a few loaves and fish. He has given his own disciples a glimpse of his power in being able to walk across the sea. And finally he has done the unprecedented – he has healed a man born blind. Many of these actions have been shown to have resonance with the wider Graeco-Roman culture as well as antecedents in the Hebrew Scriptures. The primary background for assessment of these claims will be the Hebrew Scriptures and the fullest appreciation of Jesus' person and work will be gained from a reading against that background (Jn 4.22). The language of σημεῖον is essential to the point being made at the general level of a prophet, the intermediate level of 'the prophet', the advanced level of the Messiah and the highest level of divine claim.

However, an entry point is provided in the signs, individually and cumulatively, for a wide range of readers to appreciate the significance of Jesus' identity as the divine Messiah of Israel. This is chiefly cashed out in terms of life. At the same time rival life-givers from the contemporary culture are compared and found wanting through the activity of Jesus. This aspect continues to be supported by the general context of statements that point to the uniqueness of Christ. These include the 'I am' statements (6.20, 35; 8.12, 58; 9.5; 10.11), which have been noted as also having a resonance with some of the statements attributed to Isis. Jesus' statement concerning himself as the good shepherd (10.14) also resonates in a culture where leaders were historically known as shepherds.[125] Numerous incidental remarks pointing to Jesus' uniqueness continue to create a web of references that point to his unique relationship to the Father and the necessity of attachment to him exclusively as the means to attain life (5.26; 6.40, 51, 68; 7.37; 8.31–2, 36). The signs and their particular resonance are located within this general presentation and ground it in comparisons with specific figures.

The signs continue to attest the identity of Jesus as the divine messiah of Israel, manifest the life that he brings and subtly provide a point of contrast with alternative life givers. However, Jesus is not just presented as one option amongst others. The presentation of his claims in the context of Jewish monotheism immediately makes his claim an exclusive one and this is reinforced by the general web of language that laces the Gospel testifying to the uniqueness of his identity and mission. The signs remain an integral component of the rhetorical thrust of the Gospel enabling a varied audience to access, and grow in depth of understanding of, the truth concerning Jesus. The final actions of Jesus' public career, as recorded by John, await their analysis.

---

[125] The primary background for this statement is the presentation of the false shepherds (Ezek 34.1–10) of Israel but nonetheless the possibility of secondary resonance is there; cf. Plato, *Rep.* 345 c-e; Homer, *Il.* 2.243, 254; Epictetus, *Diatr.* 3.22.35.

Chapter 5

Signs of Life: σημεῖον in John 11–12

5.1 Overview of Chapters 11–12

Chapters 11 and 12 bring to a climax the public ministry of Jesus and describe
the events that are the catalyst for the final journey to the cross. The section
therefore looks both backwards and forwards. The raising of Lazarus from the
dead, as well as being the climax in the series of signs performed by Jesus,
precipitates the plot of the Jews to kill Jesus (11.45–53) and foreshadows
Jesus' own death and resurrection. Chapter 12 brings the narrative of the
Gospel thus far to a climax. Jesus is anointed for his burial (12.7) before
entering Jerusalem, acclaimed as a King (12.12–16). The request of some
Greeks to see him indicates to Jesus that the hour of glory has arrived and this
is interpreted as a fruitful death for many (12.23–24, 32), and the judgement
of this world and its ruler (12.30–32). John is setting out a number of
perspectives to help the reader understand the significance of Jesus' coming
death, which is approaching as the climax of the narrative.

The 'trial' conducted through the previous chapters has ebbed and flowed
with the various parties taking the place of both accuser and accused. In this
section, the religious leaders pass a sentence of death (11.53), but Jesus has
the last word as the ultimate judge (12.44–50). It is the response to his word
that renders the positive verdict of life or its negative counterpart.[1] The final
section of chapter 12 reflects on the response to Jesus in both sign (12.37–43)
and word (12.44–50).

5.2 The Occurrences of σημεῖον

5.2.1 The Occurrences of σημεῖον: Text to Reader

There are only three occurrences of σημεῖον in this section. The first (11.47)
attests to the volume of signs that Jesus is acknowledged to have performed
and implies that the raising of Lazarus is a σημεῖον. This statement occurs in
the context of some rather more oblique references to the acts of Jesus that
will also be considered (11.45–46). The second occurrence (12.18) clearly

---

[1] Cf. Lincoln (2000: 110).

labels the raising of Lazarus as a sign, and the third (12.37) introduces an important discussion concerning the apparent failure of Jesus' signs and his mission in the face of the overwhelming response of unbelief. There is also an instance of the cognate verb σημαίνω in chapter 12 to be considered (12.33). There are no references to ἔργον in the section.

5.2.1.1 Seeing the Signs (Jn 11.45–47)

The references in this section continue many of the already-established trajectories. The first more oblique references occur in 11.45–46. Immediately following the raising of Lazarus, it is stated that many of the Jews, who saw what Jesus did, believed in him. The combination of 'many', 'seeing the things that he did',[2] and 'believing' is enough to suggest that the raising of Lazarus is to be seen as one more of the Johannine signs (cf. the echoes of the various elements in previous statements, 2.23; 4.45; 6.2, 14; 7.31). The general pattern of narratorial comments referring to the deeds of Jesus being in the plural is maintained in these remarks. The volume of Jesus' signs is kept before the reader.

The familiar division caused by Jesus' signs is also recorded in these verses. The belief of many is recorded but the response of others is to report to the Pharisees (v. 46). In view of the rising opposition to Jesus from the Pharisees, this can only be ominous. The acknowledgement by the Pharisees that Jesus is doing many σημεῖα (11.47) confirms the labelling of the raising of Lazarus as a σημεῖον, while the plural accords with the other summary statements in the Gospel.

This statement graphically illustrates the success and failure of the signs. On the one hand, it is clear that the magnitude and quantity of signs alluded to throughout the narrative mean that not even hostile observers can deny that they have been performed (11.47). On the other hand, there is no believing response. The reading of the signs is again the issue. The Jewish leaders see the signs as indicating a prophetic figure, perhaps similar to the 'sign

---

[2] When it comes to the phrase ἃ ἐποίησεν (11.45) there is divided manuscript evidence as to whether the relative pronoun ought to be plural or singular (ὅ—$\mathfrak{P}^{66*}$ A^c B C* D f^1 e; ἃ—$\mathfrak{P}^{6,\,45}$ ℵ A* L W Θ Ψ f^{13}; ὅσα—$\mathfrak{P}^{66c}$). The plural is unexpected in view of the immediate context, suggesting that it would be the slightly more difficult reading. It is by no means a clear decision. The accommodation could be to the better attested plural in v. 46 as well as the plurals present in other similar summaries. However, the immediate context of the raising of Lazarus and the corrections in A and C^2, that add in the word σημεῖον, suggest that the plural was most likely original. Again, the cumulative nature of the case made by the signs is subtly reinforced. The correction to ὅσα in $\mathfrak{P}^{66c}$ is also interesting in view of the stress on quality or quantity that is implied. Similar confusion exists amongst the manuscripts for v. 46. The weight of external evidence favours the plural but the singular is attested (C D M) and ὅσα is also present (A K f^{13}).

prophets' mentioned by Josephus. Their view concerning Jesus' prophetic ministry has already been made clear in chapters 7–8 where the discussion revolved around Jesus 'leading the people astray' (7.12, 47). In their eyes, he is a false prophet on the basis of his supposed Sabbath violation. The perspective of Jesus' opponents is restricted to the potential consequences of the following that Jesus is gathering with respect to the political future of the nation (11.48). The signs indicate to them that Jesus is a threat to the stability of the relationship with the Romans because of the following he is attracting. As Caiaphas sees it, ridding themselves of this troublemaker will only bring good to the nation (11.49–50). The signs are now instrumental to the narrative line that leads to the death of Jesus.[3] The frame of reference in which the signs are read is vital for their correct understanding. Caiaphas and the gathered council see the signs only from a political perspective and are keen to preserve their relationship with the Romans (cf. 5.44). The reader is urged to see the signs from the perspective of the plan of God revealed in the Hebrew Scriptures (5.46).

5.2.1.2 Signs and the Hour (Jn 12.18)

The connections with the Lazarus incident continue in chapter 12 as a large crowd come to Bethany to see both Jesus and Lazarus. The signs are still attracting a following (12.9). The connection between signs and belief is reinforced as the reader is informed of the plot to kill Lazarus, a plot that is formed because of the response to Jesus (12.11). The crowds that greet Jesus' arrival in Jerusalem are also attributed to the impression caused by the signs of Jesus, specifically his raising of Lazarus from the dead (12.17–18). Here the raising of Lazarus is explicitly labelled as a σημεῖον. The crowd is a mix of those who have seen the sign and those who have heard the testimony to the sign. While there will be some doubt cast on their response at a later point, at this moment it appears that those who have heard the testimony to the sign follow as well. The response of the crowd is dramatic enough for the Pharisees to comment that the whole world has gone after Jesus (12.19).[4]

That the signs attract, in a literal sense, the whole world is confirmed in the next verse when reference is made to the Greeks who have come to see Jesus. No doubt godfearers or proselytes, they are nonetheless described as Greeks and are representative of the gentile world.[5] Their request to see Jesus precipitates his announcement of the hour that has been anticipated through

---

[3] Bittner (1987: 171–3, 286) correctly notes that these verses specifically relate the plot to kill Jesus to the performance of his signs.

[4] Lincoln (2000: 105) notes that the issue is still discussed in terms of the tests for a false prophet with the echo of Deut. 13.1–11 in the statement by the Pharisees.

[5] Moloney 1996: 186–7. For a detailed discussion of their identity, see Kossen (1970).

the Gospel (12.23; cf. 2.4; 7.30; 8.20). While the connection with the signs is not explicit, the juxtaposition is striking. The signs are truly seen by 'all'.

The request of the Greeks is significant to Jesus in that it signals the arrival of the anticipated ὥρα. This moment has been in prospect since 2.4 and a sense of rising anticipation concerning its advent has been created in the narrative (cf. 4.21; 5.25, 28; 7.30; 8.20[6]). The hour that has been anticipated is then strongly linked to the concept of glory. In response to his request that the Father glorify his name, Jesus is told that the Father has glorified it and will glorify it (12.28). The aorist ἐδόξασα looks back over the ministry of Jesus and picks up the references to glory that occur at 2.11 and then at the beginning of chapter 11. The statement reminds the reader that the Father has been glorifying himself in the ministry of Jesus, especially in the signs he has performed. The signs are the work of the Father through the Son and the glory revealed is, as foreshadowed in the prologue, the glory of the μονογενοῦς παρὰ πατρός (1.14). The future δοξάσω looks forward to the next major event looming on the horizon, which Jesus will describe as his lifting up. This significant event is described as the judgement of the ruler of the world (12.31) and an event that draws 'all people' to him (12.32). The supremacy of Jesus is once more subtly reinforced by both of these statements. The judgement over the ruler of the world seems to imply a victory over cosmic forces of evil.[7] The ruler of the world (cf 14.30; 16.11) appears to be identified with the devil (13.1) or Satan (13.27), although this is nowhere explicitly stated. In any case, the comprehensive nature of the statement reinforces Jesus' supremacy.

John explains Jesus' statement concerning his lifting up as signifying (σημαίνω) the kind of death he was about to die (12.33). This is the first of three uses of this verb in the Gospel (cf. 18.32; 21.19). In each cases the word appears in an aside. The use of a verb cognate with σημεῖον is significant, especially from a writer who chooses his words carefully. In 12.33 and 18.32 a subtle connection is established between the death of Jesus on the cross and the language of σημεῖον. The death of Jesus, described as being lifted up, is also linked to the idea of glory in the advent of the Gospel's fateful hour (12.23). The connections established between the hour, glory, the lifting up of Jesus, the cross, and language cognate with σημεῖον lead the reader to view the death of Jesus as a σημεῖον.

There is a further link to be explored with the statement in chapter 3.14–5, which illustrated the lifting up of the Son of Man by the lifting of the bronze serpent in the Num 21 account. The explicit connection between 3.14 and 12.32–3 is established through the use of the verb ὑψόω. However a more

---

[6] For an illuminating discussion of the various nuances of the use of ὥρα in the Gospel see Brown (1966: 517-8).

[7] Cf. Kovacs (1995).

implicit connection with the language of σημεῖον is also noted, when it is recalled that the serpent was lifted up on a σημεῖον in the wilderness (Num 21.8–9). These further suggest that the death of Jesus is being subtly presented as a σημεῖον.[8]

In the light of the background of the Hebrew Scriptures, a further messianic connection may be discerned. It has already been suggested, following Bittner, that the connection between the Messiah and the performing of signs draws on material in Isaiah.[9] This connection may be further exploited. In Isaiah 11.10–12 it is promised that the Lord will lift up a σημεῖον before the nations in order to assemble the dispersed people of Israel.[10] This is stated in the context of a passage that traces the movement from the overthrow of the Assyrian kingdom to the setting up of the messianic kingdom. The reference is to a Davidic figure (11.1) and also refers to the idealised figure met in Isaiah 9. The endowment of this messianic figure with the Spirit will establish his fitness to rule (Isa 11.2–4). The effect of his rule will be a universal peace that moves beyond the borders of Israel to the entire earth as the knowledge of the true God fills the earth (Isa 11.6–9).

In Isa 11.10-16, a day is anticipated when this figure will reign over the nations. All of this will happen as the 'root of Jesse', the messianic figure referred to throughout the chapter, is raised as a σημεῖον before the nations (Isa 11.12) and gathers the dispersed people of God. According to Isaiah the nations will enquire of the one who is raised to rule over them, and will find light and salvation (Isa 42.6–7; 49.6–7). The one who is raised to rule is also a judge according to the Isa 11.3–4. The motifs of raising, drawing the nations, and judgement are all present in John 12, while the Isaianic 'day' perhaps finds its reflex in the Johannine ὥρα.[11] It seems, then, that the death of Jesus on the cross, as the Messiah of Israel, is the place where the σημεῖον promised in Isaiah 11 is lifted before the nations. This sign will draw all people, the nations and the people of Israel. It is the place where life may be found for the people of God and the place where judgement will occur for the

---

[8] Cf. also Charlier (1959: 445–7) and Glasson (1963: 38–39) who tentatively explore these connections. Brown (1966: 468) and Schnackenburg (1968: 520) resist the idea of describing the events of the cross as a σημεῖον while Frey (1994b: 191–4) denies the connection with 3.14 (although he appears to tentatively endorse it in 1994a: 259).

[9] See p. 84.

[10] The word translated σημεῖον in the Septuagint is not the usual אוֹת but rather נֵס. However, there appears to be little difference between the two in the context of this particular usage (Cf. Blenkinsopp, 2000a: 267). The LXX reading tracks a different path to the MT with respect to the translation of Isaiah 11.10. The LXX reads καὶ ὁ ἀνιστάμενος ἄρχειν ἐθνῶν as a translation of the MT שֹׁרֶשׁ יִשַׁי אֲשֶׁר עֹמֵד לְנֵס עַמִּים. This appears to interpret the MT in a way that preserves the priority of Israel over the Gentiles in the future rule of God. However the general pattern is clear and 11.12 is explicit concerning σημεῖον.

[11] Cf. Bittner (1987: 245–258).

world.[12] If these connections are accurately perceived then there is further
evidence of a major debt owed to the thought of Isaiah for the structure as
well as detail of the presentation of Jesus in the Fourth Gospel. This is seen
again as John reflects upon the apparent failure of the signs with the help of
Isaiah in the next reference to σημεῖον.

5.2.1.3 The Failure of the Signs? (Jn 12.37)

The final mention of the term σημεῖον in the first 'half' of the Gospel occurs
at 12.37. This is an important occurrence as John reflects on the apparent
failure of the signs to produce belief and seeks to justify this failure
theologically. The verses are reminiscent of Moses's words to Israel in Deut
29.2–4.[13] There, Israel is described as not believing, despite the evidence of
the signs and wonders of God. They do not believe because the Lord had not
yet given them eyes to see, ears to hear and hearts to believe. In the light of
this echo the recapitulation of the interaction between the λόγος and οἱ ἴδιοι
in the history of Israel (1.1–11), in the story of Jesus and the Jews, is
complete. The supreme revelation of God, in his Son, is rejected. At the same
time, the sovereignty of God, asserted in Deut 29.2–4, will also be echoed in
the present circumstances described in the Gospel.

The extended editorial comment in 12.37–43 appears at a key moment in
the course of the Gospel narrative. This is a 'summary' moment as the public
ministry of Jesus appears to conclude and he prepares to turn to his own
disciples (13.1). As the public ministry is evaluated, it is the presence and
apparent failure of the signs that is the focus of attention. Once more a
qualifier is attached to the mention of σημεῖα, though there is an ambiguity
in the use of τοσαῦτα that means that it could be emphasising either the
quantity or quality of the σημεῖα performed.[14] The quality and quantity of
signs performed by Jesus renders the unbelieving response even more
incredible in John's eyes and necessitates an explanation.

The undifferentiated nature of the audience in view (αὐτῶν) suggests that
this blanket statement is intended as a survey of the whole ministry, even
though the lack of response in terms of belief seems to be particularly acute

---

[12] The final occurrence of σημαίνω occurs in 21.19 where the statement Jesus makes to
Peter is again interpreted in a narrative aside as indicating what kind of a death he was to
face. This appears to be inconsistent with the usage described above. However, this final
occurrence suggests a death suffered for Christ's sake and the recurrence of the verb may
indicate that crucifixion is in mind. The confluence of language akin to σημεῖον and the
language of glory is intriguing especially as it applies to one of Jesus' disciples in the context
of a chapter that leads out from the Gospel to the time beyond the events of Jesus' life. This is
perhaps a hint that amongst the greater works of this disciple will be a death that literally
follows the path of his master and glorifies God.

[13] Brown 1966: 485.

[14] BDAG: 'τοσοῦτος', 1012.

amongst the leadership of the Jews. The comprehensive nature of this summary will be qualified shortly as John does go on to speak of those who believe (12.42), but initially the inexplicable rejection of the ministry of Jesus is the focus of attention.

The statement in 12.37 testifies to the apparently overwhelming nature of the evidence presented in the signs. This confirms the Gospel's positive stance to the relationship between signs and faith. Signs are intended to lead to faith so an explanation for the lack of response needs to be given. The signs, while impressive, are apparently not universally compelling. The same sign can be understood as evidence for the divine connections of Jesus, his sinfulness (9.16–17), or as evidence of a political threat. How can this be accounted for?

The verses cited from Isaiah come from two passages. The first quotation from Isa 53.1 is applied to both the words (τῇ ἀκοῇ ἡμῶν) and deeds of Jesus (ὁ βραχίων κυρίου; cf. Exod 6.6; Deut 5.15) and the lack of response to his ministry as embodied in both. Even at this point, the signs of Jesus remain in view as the basis for response from the crowds. The arm of the Lord is revealed in the deeds of Jesus. The next quotation from Isaiah 6.10 is introduced to explain why it was impossible for 'them' to believe. This is attributed to the work of God in blinding them and hardening their hearts. The quotation from Isaiah has been modified to emphasise seeing, doubtless in the light of the reference to signs and the discussion of light and blindness in chapter 9.[15] The action of God in the blinding and hardening is emphasised by the use of the active voice as opposed to the passives in the LXX.

The signs are not disparaged by these references. The difficulty in reading the signs is attributed to hard hearts and blind eyes and the fact that the Lord has not opened them. Throughout the Gospel, the problem of unbelief in Jesus has been approached from a variety of angles, as many obstacles to the one recommended response of believing have been presented.[16] A fundamental problem with humanity was hinted at from the very beginning of the Gospel (1.5, 10, 11) and has been further elaborated by the continual failure of observers to read the signs correctly and respond appropriately. This is explained from the human side in terms of the wrong seeking of glory (5.44; 12.43), origins (8.44–5; 10.26), and fear (7.13; 12.42). It is now explained from the divine side in terms of God's sovereignty. Both belief and unbelief

---

[15] While the first quotation is verbatim from the LXX the second appears to reflect neither the LXX nor the MT to any great degree. See also Beasley-Murray (1987: 216). Menken (1996: 121) suggests that the evangelist made his own translation of the Hebrew text.

[16] Contra Culpepper (1983: 146–8), faith is not presented in the Gospel in terms of stages or types. One either believes or not. The sign narratives present people moving from unbelief to belief. All assessments of Jesus short of the confession required are not so much types of faith, as simply inadequate. Cf. Henaut (1990: 297).

are described as a consequence of the activity of God. This was earlier hinted at in the discussion with Nicodemus (3.5; cf. 1.12–13). It has been hinted at in various exchanges through the course of the narrative (6.44, 65; 8.47; 10.26) and now surfaces again in this reflection. The problem is not with signs as such. They are presented with the purpose of provoking belief. The signs participate in the expressed purpose of Jesus' mission (12.47). However, the signs can be ignored, misconstrued and rejected, as can his words; as can Jesus himself.[17] This is now accounted for in terms of the activity of God.

The predestinarian thought of the quotations from Isaiah is not presented as the only perspective at this stage. Immediately John goes on to speak of those who do believe. This is prefaced by the strong adversative phrase ὅμως μέντοι as belief is recorded amongst the rulers.[18] The response of many through the Gospel is acknowledged here. However a shadow is cast over this belief almost immediately as the failure of these leaders to confess for fear of the Pharisees is recorded. The further reason is offered that this is done because of the love of the glory of men rather than the glory of God (12.43). The contrast is striking in that there has just been a reference to the prophet who saw the glory of God and spoke of him (12.41).[19] The failure of belief is attributed to a problem of allegiance. The problem is not confined to a particular historical setting but typifies Jesus' opponents who represent the κόσμος in its opposition to God and his son.[20] To be part of the κόσμος is to prefer the glory that comes from men rather than the glory that comes from God (11.43). This explanation joins the other explanations of unbelief posed from the human side. Together they are presented in the Gospel alongside the more overtly theological examination of unbelief found in vss. 37–40 and allowed to stand in tension. The outlining, and resolution, of this anthropological dilemma occurs in the Gospel from the twinned perspectives of divine sovereignty and human responsibility. Neither is compromised or reduced at the expense of the other.[21] When exploring the function of the σημεῖα this tension ought to be preserved. On the one hand, the Gospel

---

[17] This is reflected in the two sections that complete the chapter. 12.37–43 focuses on reaction to Jesus' signs while in vss. 44–50 Jesus himself sums up the issues in terms of his words.

[18] Schnackenburg (1980: 417) comments on the 'unusual emphasis' of this phrase.

[19] Perhaps this verse gives a clue as to part of the motivation for John in writing this Gospel. The verse echoes 1.14 and suggests that, like Isaiah, John saw Jesus' glory and spoke of him. The reference to Isa 53.1 in 12.38 further suggests that the glory that Isaiah saw was the glory of the suffering servant and focuses attention on the death of Jesus as the hour of glory.

[20] This identification is based on the interplay of stories observed in the prologue to the Gospel; see pp. 12–14. Culpepper (1983: 129) puts it well, 'Through the Jews, John explores the heart and soul of unbelief'.

[21] Carson (1981: 177–198) explores this tension in the Fourth Gospel at some depth.

suggests that the nature of the σημεῖα is such that there is no ambiguity concerning their meaning (10.25; 12.37). On the other hand, the reaction of the authorities, and even perhaps the choice of the term, suggests some ambiguity that requires an accumulation of signs to convince. The σημεῖα can be interpreted differently according to the framework in which they are situated (cf. 9.16–17).[22] This even applies to the framework of the Hebrew Scriptures as the texts from Deuteronomy are apparently used to assess Jesus' activity. The issue of signs, meaning, faith, response and predestination needs to be viewed from the two perspectives. The lack of ambiguity means that lack of response can only be ultimately seen in terms of God's activity. The ambiguity means that there are a variety of reasons posed for failure to respond. The signs can even be acknowledged by the observer (cf. 12.47) and yet their significance resisted. The narrative of the Gospel invites the reader to share and maintain the perspective that enables the signs to be seen and responded to appropriately.

5.2.2 The Occurrences of σημεῖον: Reader to Text

There is little further to add to previous discussions of the general language of σημεῖον. The language continues to be embedded in the context of a narrative that draws on the imagery, theology and story line of the Hebrew Scriptures. Perhaps at this point it is worth underlining this point and emphasising that this occurs at an overt and covert level. Overtly, the language of σημεῖον continues to draw on the use in the Scriptures of Israel, but it has also drawn, covertly, on a thematic/metaphorical understanding of the use of the language, especially from the wirings of Isaiah. These observations point to a profound understanding and appropriation of the Scriptures of Israel by John.

The rhetorical/legal connotations of σημεῖον in the wider culture continue to inform the reading of the forensic motif in the Gospel as well as contribute to its development. The 'case' has been laid out before the reader through the narrative and Jesus' final words of appeal summarise the issues of life and judgement that are at stake. The signs are not mentioned in this final statement but they undergird its central proposition. As the expression of the forensic motif in the public ministry comes to a close with Jesus' final 'appeal' in chapter 12 (12.44–50) the reader is well aware that his performance of the signs is part and parcel of his work of revealing the Father. While Jesus emphasises his words (12.47–8) the reader knows that the identity of the Father and the Son has also been based on the works or signs they share (cf. 10. 37–38).

---

[22] Bittner's (1987: 286–90) stress on the unambiguous nature of the signs in view of their background in the Hebrew Scriptures needs to be modified by this observation.

Finally, the presence of the Greeks in the narrative leaves an opening for the Graeco-Roman reader to find their way into the narrative.[23] Jesus is the Jewish Messiah, but his interest is in all people groups as the narrative has explicitly stated (3.16; 4.42) and as the Isaianic background implies.

5.3 The Sign Narratives

5.3.1.1 The Raising of Lazarus (11.1–44): Writing the Sign

This narrative account presents a climax to the sequence of powerful acts that Jesus has performed through chapters 1–12. Two features of this narrative immediately stand out. The first is that the 'pattern' of event followed by discourse is reversed in this narrative. The significance of the event is spelled out via a series of dialogues with the characters involved in the incident, prior to the powerful action of Jesus.[24] This has led some to suggest that the actual miracle itself is an anti-climax, being almost unnecessary, in light of the confession made by Martha (11.27), which brings the story to its climax.[25] However, this view underestimates the movement of the story. Lazarus's emergence from the tomb is the climax to which everything in the story has been heading. He was no doubt grateful that the point could not finally have been made without his being raised from the tomb. This inversion of the sequence of explanatory discourse and sign prepares the reader for the vastly extended sequence of dialogue and discourse in chapters 13–17 that prefaces the final and climactic sign of the Gospel, the death and resurrection of Jesus.

The second feature is the proliferation of names in the narrative. Aside from the disciples in chapter 6 no other character except Jesus has been individually named. Groups have been named (the Jews, the Pharisees, and the crowds) but the previous beneficiaries of the signs have all been anonymous. The story of Lazarus is characterised by named people in a situation of distress that would be familiar to any reader in the ancient world. The effect of this feature is to draw the reader into the heart of the incident. The reader is asked to view the incident through the eyes of a variety of characters and is placed in the village to feel the distress arising from the situation. The alignment with the events and the emotions involved is profound.

The conventional beginning of chapter 11 mentions a name, a setting and an illness, immediately setting the reader's expectations for another

---

[23] Frey (1996a: 257–263) points out the representative function of the Greeks and their importance for the Asia Minor addressees of the Gospel.

[24] Culpepper (1983: 73) comments on the impossibility of separating out sign and discourse in this account.

[25] Bultmann (1971: 409) calls it a minor miracle; see also Becker (1969: 146–7).

demonstration of divine power by Jesus. A tragedy within a family unit is quickly established. The puzzling reference to Mary in v. 2 introduces a new character and mentions an event that has not yet occurred in the narrative. The reader is taken into the Lazarus story with this new information, wondering what the anointing of Jesus might mean. The reference also invites the reader to eventually see the anointing of Jesus (12.1–7) as related to the complex of events that is unfolding. At the same time an intimacy is suggested by the act described in v. 2 that contributes to the expressions of affection that will immediately be encountered in the narrative. The reference to this action along with the names signals to the reader that there is a closer personal relationship between Jesus and the other characters in the story than has previously been the case in the sign narratives.

No indication of Lazarus' actual condition is given although the repeated references to his illness (11.1, 2, 3) indicate a poor prognosis. The relationship between Jesus and the ailing Lazarus is also spelled out for the reader in v. 3. The ominous note is softened somewhat when Jesus mentions that this illness will not lead to death but will rather bring glory to God (11.4). At this point, the reader might expect that a healing story would follow. The reference to glory recalls the strong statement made at 2.11 and suggests that the incident to follow forms an inclusio with this first sign. The expectation is that Jesus will effect a cure and that this will fall into the familiar pattern of a sign that brings glory to Jesus. The connection between the glory of God and the glory of Jesus is reinforced by this verse. The signs are the work of the Father, performed by Jesus. They manifest his identity as the divine Son.

Alignment of the reader with the characters in the narrative is achieved through the use of their names and the description of their relationship with Jesus. Lazarus is described as 'the one whom you love' (11.3) and then Jesus is explicitly described as loving the members of the family (11.5). The emotional temperature of the scenario is raised, as it becomes apparent that for Jesus there is a very personal element in the situation before him. At the same time, the reader's sympathy for the family is further aroused through these statements. The introduction of the language of love is also remarkable in the sense that Jesus has not been the subject of this verb previously. Such language recalls the statement made back in John 3.16 where God is first mentioned as acting in the Gospel. It is from his love that he acts to send forth his Son on a mission to bring life.

A potentially jarring note is then struck as Jesus decides to remain for two more days in the place where he has received the news. The reader is not necessarily alarmed by this development as it has been shown earlier that Jesus has power to heal from a distance. The reader might also assume that Jesus, who has already evinced supernatural knowledge of some circumstances, and has already said that this will not lead to death, can perceive the course of the illness and is in no hurry. Similar delays from previous narratives can also be recalled and the general impression that Jesus acts very much in accordance with his own programme is reinforced.[26]

The subsequent decision to go to Judea is treated with some surprise by the disciples (11.8). Judea is, by now, clearly a place of opposition. The subject of death has already been raised by Jesus' earlier statement concerning the fact that this illness will not result in death. It is raised again, as Jesus' own possible demise is hinted at in the disciples' words (11.8). The spectre of death is slowly making its way into the narrative and makes its presence felt once again as Jesus informs the disciples that Lazarus has fallen asleep. The disciples fail to understand that Jesus is referring to Lazarus's death.[27] The narrator points out their lack of understanding (11.13) and then, in recording Jesus' statement concerning Lazarus's death, makes clear that death has made its presence unequivocally felt. The reader might well be surprised. Jesus has previously stated that this illness would not lead to death and yet he now reports that Lazarus has died. He is going to risk his own life in order to go to him and wake him up. The strangeness of this conversation is furthered when Jesus says that he is glad, for the disciples' sake, that he was not there (11.15) and this will help them to believe. The connection between the disciples' believing and the illness of Lazarus as leading to the glorification of the Father and Son (11.4) further recalls 2.11 and sets the scene for a major event.

The pall of death that hangs over the narrative is reinforced by Thomas who states, on behalf of the disciples, that they will go with Jesus to die with him (11.16). At the end of this first movement of the story, the presence of death has been established. The reader has been aligned with the plight of the family facing serious illness and it has suddenly taken a turn for the worse. An expectation has also been established that Jesus will act in this situation that has claimed the life of his friend, and that his action poses considerable danger for both his own life and that of his disciples.

Jesus approaches the village and a person who is certainly dead (v. 17).[28] The focus of the next movement in the narrative is a conversation with Martha. Death is again prominent in the conversation between Jesus and Martha. The remarks of Martha serve to demonstrate the impact of death on those around the deceased. The passion in her remark is hinted at in the

---

[26] See Giblin (1980: 210).

[27] See Culpepper (1983: 152–64) for a discussion of these misunderstandings and their function in providing an opportunity for further clarification of spiritual truths and to draw the reader into occupying the position of an 'insider'.

[28] For background to the belief that the soul finally leaves the dead person's body on the fourth day of burial, see *Gen. Rab.* 100; *Lev. Rab.* 18.1; cf. Strack-Billerbeck II 544-5. These traditions are later than the Gospel and doubt has been expressed whether they would have been known. In any case four days is a lengthy period and there can be little doubt the length of time indicates certain death and probably the beginning stages of bodily decomposition.

emphatic μου at the end of her statement to Jesus, which also implies a mild rebuke (11.21). Martha then voices an implied request that Jesus do something as she acknowledges his closeness to God and the potential for something occurring as a result of that relationship (11.22).

The discussion then shifts to a contemplation of the possibility of life. Jesus' statement that her brother will rise (echoing Martha's emphatic μου with an emphatic σου; 11.23) is understood by Martha to be a reflection of standard Jewish belief concerning the resurrection of the pious. The point of the whole narration is then made in Jesus' climactic words concerning himself as the personal locus of resurrection and life (11.24–5). The strong claim made in this statement echoes previous such statements (6.35, 53–4; 8.12; 9.5) and highlights the extremely personal nature of these references. The thought prompted by the progression of the dialogues in chapters 5 and 6 is advanced and brought to a climax by the statement in 11.25–26. Previously Jesus has claimed to be able to give life to whomever he wishes (5.21), and that life comes through the eating of his flesh and the drinking of his blood (6.53–56). Life, intimated in the concept of the resurrection, is now stated to personally reside in him and the eschatological dimension recognised in terms of Jewish thinking is closely associated as well. The two opposing dimensions of life and death are brought together and the defeat of death is promised in Jesus' words of 11.25–6.

Martha's resounding affirmation of belief in Jesus (11.27) successfully concludes this exchange. However, the brother still lies in the grave.

The interaction is repeated with the other sister, Mary. In similar fashion to Martha, Mary greets Jesus outside the village. She falls at his feet, recalling the narrator's proleptic comments about her anointing of Jesus and indicating the intimacy of relationship suggested by that action. The almost exact repetition of Martha's words has the effect of reinforcing the pathos of the scene as well as reminding the reader of the power of Jesus. He could perhaps have done something but can he do anything now? The cumulative effect of these questions is to suggest that Jesus could have prevented the death but raises the issue of whether he can do anything in the face of death.

The reader is then given a rare account of the emotional response of Jesus in a situation. He is described as ἐνεβριμήσατο τῷ πνεύματι καὶ ἐτάραξεν ἑαυτόν. The verb ἐμβριμάομαι usually denotes a response of anger or indignation,[29] while the next phrase ἐτάραξεν ἑαυτόν is frequently translated 'troubled within himself'. Beasley-Murray points to the divergence in the English and German traditions in interpreting it.[30] English interpretations have tended to transfer the sense of being troubled from the second phrase on to the verb ἐμβριμάομαι while the German tradition has

---

[29] BDAG: 'ἐμβριμάομαι', 322.
[30] Beasley-Murray 1987: 192-3.

stayed with the attested meaning of anger and indignation. The English version tends to emphasise Jesus' internal emotional state, while the German version looks to Jesus' reaction to the matter of death and lack of faith around him.

The immediate context of v. 33 is Jesus' observation of the weeping and mourning of those around him. He has also been told twice that if he had been there Lazarus would not have died. This statement probably implies that now it is too late. The widest context has been saturated with the presence of death. The attested sense of ἐμβριμάομαι is to be followed. Jesus' anger appears to be aroused at the scene of mourning around him.[31] This is most likely to be in response to the despair that he sees death bringing and the consequences for the response of those around to himself. As he confronts the death of Lazarus, a death that he knows will end in glory (11.4) he sees the trust of his friends in his ability seemingly evaporate. The phrase ἐτάραξεν ἑαυτόν ought to be translated in its active sense as Jesus rouses himself for a confrontation with death.[32] This is also suggested by his following request to be shown the tomb where Lazarus lies (11.34).

Jesus' ability in the situation is once more questioned by onlookers in v 37. In v. 38 his anger is reported once more as he moves towards the tomb and the final confrontation with death for which the narrative has been preparing.

Jesus approaches the tomb and commands that the stone be removed (11.39). The previous impression given by Martha's response to Jesus is recast as she questions the wisdom of removing the stone in view of the obvious fact that the body will be decaying. Again the fact of death is emphasised in that Lazarus is simply referred to as τοῦ τετελευτηκότος (11.39). Martha's response casts doubt not on the sincerity of her previous response to Jesus but rather its level of insight and suggests that she like every other character in the Gospel has some way to go before grasping fully the truth concerning Jesus. Jesus' reference to the glory of God (11.40) reminds the reader of the foundational statement that Jesus has made concerning this glory and its relationship to the action that he is about to perform (11.4). The connection between signs and glory is affirmed once more.

The stone is removed but there remains one final delay. The suspense becomes unbearable as Jesus addresses his Father. Jesus explicitly connects his work to that of the Father and the goal of a believing response from those around stated. The reader is reminded of the evidential value of a sign that points to the divine identity of Jesus as well as encouraged to make the appropriate response of belief.

---

[31] Schnackenburg 1980: 335.

[32] Bevan (1932: 187–8) makes a similar suggestion. Calvin (1994: 281) is dramatic, 'Christ does not come to the tomb as an idle spectator, but like a wrestler preparing for the contest'.

Finally the moment comes, not as an anti-climax, but as the culmination of the story that has been building in suspenseful fashion. The dead man receives his name back and is addressed as living as Jesus commands him to come out of the tomb (11.43). Lazarus is the one whose name is known by the good shepherd (Jn. 10.16) and therefore given life at the sound of the voice of Jesus (Jn. 5.25). The death of Lazarus is mentioned one final time as he comes out of the tomb bound in his grave-clothes (11.44). Jesus is demonstrated as the life-giver in this final and climactic demonstration of his identity, power, and mission.

The implications of the Lazarus story continue to echo through the narrative. John 11.45–46 provides a report of the response to the action of Jesus which has the effect of providing a coda to the Lazarus narrative and also introducing the next section of the Gospel where the plan to put Jesus to death is precipitated (11.47–54). The now customary response of belief is recorded in v. 45. This creates an echo of the testimony concerning John in 10.40–42 and in effect creates a frame for the Lazarus incident. This frame is further reinforced with the mention of the many signs that Jesus is doing (11.47; cf. the statement that John did no signs).[33]

The theme of death is continued in this next section and then the further incident connected with Lazarus (12.1-11). The chief priests and Pharisees decide that it would be expedient for one man to die for the whole nation (11.50). The narrator interprets Caiaphas's comment as referring to Jesus' death (11.51–2). Life for Lazarus looks to mean death for Jesus.

In the account of the anointing of Jesus by Mary (12.1-11), death is again prominent. A meal is eaten as the Passover draws near, the Passover already having been connected with death in its previous mentions (cf. 2.13; 21–2; cf. 6.4; 6.51, 54-6, 62). Lazarus is there (12.2) and the reminder is given that Jesus raised him from the dead (12.9). Jesus' own death is anticipated as he is anointed for the day of his burial (12.7).

At the conclusion of the Lazarus account, the presentation of Jesus as a life-giver has been brought to a climax. Previously he has defeated death-dealing diseases. In this narrative, he defeats death itself, raising the body of the one he loved back to life. The events have been set in motion that will now lead to his own death. This will happen in the final sign of the Gospel; the sign to which the other signs have pointed. This raising of Lazarus leads to the cross in terms of both the plot and thematic development of the story.

While the other healing narratives have focussed the reader's attention on the issue of death and Jesus' power with respect to it, this narrative does so

---

[33] Frey (2000: 408-11) points this out. He further suggests that the framing reinforces the fact that the resurrection of Lazarus is a sign which ought to bring about belief and, on the basis of 10.42 prompting the recall of John 1.29, encourages the reader to understand the Lazarus account within the parameters of Jesus' death as substitutionary.

much more directly. The central issue in this narrative is death. Several of the other narratives have dealt with conditions that could lead to death or are closely associated with death. In this incident there is no indication of the condition that caused the death but only its presence. The naming of the characters and the repeated recording of their reactions of grief have drawn the reader right into the account so that close identification with the issue of death and its consequences is achieved. The alignment brought about by the text is not with the dead man but rather with those around. This is a brilliant move. It is difficult to identify with a dead man but one can certainly identify with those who have lost a loved one. The scenes of mourning would be familiar to the readers of the Gospel, who lived in a world of short life expectancy. It would be only with wonder that the presentation of Jesus as the life giver par excellence would be received.

5.3.1.2 The Raising of Lazarus (11.1–44): Reading the Sign

As has already been noted, in terms of statistics, death was a prominent reality in the first century Graeco-Roman world. While it is difficult to reconstruct mortality rates or life expectancy for the Roman world with any certainty there appears to be a broad consensus that Roman life expectancy at birth was twenty-five years.[34] Death was such an ever-present reality that Seneca could write 'Most men ebb and flow in wretchedness between the fear of death and the hardships of life (*Ep.* 4.5).[35] He further advised waking with the thought that 'if God is pleased to add another day, we should welcome it with glad hearts…When a man has said: "I have lived!", every morning he arises he receives a bonus' (*Ep.* 12.10).

Death was a threat from above and below. While the Roman Imperial ideology proclaimed the Emperor as the provider of life and peace this was, literally, a two edged sword as Augustus's triumph was founded on military might and violent destruction.[36] There are testimonies to Rome's insatiable

---

[34] Frier (2000: 788) notes that this conclusion rests less on evidence from the period than the reasonable conviction that comparisons can be made with the lowest levels of pre-modern populations. The problems concern the exaggeration of ages on gravestones, poor memory, and the fact that lengthy ages are generally recorded in the literature due to the abnormality of the ages reached.

[35] This echoes the thought of Euripides 'Know that death is a debt that we must all pay' (*Alc.* 419, trans. A.S. Way; cf. Horace, *Carm.* 1.4.13). A similar note of resignation is expressed in *P.Oxy* 115 l. 9–10 (2nd A.D.) 'but still there is nothing one can do in the face of such trouble' (trans. B.P. Grenfell & A.S. Hunt).

[36] Tacitus, *Ann.* 1.10.4, 'After [Augustus] there had been undoubtedly peace, but peace with bloodshed' (trans. C.H. Moore & J. Jackson). Cf. also the speech placed on the lips of Calgacus concerning the Roman conquerors of Britain; 'to plunder, butcher, steal, these things they misname empire: they make desolation and they call it peace' (*Agr.* 31.2, trans. M. Hutton & R.M. Ogilvie).

avarice amongst writers of the first century,[37] while later emperors are remembered as much for their cruelties and slaughter as their political achievements.[38] Disease, epidemics, poor nutrition, low levels of wages, substandard sanitary conditions, and no strategy for the primary prevention of disease or improved living conditions all made their contribution to the high mortality rate.[39]

Help to escape from the threat of death was sought from three major sources—physicians, gods and magicians. The physicians tried to alleviate suffering where they could but much of their time was spent gathering data that would enable them to give a prognosis predicting whether the ill person would live or die (Hippocrates, *Progn.* 1; 20; 24; 25). However they could only help in certain situations and they spent much time discerning the situations in which they could help (Hippocrates, *De arte* 3; 8). The gods were turned to, especially Asclepius the healing god.[40] However, it was perceived that the gods could not always help, especially if it was a person's time to die.[41] The third option was to turn to magicians.[42] Magicians could apparently predict the outcome of an illness or they could hope 'to drag out their life with food and drink and magic spells, trying to keep death out of the way' (Euripides, *Suppl.* 1109–113). Magicians would be considered especially useful if it was thought that the disease was caused by another magic spell.[43] Some spells also appear to be related to attempts at raising the dead.[44]

---

[37] Propertius, *Eleg.* 3.5.10–12; Petronius, *Satyr.* 119.1–3. See also Wengst (1987: 7–54), Bolt (1998: 53–5).

[38] Pliny *Nat.* 30.5; Suetonius regularly presents the excesses of his imperial subjects.

[39] See Frier (2000: 792–4).

[40] Cf. *P.Oxy* 1381(2nd A.D.) ll. 51–7; 'for the god is disposed to confer benefits, since even those whose pious ardour is only for the moment are repeatedly preserved by him after the healing art has failed against diseases which have overtaken them' (trans. B.P. Grenfell & A.S. Hunt).

[41] *Anth.graec.* 7.8, 'why should we sigh for our dead sons, when not even the gods have power to protect their children from death' (trans. W.R. Paton). Cf. Homer, *Od.* 3.236–9; Euripides, *Hipp.* 1473; *Alc.* 22.

[42] Plutarch, *De fac.* 920B, 'people with chronic diseases, when they have despaired of ordinary remedies and customary regimens, turn to expiations and amulets and dreams' (trans. H. Cherniss & W.C. Helmbold); cf also Thucydides, *Hist.* 2.47; Hippocrates, *Morb. sacr.* 4; Sir 38.1–15.

[43] Bolt 1998: 62. Pliny points out that magic is also a threat to life, testifying 'there is no one who is not afraid of curses and binding spells' (trans. W.H.S. Jones) (*Nat.* 28.4.19). There are references to curse tablets and magical spells in Tacitus, *Ann.* 2.69, 3.13, 4.52, 16.31; Suetonius, *Cal.* 4.3.

[44] Though these are difficult to interpret; see the discussion in Bolt (1998: 62–3).

There was a wide range of perspectives on life after death in the ancient world.[45] A very general progression is noted that begins with the ancient idea that the dead retained some kind of shadowy existence in their tombs and that they could be used as a positive force for those who were still alive if they were kept happy with offerings. The next 'stage' saw the development of the idea of a collective dwelling of the dead (Hades) and finally more explicit concepts of life after death developed.[46] Of course, such a developmental model can only be general and, doubtless, all three ideas co-existed. In addition, there were philosophical views from the Stoics and Epicureans that contemplated death in terms of nothingness or absorption into the impersonal life of the universe. On either account, the challenge was to live life in a state of detachment from the things of this world so as to be able to bid them farewell easily when the time came to die.[47] However, these more resigned sentiments may well be exceptional.[48]

The more radical views of the possibility of life after death occur under the name of Orphism with two schools distinguished under this heading. The first involved the figure of Pythagoras and entertained notions of the release of the soul from the body at death and its progress either to the upper realms or a state of hovering around the bodily realms.[49] It was also believed that a good man's soul might live forever in some kind of celestial bliss, while less pure souls entered the air and hovered around earth as ghosts or after a time of purgation might return to yet another episode of bodily existence (Plutarch, *Sera.* 564A-B; 565A-566A).

The Mystery cults offered a second and better alternative for many people, as Cicero's comment implies 'Nothing is better than those mysteries…we have learned from them the basic fundamentals of life, and have grasped the basis not only for living with joy but also for dying with a better hope' (Cicero, *Leg. man.* 2.14.36, trans. H.G. Hodge). Traditional religion connected immortality with the gods but the mysteries, especially in the first century those associated with Demeter and Dionysus, made immortality accessible to the ordinary person. The basis of hope in the mysteries was situated in the action of the individual being initiated in a ceremony. The details are obscure but it seems that some near death experience was re-

---

[45] Black (1984: 416–8) has a succinct summary

[46] Burkert 1985: 190–215.

[47] Several epitaphs express this sentiment most eloquently, 'I was not, I was, I am not, I don't care', (*IG* 14.2190; cf. *CIL* 13.530; trans. Lattimore [1962: 84]; 'We are mortals, not immortals' (*CIL* 11. 856), 'When life ends, all things perish and turn to nothing' (*CLE* 1. 420), 'We are and were nothing. Look reader how swiftly we mortals pass from nothing to nothing' (*CE* 1495.1-2; Lattimore [1962: 83]; trans. Toynbee [1971: 285 n. 67-9]). Lattimore (1962: 83–85) has several more examples.

[48] Toynbee 1971: 34.

[49] Burkert 1985: 300–1.

enacted, which may actually have been life threatening, after which the promise of a blessed afterlife was the initiate's (Apuleius, *Metam.* 11.6). Gold leaves have been discovered in initiates' tombs. Their meaning also remains obscure, but they appear to give instructions to the dead about the path to follow in the next world and express confidence concerning a future beyond the grave.[50]

There were opposing views concerning the body with respect to life and death. In the tradition of Homer, real life was bodily life and the afterlife could not properly be called life at all. At death the soul moved away from the body as its sinews were no longer able to hold the flesh and bones together (*Od.* 11.218–9). It went into the afterlife as a shadow, not a material body. Orphic views privileged the soul over the body and said, at death, that the soul returned to the air while the body remained on the ground. Any sense of apotheosis (movement to divine rank beyond death), as was posited for the emperors, was not embodied but involved only the soul. The body was burned away on the funeral pyre so that the soul could ascend to the Gods (Apollodorus, *Bib.* 2.7.7; Lucian, *Peregr.* 4, 6, 30, 33; *Anth. graec* 16.185). Heaven was the domain of souls and not bodies. In contrast, there are a few hints in the Hebrew Scriptures and associated writings that suggest the contemplation of some form of embodied existence beyond death (Isa 26.9; Dan 12.2–3; 2 Macc 7.9, 14; Pss 2.31, 3.12; 13.11; 14.9–10).

When it comes to the possibility of a body returning to life after death the general view seems to have been that this was almost impossible (Homer, *Il.* 24.551; 24.756, 21.56; Aeschylus, *Eum.* 645–51, *Ag.* 568–9; Sophocles *El.* 138–9; Euripides *Hel.* 1285–7; Herodotus, *Hist.* 3.62.3; Aristotle *De an.* 1.3.406b; cf. also the evidence of the Hebrew Scriptures: 2 Sam 12.22–23; Ps 88.10–12). There are, however, isolated reports of dead people returning to life. In the Hebrew Scriptures there is the miracle tradition involving both Elijah and Elisha (1 Kgs 17.17–24; 2 Kgs 4.18–37), who are involved in the apparent resurrection of a dead boy. From the legends of the Graeco-Roman world, there are a number of reports concerning the god Asclepius returning a variety of figures to life (Pindar, *Pyth.* 3.50–62; Lucian *Salt.* 45; Pliny, *Nat.* 29.1.3; Pausanias, *Descr.* 2.26.5; 2.27.4; Apollodorus, *Bib.* 3.10.3; though note the variety of reports concerning this legend that are recorded by Sextus Empiricus, *Math.* 1.261). Pliny also provides a list of a number of people who revived on the funeral biers, often with short-lived results (*Nat.* 7.51–52). There are also reports involving the physician Asclepiades (Pliny, *Nat.*

---

[50] J.E. Harrison (1903: 575–90) has a lengthy discussion. Cf. Burkert (1985: 293–6), who quotes the poignant sentiments expressed on one of these leaves, 'I flew away from the circle of heavy grief and pains…I dived beneath the lap of the mistress, the chthonic queen'. This is followed by the claim, 'Happy and blessed one, god you will be instead of a mortal'. The leaves date to the fourth century BC.

7.37.124), the philosopher Empedocles (Diogenes Laertius, *Vita* 8.67) and Apollonius of Tyana (Philostratus, *Vita Apoll.* 4.45) that involve the apparent raising of the dead. One final account that involves the use of magic comes from the writings of Apuleis. He describes the work of Zatchlas, an Egyptian prophet, who is contracted to bring back the spirit of a recently deceased young man and to reanimate his corpse. The corpse is reanimated and tells of the circumstances of his death (*Metam.* 2.29–30).[51] These isolated incidents suggest the possible existence of a conceptual framework for grasping the idea of a temporary return to existence before dying again. However, it must be kept in mind that most of these reports do not involve a definite description of death in the sense that the individuals involved are either not yet buried or cremated and, as such, have not entered the 'realm of the dead'.

In the midst of a variety of views concerning both death and the possibilities beyond, this story has peculiar resonance. Jesus raises to life a young man who has been in the tomb for four days. Under any contemporary system of belief, his spirit has left his body. Jesus resurrects the corpse by command and demands that the dead man be released. It is not just a temporary reanimation. A later account confirms the reality of the incident as the young man is described sitting with his friends at a meal (12.2).

Within a Jewish framework as articulated by Jesus and Martha in their conversation, this event suggests that the promises of the end times have been enacted in the present. For all readers this is an extraordinary story highlighted by the fact that the narrative emphasised the grief and hopelessness associated with the event. The reader is helped to feel a little of the impact of the role of the Jesus as life-giver and is given a graphic illustration of the goal of his ministry. This is an illustration that both precipitates and interprets Jesus' own death and resurrection in the context of the narrative of the Fourth Gospel.

5.4 Summary

Throughout the entire section, from chapter five through to chapter twelve, the language of σημεῖον and the narratives designated as σημεῖα have been prominent. The narratives have provided structure to this section and visible demonstrations of the teaching of the Gospel regarding Jesus, his identity and mission. They have also provided a point from which further extended

---

[51] There are also isolated examples of spells aimed at reanimation of bodies, which possibly hint at an attempt at resurrection., e.g. PGM XII. 278–283 (A.D. 346). 'I conjure you, spirit coming in the air, enter, inspire, empower, resurrect (διαέγειρον) by the power of the eternal god, this body; and let it walk about in this place, for I am he who acts with the power of Thayth, the holy god' (trans. Betz 1986: 180).

discourses expounding this can take place. All of this has formed a unity of word and work attesting to the identity and mission of the sent Son. The signs are meant to convince the onlooker of the truths concerning Jesus and it is their apparent failure that prompts the extended reflection via the prophet Isaiah at the end of the whole section as the account of Jesus' public ministry is summarised and evaluated.

The sequence of signs in chapters five to twelve began and ended with a reminder that in them was displayed the glory of God (2.11; 11.4, 40), expressed in the prologue to the Gospel as the glory of the unique one from the Father, full of truth and grace. The very first sign indicated that the appropriate response to the signs is faith and this has been present in the responses of characters throughout the narratives.

The trial metaphor that has been noted as a key feature of this Gospel's presentation has been prominent throughout this section. The signs have played their part as a cumulative set of witnesses to the claims of Jesus. The consistent references to the quantity and quality of σημεῖα in the ministry of Jesus has played on the rhetorical usage of σημεῖον and the notion of cumulative proof.

Different facets of Jesus' person and mission have been demonstrated through the various accounts but supremely attention has been paid to the fact that he is the one who brings life. He has saved people from the brink of death, from conditions that would have been recognised as a living death and has even robbed a grave of its human booty. He has provided an abundance of two of the staples of life. He has also demonstrated an ability to walk on the sea that would normally be associated only with the divine.

From a wide number of possibilities a small range of σημεῖα have been chosen for both their spectacular qualities and their representative nature. In each of these narratives, a point of contact is established between the story of Jesus and the 'real world'. He is shown dealing with the problems of everyday existence. At the same time, it has been observed that many of the signs would have stimulated interest at a further level given the cultural repertoire of the audience. A subtle polemic against some of the more popular rival gods of the age has been detected. This has operated within a general context where the uniqueness of Jesus is continually implied. In John 11–12 this presentation is continued. His coming actions are said to be a judgement on the ruler of this world and he will draw all people to himself (12.31–32). Jesus final speech (12.44–50) emphasises his unique role in revealing God (12.44–45), saving the world (12.47) and providing the grounds for judgement (12.48). The magnitude of Jesus' acts generally and the insistence upon his uniqueness as the revealer of God is juxtaposed with a number of pretenders. Glory is to go to the Son alone and through him to the Father who has sent him.

It has also been observed that in many of the σημεῖα accounts, and occasional attached discourses, the shadow of the cross grows increasingly prominent. The sign narratives prepare the reader, as do the rest of the contents of the Gospel for an understanding of *the* event of the Gospel—the death and resurrection of Jesus. The forensic theme of the Gospel also prepares for this event. The final trial of Jesus before the Gentile representatives of the κόσμος is still to take place. The signs therefore take their place also in the exposition of this seminal event. The narrative has prepared the reader to understand that this final complex of events, the death and resurrection of Jesus is to be seen as a sign as well. It is time then to turn to the final section of the Gospel where an extensive discourse provides the platform for interpreting the climactic sign of the Fourth Gospel.

Chapter 6

The 'Sign of Signs': σημεῖον in John 13–21

6.1 Overview of Chapters 13–21

In this section, attention turns to the death and resurrection of Jesus, the 'sign of signs'.[1] What has been looming with increasing intensity throughout the Gospel comes into clear focus, as it becomes apparent that everything recorded in the Gospel has been orientated towards helping the reader understand the detail and importance of this moment. Before moving to recount the actual events, John takes time to present a further extended reflection upon 'the hour' (12.23, 27) as Jesus turns to his own disciples (13.1). This is achieved via a sequence of symbolic actions (13.1–38) followed by an extended discourse (Chs. 14–16). Through this material, the reader is prepared to understand the coming events as Jesus' return to the Father (13.1) and an action of service that brings cleansing (13.7–11). In addition, the way will be opened for his followers to go to the Father (14.1–14), and a further phase of his mission will be initiated. This further phase will be accomplished through the disciples with the aid of the Paraclete (14.15; 15.26–16.15). The disciples are promised peace (14.27; 16.33) and joy (16.20–24) through the work of the Son, which is also described in terms of an overcoming of the world (16.33). These perspectives are added to other clues that have been given to the reader to prepare them to understand the significance of the death and resurrection (cf. 2.18–22; 3.14–16; 6.51; 8.28; 10.15–18; 12.23–24, 31–32).

In terms of the persuasive intention of the Gospel, the section can also be seen to exercise an apologetic function concerning the future role of the disciples as the appointed witnesses to Jesus (15.27). While this role applies generally to all the disciples addressed by the statement, it has specific implications for the reception of the Fourth Gospel itself. A guarantee is offered concerning the veracity and reliability of the contents of the Gospel. It can be relied upon because it is the testimony of one of the appointed witnesses who was with Jesus from the beginning. This witness, like the other witnesses, is empowered by the Spirit to provide the details of Jesus' life as well as their authoritative interpretation (14.26; 16.13). The reader is encouraged to be confident in the veracity and reliability of the Gospel.

---

[1] The phrase comes from Østenstad (1998: 111).

To this end, it is the 'Beloved Disciple' (13.23) who emerges as a key figure in the latter chapters of the Gospel and it is his testimony that apparently stands behind the Gospel (19.35; 21.24),[2] whether as source or actual author. The title indicates that the 'Beloved Disciple' is one of Jesus' own who is loved to the end and has been shown all things (13.1, 21; 14.15). He is a representative of the authentic witness of those who have been with Jesus from the beginning (15.27), who saw and can therefore testify to his glory (1.14). The appeal to believe in Jesus and its concomitant opportunity to become a child of God (1.12) and enjoy abundant life (10.10) will continue to be proclaimed through the witness of the Beloved Disciple in the Fourth Gospel. The testimony of the 'Beloved Disciple', and that of the disciples that he exemplifies, will also carry on the trial that Jesus has been conducting against the world in the power of the Spirit (16.4–15). All of this material points forward to the time after the resurrection when the Spirit is given and the mission of the Son of God will be carried on through his appointed representatives.

John 13–17 further informs the presentation of the events of the death and resurrection of Jesus. In a sense, the pattern observed with respect to the raising of Lazarus continues in that the sign is prepared for in the discourse that precedes its presentation. However, the nature of the death and resurrection as the climactic final sign in the Gospel means also that the whole of what precedes, the public ministry of Jesus and especially the individual sign narratives has been preparing the reader to encounter the death and resurrection narratives.

6.2 The Occurrences of σημεῖον

In this final section only one specific reference to σημεῖον occurs (20.30–31). This reference will provide a vantage point from which to assess the overall use and intended impact of the σημεῖον language in the Gospel. This final reference suggests that the death and resurrection of Jesus, together, constitute both a sign and the culmination of the signs presented throughout the Gospel. There are, however, some important references to ἔργον that will also need to be considered as part of the overall presentation of Johannine signs. This is necessary given the overlap between these terms as suggested by the discussion in John 5.[3] These references occur at 14.10–12 and 15.24. While familiar themes recur in these references, some new perspectives are added to an understanding of the meaning and function of σημεῖον

---

[2] Bauckham 1993b: 40.
[3] See pp. 79–81.

In a departure from the analysis of the previous three chapters, the general references will be dealt with under the single heading 'text-to-reader and will not be considered from the perspective of 'reader-to-text'. The points made in the previous 'reader-to-text' sections remain valid for the following analysis and it is not necessary, therefore, to repeat them here.

6.2.1 *'Believe the Works' (Jn 14.10–12)*

In the dialogue sequence of chapter 14, Jesus replies with a series of statements to Philip's request to him to show them the Father. This request and Jesus' incredulous response together demonstrate the significant lack of understanding of the disciples despite all that they have seen and heard. In reply, Jesus points again to the testimony of his words and works, repeating his arguments from the debates of John 5 and John 10. John 14.10 brings the two aspects of Jesus' ministry into close association but, as the following vss. 11–12 show, the two are not collapsed into one another. Verse 11, especially, distinguishes Jesus' words from his works. Jesus urges belief that the Father is in him and he is in the Father. Once he has made this statement, he then distinguishes this from the 'testimony' of the works.[4] The evidential sense of the works feeds into thinking about the signs once more.

The signs appear to be the referent of the use of ἔργα in v. 11, especially in the light of the echo of the similar statement made earlier (10.38). The echo of this appeal together with the reiteration of the arguments of John 5, both presented before the Jews, forces a further revaluation of the understanding of the disciples. They have remained with Jesus, but their lack of understanding is alarming. The reader looks for some kind of help to enable them to pierce the fog of misunderstanding in which they struggle. This will be forthcoming in the promises concerning the Paraclete. The echo of the earlier passage (10.38) is striking. The same 'evidence' is offered to the Jewish outsider and the disciple. The works or signs of Jesus are seen to be useful in convincing both audiences.

An even more startling statement appears in the next verse when Jesus promises that the one who believes in him will do his ἔργα, and greater (μείζονα), because he goes to the Father (14.12). This is a surprising reference and, on the grounds of the perceived connection between signs and works thus far, seems to imply the possibility that the disciples of Jesus will perform deeds similar to those he performed. Given the magnitude of Jesus' signs it is difficult to see what these actions might be. Two considerations help to give a perspective on this statement.

---

[4] The phrase εἰ δὲ μή makes the distinction clear. The works are also emphasised through the placement of αὐτά, 'the works themselves'.

First, ἔργα appears to include but not be limited to the σημεῖα. This has been seen especially in John 5 where the works of the Son were broadened to include the giving of life and the execution of judgement.

Secondly, the basis on which the disciples will perform these greater works is the return of Jesus to the Father. The greater works are performed by the disciples in a distinctly eschatological framework of understanding, which anticipates an era of clarity and power in the proclamation of Jesus enabled by the giving of the Spirit.[5] It is clear, as Jesus goes on to teach, that he will continue his work in the world with and through the disciples following his return to the Father. The disciples are promised Jesus' support in response to their prayers, addressed in his name, and answered by him to the Father's glory (14.13–14). The mission of bringing life remains the same both before and after the departure of Jesus to the Father. The difference is that the work of Christ is completed and the Spirit is given. Both of these facts provide the context in which the disciples do the greater works; or, rather, Jesus continues his work through them. While this may include actions that approximate the actions designated σημεῖα by John, this particular term is reserved for the actions of Jesus in the Gospel. This is because of the specific messianic nature of the signs and their accrediting of Jesus' divine identity and mission from the Father in the Gospel's narrative.

The possibility is not precluded of the disciple's performing miraculous works similar to those performed by Jesus. However, the general thrust of the farewell discourse suggests that the chief means that the disciples will use to do the 'greater works' will be their message of testimony concerning Jesus. Like so many others in the Gospel, the disciples' role is chiefly to testify to Jesus (15.26–27; 17.20; 19.35; 21.24).[6] This message will continue the work of judgement that has been inaugurated in the ministry of Jesus, a work that includes both bringing life and confirming condemnation,. The 'greater works' of the disciples will therefore be performed in the context of the continuation of the trial that has characterised the ministry of Jesus (16.8–11). The signs of Jesus will continue to have their place to play in this ongoing trial as they form an essential part of the testimony of the disciples to Jesus before the κόσμος. The written Gospel, insofar as it bears testimony to Jesus, is a part of the programme of greater works.

A final consideration of the nature of the 'greater works' comes in the post-resurrection commissioning of the disciples (20.19–23). Jesus breathes on them, commands that they receive the Spirit, and then commissions them with the task of either forgiving sins or withholding forgiveness. They are commissioned to impart life or confirm judgement (cf. 5.20–23).

---

[5] Barrett 1978: 460. Carson (1991: 495–6) emphasises the power and clarity of the disciples' ministry following Jesus' glorification.

[6] Cf. Köstenberger (1998: 170).

6.2.2 Signs and Judgement (Jn 15.22–24)

A further significant reference occurs at Jn 15.22–24 where Jesus is speaking of the hatred of the world towards himself and his disciples. In two parallel statements, Jesus refers to the effects of his words and his works as providing a basis for judgement on the κόσμος. A distinction between the words and works of Jesus is maintained at the same time as their overlapping function is clearly acknowledged. Both the words and works of Jesus render those who have heard and seen him responsible for their own rejection of him. However, as in the previous passages where the two are closely connected, their distinction is also maintained (10.37–38; 14.10–12). The words are not works. This is brought out by the use of the verb ποιέω and the fact that the works were seen (ὁράω). The basic unity of the words and works is not found in the fact that the words are considered the works of Jesus, but rather in the fact that it Jesus who speaks the words and it is Jesus who performs the works. It is the identity of his person perfectly expressed in his words given him by the Father and his works shown him by the Father that is the point.

Jesus says that he has come and performed works that no one else has done. The signs of Jesus, being part of the broader category of works, fall under the compass of 15.22–24 and its import. The unprecedented nature of his works mentioned in this reference (15.24) recalls the statement made concerning his healing of the man born blind (9.32) and alludes to the other powerful actions as well. The details in each of the sign narratives that point to their extraordinary nature are recalled, as well as the qualifiers present in the various narrative summaries of Jesus' ministry that mentioned the quantity and quality of his signs (7.31; 9.16; 12.37). While the σημεῖα and the ἔργα might not be entirely synonymous, it is clear that the signs in the narrative are the focal point of what Jesus describes as his works.

The passage is a powerful statement as first the words of Jesus and then his works are organised around the central accusation, 'whoever hates me, hates my Father also' (15.23). This hatred and, therefore, turning away from the offer of life is all the more tragic and culpable because of the power and convincing nature of his works. The works/signs of Jesus are, therefore, intimately connected with the negative judgement that occurs in the context of Jesus' mission. They reveal the Father in the Son and render the observer with no excuse for a negative response. The perfect tenses used in 15.24 point to the completeness of the revelation in the works of Jesus and the implacability of the response from those who reject this.

The signs, as the expression of Jesus' work and identity in the κόσμος, perform a revelatory and divisive function. They have enabled the onlookers to see Jesus and the Father and to reject them both (15.24). The σημεῖα, as an expression of Jesus' identity and work in the world, render judgement in the negative sense. This is not the major accent of the Gospel but it is a reality nonetheless. Although the Son has not come to judge but rather to save (12.47), the fact of his coming and identifying himself renders culpable all those who refuse to accept his identity and mission. The double-edged nature of Jesus' ministry was outlined in Jesus' statement in John 5 where he pointed to the greater works of giving life and executing judgement, that the Father has given over to him.

Both the references 14.11-12 and 15.22-24 occur in a section that also intersects with the trial theme that has been present throughout the Gospel. In John 14–16, it is clear that the disciples are being prepared for their role in the continuation of the trial of the κόσμος that has been conducted throughout the course of the Gospel.[7] They have been chosen to bear witness to Jesus because they have been with Jesus from the beginning (15.27). They have seen the signs and heard the words and can therefore bear testimony to the entire ministry of Jesus. They will be aided in their testimony by the presence of the Paraclete who will lead them into all truth and help them both to understand and to testify to Jesus.

Their verbal testimony will be a synthesis of eyewitness narration and confession under the inspiration of the Spirit.[8] The significance of the events is brought out at the same time as they are narrated. As these events are narrated, they will continue to exercise their function of revealing Jesus and provoking a response that either leads to life or condemnation. This will occur as they continue to present the positive message concerning Christ who was sent to bring life to the world (3.16; 12.46). The signs will continue to exercise their role in Jesus' ministry for all readers/hearers of the testimony that is preserved in the Gospel.

6.2.3 Signs and the Purpose of the Gospel (Jn 20.30–31)

The final reference in the Gospel to σημεῖον occurs at 20.30–31 in the immediate context of the post resurrection appearances to the disciples, especially Thomas. Thomas's profession of faith provides the movement to faith that has been a feature of the previous sign narratives and provides a climax to the death and resurrection account as well as to the Gospel as whole. The statement in 20.30–31 then follows. This statement bristles with difficulties that are well known but these difficulties ought not to mask the simple observation that 20.30–31 is a statement of intention, addressed to the

---

[7] As expounded in some detail by Lincoln (2000: 110-123).

[8] The two poles of testimony according to Ricoeur (1980). See Lincoln (2000: 340–53) for an exposition. The testimony of the disciples extends beyond a verbal proclamation, though this would appear to be its focus. Jesus has earlier spoken of their love for one another (Jn 13.35). The possibility of powerful works is also suggested by 14.12.

audience, that indicates the purpose for the Gospel's production.[9] The appearance of σημεῖα in this context indicates the importance of this language for the Gospel's persuasive strategy, as well as its prominence in the overall theological thought of John. An examination of the details of this statement will bring together some of the threads from the previous examination of the language of σημεῖον throughout the Gospel.

6.2.3.1 'These Signs are Written'

The first part of the statement refers to the πολλά...καὶ ἄλλα σημεῖα that Jesus performed that have not been recorded. The general impression given by the recurrence through the Gospel of the plural σημεῖα, that Jesus ministry is characterised by signs, is reinforced. A selection process has clearly been undertaken in the Gospel's presentation of the σημεῖα.

The appearance of σημεῖα after a relatively lengthy absence from the narrative has prompted discussion as to its precise denotation, particularly when the words of Jesus appear to be excluded from the overall purpose statement of the Gospel. While this might simply point to the importance of the σημεῖα for the contents and purposes of the Gospel, it may also indicate a broadening of the concept referred to by the term.[10] A variety of options for the denotation of σημεῖον in this verse are countenanced by exegetes. Some believe that the reference is only to the resurrection appearances,[11] others that it is only the events of chapters 1–12, miraculous[12] or otherwise.[13] Some consider only the resurrection appearances and the miracles prior to chapter 12, while others include the death and resurrection as a complex event.[14] Finally, some consider the entire ministry of Jesus, his words and works, to be

---

[9] Cf. the comments of Warner (1990: 153).

[10] As observed amongst others by van Belle (1998: 320). Nicol (1972: 115) comments on the 'surprising elasticity' of the concept in this verse.

[11] As suggested for example by Hoskyns (1954: 655-6), Minear (1983: 90), O'Day (1995: 851), Kammler (1996).

[12] This is stated by, amongst others, Bultmann (1971: 114, n. 1), Ashton (1991: 521), Welck (1994: 50), Morris (1995: 608). Often this appears to be simply assumed by exegetes, cf. the title of Bammel (1965), '"John Did No Miracle": John 10.41'.

[13] Some exegetes, observing that there is nothing inherent in the word σημεῖον that denotes the miraculous include other incidents, especially the cleansing of the temple, e.g. Dodd (1954:141–2), who also includes the footwashing and Köstenberger (1995: 91).

[14] Dodd (1954: 439) and Carson (1991: 661) are amongst those who include the death and resurrection. Brown (1970: 1058), Schnackenburg (1982: 337) and Beasley-Murray (1987: 387) represent those who acknowledge the reference to σημεῖα encompasses the entire Gospel but they resist seeing the death and resurrection in sign terms, preferring instead a reference to the resurrection appearances. Bittner (1987: 320) concedes this as a possibility but postpones a decision.

intended.[15] The position adopted here is that the reference is to the miraculous events prior to chapter 12 as well as the death and resurrection considered as a complex event. This position is adopted for the following reasons.

First, the mention of the disciples as the chief audience for the signs in 20.30–31 emphasises the focus on the disciples throughout the resurrection appearances. This suggests that the immediately preceding events are included in the remit of the statement. The close connection between the events described involving Thomas, and the statement of 20.30-31 supports this view.[16] The particle οὖν logically connects the Thomas narrative and normally implies a close connection in the narrative.[17] There is also a thematic connection established through the repetition of πιστεύω in vv. 29–30.[18] The address appears to have in mind specifically those who have not seen, as Thomas and the disciples did, and are therefore reliant on the testimony recorded in the Gospel.

Secondly, while 20.30–31 includes the events immediately prior, the referent of σημεῖα is not restricted to these events. A number of considerations suggest that this is unlikely. The earlier occurrence of the events termed signs and the term itself are sufficiently striking to suggest that a later occurrence of the term, even as apparently isolated as that in 20.30 could not help but recall the earlier predominant usage. In this sense there may be said to exist a 'discourse trace' of the word σημεῖον that ensures some recollection by the reader of the earlier occurrences and therefore association with the present usage. This is all the more likely in view of the use of the term in explicit editorial comments (2.11; 2.23; 4.54; 12.37). Further, the reference to ἐν τῷ βιβλίῳ τούτῳ indicates that the statement is intended to cover the contents of the entire work. Also, the mention of the disciples recalls their presence at five of the seven events designated as signs in the first half of the Gospel (2.11; 6.3; 6.16; 9.2; 11.16).[19] The disciples are highlighted in John 20.20–31, not only because they have been immediately present in the narrative, but also to highlight their role as the ongoing witnesses to Jesus. They have been with him from the beginning (15.27) and are therefore the authoritative witnesses to the ministry of Jesus expressed in

---

[15] Bultmann (1971: 452, 698) famously sees the σημεῖα as encompassing the words of Jesus. This expanded sense of σημεῖα in 20.30 is also the position of Reinhartz (1983: 33–42), Van Belle (1998: 320), and Lincoln (2000: 176).

[16] Schnelle 1987: 139.

[17] Carson (1991: 661) points this out. The analysis of the Johannine use of particles by Buth (1992) bears out this observation.

[18] Van Belle 1998: 309.

[19] It is likely that they are also assumed to be present at Cana in 4.46–54. It is only at the healing of the man at the pool (5.1–17) that there is no reason given in the context to assume their presence.

the signs. Σημεῖα refers to both the resurrection appearances and the events of chapters 1–12.

Thirdly, the Gospel's usage suggests that the denotation of σημεῖα is restricted to those occurrences that would fall under the rubric of miracle. In the case of five of these signs this is clear on the basis of the explicit and implicit identification in the text (2.11; 4.54; 6.14; 9.16; 12.18). It has been suggested that the healing of the man at the pool in John 5 and the action of Jesus walking on the water are also to be included.[20] The temple cleansing is excluded.[21]

Fourthly, the death and resurrection are portrayed as a complex event in the Gospel. It is clear from very early on that the resurrection is presented as the necessary complement to the death of Jesus (2.19; cf. 10.11–18). The references to the hour of Jesus' glory and to his lifting up, that have the event of the cross as their focus, stretch beyond the cross to encompass the resurrection. In view of the presentation of the farewell discourses of these events as a return to the Father, the ascension to the Father, though not portrayed is probably also to be included. As Lincoln notes, for the implied author, 'Jesus' death, resurrection and ascension are all stages in the one event of glorification and together constitute the one hour of glory'.[22] The accumulation of hints pointing towards the identification of this complex event in sign terms includes the response to the demand for a sign in explicit terms of the death and resurrection in 2.18–19 and the implicit reference to σημεῖον in the reference to the lifting of the snake in 3.14–5. Jesus has been increasingly identified with the material substance of the signs through chapters 5–12, especially in the ἐγώ εἰμι statements with predicate. The use of the verb σημαίνω in chapter 12 and 18 has provided another subtle verbal connection. Finally, the re-introduction of the term σημεῖα after a lengthy absence and, consequently, its prominence in the Gospel, is best explained by the fact that the death and resurrection are considered to be a sign.[23]

The strongest arguments against the identification of the events post chapter 12 as a sign are that the death and resurrection of Jesus are apparently not explicitly labelled as such and that they are so climactic that they are of a different order to the previous events. This view is expressed most eloquently by Barrett who says concerning the cross that,

> it is not a σημεῖον and it is not called a σημεῖον, because it is not merely a token of something other than itself; this event is the thing it signifies...The matter may be expressed by saying through the gospel the course of events has taken place, as it were, in front of a mirror, and on a line intersecting the mirror. As the events themselves move

---

[20] See pp. 82, 84.

[21] See p.p. 51-2.

[22] Lincoln 1998: 131.

[23] Carson 1991: 661.

nearer to the mirror, the images of the events, which we may take to represent the eternal realities portrayed by them, correspondingly move nearer to the mirror and become clearer and clearer. Finally, object and image coincide in the surface of the mirror. So, in the death and resurrection of Jesus, signs and meaning coincide.[24]

It has already been suggested that there are enough implied links for the identification of the death and resurrection as the final and climactic sign. Perhaps the force of Barrett's eloquent observation can be felt without conceding his whole point that the death and resurrection are not signs. There is a sense in which the other signs do lead up to and anticipate the events of the death and resurrection narratives. It is, however, in the culmination of the σημεῖα events in the death and resurrection that the final piece of the jigsaw is placed and the rhetorical aim of the Gospel as expressed in 20.30–31 is considered accomplished. The death and resurrection of Jesus operates in a similar way to all the other signs in that it enacts what it is speaking about but at the same time it is the culmination of the previous signs. It is perhaps the point where sign and meaning most closely coincide, but it nonetheless retains its sign nature in the context of Johannine thought. It provides the basis, albeit ultimate, for seeing the message of the Gospel as summarised in 20.30–31. Even this sign points ultimately beyond itself to the truth expressed in the Gospel that Jesus is the divine son and life-giving messiah. The death and resurrection of Jesus can operate like any of the other signs. It can be 'seen' (in this case by the reader) and its significance can either be appreciated by coming to believe or missed through a refusal to come to faith.

Finally, a number of considerations suggest that to understand an expanded sense of σημεῖον in 20.30-31, i.e. as including all the words and deeds of Jesus recorded in the Gospel, is erroneous. The argument concerning the broadened reference of σημεῖον in vs. 30 is mainly based on the close relationship observed between the works of Jesus and the signs, and the related observation that some of the plural forms of ἔργον appear to encompass both the words and works of Jesus (esp. 14.10–11, 15.22–24).[25] However, the previous examination of these references revealed that a careful distinction is maintained throughout the Gospel between the words and works of Jesus. At times, they appear to be interchangeable but a distinction is definitely made. There is a basic unity expressed between the words and works of Jesus but no identity.[26] Any attempt to broaden the reference of σημεῖα in its final occurrence fails to convince on the cumulative weight of

---

[24] Barrett 1978: 78.

[25] In his exegesis of the various passages that support this conclusion, Ensor (1996: 239–40) points out the difficulty of coming to a final conclusion about the referent of ἔργα. In his examination of 5.36 and 10.25, 32, 37 he does suggest that the miracles of Jesus appear to be primarily in mind.

[26] Cf. the conclusions of de Jonge (1977: 136).

past usage and the distinctions established between the signs/works of Jesus and his words.

The call is to the readers, whoever they might be, to believe. The textual problem of these verses is notorious. The debate concerns whether the verbal form of πιστεύω is in the present or aorist subjunctive. The external evidence is finely balanced with most exegetes hesitant to be dogmatic. The aorist is attested in earlier and disparate manuscripts: $\aleph^c$ A C D K L W Δ Π Ψ and numerous minuscules. The present subjunctive is recorded in the early $\mathfrak{P}^{66}$ though there it is unclear due to the condition of the text. It also appears in the original version of $\aleph$ and is known in various textual traditions B Θ. An examination of the photographs of $\mathfrak{P}^{66}$ suggests that the present subjunctive is most likely original in view of the available space.[27] This, and the fact that the aorist is a correction in $\aleph$, shifts the weight of probability on external grounds to the present subjunctive being the original reading.[28]

It is difficult to draw any firm conclusions from the textual evidence alone. It is sometimes considered that if the verb is in the present subjunctive then believers must be in view with a pastoral/encouragement purpose implied, and if it is in the aorist subjunctive then non-believers with a missionary purpose are implied.[29] However, the ambiguity of usage of both the present and aorist forms of the subjunctive with respect to this issue is attested at earlier points in the Gospel where the context is determinative (e.g. 6.29; 11.15; 11.40; 14.29). The decision must be based on wider evidence and in this case the evidence of the narrative is ambiguous. The focus on the disciples in this verse and through the farewell discourses suggests that the strengthening of the believer is the focus. The assumption that the reader appears at certain points to be expected to be familiar with many of the details of the story also suggests an informed, if not believing, audience. In contrast, the stress on witness through the Gospel is amenable to a more overtly evangelistic purpose.[30] The many narratives that trace the movement from unbelief to belief appear to be aimed at achieving the same transition in the reader to the same conclusion.[31] On balance, the best solution might be to suggest that the writer is interested, more generally, in nurturing faith in Jesus. The most likely initial place of reception of the Gospel is in the midst of the Christian congregation. This suggests that the Gospel message seeks to strengthen Christian faith and commitment. This need not preclude an

---

[27] Martin & Barns: 1962, Plate 145.

[28] So too Fee (1992).

[29] Brown (1970: 1056) infers on the basis of the present that 'the readers of the Gospel are already Christian believers'.

[30] Lincoln (2000: 179) disputes the connection made by some scholars between the trial motif and an evangelistic purpose.

[31] As Henaut (1990: 297–8) suggests.

application to outsiders present or the Gospel itself providing the resources for the members of the congregation to use in their conversations with neighbours concerning Jesus. The signs enable an initial response of faith in Jesus and will nourish the continual maintenance of this posture towards him.[32]

Finally, this belief has specific content and specific consequences. Jesus is to be believed in as the divine Messiah.[33] Throughout the Gospel there have been a number of references placing the signs at the heart of the Gospel's testimony to Jesus as the Messiah (most explicitly 7.31; cf. 10. 22–25, 37–38) but there is an added dimension to this confession. Jesus is a particular kind of Messiah and the phrase 'Son of God' expresses this. The expression is more than a synonym, particularly since it comes at the end of a Gospel which has been introduced with the eternal perspective of the prologue. Jesus is continually portrayed as expressing a distinct filial consciousness through the prominent use of 'Father' and 'Son' throughout the Gospel. The title, occurring immediately following a climactic confession of the divinity of Jesus (20.29), functions to further define what is meant by the term Messiah. Jesus must be confessed as the divine Messiah. The signs that enable the

---

[32] The understanding expressed here is akin to the expanded sense of mission explored by Okure (1988: 292–4).

[33] This reading has been challenged by Carson (1987) and, more recently, Jackson (1999: 18–20) who suggest that the purpose statement is better read as asking for belief that the Messiah is Jesus. Carson's key argument is a grammatical one and draws on the criticism of the work of McGaughy by Goetchius (1976). McGaughy (1972) found that in the type of construction that occurs in 20.31, where a subject and predicate nominative are linked by a verb, the subject is likely to be marked by the use of the article, where other clear markers are not present. He suggested that there were five exceptions to this in the NT: John 20.31; 1 Jn 2.22; 4.15; 5.1,5, all having the anarthrous Ἰησοῦς as their subject due to their confessional nature. Carson suggests that these are not in fact exceptions and that other passages in the New Testament confirm the general rule proposed. In his review of the New Testament evidence and discussion of the phenomenon, Wallace (1996: 40–48) suggests that the evidence in the New Testament is at least ambiguous and tends to run in the opposite direction than that envisaged by Carson so that in the grammatical situation presented in 20.31 word order may in fact be determinative. His criticism is not as strong as it appears though. His argument depends in part on the 'exceptions' to McCaughey's work that appear in 1 Jn, which Wallace suggests is clearly written to Gentile Christians on the basis of 5.21. As Carson argues, however, these may not be exceptions and it is not clear how determinative 5.21 can be for a Gentile audience of the letter. Carson's position is challenged on narrative grounds by Brownson (1995: 214) who suggests that while 'Messiah' is obviously an important category throughout the Gospel, the identity of Jesus is clearly at the forefront of every discussion. He is the 'subject' of the book that has been written. Cf. Lincoln (2000: 177) and also the comments on the confessional nature of the verse (and those in 1 John) and the comparison made with 1.49 and 11.27 by Pryor (1991: 204, n.222). As plausible as Carson's reading initially appears, it must be questioned on literary grounds with the grammatical considerations still open.

confession of Jesus as the Messiah also enable this understanding of the confession to be made. They point to his divine nature as τὸν υἱὸν τὸν μονογενῆ (3.16; cf. 1.14).

The result of this confession is life for those who believe. The life on offer has been illustrated by the sign narratives, which have presented Jesus as the life-giver in a comprehensive sense.

This final statement also points to the uniqueness of Jesus. The life promised in the Gospel comes in his name only. This caps the further development of this theme through the farewell narratives. A brace of 'I am' statements (14.6; 15.1) join the declaration that to see Jesus is to see the Father. Jesus promises to give a peace that the world cannot give (14.27) in the context of an empire that claimed to have brought peace to all.[34] He claims to have overcome the world (16.33).

6.2.3.2 Summary

The σημεῖα referred to throughout the Gospel are the recorded powerful deeds of Jesus performed before the κόσμος and especially the disciples, through whom these deeds will continue to be presented to the κόσμος. They, therefore, include the public death of Jesus on the cross and his resurrection appearances before the disciples. 20.30–31 are key verses for understanding the significance and function of the signs in the Gospel. Σημεῖον is a term that has been chosen by the narrator for the purposes of communication with the reader. It is clear that the sign narratives have been deliberately recorded for a specific purpose within the context of the Gospel. Ultimately they point to Jesus' identity as the divine Son, sent by the Father to do his work. The signs point to Jesus' identity in the context of the legal motif that is so prominent in the Gospel and in the context of the matrix of expectations concerning the work of God with his people. They are integral to the achievement of the Gospel's purposes and are clearly intended to lead to the faith that is the overall goal of the writing of the Gospel. While the signs are performed publicly, this verse points to the importance of the disciples as their audience. It is through the witness of this authorised audience (15.27; 17.18; 20.21) that the testimony of Jesus presented in the signs will be proclaimed to the world and to those who will believe through their testimony (17.20). The signs remain an integral part of the testimony to Jesus through the ongoing witness of the disciples, especially as recorded in this particular work.

---

[34] The study by Wengst (1987) explores the claims of the *Pax Romana* as well as the dark side to its achievement.

6.2.4 John 21.24–25

While σημεῖα is not explicitly mentioned, the general reference of ἄλλα πολλὰ ἃ ἐποίησεν is reminiscent of previous summary statements concerning the multiple events and signs performed in Jesus ministry. The reader might perceive an oblique reference to the signs as being included in the remit of this statement. If so, the reader leaves the Gospel with a final reminder of the abundance of evidence present for the claims made concerning Jesus. The hyperbole of the final statement, while possibly conventional,[35] reinforces the point made throughout the Gospel in the references made to the multiple signs of Jesus.

6.3 The Sign Narratives

6.3.1.1 The Death and Resurrection of Jesus (Jn 18–20): Writing the Sign

The death and resurrection of Jesus are, together, the final and climactic Johannine sign. A brief examination, therefore, of some of the principal features of the death and resurrection narratives will explore how these signs bring to both fruition and climax many of the elements presented in the earlier signs. This examination will take in the arrest and trial narratives as the necessary prelude to the actual crucifixion of Jesus. The account of the passion will make its own contribution to the forensic motif pursued throughout the Gospel, to the presentation of Jesus as life-giving divine Messiah, and to the implicit critique made of possible alternatives.

The first point to be observed in terms of the forensic motif of the Gospel is that this is where a formal trial of Jesus takes place.[36] It is noteworthy that this takes place before a representative of Roman rule. Throughout the Gospel, an informal trial of Jesus has been conducted before the Jews. This is reprised briefly in the meeting recorded before Annas in John 18 but the most explicit trial takes place before Pilate. In terms of the Johannine presentation this has the effect of having Jesus tried before the world in a comprehensive sense and universalises the issues that have previously been presented in a Jewish context.[37] In the brief episode before Annas, Jesus is questioned concerning his teaching and his disciples. The signs are not discussed. It has already been conceded that these have been performed. The question of what

---

[35] Bultmann (1971: 718) compares this verse with ancient rhetorical conventions that he cites as parallels for 20.30–31. The parallels appear to be much closer to 21.24–5 than they do to 20.30–31.

[36] Surprisingly Harvey (1976) does not deal with this as part of his study on the trial theme in the Gospel, preferring to concentrate on the informal proceedings before the Jews.

[37] Söding 1996: 37.

they signify is at issue. The dispute is over his teaching and the political implications of his gathering of disciples.

The signs do not feature in the trial before Pilate either. The discussions between Jesus and Pilate focus on issues of authority and questions of truth. As in the trial before the Jews, the roles of accused and judge are inverted at various points in the narrative as Jesus emerges as the judge of Pilate. It is clear that Jesus' innocence is maintained (18.23, 38; 19.4, 6) and his eventual death occurs more as a result of political intrigue, self-preservation and callous indifference to the rule of law than as a consequence of anything else.

The account of the arrest, trial and death of Jesus contains a variety of scenes and characters that present a number of perspectives through which the reader can view the event. The lengthy farewell discourses place the reader into the shoes of the disciples, 'hearing' Jesus' final words. The identification engendered here persists into the arrest scene where Jesus protects his disciples by giving himself up for them. Later it is recorded that the disciples disappear with the exception of Peter and 'another disciple'. Eventually these two are no loner visible either as the lengthy account of Jesus' trial before Pilate is recounted. The 'Beloved Disciple' reappears at the foot of the cross and the reader is invited to stand here with him to observe Jesus' last words and actions. The constant shifting of perspective makes sympathy with one individual view difficult and the reader is consequently thrust more into the role of a general observer of all that is occurring and forced to consider the significance of the events unfolding from a more objective perspective.

Throughout this account the narrator adds interpretative comments that help the reader to understand the significance of the actions as they unfold. Of particular importance are a series of asides that stress the fact that the events unfolding are the fulfilment of Scripture (19.24, 28, 36, 37).[38] This final sign is to be understood as the fulfilment of the plan of God as announced in the Hebrew Scriptures.

The events of the resurrection are focalised through Mary Magdalene and several of the disciples. The reader is enabled to feel the bewilderment and joy of Mary, the amazement of the disciples as Jesus appears amongst them and Thomas' scepticism and final coming to faith in the Gospel's climactic confession. The blessing pronounced on those who will believe without seeing (20.29) would have special resonance for the later hearer of the Gospel, whose access to Jesus and the events of his life is mediated through the testimony of this Gospel.

---

[38] Evans (1982) notes that the language of fulfilment predominates in these citations and others in chapters 13–21. This use appears aimed at proving that the 'disgrace of the crucifixion was Jesus' very purpose' (p. 83)

The account of the arrest, trial and death of Jesus present him and his mission under three main images, those of shepherd, king and lamb.[39] In the combination of these can be seen the presentation of the significance of his death as the life-giving Messiah. It is particularly in the arrest scenes that Jesus is presented as the shepherd drawing on his own extended metaphor detailed in John 10. Jesus offers himself for arrest in place of his disciples (18.8). He protects his own from those who have come to kill and destroy (10.10). The detail of the location of this scene, with Jesus standing at the entrance of the garden, suggests the imagery from John 10 as well.[40] The reader is reminded of Jesus' own words, emphasising the prophetic nature of his ministry as well as emphasising again his role as the good shepherd laying down his life for the sheep (18.9; cf. 17.12; 10.28).

In his death on the cross Jesus is presented as the Lamb of God, recalling the seminal statement by John at 1.29. This is alluded to through the repeated references to the Passover setting of the death of Jesus (19.14, 31).[41] Other details such as the hyssop used to hold the wine given to slake Jesus' thirst (19.29; cf. Exod 12.22) and the unbroken bones, emphasised by the citation of Scripture (19.33, 37; cf. Exod 12.46; Num 9.12), further suggest this theme.

In the presentation of Jesus as the Passover victim an important implicit link with the sign language of Exodus is forged.[42] The event that is commemorated by the Passover was the climax of the signs visited upon Egypt as a judgement against them and the means of liberation of the people of Israel. Aside from any propitiatory elements that might be alluded to in the symbolism, this event is also described in the Exodus account as a judgement on the gods of Egypt (Ex 12.12). The events of 'the hour' have been described in the Gospel as the judgement of 'the ruler of this world' (12.31), perhaps echoing this aspect of the Passover symbolism as well as emphasising the dual focus of the cross as a place of salvation and judgement. The event the Passover commemorates was a judgement on the gods of Egypt in that they were shown to be powerless to prevent the loss of life of the first born of Egypt. In the case of the Fourth Gospel's presentation of the cross, the judgement comes whereby the actions of Jesus are shown to deliver what other gods promised—life. The ruler of this world is shown to be powerless as Jesus rises from the dead and provides life for those who believe in him.

---

[39] Stibbe 1993: 179.

[40] Stibbe (1992: 102–4) points out the way in which the setting of the scene in the garden recalls the good shepherd discourse.

[41] The timing difficulties of this event in relation to the synoptic presentation are well-known. For two alternative suggested solutions see Blomberg (2001: 246–7) and Instone-Brewer (2001). Whatever solution is proposed (or ignored) the Passover context of the Johannine account is clear.

[42] This link further supports the observations by Porter (1994: 406) concerning the significance of the Passover theme in the Fourth Gospel.

The presentation of Jesus as the life-giver is also explicitly maintained in the narrative of the crucifixion. This is especially highlighted following the death of Jesus. His side is pierced and it is observed that blood and water run out (19.34). The importance of this incident for the narrator is reflected in the solemn comment of testimony that immediately follows its occurrence (19.35). While blood might be expected from such a wound, the water is unexpected and prompts reflection on the previous imagery associated with water through the Gospel. Water is a prominent feature of the Gospel story associated with life, cleansing and supremely the Holy Spirit.[43] As well as being a part of a complex of events that attest to the fact of Jesus' death, the flow of blood and water is a testimony to the significance of the death.[44] The outpouring of water and blood comes to symbolise the life and cleansing offered through Jesus. As he is lifted up on the cross Jesus is again portrayed as the life-giver.

The dominant theme of the trial narrative before Pilate is the presentation of Jesus as king. Kingship is implicitly expressed in the way that Jesus is depicted as being in control throughout the entire sequence of events but it is emphasised in the trial before Pilate where the language of kingship is prominent (esp. from 18.33–19.12). The choice between the kingdom of God and the kingdom of Caesar is vividly presented in the debate that occurs between their respective representatives. This is particularly acute in two key scenes where the language of kingship is especially prominent (18.33–38a; 19.9–11). These passages occur within the context of seven scenes of dialogue between Jesus, Pilate and the Jews in the prelude to the death of Jesus.[45] In the first of these significant scenes, 18.33–38a, Pilate calls Jesus and addresses the question of kingship directly (18.33). In responding as Jesus does with a question, he immediately reverses the roles becoming Pilate's judge in the situation. The specific detail of the nature of Jesus' kingship is addressed in vss. 36–37 as Jesus accepts the title but qualifies the nature of his kingship in both negative and positive terms. His kingdom is not to be construed in the terms with which Pilate is accustomed. The evidence for this is the arrest of Jesus and the fact that he has no soldiers with swords. At his arrest he specifically eschewed the use of violence by his followers (18.10–11).

The more positive statement concerning his kingship is then made in v. 37 when he declares that he has come into the world in order to be a king. However, he defines his Kingship as concerned with testimony to the truth

---

[43] See C.R.Koester (1995: 167–83).

[44] Lincoln (2000: 388) points out that Jesus' death is attested by the events recorded in 19.30–33

[45] See Brown (1970: 859) for a representation of the seven scenes that make up this sequence.

and his kingdom comprised of followers who are 'of the truth'. This statement in v. 39 is significant in two respects. First, it is made before the bearer of Roman Imperial power. A clash of kingships is implicit at this point, though Pilate's subsequent attempts to release Jesus demonstrates that he, at least at this point, sees no threat from such a kingdom. Pilate's reply τί ἐστιν ἀλήθεια; exposes him, and the world he represents, as not concerned with pursuing the truth. When put on trial, Pilate aligns himself with the world that the Jews represent and the opposition of the entire 'world' to Jesus is complete. There is no justice to be found (v. 38b) and subsequently an innocent man is sacrificed for political gain in the delicate balance of power played out between Pilate and the Jews.

Secondly, it is clear that the nature of Jesus' kingship is involved with testimony to the truth. This is consonant with the presentation of Jesus as Messiah and echoes Isa 55.4 where the Messiah is made to be testimony amongst the Gentiles.[46] This allusion to Isa 55.4 is one of several allusions to material from Isaiah 55 (cf. 4.15; 6.27; 7.37; 12.9) through the Gospel.[47] In Isa 55.4 the descendant of David is presented as the one who will interpret Yahweh's will to the world. Similar thoughts occur in Isa 43 where the nations are called to hear the testimony concerning Yahweh and will be forced to declare that it is true (Isa 43.9–10). All of this is in the context of an absolute claim by Yahweh to be the one true God (Isa 43.11). In the Fourth Gospel, Jesus is the truthful witness to his Father. He speaks what he has heard the Father say (8.26; 12.50). Jesus testifies to the reality of the Father, his sovereignty and his purposes. He now declares this before the Gentiles. Lincoln notes the connections between the idea of witnessing to the truth and the further presentation of Jesus as a judge in the situation. Isaiah once more provides useful background understanding. The Davidic king of Isa. 11 is also a judge (Isa 11.3–4).[48] This is the same passage that goes on to note how this king will be a σημεῖον for the nations (LXX Isa 11.12).

The second passage, 19.9–11, is a reprise of this earlier discussion after Jesus has been scourged and presented in mocking fashion to the Jews as their King (19.1–5). Pilate is affronted when the Jews declare that Jesus has claimed himself to be a Son of God (19.7). This statement seems to prompt from Pilate the realisation that there may be more going on than a mere political trial and he hastens to question Jesus again. The reader is reminded that the issue of Jesus' kingship is to be judged in terms of his wider claim to have come from God. The reader already knows the answer to Pilate's question πόθεν εἶ σύ (cf. 7.27–8; 8.14; 9.29–30) though for Pilate there is no reply. Pilate boasts of his own power in the situation (19.10) but is

---

[46] Derrett 1989: 192.
[47] Dahms (1981) also explores this connection.
[48] Lincoln 2000: 51, 135.

rebuffed by Jesus. Pilate's power in the situation is cast into the perspective of the kingdom that Jesus represents. So too is, by implication, the Roman imperial system that he represents. Jesus has made a dual claim regarding his kingship. He has admitted that he is a king but has pointed to the different nature of the rule that he exercises. He has come as a King to testify to the truth. He has also claimed that the alternative rule or kingdom that he represents is the supreme rule and authority even in the apparently weak situation in which he is now placed. He has moved the discussion of his Kingship into divine categories. Pilate, despite all his pretensions to power, is claimed to be at the disposal of the sovereign one from above, whom the reader knows Jesus represents.

The theme of kingship is also stressed when the Roman soldiers ironically acclaim him as such (19.1–3) and then as Pilate presents Jesus as the Jews' king (19.14). The final movement in this presentation comes with the words of the Jews who decide between the two types of power displayed in the whole scene. They declare that they have no king but Caesar (19.15). The Jews play upon the threat to Caesar by a rival king and combine this with the statement concerning friendship with Caesar. This is enough to force Pilate to finally act. The echo of Jesus' statement to his disciples that they are his friends (15.14–15) provides the reader with the choice of friendship with Caesar or friendship with Christ. This is clearly stated in v. 12 where the Jews state that anyone who sets himself up as a king sets himself against Caesar and is therefore not Caesar's friend.

The various hints presenting Jesus as an imperial figure, which have been given through the Gospel, come to a head here as the choice is starkly presented and then decided by the Jews in their fateful words that they have no king but Caesar (19.15). Lincoln notes further echoes from Isaiah in this statement where the unique claim of Yahweh's exclusive Lordship rings out (Isa 43.11; 45.21). The Jews have given up their status as God's chosen people and Pilate is ultimately shown by the narrative to be as powerless as the gods of the nations (Isa 44.10; 45.20; 46.7).[49] This 'ruler of the world' and the system he represents is judged by Jesus, the king who bears witness to the truth.

The question in the dialogue with Pilate is not whether Jesus' kingship exists but how it exists. Ultimately, it is a kingship that is not of the world but it exists in the world. It sets before the world a sovereignty that fundamentally surpasses every other kind of sovereignty because it comes from above.[50] The confrontation with the world is acknowledged and a different kind of peace, life and freedom is offered in the Gospel, through the ministry of Jesus.

---

[49] Lincoln 2000: 138.
[50] The discussion by Rensberger (1989: 97) is penetrating on these matters.

The final note in the presentation of Jesus as king is struck when the *titulus* announces Jesus in his death, as the king of the Jews. The universality of this declaration in the multiple languages of the *titulus* hints at the broader implications of the raising of the King of the Jews. The Messiah is raised as a σημεῖον before the nations (Isa 11.12).

The three images of shepherd, lamb, and king combine to give a rich perspective on the death of Jesus. These events may appear to be a long way from the thought of the signs in the Gospel. To think so would be a mistake. The sign language and narratives have together combined to make their contribution to these perspectives on the death of Jesus. In them, the royal claims of Jesus have been made and the offer of life held out. They have foreshadowed the cross of Jesus in this respect and have pointed to the deeper significance of this action. The signs have also intimated the divine identity and glory of Jesus in their discourse. This king is not one more political rival or messianic pretender to be judged and found wanting at the bar of Roman jurisprudence. This is the divine Son who as the good shepherd lays down his life for the sheep; as the Passover lamb enables the forgiveness of sins and pronounces judgement on the gods of this world; and as the king, rules in glory in the humiliation of the cross.

6.3.1.1a The Resurrection Account

The resurrection account moves through a sequence of scenes adding progressive detail to reveal to the reader what has happened. The first scene 20.1–2 focuses, through Mary Magdalene, on the empty tomb. There is no suggestion in Mary's mind of anything other than a grave robbery or at least the removal of the body by persons unknown. The hint is offered that she is not alone in her view of this (οἴδαμεν, 20.2) suggesting the requisite two witnesses to such an event. The second scene (20.3–10) sees the two disciples run to the tomb to observe its contents: the grave-clothes and the separated and rolled headcloth. A further two witnesses are mentioned. The beloved disciple concludes, based upon his observation of the material in the tomb, that Jesus has risen from the dead. He reaches this conclusion without the benefit of the interpretation of Scripture (20.9). The comment concerning Scripture points forward to the importance of later reflection upon the Hebrew Scriptures for the provision of a framework in which to understand these events. The opening two scenes establish the emptiness of the tomb as the presupposition of all that is to come. The presence of the grave-cloths cannot help but recall the scene of Lazarus exiting his tomb wrapped in the clothes of death and still requiring release. Here, the grave clothes lie empty.

The next scene (20.11–18) records the first of four post-resurrection appearances as Jesus speaks to Mary Magdalene. The initial trouble that Mary has in identifying Jesus (20.15) indicates to the reader the extraordinary nature of what has happened. The ambiguity concerning the body of Jesus is expressed in the narrative of each of the next three appearances as well. Jesus' body is corporeal in that both Mary and Thomas can touch it (20.17, 27). However, it also appears to be able to either move through walls or relocate itself in space unnaturally (20.19). The body is clearly that of Jesus. It bears his scars (20.27) but it also appears that recognition of the body can be withheld (20.14).

The accounts are redolent with the vocabulary of seeing (20. 14, 18, 21, 25, 27) and it is clear that the reader is to grasp that Jesus has been seen by the disciples alive in bodily form. Details scattered throughout these narratives recall details from earlier in the Gospel. The calling of Mary by name recalls Jesus' saying concerning the good shepherd and his knowledge of his sheep (10.14, 27). His greeting of peace recalls his earlier promise to the disciples (14.27; 16.33). These details serve to emphasise the continuity between the risen Jesus and the Jesus of the earlier narrative.

The commissioning of the disciples (20.19–23) is an important moment. Jesus breathes on them in a manner reminiscent of both the creation account and the resurrection of the barren Israel (ἐμφυσάω, cf. Gen 2.7; Ezek 37.9 LXX). Recreated, the disciples are sent with a message of the forgiveness of sins (20.23) and a circle is closed with the statement concerning the Lamb of God from the beginning of the Gospel. The manner in which the sins of the world are to be taken away has been demonstrated in the events of the cross at the Passover. It will be on the basis of their testimony to Jesus, his life, death, and resurrection that the forgiveness of sins can be pronounced as given or withheld. With this brief statement (vv. 21–23) a further dimension of the meaning of the cross is revealed. It is the place where forgiveness has been made possible. The solution to the world's plight, hinted at in 1.29, is foreshadowed and the basis on which one can become a child of God is stated.

The sending of the disciples recalls the earlier references to their mission in the farewell narratives. Jesus tells them that they must testify to him and that this will be a part of the ongoing trial of the world that continues to bring life and judgement (16.5–11). The breathing of the Spirit recalls the promises concerning the Paraclete to aid them in this task (14.25; 15.26–7; 16.13). The disciples' task is to bear witness to Jesus as they are sent.[51]

---

[51] Perhaps here, one final reference from Isaiah lies in the background. In Isaiah 66 a remnant of rebellious Israel is rescued from the wrath of Yahweh and sent to the nations to declare his glory (66.19). They will have signs placed upon them (66.19). The disciples, as they are sent, bear the signs of Jesus in their proclamation. As they witness to Jesus, they set the sign of the Messiah raised on his cross in the midst of the nations bringing salvation as a light to all nations (Isa 49.6).

The sequence of appearances in chapter 20 is brought to a climax with the appearance to Thomas. Thomas's demand to see Jesus is met and belief is urged from him in response. His confession is the full confession that takes the reader back to the insight communicated in the prologue that Jesus is the divine Son. In this confession the Fourth Gospel both reaches its climax and returns to its starting point. The final sign has been met with belief. The anticipation of many others echoing that belief is implied as Jesus pronounces a blessing on all who believe without seeing (20.29). The readers are addressed over the head of Thomas at this point. Future readers of the testimony of the Gospel will have to 'see' the signs in the report of the witnesses and they will come to belief on the basis of this and not the actual seeing of Jesus. They will, however, be counted as blessed and will express neither an inferior or superior faith. It will simply be on a different basis to the original disciples.

The combined death and resurrection account has portrayed the climactic sign of the Gospel. It has been extensively prepared for by the rest of the Gospel and its significance emphasised in the wealth of detail contained in the account itself. It is the culmination of the σημεῖα recorded in the Gospel. The ambiguity of 'lifting up' is exploited to the full as Jesus is raised up as the final sign in the Gospel; a sign that reveals the divine Messiah as saviour of the world, promises life, and draws forth the climactic statement of faith in the Gospel.

6.3.1.2 The Death and Resurrection of Jesus (Jn 18–20): Reading the Sign

Hengel's extensive examination of ancient literature portrays the ancient world's view of crucifixion.[52] His study reveals that it was a punishment for slaves (Cicero, *Verr.* 2.5.168), prisoners of war (Josephus *B.J.* 5.451), bandits (Josephus, *B.J.* 2.253) and revolutionaries (Josephus *A.J.* 17.295). The humiliation was carried out via a process of public trial (Cicero, *Rab. Perd.* 9–17), flogging and torture (Josephus *B.J.* 5.449–521; Livy, *Hist.* 22.13.19), naked exposure (Diodorus Siculus, *Hist.* 33.15.1), the mocking and ridiculing of the victim by crowds (Philo *Spec.* 3.160) and, frequently, denial of honourable burial (Pliny, *Nat.* 36.107–8). This most dreadful and symbolic death proclaimed the victory of Rome and her gods over those who would oppose her and was a shameful death in a culture where it is frequently asserted matters of honour and shame were critical.[53]

---

[52] Hengel 1977.

[53] Moxnes (1983) has a general introduction while Lincoln (2000: 285–300) considers the impact of the trial motif in the light of the concepts of shame and honour. See pp. 287–90 for specific reflections on the crucifixion narrative.

John however chooses to portray this as the moment of the glorification of Jesus throughout the Gospel (7.39; 12.28; 17.5; 21.19). This is achieved in the passion narrative itself through the invoking of the three motifs described above. Throughout the passion narrative Jesus is revealed as in control of all the circumstances surrounding his arrest, through to his encounters with Pilate to his crucifixion and death where he gives up his spirit. His portrayal in the narrative as the shepherd, lamb and king also work to invert the values of the cross as popularly understood so that the reader is asked to consider this most shameful death as the glorification suggested by the narrator. At the deepest level of the narrative the reader has been educated into seeing that what is occurring is the work of the Father (4.39; 17.5) and that Jesus is seeking the honour of the Father in his death. The reader is able to see that many details of the ordeal that Jesus goes through which are meant to humiliate him actually acclaim his true status in an ironic fashion. This is especially true for his mock investiture by the soldiers where he is dressed and hailed in the manner of Roman rulers.[54] In these and many other details, John inverts the normal reading of the cross so that it is 'the hour' of Jesus' glory.[55] The resurrection of Jesus is an overturning of the verdict of the cross in both a political and religious sense.

One of the keynotes of the presentation of Jesus' death is the stress on kingship. This theme obviously relates in the Jewish context to the Messiah but it is surprising that the most sustained discussion of the kingship of Jesus occurs in dialogue with the Roman authorities. In a narrative some things only become clear from the vantage point of the end and it is suggested that this is the case with respect to the trial and death of Jesus. The clearly posed choice offered to the Jews between their 'King' and Caesar underlines the implicit comparison and contrast that has been made throughout the Gospel between the figure of Jesus and the Roman emperor.

It has been noted that, at various points, the σημεῖα narratives contain features that might conceivably create a resonance with the activities of various emperors or with their general role.[56] Other phrases and concepts occur at various points in the narrative that also appear to resonate with the language and ideology of the imperial cult.[57] As Jesus is raised on the cross, it

---

[54] Neyrey 1995b: 125.

[55] Neyrey 1995b: 126.

[56] These features have included some correspondences with healings reported to have been performed by Vespasian as well as the presentation of Jesus as a benefactor in the feeding signs.

[57] Such features include the acclamation of Jesus as 'truly the saviour of the world' (4.42); the entry into Jerusalem (MacCormack 1972: 723); the later reference to Jesus as Lord and God (20.29); and the references to ζωή, εἰρήνη, λόγος and ἀρχή (see below). Cf. C.R. Koester (1990), Cassidy (1992), Tilborg (1996: 165–219), and Van Den Heever (1998: 660–667) for further details and discussion.

is clear that, according to John, he is enthroned as a King. In the trial and death of Jesus, the implicit presentation of Jesus in imperial terms comes into focus. These hints and echoes are gathered together into a portrait that sees Jesus portrayed in terms reminiscent of the Emperors of Rome and at the same time providing an alternative. This is a significant presentation in view of the growing popularity of the imperial cult throughout the first century.

The presence and prevalence of imperial worship has been clearly established. In one of the more significant works in this area, Price shows that the presence of the imperial cult would have been encountered wherever one travelled in the empire in the form of rituals, statues and festivals.[58] The importance of the cult is increasingly acknowledged in the Eastern Empire as a means of both maintaining and negotiating Roman Imperial power.

The important observation for the study of the Fourth Gospel is not so much the religious practices associated with the cult as the ideology or world view promoted concerning the Emperor and the Roman Empire that was intimately connected with it.[59] This was structured and maintained by the way that the cult was very much embedded in the fabric of everyday life. This ideology was encountered in the praises of historians and poets, the coins handled in every day commerce, the structures of Roman taxation and government, and civic inscriptions. These combined to present an ideology that spoke of sovereign power akin to the divine, exercised through the Imperial office, upon which depended the well being of society.[60]

Two foundational elements to this 'structuring' are the apotheosis of the Emperor and the complex web of beliefs that were expressed concerning the Augustan achievements in creating the empire. While the extent of divine honours paid Julius Caesar during his life is disputed, there is no doubt concerning the fact that following his death he was seen as raised to the level of deity (cf. *SIG* III.760; *SEG* XIV.474; see also Cicero *Phil.* 1.110; Suet, *Jul.* 76.1). While a long history of veneration of individuals in the Greek east

---

[58] Price 1984a: 2. He has maps with the distribution of temples, theatres and inscriptions on pp. xxi-xxvi. The map is a collation of sites over time so the distribution and presence in the late first century is not clear. Mitchell (1993: 100), writing about Anatolia, comments that 'The diffusion of the cult of Augustus and of other members of his family in Asia Minor and throughout the Greek east from the beginning of the Empire was rapid, indeed almost instantaneous'. See also the survey by Winter (1994: 93–103). From the point of view of the Fourth Gospel it is interesting to note the large amount of evidence for the long term presence of the cult in Ephesus, Tilborg (1996: 174–212). Imperial presence and the associated cult would have been a shared and prevalent reality.

[59] According to Price (1984a: 248), the symbolism of the cult not only 'evoked a picture of the relationship between the emperor and the gods, but [it] was also structuring; it imposed a definition of the world. The imperial cult, along with politics and diplomacy, constructed the reality of the Roman Empire'. See also Alistair Kee (1985: 114–8).

[60] Carter (2000: 38-40)

made such a move 'natural' there was some reluctance in Rome to accord
divine honours to individuals until after their death.[61] However, the apotheosis
of Julius made it possible for Augustus to be spoken of as the Son of God
(*P.Oxy* 1453 1. 11; *OGIS* 655.2), as were many subsequent Emperors.

The Imperial ideology mainly drew on Augustan mythology that suggested
that the dawn of a new era had occurred with the advent of the Augustan
dynasty.[62] In his person, Augustus combined both secular and religious roles
of leadership, providing in his person and rule peace and stability following
the difficult days of the end of the Republic. This is celebrated in poetry and
inscription.[63] Fears argues that with the aid of the imperial cult a myth of
supernatural character was also formed that supplied 'an image of the ruler as
the visible embodiment of cosmic order, divinely ordained to ensure the
prosperity of the human race'.[64] This was reinforced in Stoic circles where the
emperor was seen as the embodiment of the divine logos.[65]

Two key features of this new era were life and peace. The sense of a new
beginning to life itself is reflected famously in the inscriptions erected by the
Council of Asia celebrating the birthday of Augustus.[66] In these inscriptions,
the calendar is conformed to the birth of Augustus, which is described as
initiating the beginning of all things. Consequently, his birthday is marked as
the beginning of good news for the world. Augustus is further described as the
source of all good things and a giver of life. 'Therefore (perhaps) each person
would justly consider that this (event) has been for himself the beginning of
life and of living (ἀρχὴν τοῦ βίου καὶ τῆς ζωῆς), which is the limit and

---

[61] At the funeral of the emperor their soul was believed to ascend to heaven as their body
burned. It had to be 'witnessed' and then the senate decreed the Emperor as *divus*. In time an
eagle was released from a cage atop the burning funeral pyre to symbolise the ascent of the
Emperor's soul to the gods (Herodian *Hist.* 4.1–11; Lucian *Peregr.* 39).

[62] Klauck (2000: 301) almost spares his readers a chapter on the imperial cult when he
states that he could almost be contented with the assessment of Taeger that the model
provided by Augustus 'remained determinative for the external form given to the imperial
cult for about three hundred years'.

[63] Expressions of this ideology are seen famously in Virgil's writings. In the fourth
Eclogue Augustus' birth is spoken of in what might be called messianic terms. Virgil writes
of how the 'great line of centuries begins anew' (*Ecl.* 4.5), the earth will be released from its
continuing dread and the child to be born will have the gift of divine life and will rule a world
to which peace has been brought. Though originally referring to the child of Antony and
Octavia, by the time that Virgil had written the Aeneid and come into the orbit of Octavian
the child of the poem was identified as Augustus (*Aen.* 6.791–94; cf also *Georg.* 1.24–42).

[64] Fears 1981a: 9. His interest is primarily in the role of Jupiter in the construction of this
myth.

[65] See the discussion by Chesnut (1978) who suggests that in Roman political theory a
widespread and important tradition developed that saw the emperor as the embodiment or
agent or representative on earth of the Law or Reason or Logos of God. See especially his
exposition of Plutarch (1321–4). Cf. Brent (1999: 44–50).

[66] Ehrenberg & Jones (1976) § 98.

end of regret at having been born'.[67] This picture is reflected in the comments of others as well within the empire. Philo expresses similar language and hopes in his approach to Gaius. While critical of Gaius he is expansive concerning Augustus (*Legat.* 143–7),

> the whole human race exhausted by mutual slaughter was on the verge of utter destruction, had it not been for one man and leader Augustus whom men fitly call the averter of evil. This is the Caesar who calmed the torrential storms on every side, who healed the pestilences common to the Greeks and barbarians...This is he who not only loosed but broke the chains, which had shackled and pressed so hard on the habitable world...(144–5, trans. F.Colson).

Suetonius (*Aug.* 98.2) describes the scene as Augustus sailed past Puteoli,

> it happened that from an Alexandrian ship...the passengers and crew, clad in white, crowned with garlands and burning incense, lavished upon him good wishes and the highest praise, saying that it was through him they lived...and through him they enjoyed their liberty and their fortunes (trans. J.C. Rolfe).[68]

This golden age was not only marked by life but also by peace.[69] Augustus in his *Res Gestae* refers to the fact during his reign the doors to the temple of Janus were closed three times, an event that was only supposed to occur in times of peace (*Res Gest. divi Aug.* 13). An altar, the Ara Pacis, was erected to him and the iconography on this altar celebrates the return of a golden age marked by peace amongst other blessings. Inscriptions that have been found in a number of cities in Asia Minor celebrate a time of peace that is an end to all war (Ehrenberg & Jones § 98.b. 1. 36), while in Halicarnassus Augustus is lauded as the saviour of the human race (σωτῆρα τοῦ κο[ι|ν]οῦ τῶν ἀνθρώπων γένους [Ehrenberg & Jones § 98a]).

The Augustan ideology was inherited and exploited by later emperors. Gaius is accused of taking the imperial claims to divinity a little too seriously by Philo (*Legat.* 93–97; 162; 357). Seneca lauds Nero in terms reminiscent of Augustus (*De Clem* 1.1.2). Vespasian's own rule is stabilised by a series of

---

[67] Trans. Sherk (1984: § 101.iv 9–11); Ehrenberg & Jones § 98.

[68] Seneca (*Polyb.* 7.4) also points in this direction. He also describes Nero as the arbiter of life and death (*Clem.* 1.1.2; 1.26.5). Aristides represents the high point of this adulation in his oration concerning Rome which is riddled with praise for Rome (and by extension) the emperor's role in bringing order, peace and life to a troubled world: 'one would suppose that before your empire everything was in confusion, topsy-turvy, and completely disorganized, but that when you took charge, the confusion and faction ceased and there entered in universal order and a glorious light in life and government and the laws came to the fore and the altars of the gods were believed in' (*Eul.* 103, trans. C.A. Behr) He lauds the benefits of Roman rule as including justice (31–39), absence of envy and hatred (65), presence of order (81, 87), material gifts and security (98, 100).

[69] Wengst (1987) has an extensive examination of the *Pax Romana*.

signs as well as by trading on the divine implications of his person (Tacitus, *Hist.*; 1.3; 1.10; 2.73–81; 4.3; 4.81; cf. also Suetonius, *Vesp.* 5.2–6; Cassius Dio, *Hist.* 64.9.1; 65.1.2–4, 8.1–2; Josephus *B.J.* 1.23; 4.263; 3.401–4).[70] Josephus associates the rise of Vespasian (and the Romans) with the manifest will of God (*B.J.* 2.390–1; 4.622; 5.368, 378). There is also the suggestion in Revelation 13.13–15 that signs or miracles were manufactured in the service of the promotion of the imperial cult.[71] Finally, it appears clear that Domitian aggressively pursued the divine implications of the imperial cult during his rule. Suetonius, *Domit.* 13.1–2 records Domitian being addressed as 'Lord and God'. Martial (*Epig.* 5.5; 7.5.1–6; 3.4.8–9; 8.2.6–7; 8.2.1–5; 9.28.7–8; 66.3–4) and Statius (*Silv.* 3.4.20; 4.2.14) provide abundant evidence for Domitian's titles and status.[72]

It is difficult to assess how the emperor was viewed with respect to his divinity and what this actually meant for participants in the cult. However, the presence of a strong web of belief around his person and the connecting of him with the advent of the golden age of the empire, and its maintenance, seems certain. It would have been difficult for any person living in the late first century to be unaware of the claims of the empire and the position of the emperor, if not amongst the gods, then certainly as a major mediator of the benefits of life and peace.

As a rival to the imperial figure, Jesus promises and in his signs demonstrates he can deliver life and peace. However, he is crucified in a manner that is reserved for slaves and for insurrectionists. He dies a political death, which must also have had religious implications. The cross proclaimed the triumph of Rome and her gods. It proclaimed the powerful control that Rome had over life and death for her enemies. All would-be kings and gods were subject to her control as represented in this public and humiliating method of execution.

Jesus is enthroned as king on the cross subverting ideas of kingship and demonstrating in graphic fashion that his kingship is truly not of this world. He rises from death and proves the superiority of his kingship and the programme he represents. Even the great Domitian is helpless in the face of death as Statius suggests while lamenting the death of the Secretary of State's wife.[73] Jesus has already raised a friend from death and will, himself, not be

---

[70] K. Scott (1975: 25–32) has an extensive discussion.

[71] Though this is speculative; see Scherrer (1984) and Bauckham (1993a: 17).

[72] Domitian is described by Statius as the ruler of the waves and earth (*Theb.* 1.31; cf. *Silv.* 4.2.14), a friend to peace and a bringer of joy (4.3.134–5). K. Scott (1933: 259) suggests that Statius' *Silvae* is a 'veritable repertoire of the forms and characteristic ideas of the Roman imperial cult'

[73] Statius, *Silv.* 5.1: 'Is there the aught that Caesar may not do? What tarrying could there have come to mortal lives, if thou, O Sire, hadst been all-powerful! far away would Death be groaning, imprisoned in the unseeing pit' (trans. J.A. Mozley).

removed by death since he rises. Consequently his supporters need not fear Roman power, need not be cowed by Augustan ideology, and ought not be seduced by the everyday fabric of the cult that proclaimed an inferior rival to the God and Father revealed in Jesus Christ. They are to remain friends of Jesus and not desire to become Caesar's friend.

For many in the Graeco-Roman world the idea of a bodily resurrection was a fantastic notion and against nature (Plutarch *Rom.* 28.4, 7–8). John's narrative leaves few alternatives to consider. The development of a Hero cult demanded that the body stay in the tomb and the hero's power was localised around that site.[74] The resurrection appearances show that Jesus' tomb has been decisively emptied. It is not a translation story. The stories of people who disappeared, or were translated to other locations either on or under earth or in heaven, did not normally have a tomb because they did not need one. To be translated was to avoid death altogether.[75] A man of great virtue might join the gods (Cicero *Rep.* 2.17; Sir. 45.4–5), while others would be reincarnated. The funeral pyre burned the body away so the immortal part could ascend to the Gods (Apollodorus, *Bib.* 2.7.7; Lucian *Hermot.* 7; cf. *Peregr.* 4, 6, 30, 33).

The Johannine narrative suggests none of these options. This is an extraordinary occurrence and the ambiguity concerning the nature of Jesus' body makes it all the more peculiar. One thing is clear though. A crucified body has come back to life.

6.4 Summary

It has been noted that many of the themes concerning the signs in the first half of the Gospel have been maintained in the two clusters of references to works in the farewell discourses. The signs of Jesus, insofar as they are included within the designation of works, are set before the disciples and commended as leading them to belief. They will continue therefore to help the disciples maintain their belief in Jesus. The identification of the Father and the Son has been emphasised also in Jesus' statement that in his works he and the Father are seen and if they are rejected then both he and the Father are hated (15.24). So, the signs play an important role in rendering those that see them without excuse for their rejection of Jesus. As well as manifesting the life that Jesus brings the signs also play a part in the judgement that is the dark consequence of his mission.

The final mention of σημεῖον in the Gospel occurs at a highly significant point as a purpose statement for the whole Gospel is laid out. The forensic

---

[74] Bolt 1996: 32–3.
[75] Bolt 1996: 34–7.

connotations continue to be a factor in the Gospel's use as again the plurality of signs is referred to. The reader is reminded that there is sufficient evidence for the claims made concerning Jesus to inspire the appropriate response of belief.

The relationship between this final culminating sign and the previous signs mentioned in the Gospel is recursive. The death and resurrection of Jesus relies on the insights imparted by the other signs for its impact. In these signs the identity of Jesus as the divine Messiah has been hinted at and patiently built up as this truth has been stated and explored from a number of angles. At the same time, the life-giving mission of Jesus has also been graphically illustrated by the material nature of the signs themselves. Hints have also been noted that suggest that there is a subtle critique in the sign narratives of other would be life givers.

These signs need, however, the final fulfilment of the death and resurrection of Jesus to complete the portrait they have painted. The signs that Jesus performed have been noted as increasingly indicating that their reference is to him personally. Now in the death and resurrection this is realised as Jesus is the sign—he is lifted up in the death and resurrection and declared to be Lord and God; those who look to him will find life.

The whole narrative has been shaped to highlight the significance of the moment where Jesus is lifted up. The Gospel now continues this lifting up of Jesus before all who will read it in the hope that they be drawn to the Son of God and enjoy life.

Chapter 7

Conclusions

It is appropriate at this point to take some account of the insights gained by this study of the rhetorical impact of σημεῖα in the Gospel according to John and to reflect a little more widely on issues that have arisen from this pursuit. The study was initially undertaken on the basis that the prominence of the term σημεῖον in the Fourth Gospel poses questions as to the reasons for its choice and also invites ongoing reflection concerning its function in the gospel narrative and its rhetorical impact. In order to approach these questions an audience-oriented narrative analysis (text-to-reader) was combined with an examination of aspects of the audience's cultural repertoire (reader-to-text) that appeared to relate to vocabulary and situations portrayed in the text of the Gospel.

From the point of view of 'text-to-reader', seventeen occurrences of the word σημεῖον were examined together with the narratives designated by the term. The network of understanding created by the seventeen occurrences of σημεῖον provides the broad, general framework within which the individual narratives are to be read. Links between the terms σημεῖον and ἔργον were also noted and the relationship of these terms to the trial motif that is prominent in the Gospel narrative was explored at length. The σημεῖα narratives were examined for the way in which they align the reader with the situations portrayed in them and also alert the reader to the significance of these events in the wider context and themes of the Gospel.

From the point of view of 'reader-to-text', the use of the term σημεῖον in the broader cultural context was surveyed. It was noted that while it had a wide range of use, there was a considerable history of use in religious contexts. A further use of the word, denoting a soft kind of proof, was noted in persuasive or argumentative contexts. This use was also noted in rhetorical texts, which suggested that it was also known in legal contexts. Both of these connotations are exploited in the argument of the Gospel. The specific situations and vocabulary of the sign narratives were also examined for possible resonance in the broader cultural context.

The findings of this study may be summarised under the headings of the following two sections.

7.1 σημεῖα in the Fourth Gospel

The investigation revealed a rich, multi-faceted perspective on the σημεῖα in the Fourth Gospel. The σημεῖα are actions, performed by Jesus, that attest his identity as the divine Messiah, who is sent by the Father to bring life to the world. They are an essential part of the Gospel's presentation and the cumulative weight of their presentation is intended to prompt a response of faith in Jesus by the reader. This presentation is reinforced by being embedded in the context of an extended trial metaphor that is predominant in the Gospel's narrative. The signs form an important part of the testimony to the truth of Jesus' claims concerning himself in this trial. This was reinforced in the narrative through the association of σημεῖον with ἔργον, a term which is prominent in the trial motif throughout the Gospel. A positive believing response to the revelation of the Son in his signs secures a judgement that leads to life. However, this aspect of the Gospel's presentation meant that the signs also functioned as part of the lawsuit conducted by God against the κόσμος and provided clear grounds on which a negative verdict might be rendered on the culpable rejection of the Son. In this sense the σημεῖα have the same effects as the words of Jesus and Jesus himself. There is a perfect unity amongst Jesus' person, words and actions that makes any attempt to prioritise word or deed over one another unintelligible.

The general references to σημεῖον in the context of the trial motif create the broader context within which the σημεῖα narratives are to be read. From a literary and rhetorical perspective, the σημεῖα narratives are a collection of cumulative proofs in the trial conducted with respect to the reader. In each of them the divine glory of Jesus is revealed. The placement and function of the signs follows the contours of the narrative.

The initial two signs begin by attesting the identity of Jesus in the opening four chapters of the Gospel and then four of the following five σημεῖα become used in a more 'aggressive' and symbolic fashion in a series of controversies with the Jews.

The signs and their accompanying discourses or dialogues test and sift the response to Jesus' ministry. In each of the sign narratives care is taken to align the reader sympathetically with the characters and situations involved so that the impact of the incidents is not only acknowledged but also felt. Jesus interacts with (extreme) examples of familiar situations of distress—sickness, blindness and terminal illness, situations of hunger and social embarrassment and finally death itself. The implications of his life-giving mission are graphically depicted in each of the sign narratives. They illustrate the significance of his work at the same time as they manifest its actual consequences. The desired response of faith is presented in each of the narratives, encouraging the reader to either make or affirm the same response.

The general references to σημεῖον and the σημεῖα narratives converge in their focus on the death and resurrection of Jesus, which is the climactic sign in the Gospel. This complex sign has been anticipated throughout the narrative and, in each of the preceding sign narratives, its significance has been foreshadowed. While there is a sense in which this event stands outside the sequence of narratives as their culmination, there is also an important sense in which it, too, is a sign that points to the truth of Jesus as the divine Messiah, sent by God to bring life to the κόσμος. The prominent themes of shepherd, lamb and king in the Passion Narratives point to this understanding. The understanding of Jesus as the sent life-giver is further emphasised by the resurrection narratives that show him breathing life into his disciples and sending them out to continue his mission. He is finally acclaimed in the confession that the whole Gospel has been anticipating as Thomas recognises his 'Lord and God' (20.29).

Finally, the σημεῖα invite an implicit comparison with rival would-be life-givers. This thread culminated, it was suggested, in an implicit comparison with the Roman emperor. The audience of the Gospel lived in a world full of gods. The presentation of the Son of God, the only one who has seen God, the unique Son of the Father, would have been controversial in a polytheistic society. Jesus is presented as the unique Son of the God of the Jews. This claim is controversial in both the Jewish monotheistic context and in the broader polytheistic context. It also constitutes a claim with implications for the whole of a culture where the religious and political are inextricably intertwined in the figure of the emperor and his significance as a religious and political figure for guaranteeing the good order of the empire. The signs point to the only true God worthy of worship and dependence—the only true king and the only true giver of life.

The σημεῖα function in the Gospel to identify Jesus as the divine Messiah, illustrate his mission as the true life-giver and provide a point of comparison and contrast with rivals.

7.2 σημεῖον and the Rhetorical Impact of the Fourth Gospel

The stated goal of the Gospel is to draw out from the reader a response of belief to the story of Jesus. In order to do this John has chosen a word that has resonance in a number of areas and placed it near to the heart of his presentation. The confluence of the two directions of approach to the Gospel investigated in this study enable the rhetorical impact of this well chosen term and the narratives it designates to be better appreciated.

First, the σημεῖα engage the reader at two levels. At a more cognitive level the presentation of Jesus' σημεῖα in the context of the forensic motif invites appraisal and evaluation of his deeds and claims. The general references to the ministry of Jesus as containing signs stressed their plurality and quality. The embedding of this language and the σημεῖα narratives in the forensic motif provides opportunity for a series of objections to be raised and refuted or rejected during the course of the narrative. In the sign narratives themselves there are often impartial witnesses that affirm the performing of the σημεῖα. The reader is drawn into the drama of the trial conducted before them and forced to make a decision on the evidence presented in the signs.

A second level of engagement is made possible through the σημεῖα narratives themselves. They not only provide the basis for that decision but also illustrate the significance of the decision made to embrace the only life-giving alternative. This decision is to be made continually as the reader encounters Jesus throughout the Gospel. The alignment of the reader with the individuals and situations portrayed enables the reader to enter the story at a more emotional and visceral level and feel the consequences of Jesus being the life giving Messiah as well as understand this concept.

Secondly, a point of entry into the gospel story is provided for a diverse audience to grasp and grow in the understanding of the twin perspectives that salvation is from the Jews and that Jesus is truly the saviour of the world.

The background use in the Hebrew Scriptures has been noted throughout as the σημεῖα attest the chosen representative of God. This use draws on the attesting function of the signs in the seminal exodus narratives and the prophetic narratives. On the larger scale, the role of the signs in alerting Israel, the enemies of God, and eventually the whole earth to the glory and reality of God is foundational for understanding the use of the term. The more symbolic function appears to draw on the sign narratives that cluster in the prophetic works. These operated as more than a visual aid to the prophets' message but had the nature of proclamation about them, sharing in the events they symbolically portrayed. In a similar fashion the σημεῖα in the Gospel do not just symbolise life but actually bring life. Finally the σημεῖα are also a feature of messianic expectation testifying to the Spirit-anointed one of Isaiah 11, 42, and 61 who would do things similar to the signs recorded in the Gospel and even be raised as a sign himself before the nations to collect the children of God. This gathered remnant would themselves be sent with signs to continue to gather the people of God from throughout the earth (Isa 66.19). In terms of the early audience, those familiar with the details of the presentation in the Hebrew Scriptures are well placed to appreciate the resonance and depth of understanding to the portrait of Christ presented.

The term σημεῖον provides an entry point for those without this wealth of background also to access the message of the Gospel. A wide audience is also enabled to grasp the function of the σημεῖον references in the narrative through its embedding in the forensic motif that is prominent in the Gospel's discourse. The term σημεῖον itself was seen to be amenable to this kind of usage in that it has a function of proof in rhetorical and therefore legal usage. It suggests a 'soft' kind of proof that may require an accumulation of such 'proofs' in order to make the point. It was noted that the continual indeterminate references to σημεῖα in the plural as well as the accumulation of narrated σημεῖα in the narrative both reflected this understanding and therefore contributed to the forensic motif in the Gospel. For the reader familiar with the more pagan notion of a sign that directly communicated information from the gods and requires an interpreter, this nuance and its setting within the forensic motif of the Gospel exerts a control on the understanding of the term and leads the reader gently in the right direction, while the dialogues and discourses provide a sense of interpretation for several of the signs.

In each σημεῖον narrative the connotations of the sign in the wider cultural context reinforced the basic message of life offered. Each σημεῖον narrative presents Jesus as a giver of life. For those with the informed background described above, the signs would have been seen as tokens of the life indicating the advent of the Messiah. However, the compass of the signs was wide enough for the message of life, broadly speaking, to be appropriated quite widely through the culture. At the same time resonance was noted with other potential life-givers in the surrounding world. Jesus is presented as the unique giver of life. It was suggested that through the Gospel the figure of the Roman emperor emerged as a particular focus for this implicit comparison.

The signs of Jesus are of fundamental importance in the rhetorical strategy of the Fourth Gospel. It is only those who truly see the signs of Jesus who will come to believe. The author of the Gospel seeks to facilitate this true seeing, as far as it is possible humanly speaking, by presenting the signs persuasively and clearly. The community of faith will also continue to be fed by the signs of Jesus as he is presented in all his depth and glory in his words and works in John's account.

It is the negotiation between the conceptual background of the text and the cultural foreground of this diversity of audience that accounts for the prominence of this term in the Fourth Gospel. The language of σημεῖον bridges admirably the world behind the text and the world in front of the text. The usage is theologically reflective in that it draws on a term that is significant in the Hebrew Scriptures as outlined above. It is christologically focussed as the collocation of themes from the Hebrew Scriptures comes to a point in the portrayal of Jesus in the Fourth Gospel as the divine Messiah. Finally, the usage is audience aware. By emphasising the term σημεῖον with its connotations of proof and embedding it in the forensic motif of the Gospel access to faith in the Messiah of Israel is opened to a wide audience.

7.3 Thinking Further

In terms of previous research on the σημεῖα in the Fourth Gospel, this study has contributed at a broad level and at the level of detail. At the broad level the approach adopted has yielded a fresh and more integrated perspective on the role of the σημεῖα in the Fourth Gospel. As has been already suggested, previous research has tended to focus on the question of sources and their identification. The few studies that have not done this have considered the background, or use of the term, in isolation from the potential impact on the audience in front of the text.[1] This thesis contributes a much needed analysis of the σημεῖον language and narratives from a literary point of view. In particular the relationship between the general references to σημεῖον and the specific sign narratives has been explored at greater depth than before and the relationship between this strand of the Gospel's presentation and other narrative strands, especially the trial motif, further illuminates the integrated nature of the Gospel's narrative.

The combination of narrative analysis and socio-historical description in this study bridges the divide between the implied reader in the text and the early audience of the text. This has enabled a greater appreciation of the rhetorical impact of the Gospel's content and argument. The integrated perspective presented here takes into account the literary context of the language and narratives, their theological background and the cultural context into which they are communicated. This has enabled a rich analysis keeping in mind author, text and reader. This overall approach has demonstrated how the 'spiritual Gospel' also 'keeps its feet firmly on the ground' with respect to its audience, providing in the σημεῖα the resources for identifying the true life-giver in the midst of a world of death and competing alternatives.

There appears to be further scope for appreciating the rhetorical impact of other prominent vocabulary and themes in the study of the Fourth Gospel. One area where this might be pursued concerns the possible connection between the σημεῖον narratives and the world of magical practice. Many conditions in the ancient world were treated, and caused, by magical spells. Investigation into the resonance of the vocabulary and situations with this area might shed light on the absence of exorcisms in the Gospel, especially in the light of the strong 'name' theology of the Gospel and the importance of names in magical practice.

At a more detailed level, the relationship of the σημεῖα language and narratives was related to the prominent trial motif, further illuminating this important literary construct. This is an advance on previous studies that have either failed to pursue this connection or treated it in perfunctory fashion. At the same time, the importance of this motif through the Gospel is reinforced,

---

[1] See pp. 1–5.

strengthening its claim to be the major integrating motif of the Johannine presentation.[2] The connection of the signs to this theme, and their resulting role as witnesses to the identity of Jesus, shows that the value of the signs at an evidential level is not to be despised in favour of a more exotic spiritual/symbolic understanding. With respect to this forensic connection it also needs to be pointed out that in terms of specific research on the σημεῖα this study aligns itself with the more recent scholarship that sees no conflict between word and deed in the Gospel's presentation and views the relationship between sign and faith as positive.[3] However, the relationship between this perspective and the perspective of the Gospel that suggests that no one can 'read' the signs truly without the aid of the Spirit of God remains to be comprehensively enunciated.

The integration of elements of the sign narratives into the theme of comparison with the imperial cult makes an important contribution to the growing number of studies investigating the relationship between the Fourth Gospel and that cult.[4] At an even more detailed level, the presence of such a comparison raises the possibilities for further examination of the sayings concerning the ruler of the world (12.32; 14.30; 16.11) and the possible connections this has with the imperial cult. There may be further scope for investigating to what extent the figure of Caesar might be seen as a vehicle for portraying the Gospel's Christology by way of comparison and contrast. The polemical aspect to the presentation of the σημεῖα that has been discerned is worthy of further investigation in its own right. This has been prominent concerning the Gospel's approach to the Jews but there remains to be investigated this broader aspect of polemic, and its relationship to the Johannine view of the κόσμος.

This study has also contributed to thinking about characterisation in John. It has been stressed in this thesis that the characters in the sign narratives are a point of identification with respect to more than their response of faith to Jesus, although this is undoubtedly on view. The use of various techniques in the text to align the audience with their plight, together with the connections established in the broader cultural context shows that these characters depict real people in situations with which the audience could readily identify. Further thinking on Johannine characterisation ought to be broadened to include the insights that arise from the consideration of focalisation and audience alignment in the thesis.

Due to constraints of space and a broader interest, very little attention was paid to the possible relationship between the presentation of the signs in the Synoptics and John. If knowledge of the synoptic tradition can be assumed as

---

[2] As suggested in the comprehensive analysis by Lincoln (2000: see especially pp. 140-50).
[3] See for example Bittner (1987: 130-1), Johns and Miller (1994), Thompson (1988: 69-81).
[4] See for example Cassidy (1992), van den Heever (1998).

part of the repertoire of at least part of John's audience, then the implications for their 'hearing' of this language in both John and the Synoptics also remains to be explored.

7.4 Jesus: The True Life-Giver

The craft of John's narrative continues to be explored and appreciated, not only in its own right but also in terms of its persuasive impact. This study has contributed to this interest with respect to the σημεῖον language and narratives. John's aim is to convince his readers that Jesus is the divine Messiah of Israel. The term σημεῖον is essential to that purpose as John presents Jesus in his σημεῖα and arranges them in the overall context of his narrative to convince his audience of this fact. Not only is Jesus shown to be the divine Messiah but the implications are also demonstrated. He is repeatedly shown to be the only one who can bring life to the real world of the Gospel's audience—a world that is marked by death and full of false alternatives promising life. This is a message that remains relevant and it is from John's method of communication, remaining faithful to the background and content of the message and yet finding ways to connect that message with the contemporary audience, that those who wish to proclaim his message afresh can continue to learn.

Bibliography

1. Reference Works

ALEXANDER, P. H. *et al.* (eds.), 1999. *The SBL Handbook of Style for Ancient Near Eastern, Biblical, and Early Christian Studies* (Peabody, Mass.: Hendrickson).

BORING, M.E., K. BERGER, C. COLPE (eds.), 1995. *Hellenistic Commentary to the New Testament* (Nashville; Abingdon Press).

CLINES, D. J. A., 1997. *The Sheffield Manual for Authors & Editors in Biblical Studies* (Manuals 12; Sheffield: Sheffield Academic Press).

DANKER, F. W. (rev. & ed.), 2000. *A Greek-English Lexicon of the New Testament and other Early Christian Literature. Third Edition. BDAG* (based on Walter Bauer's *Griechisch-deutsches Wörterbuch zu den Schriften des Neuen Testaments und der frühchristlichen Literatur,* 6th edn, and on previous English editions by W.F. Arndt, F.W. Gringrich, and F.W. Danker; Chicago: University of Chicago Press, 3rd edn).

FUNK, R. (ed.), 1961. *A Greek Grammar of the New Testament and Other Early Christian Literature, F. Blass and A. Debrunner: A Translation and Revision of the ninth-tenth German edition incorporating supplementary notes of A. Debrunner* (Chicago: Chicago University Press).

HATCH, E. & H. A. REDPATH (eds.), 1998. *A Concordance to the Septuagint and the Other Greek Versions of the Old Testament (Including the Apocryphal Books)* (Introd. R.A Kraft & E. Tov; Hebrew/Aramaic index by Takamitsu Muraoka; Grand Rapids: Baker, 2nd edn).

HORNBLOWER, S. & A. SPAWFORTH (eds.), 1996. *The Oxford Classical Dictionary* (Oxford: Oxford University Press; 1996, 2nd edn).

LIDDELL, H. G. & R. SCOTT, 1996. *A Greek-English Lexicon* (rev. H.S. Jones, with R. McKenzie; rev. supp. edited by P.G.W. Clare with A.A. Thompson; Oxford: Clarendon Press, 1996, 9th edn).

LOUW, J. P. & E. A. NIDA (eds.), 1988. *Greek-English Lexicon of the New Testament Based on Semantic Domains* (2 vols.; New York: United Bible Societies).

SWANSON, R. (ed.), 1995. *New Testament Greek Manuscripts: Variant Readings Arranged in Horizontal Lines Against Codex Vaticanus: John* (Sheffield: Sheffield Academic Press).

WALLACE, D. B., 1996. *Greek Grammar Beyond the Basics. An Exegetical Syntax of the New Testament* (Grand Rapids: Zondervan, 1996).

2. Primary Sources

2.1 Biblical and Associated Texts

BRENTON, SIR L. C. L., 1998. The Septuagint with Apocrypha: Greek and English (Peabody, Mass.: Hendrickson, 1998).

CHARLESWORTH, J. C. (ed.), 1983, 1985. *The Old Testament Pseudepigrapha* (2 vols.; London: Darton, Longman & Todd).

ELLIGER, K & W. RUDOLPH (eds.), 1967/1977. *Biblia Hebraica Stuttgartensia* (rev. W. Rudolph & H.P. Rüger; Stuttgart: Deutsche Bibelgesellschaft, 3rd edn).

GARCIA MARTÍNEZ, F. & E. J. C. TIGCHELAAR (eds.), 1997-8. *The Dead Sea Scrolls Study Edition* (2 vols.; Leiden: Brill).

MARTIN V. & J. W. B. BARNS, 1962. *Papyrus Bodmer II, Supplément Evangile de Jean chap. 14-21. Nouvelle édition augmentée et corrigée avec reproduction photographique complète du manuscrit (chap 1-21)* (Cologny-Genève: Bibliotheca Bodmeriana).

NESTLE, E. & K. ALAND (eds.), 1993. *Novum Testamentum Graece* (Stuttgart: Deutsche Gesellschaft, 27th edn).

NEUSNER, J., 1985. *Genesis Rabbah: The Judaic Commentary to the Book of Genesis. A New American Translation III Parashiyyot Sixty-Eight through One Hundred on Genesis 28.10 to 50.26* (Brown Judaic Studies 106; Atlanta: Scholars Press, 1985).

—, 1997. *The Components of the Rabbinic Documents From the Whole to the Parts X: Leviticus Rabbah II Parashiyyot Eighteen through Thirty Seven* (USF Academic Commentary Series 96; Atlanta: Scholars Press, 1997).

RAHLFS, A. (ed.), 1952. *Septuaginta* (2 vols; Stuttgart: Privilegierte Württembergische Bibelanstalt, 1952, 5th edn).

ZIEGLER, J., 1939. *Isaias* (Septuaginta Vetus Testamentum Graecum; Societatis Litteratum Gottingensis XIV; Göttingen: Vandenhoeck & Ruprecht, 1939).

2.2 *Graeco-Roman Literary Sources*

Achilles Tatius
S. GASELEE, *Achilles Tatius* (LCL; Cambridge, Mass. & London: Harvard University Press & W. Heinemann, 1917, rev. 1969, repr. 1984).

Aelian
A. F. SCHOLFIELD, *Aelian on the Characteristics of Animals II: Bks VI–XI* (LCL; Cambridge, Mass. & London: Harvard University Press & W. Heinemann, 1958, repr. 1971).

Aelius Aristides
C. A. BEHR, *P. Aelius Aristides. The Complete Works II. Orations XVII–LIII* (Leiden: Brill, 1981).

Aeschylus
H. W. SMYTH, *Aeschylus II: Agamemnon Libation-Bearers. Eumenides. Fragments* (LCL; Cambridge, Mass. & London: Harvard University Press & W. Heinemann, 1926, repr. 1983).

Anthologia Graeca
W. R. PATON, *The Greek Anthology V* (LCL; Cambridge, Mass. & London: Harvard University Press & W. Heinemann, 1918, repr. 1979).

Apollodorus
J. G. FRAZER, Apollodorus: The Library (LCL; 2 vols.; Cambridge, Mass. & London: Harvard University Press & W. Heinemann, 1921).

Apollonius Rhodius
R. C. SEATON, *Apollonius Rhodius, The Argonautica* (LCL; Cambridge, Mass. & London: Harvard University Press & W. Heinemann, 1912).

Appian
H. WHITE, *Appian's Roman History I* (LCL: Cambridge, Mass. & London: Harvard
    University Press & W. Heinemann, 1912).

Apuleius
J. A. HANSON, *Apuleius Metamorphoses I: Bks 1–6* (LCL; Cambridge, Mass. & London:
    Harvard University Press & W. Heinemann, 1989).

Aretaeus
F. ADAMS (ed.; trans.) *The Extant Works of Aretaeus the Cappadocian* (London: 1856).
K. HUDE, *Aretaeus*, in *Corpus medicorum Graecorum II* (Berlin: Akadamie-Verlag, 2nd edn.,
    1958).

Aristophanes
B. B. ROGERS, *Aristophanes I: The Acharnians. The Knights. The Clouds. The Wasps* (LCL;
    3 vols.; Cambridge, Mass. & London: Harvard University Press & W. Heinemann,
    1924).

Aristotle
W. S. HETT, *Aristotle On the Soul. Parva Naturalia. On Breath* (LCL; Cambridge, Mass. &
    London: Harvard University Press & W. Heinemann, 1936, rev. 1957).
H. P. COOKE & H. TREDENNICK, *Aristotle. The Categories of Interpretation. Prior Analytics*
    (LCL; Cambridge, Mass. & London: Harvard University Press & W. Heinemann,
    1938).
J. H. FREESE, *Aristotle. The "Art" of Rhetoric* (LCL; Cambridge, Mass. & London: Harvard
    University Press & W. Heinemann, 1926).

Artemidorus
R. J. WHITE, *The Interpretation of Dreams: Oneirocritica by Artemidorus* (trans. & comm.;
    Noyes Classical Studies: Park Ridge, N.J.: Noyes Press, 1975).

Athenaeus
C. B. GULICK, *Athenaeus, The Deipnosophists I* (LCL; 7 vols.; Cambridge, Mass. & London:
    Harvard University Press & W. Heinemann, 1927–41).

Chrysostom
P. SCHAFF (ed.), *St. Chrysostom, The Nicene and Post-Nicene Fathers Vol. 14* (Grand Rapids:
    Eerdmans, 1975).

Cicero
W. H. FALCONER, *Cicero. De senectute, De amicitia, De divinatione* (LCL: Cambridge,
    Mass. & London: Harvard University Press & W. Heinemann, 1923).
C. W. KEYS, *Cicero. De Republica. De Legibus* (LCL; London & New York: W. Heinemann
    & G.P. Putnam's Sons, 1928).
H. G. HODGE, *Cicero. The Speeches. Pro Lege Manilia. Pro Caecina. Pro Cluentio. Pro
    Rabirio Perduellionis* (LCL: Cambridge, Mass. & London: Harvard University Press
    & W. Heinemann, 1927).
L. H. G. GREENWOOD, *Cicero. The Verrine Orations I. Against Caecilius. Against Verres I,
    II.i, ii* (LCL: Cambridge, Mass. & London: Harvard University Press & W.
    Heinemann, 1928).

L. H. G. GREENWOOD, *Cicero. The Verrine Orations II. Against Verres II* (LCL: Cambridge, Mass. & London: Harvard University Press & W. Heinemann, 1935).

H. RACKHAM, *Cicero. De Finibus Bonorum et Malorum* (LCL: Cambridge, Mass. & London: Harvard University Press & W. Heinemann, 1914, 2nd edn 1931).

J. E. KING, *Cicero. Tusculan Disputations* (LCL: Cambridge, Mass. & London: Harvard University Press & W. Heinemann, 1927, rev. 1945).

R. GARDNER, *Cicero. The Speeches. Pro Sestio. In Vatinum* (LCL: Cambridge, Mass. & London: Harvard University Press & W. Heinemann, 1958).

Columella

H. BOYD et al., *Lucius Junius Moderatus Columella, On Agriculture I: Res Rustica I–IV* (LCL; 2 vols.; Cambridge, Mass. & London: Harvard University Press & W. Heinemann, 1941, 1954).

Demosthenes

J. H. VINCE, *Demosthenes I: Olynthiacs, Philippics Minor Public Speeches Speech Against Leptines I–XVII, XX* (LCL; Cambridge, Mass. & London: Harvard University Press & W. Heinemann, 1930).

C. A. VINCE & J. H. VINCE, *Demosthenes II: De Corona De Falsa Legatione XVIII, XIX* (LCL; Cambridge, Mass. & London: Harvard University Press & W. Heinemann, 1926).

A. T. MURRAY, *Demosthenes IV: Private Orations XXVII–XL* (LCL; Cambridge, Mass. & London: Harvard University Press & W. Heinemann, 1936).

A. T. MURRAY, *Demosthenes V: Private Orations XLI–XLIX* (LCL; Cambridge, Mass. & London: Harvard University Press & W. Heinemann, 1939).

A. T. MURRAY, *Demosthenes VI: Private Orations L–LVIII In Neaeram LIX* (LCL; Cambridge, Mass. & London: Harvard University Press & W. Heinemann, 1939).

Dio Cassius

E. CARY & H. B. FOSTER, *Dio's Roman History* (LCL; 9 vols.; Cambridge, Mass. & London: Harvard University Press & W. Heinemann, 1914–27).

Dio Chrysostom

J. W. COHOON et al., *Dio Chrysostom* (LCL; 5 vols.; Cambridge, Mass. & London: Harvard University Press & W. Heinemann, 1932–51).

Diodorus Siculus

C. H. OLDFATHER et al., *Diodorus of Sicily* (LCL; 12 vols.; Cambridge, Mass. & London: Harvard University Press & W. Heinemann, 1933–1967).

Diogenes Laertius

R. D. HICKS, *Diogenes Laertius, Lives of Eminent Philosophers* LCL; 2 vols.; Cambridge, Mass. & London: Harvard University Press & W. Heinemann, 1925).

Dionysius of Halicarnassus

E. CARY & E. SPELMAN, *The Roman Antiquities of Dionysius of Halicarnassus* (LCL; 7 vols.; Cambridge, Mass. & London: Harvard University Press & W. Heinemann, 1937–1950).

Dioscorides

M. WELLMAN, *Pedanii Dioscuridis Anazarbei de materia medica libri quinque* (3 vols.; Berlin: Weidmann, 1907–1914).

Epictetus
W. A. OLDFATHER, *Epictetus. The Discourses as Reported by Arrian, the Manual, and Fragments* (LCL; 2 vols.; Cambridge, Mass. & London: Harvard University Press & W. Heinemann, 1925, 1928).

Euripides
A. S. WAY *et al.*, *Euripides* (LCL; 3 vols.; Cambridge, Mass. & London: Harvard University Press & W. Heinemann, 1912–2002).

Herodian
C. R. WHITTAKER, *Herodian* (LCL; 2 vols.; Cambridge, Mass. & London: Harvard University Press & W. Heinemann, 1969, 1970).

Herodotus
A. D. GODLEY, *Herodotus* (LCL; 4 vols.; Cambridge, Mass. & London: Harvard University Press & W. Heinemann, 1920–1925).

Hippocrates
W. H. S. JONES *et al.*, *Hippocrates* (LCL; 6 vols.; Cambridge, Mass. & London: Harvard University Press & W. Heinemann, 1923–1988).

Homer
A. T. MURRAY, *Homer, The Iliad* (LCL; 2 vols.; Cambridge, Mass. & London: Harvard University Press & W. Heinemann, 1924, 1925).
A. T. MURRAY, Homer, *The Odyssey* (LCL; 2 vols.; Cambridge, Mass. & London: Harvard University Press & W. Heinemann, 1919).

Horace
C.E. BENNETT, *The Odes and Epodes* (LCL: Cambridge, Mass. & London: Harvard University Press & W. Heinemann, 1914, rev. 1968).

Josephus
H. ST. J. THACKERAY, *et al.*, *Josephus* (LCL; 10 vols; Cambridge, Mass. & London: Harvard University Press & W. Heinemann, 1927–1965).

Justin Martyr
A. CLEVELAND COXE, *The Apostolic Fathers with Justin Martyr and Irenaeus. American Edition. Chronologically arranged, with Brief Notes and Prefaces* (Anti-Nicene Fathers I; Edinburgh & Grand Rapids: T&T Clark; Eerdmans, repr. 1989).

Juvenal
G. G. Ramsay, *Juvenal and Persius* (LCL; Cambridge, Mass. & London: Harvard University Press & W. Heinemann, 1918, rev. 1940).

Livy
E. T. SAGE, *Livy XI: Bks XXXVIII–XXXIX* (LCL; Cambridge, Mass. & London: Harvard University Press & W. Heinemann, 1936, repr. 1949).

Lucian
A. M. HARMON, *Lucian* (LCL; 8 vols.; Cambridge, Mass. & London: Harvard University Press & W. Heinemann, 1913–1967).

Martial

D. R. SHACKLETON BAILEY, *Martial. Epigrams* (LCL; 3 vols.; Cambridge, Mass. & London: Harvard University Press & W. Heinemann, 1993).

Menander

F. G. ALLISON, *Menander. The Principal Fragments* (LCL; London & New York: W. Heinemann & G.P. Putnam's Sons, 1921, rev. 1930).

Nonnus

W. H. D. ROUSE, *Nonnus* (LCL; 3 vols.; Cambridge, Mass. & London: Harvard University Press & W. Heinemann, 1940).

Pausanius

W. H. S. JONES, *Pausanias: Description of Greece* (LCL; 4 vols.; Cambridge, Mass. & London: Harvard University Press & W. Heinemann, 1918–1935).

Petronius

M. HESELTINE & E. H. WARMINGTON, *Petronius*; W.H.D. Rouse, *Apocolocyntosis* (LCL; Cambridge, Mass. & London: Harvard University Press & W. Heinemann, 1913, rev. 1969).

Philo

F. H. COLSON & G. H. WHITAKER, *Philo* (LCL: 10 vols.; Cambridge, Mass. & London: Harvard University Press & W. Heinemann, 1929, repr. 1981).
R. MARCUS, *Philo: Supplement I: Questions and Answers on Genesis* (LCL Cambridge, Mass. & London: Harvard University Press & W. Heinemann, 1953, repr. 1961).

Philostratus

F. C. CONYBEARE, *Philostratus: The Life of Apollonius of Tyana. The Epistles of Apollonius and the Treatise of Eusebius* (LCL: 2 vols.; Cambridge, Mass. & London: Harvard University Press & W. Heinemann, 1912).

Pindar

J. SANDYS, *The Odes of Pindar Including the Principal Fragments* (LCL: Cambridge, Mass. & London: Harvard University Press & W. Heinemann, 1914, rev. 1919, rev. 1937).
A. B. DRACHMANN, *Scholia Vetera in Pindari Carmina II. Scholia in Pythionicas.* (Leipzig: Teubner, 1905).

Plato

R. G. BURY, *Plato, Timaeus. Critias. Cleitophon, Menexenus. Epistles* (LCL: Cambridge, Mass. & London: Harvard University Press & W. Heinemann, 1929).
P. SHOREY, *Plato, The Republic I: Books. I–V* (LCL; Cambridge, Mass. & London: Harvard University Press & W. Heinemann, 1930, rev. 1937).

Plautus

P. NIXON, *Plautus: Casina, The Casket Comedy, Curculio, Epiducus, The Two Menaechmuses* (LCL: Cambridge, Mass. & London: Harvard University Press & W. Heinemann, 1917).

Pliny

H. RACKHAM *et al., Pliny, Natural History* (LCL; 10 vols.; Cambridge, Mass. & London: Harvard University Press & W. Heinemann, 1938–1962).

Plutarch
B. PERRIN, *Plutarch's Lives* (LCL; 11 vols.; Cambridge, Mass. & London: Harvard University Press & W. Heinemann, 1914–1926).
F.C. BABBITT *et al.*, *Plutarch's Moralia* (LCL; 16 vols.; Cambridge, Mass. & London: Harvard University Press & W. Heinemann, 1927–1976).

Propertius
G. P. GOOLD, Propertius. *Elegies* (LCL: Cambridge, Mass. & London: Harvard University Press, 1990).

Quintilian
D. A. RUSSELL, *Quintilian, The Orator's Education: Books 3–5* (LCL; 5 vols.; Cambridge, Mass. & London: Harvard University Press, 2001).

Rhetorica ad Herrenium
H. CAPLAN, [Cicero] *Rhetorica ad Herennium* (LCL: Cambridge. Mass. & London: Harvard University Press, 1954).

Scriptores Historiae Augustae
D. MAGIE, *The Scriptores Historiae Augustae I* (LCL; Cambridge, Mass. & London: Harvard University Press & W. Heinemann, 1921).

Seneca
M. HESELTINE & E. H. WARMINGTON, Petronius; W. H. D. ROUSE, *Apocolocyntosis* (LCL; Cambridge, Mass. & London: Harvard University Press & W. Heinemann, 1913, rev. 1969).
F. J. MILLER, *et al.*, Seneca (LCL; 10 vols.; Cambridge, Mass. & London: Harvard University Press & W. Heinemann, 1917–2002).

Sextus Empiricus
R. G. BURY, *Sextus Empiricus* (LCL; 4 vols.; Cambridge, Mass. & London: Harvard University Press & W. Heinemann, 1933–1949).

Silius Italicus
J. D. DUFF, *Silius Italicus, Punica I* (LCL: Cambridge, Mass. & London: Harvard University Press & W. Heinemann, 1927).

Sophocles
F. STORR, *Sophocles: Oedipus the King. Oedipus at Colonus. Antigone* (LCL; 2 vols.; Cambridge, Mass. & London: Harvard University Press & W. Heinemann, 1912, 1913).

Strabo
H. L. JONES, *The Geography of Strabo* (LCL; 8 vols.; Cambridge, Mass. & London: Harvard University Press & W. Heinemann, 1917–1932).

Statius
J. A. MOZLEY, *Statius I: Silvae, Thebaid I–IV* (LCL; Cambridge, Mass. & London: Harvard University Press & W. Heinemann, 1928).

Suetonius
J. C. ROLFE, *Suetonius* (LCL; 2 vols.; Cambridge, Mass. & London: Harvard University Press
& W. Heinemann, 1913, 1914).

Tacitus
M. HUTTON & R. M OGILVIE, *Agricola*; M. HUTTON & E. H. WARMINGTON, *Germania*; W.
PETERSON & M. WINTERBOTTOM, *Dialogus; Tacitus I*, (LCL: Cambridge, Mass. &
London: Harvard University Press & W. Heinemann, 1914, rev. 1970).
C. H. MOORE & J. JACKSON, *The Histories and the Annals* (LCL; 4 vols. Cambridge, Mass. &
London: Harvard University Press & W. Heinemann, 1925–1937).

Thucydides
C. F. SMITH, *Thucydides I: History of the Peloponnesian War Books I & II* (LCL:
Cambridge, Mass. & London: Harvard University Press & W. Heinemann, 1919,
rev. 1928).

Virgil
H. RUSHTON FAIRCLOUGH, *Virgil* (LCL; 2 vols.; Cambridge, Mass. & London: Harvard
University Press & W. Heinemann, 1999, 2000 rev. repr.).

2.3 Other Primary Sources

BEARD, M. et al. (eds.), 1998. *Religions of Rome. Volume 2. A Sourcebook* (Cambridge:
Cambridge University Press).
BETZ, H. D., 1992. *The Greek Magical Papyri in Translation: Including the Demotic Spells
I: Texts with an Updated Bibliography* (Chicago: University of Chicago Press, 2nd
edn.).
BROWNE, G. M. et al., 1972. *The Oxyrhynchus Papyri XLI* (London: Egypt Exploration
Society, 1972).
BÜCHELER, F., 1897. *Carmina Epigraphica Latina* (Leipzig: Teubner, 1897, repr. 1921).
CONSTANTINIDES, E., 1969. 'A Private Letter from Oxyrhynchus', *Chronique D'Égypte*
44.87: 101–105.
COTTER, W., 1999. *Miracles in Greco-Roman Antiquity. A Sourcebook for the Study of New
Testament Miracle Stories* (London: Routledge, 1999).
DITTENBERGER, W., 1982. *Sylloge Inscriptionum Graecarum* (4 Vols.; New York: Georg
Olms, orig. published 1915).
——— 1903-5. *Orientis Graeci Inscriptiones Selectae* (Leipzig: Hirzel, 1903–5).
EHRENBERG, V. & A. H. M. JONES, 1976. *Documents Illustrating the Reigns of Augustus and
Tiberius* (Oxford: The Clarendon Press· 2nd edn.).
FRIEDRICH, C. et al., 1906. *Inschriften von Priene* (Berlin: Georg Reimer).
GRANT, F. C. (ed.), 1953. *Hellenistic Religions: The Age of Syncretism* (The Library of
Liberal Arts 134; New York: The Liberal Arts Press).
GRENFELL, B. P. & A. S. HUNT, 1898 *The Oxyrhynchus Papyri I* (London: Egypt Exploration
Society).
—, 1915. *The Oxyrhynchus Papyri XI* (London: Egypt Exploration Society).
—, 1916. *The Oxyrhynchus Papyri XII* (London: Egypt Exploration Society).
—, 1920. *The Oxyrhynchus Papyri XIV* (London: Egypt Exploration Society).
HAGEDORN, U. et al., 1969. *Das Archiv des Petaus* (Papyrologia Coloniensia IV; Köln &
Opladen: Westdeutscher Verlag).
HONDIUS, J. J. et al., 1923. *Supplementum Epigraphicum Graecum* (Leyden: Sijthoff,
1923–>).

HORSLEY, G. H. R., 1981. *New Documents Illustrating Early Christianity 1: A Review of the Greek Inscriptions and Papyri published in 1976* (Macquarie University, Australia: The Ancient History Documentary Research Centre).

—, 1983. *New Documents Illustrating Early Christianity 3: A Review of the Greek Inscriptions and Papyri published in 1978* (Macquarie University, Australia: The Ancient History Documentary Research Centre).

—, 1987. *New Documents Illustrating Early Christianity 4: A Review of the Greek Inscriptions and Papyri published in 1979* (Macquarie University, Australia: The Ancient History Documentary Research Centre).

HUNT A. S. & C. C. EDGAR, 1932. *Select Papyri I: Non-Literary Papyri. Private Affairs* (LCL; Cambridge, Mass. & London: Harvard University Press & W. Heinemann, repr. 1959).

JOUGET, P. & O. GUÉRARD, 1933. 'Ostraca grecs d'Eléphantine', *Aegyptus* 13: 443–454.

KEYES, C. W., 1935. 'Four Private Letters from the Columbia Papyri', *Classical Philology* 30: 141–50.

KIRCHHOFF, A. et al., 1923. *Inscriptiones Graecae* (vols. i–xv; Berlin: Reimer, 1923–).

LATTIMORE, R., 1962. *Themes in Greek and Latin Epitaphs* (Urbana: University of Illinois Press).

LEWIS N. & M. REINHOLD, 1955. *Roman Civilization. Sourcebook II: the Empire* (New York: Harper & Row).

LIDONNICI, L. R., 1995. *The Epidaurian Miracle Inscriptions. Text, Translation and Commentary* (Atlanta: Scholars Press, 1995).

LIGHTFOOT, J. B. & J. R. HARMER (eds. & trans.), 1891. *The Apostolic Fathers. Greek Texts and English Translations of Their Writings* (rev. & ed. M.W. Holmes; Grand Rapids; Baker, rev. 1992).

LLEWELYN, S. R. & R. A. KEARSLEY, 1994. *New Documents Illustrating Early Christianity 7: A Review of the Greek Inscriptions and Papyri published in 1982–3* (Macquarie University, Australia: The Ancient History Documentary Research Centre).

MAGIE, D., 1905. *De Romanorum Juris Publici Sacrique Vocabulis Sollemnibus in Graecum Sermonem Conversis* (Leipzig: Teubner).

MEYER, M. W. (ed.), 1987. *The Ancient Mysteries A Sourcebook: Sacred Texts of the Mystery Religions of the Ancient Mediterranean World* (San Francisco: Harper & Row, 1987).

MOMMSEN, T. et al., 1862–1963. *Corpus Inscriptionum Latinarum* (Berlin: Reimer, 1862–1963).

MOULTON J. H. & G. MILLIGAN, 1930. *The Vocabulary of the New Testament Illustrated from the Papyri and Other Non-literary Sources* (London: Hodder & Stoughton).

NAVEH, J. & S. SHAKED, 1985. *Amulets and Magic Bowls. Aramaic Incantations of Late Antiquity* (Jerusalem: The Magnes Press).

SHERK, R. K. (ed. & trans.), 1984. *Rome and the Greek East to the Death of Augustus* (Translated Documents of Greece and Rome 4; Cambridge: Cambridge University Press).

—, 1988. *The Roman Empire: Augustus to Hadrian* (Translated Documents of Greece and Rome 6; Cambridge: Cambridge University Press).

STRACK, H. L. & P. BILLERBECK, 1924. *Kommentar zum Neuen Testament aus Talmud und Midrasch II. Das Evangelium nach Markus, Lukas und Johannes und die Apostelgeschichte* (Munich: C. Becksche Verlagsbuchhandlung (Oskar Beck), 1924).

VISSER, E., 1935. 'Briefe und Urkunden aus der berliner Papyrussammlung', *Aegyptus* 15: 267–76. (P. 16108).

WHITTAKER, M., 1984. *Jews & Christians: Graeco-Roman Views* (Cambridge: Cambridge University Press, 1984).
YOUTIE, H. C., 1970 'ΣΗΜΕΙΟΝ in the Papyri and Its Significance for Plato, Epistle 13 (360a – b)', *ZPE* 6: 105–116.

3. Secondary Literature

ANDERSON, P. N., 1996. *The Christology of the Fourth Gospel: Its Unity and Disunity in the Light of John 6* (WUNT 2.78; Tübingen: Mohr Siebeck).
ASHTON, J., 1991. *Understanding the Fourth Gospel* (Oxford: Clarendon Press).
1994. *Studying John: Approaches to the Fourth Gospel* (Oxford: Clarendon Press).
ASIEDU-PEPRAH, M., 2001. *Johannine Sabbath Conflicts as Juridical Controversy* (WUNT 2.132; Tübingen: Mohr Siebeck).
ATTRIDGE, H. W., 1978 'The Philosophical Critique of Religion under the Early Empire', *ANRW* 16.1: 45–78. Part 2, *Principat*, 16.1 (Edited by H. Temporini & W. Haase, New York: de Gruyter, 1978).
AUNE, D., 1980. 'Magic in Early Christianity', *ANRW* 23.2: 1507–57. Part 2, *Principat*, 23.2 (Edited by H. Temporini & W. Haase, New York: de Gruyter, 1980).
AURENHAMMER, M., 1995. 'Sculptures of Gods and Heroes from Ephesus' in H. Koester (ed.) 1995: 251–80.
BAL, M., 1983. 'The Narrating and the Focalizing: A Theory of the Agents in Narrative', *Style* 17.2: 234–69.
—, 1985. *Narratology: Introduction to the Theory of Narrative* (trans. C. van Boheemen; Toronto: University of Toronto Press, rev. edn).
BAMMEL, E., 1965. '"John did no miracle": John 10.41', in Moule 1965: 179–202.
BARNETT, P.W., 1981. 'The Jewish Sign Prophets - A.D. 40–70. Their Intentions and Origin', *NTS* 27: 679–97.
BARR, J., 1961. *The Semantics of Biblical Language* (Oxford: Oxford University Press).
BARRETT, C. K., 1947. 'John and the Old Testament', *JTS* 48: 155–69.
—, 1972. 'The Prologue of St. John's Gospel', in C. K. Barrett, *New Testament Essays* (London: SPCK, 1972): 27–48.
—, 1978. *The Gospel According to St John* (London: SPCK, 2ⁿᵈ edn).
BARTH, K., 1986. *Witness to the Word: A Commentary on John 1* (ed. W. Fürst; trans. G.W. Bromiley; Grand Rapids: Eerdmans).
BARTON, S., 1998, 'Can We Identify the Gospel Audiences?', in Bauckham 1998b: 173–94.
BAUCKHAM, R, 1985. 'The Son of Man: "A Man in My Position" or "Someone"?', 23–33.
—, 1993a. *The Theology of the Book of Revelation* (NTT; Cambridge: Cambridge University Press).
—, 1993b. 'The Beloved Disciple as Ideal Author', *JSNT* 49: 21–44.
—, 1993c. 'Papias and Polycrates on the Origin of the Fourth Gospel', *JTS* 44.1: 24–69.
—, 1998a. *God Crucified: Monotheism and Christology in the New Testament* (Grand Rapids: Eerdmans).
—, 1998b. *The Gospels for All Christians: Rethinking the Gospel Audiences* (R. Bauckham (ed.); Grand Rapids: Eerdmans).
—, 1998c. 'For Whom were the Gospels Written?' in Bauckham 1998b: 9–48.
—, 1998d. 'John for Readers of Mark', in Bauckham 1998b: 147–72.
—, 2002. 'Jewish Messianism according to the Gospel of John'. Paper presented at the Tyndale New Testament Study Group; Tyndale House, Cambridge, July 8–9, 2002.

BEARD, M. et al., 1998. *Religions of Rome Volume 1: A History* (Cambridge: Cambridge University Press).

BEASLEY-MURRAY, G. R., 1987. *John* (WBC 36; Waco: Word Books).

BECKER, J., 1969. 'Wunder und Christologie', *NTS* 16: 130–48.

BERLIN, A., 1983. *Poetics and Interpretation of Biblical Narrative* (Bible and Literature Series; Sheffield: The Almond Press).

BERNARD, J. H., 1928. *A Critical and Exegetical Commentary on the Gospel According to St John* (ICC; 2 vols.; Edinburgh: T&T Clark).

BETZ, O., 1974. 'Das Problem des Wunders bei Flavius Josephus im Vergleich zum Wunderproblem bei den Rabbinen und im Johannesevangelium', in O. Betz et al. (eds.), *Josephus-Studien: Untersuchungen zu Josephus dem antiken Judentum und dem Neuen Testament. Otto Michel zum 70. Geburtstag gewidmet* (Göttingen: Vandenhoeck & Ruprecht): 23–44.

—, 1976. 'Might', in vol. 2 of *The New International Dictionary of New Testament Theology* (ed. C. Brown; Exeter: Paternoster Press, 1976): 601-6.

—, 1993. 'σημεῖον', in vol. 3 of *Exegetical Dictionary of the New Testament* (eds. H. Balz & G. Schneider; Grand Rapids: Eerdmans): 238–41.

BEUTLER, J., 1990. 'Greeks Come to See Jesus (John 12.20ff): [Isaiah 52.15 as Background]', *Bib* 71.3: 333-347.

BEVAN, E., 1932. 'Note on Mark i 41 and John xi 33,38', *JTS* 33: 186–8.

BITTNER, W., 1987. *Jesu Zeichen im Johannesevangelium: Die Messias-Erkenntnis in Johannesevangelium vor ihrem jüdischen Hintergrund* (WUNT 2.26; Tübingen: Mohr Siebeck).

BLACK II, C. C., 1984. 'Pauline Perspectives on Death in Romans 5–8', *JBL* 103.3: 413–33.

BLENKINSOPP, J., 2000a *Isaiah 1-39* (AB 19; New York: Doubleday).

—, 2000b *Isaiah 40-55* (AB 19a; New York: Doubleday).

BLOMBERG, C. L., 2001. *The Historical Reliability of John's Gospel* (Leicester: IVP).

BOCK, D. L., 1994 *Luke 1.1-9.50* (BEC: Grand Rapids: Baker Books).

BOLT, P. G., 1991. 'The Narrative Integrity of Mark 13: 24-27" (MTh diss., Australian College of Theology, Kensington, NSW).

—, 1995. 'Mark 13: An Apocalyptic Precursor to the Passion Narrative', *RTR* 54.1: 1-16

—, 1997. '"Do you not care that we are perishing?" Jesus' Defeat of Death and Mark's Early Readers' (PhD diss., King's College, London).

—, 1998. 'Life, Death and the Afterlife in the Greco-Roman World', in Longenecker 1998: 51–79.

—, 2000. 'Feeling the Cross: Mark's Message of Atonement', *RTR* 60.1: 1–17.

BONNEY, W., 2002. *Caused to Believe: The Doubting Thomas Story as the Climax of John's Christological Narrative* (BIS 62; Leiden: Brill).

BOOMERSHINE, T. E., 1974. 'Mark, the Storyteller: A Rhetorical-Critical Investigation of Mark's Passion and Resurrection Narrative' (PhD diss., Union Theological Seminary, New York).

BOOTH, W. C., 1983. *The Rhetoric of Fiction* (London: Penguin Books, 2ⁿᵈ edn).

BORGEN, P., 1965. *Bread from Heaven: An Exegetical Study of the Concept of Manna in the Gospel of John and the Writings of Philo* (NovTSup. 10; Leiden: Brill).

—, 1970. 'God's Agent in the Fourth Gospel', in J. Neusner (ed.), *Religions in Antiquity* (Leiden: Brill): 137–48.

—, 1997. 'John 6: Tradition, Interpretation and Composition', in Culpepper 1997: 95–114.

BORMANN, L., et al. (eds.) 1994. *Religious Propaganda and Missionary Competition in the New Testament World: Essays Honoring Dieter Georgi* (NovTSup 74; Leiden: Brill, 1994).

BOTHA, P. J. J., 1988. 'God, Emperor Worship and Society: Contemporary Experiences and the Book of Revelation', *Neot* 22: 87–102.

BOWERSOCK, G. W., 1982. 'The Imperial Cult: Perceptions and Persistence', in B.F. Meyer & E.P. Sanders 1982: 171–82.

BRENT, A. 1999. *The Imperial Cult and the Development of Church Order: Concepts and Images of Authority in Paganism and Early Christianity before the Age of Cyprian* (VCSup 45; Leiden: Brill).

BROER, I. 1983. 'Noch einmal: Zur religionsgeschichtlichen "Ableitung" von Joh 2,1–11', *SNTU* 8: 103–23.

BROWN, R. E., 1966, 1970. *The Gospel According to John* (AB 29; 2 vols.; New York: Doubleday).

BROWNSON, J. V., 1995. 'John 20:31 and the Purpose of the Fourth Gospel', *RefR* 48.3: 212–16.

BULLOUGH, E., 1912. '"Psychical Distance" as a factor in Art and as an Aesthetic Principle', *Brit. Journal of Psychology* 5.2: 87–118.

BULTMANN, R., 1971. *The Gospel of John* (trans. G.R. Beasley-Murray; Oxford: Blackwell).

BURKERT, W., 1985. *Greek Religion: Archaic and Classical* (trans. J. Raffan; Oxford: Blackwell).

BURRIDGE, R. A., 1997. 'Biography' in Porter 1997: 371–92.

—, 1998. 'About People, by People, for People: Gospel Genre and Audiences', in Bauckham 1998b: 113–45.

BUTH, R., 1992. 'Οὖν, Δέ, Καί and Asyndeton in John's Gospel' in D.A. Black (ed.), *Linguistics in New Testament Interpretation* (Nashville; Broadman Press): 144–61.

BYRNE, B., 1985. 'The Faith of the Beloved Disciple and the Community in John 20', *JSNT* 23:83–97.

CALVIN, J., 1994. *John* (The Crossway Classic Commentary series; Wheaton: Crossway Books).

CAMPBELL, W. T., 2002. 'The Relationship of Signs and Belief in the Fourth Gospel' (PhD. diss.; Southwestern Baptist Theological Seminary).

CARSON, D. A., 1981. *Divine Sovereignty and Human Responsibility: Biblical Perspectives in Tension* (London: Marshall, Morgan & Scott).

—, 1985. 'Historical Tradition in the Fourth Gospel. A Response to J.S. King', *JSNT* 23: 73–81.

—, 1987. 'The Purpose of the Fourth Gospel: John 20:31 Reconsidered', *JBL* 106.4: 639–51.

—, 1991. *The Gospel According to John* (Leicester: IVP).

—, 1992. 'The Purpose of Signs and Wonders in the New Testament', in M.S. Horton (ed.), *Power Religion: The Selling Out of the Evangelical Church?* (Chicago: Moody Press): 89–118.

CARTER, W., 1999a. 'Toward an Imperial–Critical Reading of Matthew's Gospel' in E.H. Lovering Jr. (ed.), *SBL 1998 Seminar Papers (Part One)* (Atlanta: Scholars Press): 296–324.

—, 1999b. 'Contested Claims: Roman Imperial Ideology and Matthew's Gospel', *BTB* 29.2: 56–67

—, 2000. *Matthew and the Margins: A Socio-Political and Religious Reading* (JSNTSup 204; Sheffield: Sheffield Academic Press).

CASEY, M., 1999. 'Some Anti-Semitic Assumptions in the *Theological Dictionary of the New Testament*', *NovT* 61.3: 280–291.

CASSIDY, R., 1992. *John's Gospel in New Perspective: Christology and the Realities of Roman Power* (Maryknoll, NY: Orbis Books).

CASTRIOTA, D., 1998. *The Ara Pacis Augustae and the Imagery of Abundance in Later Greek and Early Roman Imperial Art* (Princeton: Princeton University Press).

CHARLIER, J-P., 1959. 'La notion de signe (ΣΗΜΕΙΟΝ) dans le IVᵉ Évangile', *RSPT* 43: 434–48.

CHESNUT, G. F., 1978. 'The Ruler and the Logos in Neopythagorean, Middle Platonic, and Late Stoic Political Philosophy', *ANRW* 16.2:1310–32. Part 2, *Principat*, 16.2 (Edited by H. Temporini & W. Haase, New York: de Gruyter, 1978).

CHILDS, B. S., 1974. *Exodus: A Commentary* (OTL; London: SCM Press).

CIHOLAS, P., 1982. 'The Socratic and Johannine SHMEION as Divine Manifestation', *PRSt* 9: 251–65.

CLARK, D. K., 1983. 'Signs in Wisdom and John', *CBQ* 45.2: 201–9.

COLE, A., 1973. *Exodus: An Introduction and Commentary* (TOTC; London: The Tyndale Press).

COLE, R. D., 2000. 'Wine', in D.N. Freedman (ed.), *Eerdmans Dictionary of the Bible* (Grand Rapids: Eerdmans): 1379–80.

COLLINS, A.Y., 1994. 'Rulers, Divine Men, and Walking on the Water (Mark 6.45–52)', in Bormann et al.: 207–27.

—, 2000. 'Mark and His Readers: The Son of God Among Greeks and Romans', *HTR* 93.2: 85–100.

COLLINS, J. J., 1995. *The Scepter and the Star: The Messiahs of the Dead Sea Scrolls and Other Ancient Literature* (ABRL; New York: Doubleday).

—, 1997. 'A Herald of Good Tidings: Isaiah 61:1–3 and Its Actualization in the Dead Sea Scrolls', in C.A. Evans & S. Talmon (eds.), *The Quest for Context and Meaning. Studies in Biblical Intertextuality in Honor of James A. Sanders* (BIS 28; Leiden: Brill).

—, 1998. 'Jesus, Messianism and the Dead Sea Scrolls', in J. Charlesworth et al. (eds.), *Qumran-Messianism: Studies on the Messianic Expectations in the Dead Sea Scrolls* (Tübingen: Mohr Siebeck): 100–119.

COLLINS, M. S., 1995. 'The Question of Doxa: a Socioliterary Reading of the Wedding at Cana', *BTB* 25.3: 100–109.

COLLINS, R. F., 1990. 'Cana (John 2.1–12) – The First of His Signs or the Key to His Signs?' in R.F. Collins, *These Things Have Been Written: Studies on the Fourth Gospel* (Louvain Theological and Pastoral Monographs; Louvain: Peeters Press): 158–82.

CONTRERAS, C. A., 1980. 'Christian Views of Paganism', *ANRW* II.23.2: 974–1022. Part 2, *Principat*, 23.2 (Edited by H. Temporini & W. Haase, New York: de Gruyter, 1980).

COOPER, K. T., 1979. 'The Best Wine: John 2:1–11', *WTJ* 42.1: 364–80.

COTTER, W., 1991. 'The Markan Sea Miracles in the Literary Context of Greco-Roman Antiquity' (PhD diss; University of St Michael's College, Toronto).

COTTERELL, P. & M. TURNER, 1989. *Linguistics and Biblical Interpretation* (London: SPCK).

CRAFFERT, P. F., 1996, 'Relationships Between Social–Scientific, Literary, and Rhetorical Interpretation of Texts', *BTB* 26.1: 45–55.

CRAPIS, C., 1988. 'Théorie des indices dans la rhétorique latine', *Versus* 50/51: 175–97.

CROOK, J. A., 1995 *Legal Advocacy in the Roman World* (London: Duckworth).

CROUCH, F. L., 1996. 'Everyone Who Sees the Son: Signs, Faith, Peirce's Semeiotics, and the Gospel of John' (PhD diss., Duke University).

CULPEPPER, R. A., 1983. *Anatomy of the Fourth Gospel: A Study in Literary Design* (Philadelphia: Fortress Press).

—, 1993. 'John 5.1–18: A Sample of a Narrative Critical Commentary', in *The Gospel of John as Literature: An Anthology of Twentieth Century Perspectives* (selected and introduced by M.G.W. Stibbe; NTTS 17; Leiden: Brill): 193–207.

—, 1997. *Critical Readings of John 6* (ed. R.A. Culpepper; BIS 22; 1997; Leiden: Brill)

—, 1998. *The Gospel and Letters of John* (IBT; Nashville: Abingdon Press).

CUSS, D., 1974. *Imperial Cult and Honorary Terms in the New Testament* (Paradosis 23; Fribourg: The University Press).

DAHL, N. A., 1962. 'The Johannine Church and History', in W. Klassen & G.F. Snyder (eds.), *Current Issues in Interpretation: Essays in Honor of Otto A. Piper* (The Preacher's Library; London: SCM): 124–142.

DAHMS, J. V., 1981. 'Isaiah 55:11 and the Gospel of John', *EQ* 53: 78–88.

DALY-DENTON, M., 1999. 'Going Beyond the Genially Open 'CF.': Intertextual Reference to the Old Testament in the New', *Mils* 44: 48–60.

—, 2000. *David in the Fourth Gospel: The Johannine Reception of the Psalms* (AGJU 47; Leiden: Brill).

D'ANGELO, M. R., 1992. 'Abba and "Father": Imperial Theology and the Jesus Traditions', *JBL* 111.4: 611–30.

DANKER, F. W., 1985. 'Politics of the New Age According to St. Luke', *CurTM* 12.6: 338–45.

—, 1988. *Jesus and the New Age: A Commentary on St Luke's Gospel* (Philadelphia: Fortress Press, rev. edn).

—, 1994. 'Matthew: A Patriot's Gospel', in Evans & Stegner 1994: 94–115.

DAVIES, W. D., 1974. *The Gospel and the Land* (Berkeley: University of California Press).

—, 1977. 'The Johannine "Signs" of Jesus', in M.J. Taylor (ed.), *A Companion to John: Readings in Johannine Theology (John's Gospel and Epistles)* (New York: Alban House): 91–115.

DAVIES, W. D. & D. C. ALLISON, 1997. *A Critical and Exegetical Commentary on The Gospel According to Saint Matthew Vol. III: Commentary on Matthew XIX–XXVIII* (Edinburgh: T&T Clark).

DE BOER, M.C., 1992. 'Narrative Criticism, Historical Criticism, and the Gospel of John', *JSNT* 47: 35–48.

DEHAVEN-SMITH, L., 1997. 'How Jesus Planned to Overthrow the Roman Empire', *RelStTh* 16: 48–59.

DE JONGE, M., 1977. *Jesus: Stranger from Heaven and Son of God: Jesus Christ and the Christians in Johannine Perspective* (ed. & trans. John E. Steely; SBLSBS 11; Missoula: Scholars Press).

DEINES, R., 1993. *Jüdische Steingefäße und pharisäische Frömmigkeit: Ein archäologisch-historischer Beitrag zum Verständnis von Joh 2,6 und der jüdischen Reinheitshalacha zur Zeit Jesu* (WUNT 2.52; Tübingen: Mohr Siebeck).

DEISSMANN, A., 1927. *Light from the Ancient East: The New Testament Illustrated by Recently Discovered Texts of the Graeco-Roman World* (trans. L.R.M. Strachan; London: Hodder & Stoughton, rev. edn).

DENNISON, W. D., 1976. 'Miracles as <<Signs>>: Their Significance for Apologetics', *BTB* 6.2–3: 190–202.

DERRETT, J. D. M., 1963. 'Water into Wine', *BZ* 7: 80–97.

——— 1989. 'Christ, King and Witness (John 18.37)', *BibeO* 31: 189–98.

DODD, C. H., 1954. *The Interpretation of the Fourth Gospel* (Cambridge: Cambridge University Press).

DUMBRELL, W. J., 1994. *The Search for Order: Biblical Eschatology in Focus* (Grand Rapids: Baker Books).

DUPREZ, A., 1970. *Jésus et les dieux guérisseurs: A propos de Jean, V* (CahRB 12; Paris: J. Gabalda).

DURHAM, J. I., 1987. *Exodus* (WBC 3; Waco: Word Books).

EBELING, G., 1971. 'Time and Word', in J.M. Robinson (ed.), *The Future of Our Religious Past: Essays in Honour of Rudolf Bultmann* (trans. C.E. Carlston & R.P. Scharlemann; London: SCM): 247–66.

ECO, U., 1981. *The Role of the Reader: Explorations in the Semiotics of Texts* (Hutchinson University Library; London: Hutchinson).

EDWARDS, R., 2003. *Discovering John* (London: SPCK).

ENSOR, P. W., 1999. *Jesus and His "Works": The Johannine Sayings in Historical Perspective* (WUNT 2.85; Tübingen: Mohr Siebeck).

ESLER, P., 1998. 'Community and Gospel in Early Christianity: A Response to Richard Bauckham's *Gospels For All Christians'*, *SJT* 51.2: 235–48.

ESSER, A., 1961. *Das Anlitz der Blindheit in der Antike: Die kulturen und medizinhistorischen Ausstrahlungen des Blindenproblems in den antiken Quellen* (JanusSup 4; Leiden: Brill, 2nd edn).

EVANS, C. A., 1981. 'The Voice From Heaven: A Note on John 12:28', *CBQ* 43.3: 405–8.

—, 1982. 'On the Quotation Formulas in the Fourth Gospel', *BZ* 26.1: 79–83.

—, 1987. 'Obduracy and the Lord's Servant: Some Observations on the Use of the Old Testament in the Fourth Gospel', in C.A. Evans & W.F. Stinespring (eds.), *Early Jewish and Christian Exegesis. Studies in Memory of William Hugh Brownlee* (Atlanta: Scholars Press): 221–36.

—, 1993. *Word and Glory. On the Exegetical and Theological Background of John's Prologue* (JSNTSup. 89; Sheffield: JSOT Press).

—, 1997. 'Jesus and the Dead Sea Scrolls from Qumran Cave 4' in C.A. Evans & P.W. Flint (eds.), *Eschatology, Messianism and the Dead Sea Scrolls* (SDSSRL; Grand Rapids: Eerdmans): 91–100.

EVANS, C. A. & W. R. STEGNER (eds.), 1994. *The Gospels and the Scriptures of Israel* (JSNTSup. 104; SSEJC 3; Sheffield: Sheffield Academic Press).

FABRY, H-J., 1998 כּס; כֹס, in vol. 9 of *Theological Dictionary of the Old Testament* (eds. G.J. Botterweck & H. Ringgren; trans. J.T. Willis et al.; 11 vols.; Grand Rapids: Eerdmans, rev. edn): 437–42.

FEARS, J. R., 1981a. 'The Cult of Jupiter and Roman Imperial Ideology', *ANRW* 17.1:1201–53. Part 2, *Principat*, 17.1 (Edited by H. Temporini &W. Haase, New York: de Gruyter, 1981).

—, 1981b. 'The Cult of Virtues and Roman Imperial Ideology', *ANRW* 17.2: 827–948. Part 2, *Principat*, 17.2 (Edited by H. Temporini & W. Haase, New York: de Gruyter, 1981).

FEE, G. D., 1992. 'On the Text and Meaning of John 20.30–31', in F. Van Segbroeck, et al. (eds.), *The Four Gospels* (Festschrift Frans Neirynck; BETL 100; 3 vols.; Leuven: Leuven University Press): 3. 2193–2205.

FERGUSON, J., 1970. *The Religions of the Roman Empire (Aspects of Greek and Roman Life*; London: Thames & Hudson).

FISHWICK, D., 1978. 'The Development of Provincial Ruler Worship in the Western Roman Empire', *ANRW* 16.2:1201–53. Part 2, *Principat*, 16.2 (Edited by H. Temporini & W. Haase, New York: de Gruyter, 1978).

FITZMYER, J., 1970. *The Gospel According to Luke* (AB 28; New York: Doubleday).

2000 *The Dead Sea Scrolls and Christian Origins* (SDSSRL; Grand Rapids: Eerdmans).

FORD, J. M., 1995. 'Jesus as Sovereign in the Passion according to John', *BTB* 25.3: 110–17.

FORMESYN, R., 1962. 'Le Sèmeion Johannique et le Sèmeion Hellénistique' *ETL* 38: 856–94.

FORTNA, R. T., 1970. *The Gospel of Signs* (Cambridge: Cambridge University Press).

—, 1975. 'Christology in the Fourth Gospel: Redaction-Critical Perspectives', *NTS* 21: 489–504.

—, 1988. *The Fourth Gospel and Its Predecessor* (Edinburgh: T&T Clark).

FREED, E. D., 1965. *Old Testament Quotations in the Gospel of John* (NovTSup 11; Leiden: Brill).

FRETHEIM, T. E., 1991. *Exodus* (IBC; Louisville: John Knox Press).

FREY, J., 1994a. 'Heiden–Griechen–Gotteskinder. Zu Gestalt und Funktion der Rede von Heiden im 4. Evangelium', in R. Feldmeier & U. Heckel (eds.), *Die Heiden: Juden, Christen und das Problem des Fremden* (WUNT 70; Tübingen: Mohr Siebeck): 228–68.

—, 1994b' "Wie Moses die Schlange in der Wüste erhöht hat..." Zur frühjüdischen Deutung der "ehernen Schlange" und ihrer christologischen Rezeption in Johannes 3,14f.', in M. Hengel &H. Löhr (eds.), *Schriftauslegung im antiken Judentum und im Urchristentum* (WUNT 73: Tübingen: Mohr Siebeck, 1994): 153–205.

—, 2000. *Die johanneische Eschatologie. Sie eschatologische Verkündigung in den johanneischen Texten III* (WUNT 117: Tübingen: Mohr Siebeck, 2000).

FRIEBEL, K. G., 1999. *Jeremiah's and Ezekiel's Sign-Acts: Rhetorical Nonverbal Communication* (JSOTSup 283; Sheffield: Sheffield Academic Press).

FRIER, B. W., 1998. 'Demography', in A.K. Bowman et al. (eds.), *The Cambridge Ancient History Vol. XI, The High Empire, A.D. 70–192* (Cambridge, Cambridge University Press, 2nd edn): 787–816.

FRIESEN, S. J., 1993. *Twice Neokoros: Ephesus, Asia, and the Cult of the Flavian Imperial Family* (Religions in the Graeco-Roman World 116; Leiden: Brill).

—, 1995. 'The Cult of the Roman Emperors in Ephesos: Temple Wardens, City Titles, and the Interpretation of the Revelation of John', in H. Koester (ed.) 1995: 229–250.

GARLAND, R., 1985. *The Greek Way of Death* (London: Duckworth).

—, 1995. *The Eye of the Beholder: Deformity and Disability in the Graeco-Roman World* (London: Duckworth).

GARNSEY, P., 1988. *Famine and Food Supply in the Graeco-Roman World: Responses to Risk and Crisis* (Cambridge: Cambridge University Press).

—, 1999. *Food and Society in Classical Antiquity* (Key Themes in Ancient History; Cambridge: Cambridge University Press).

GEORGI, D., 1986. 'Who is the True Prophet?', *HTR* 79.1–3: 100–26.

GESE, H., 1981. *Essays on Biblical Theology* (trans. K. Crim; Minneapolis: Augsburg Publishing House).

GIBLIN, C. C., 1980. 'Suggestion, Negative Response, and Positive Action in St John's Portrayal of Jesus (John 2.1–11; 4.46–54; 7.2–14; 11.1–44)', *NTS* 26: 197–211.

GIBSON, J., 1995. 'Jesus' Refusal to Produce a 'Sign' (Mk 8.11–13)', *JSNT* 38: 37–66.

GLASSON, T. F., 1963. *Moses in the Fourth Gospel* (SBT 40; London: SCM).

1964. 'The Ensign of the Son of Man (Matt. XXIV.30), *JTS* 15: 299-300.

GOETCHIUS, E. V. N., 1976. Review of L.C. McGaughy, *Toward a Descriptive Analysis of EINAI as a Linking Verb in New Testament Greek, JBL* 95: 147–9.

GOODENOUGH, E. R., 1928. 'The Political Philosophy of Hellenistic Kingship', *Yale Classical Studies* 1 (ed. A.M. Harmon; New Haven: Yale University Press): 55–105.

GRANT, R. M., 1952. *Miracle and Natural Law in Graeco-Roman Thought and Early Christian Thought* (Amsterdam: New Holland).

GRAY, R., 1993. *Prophetic Figures in Late Second Temple Jewish Palestine: The Evidence from Josephus* (Oxford: Oxford University Press).

GRAYSTON, K., 1990. *The Gospel of John* (London: Epworth Press).

GREEN, J. B., 1997. *The Gospel of Luke* (NICNT: Grand Rapids: Eerdmans).

GRIFFITHS, D. R., 1954. 'Deutero-Isaiah and the Fourth Gospel: some points of comparison', *ExpTim* 65: 355-60.

GRIGSBY, B., 1985. 'Washing in the Pool of Siloam—A Thematic Anticipation of the Johannine Cross', *NovT* 27.3: 227–35.

GRIMM, V. E., 1996. *From Feasting to Fasting, the Evolution of a Sin: Attitudes to Food In Late Antiquity* (London: Routledge).

GRMEK, M. D., 1989. *Diseases in the Ancient Greek World* (trans. M.Muellner & L. Muellner; Baltimore: The Johns Hopkins Press).

GUNDRY, R.H., 1994. *Matthew. A Commentary on His Handbook for a Mixed Church Under Persecution* (Grand Rapids; Eerdmans²).

GUTHRIE, D., 1967. 'The Importance of Signs in the Fourth Gospel', *VE* 5: 72–83.

HAENCHEN, E., 1984. *John* (ed. R. Funk & U. Busse; trans. R. Funk; Hermeneia; 2 vols.; Philadelphia: Fortress Press).

HAGENOW, G., 1982. *Aus dem Weingarten der Antike: der Wein in Dichtung, Brauchtum und Alltag* (Kulturgeschichte der antiken Welt 12; Manz am Rhein: Philipp von Zabern).

HAKOLA, R., 1999. 'A Character resurrected: Lazarus in the Fourth Gospel and Afterwards', in D. Rhoads & K. Syreeni (eds.), *Characterization in the Gospels: Reconceiving Narrative Criticism* (JSNTSup 184; Sheffield; Sheffield Academic Press): 223–263.

HANSON, A. T., 1991. *The Prophetic Gospel: A Study of John and the Old Testament* (Edinburgh: T&T Clark).

HANSON, R. P. C., 1980. 'The Christian Attitude to Pagan Religions up to the Time of Constantine the Great', *ANRW* II.23.2: 910–73. Part 2, *Principat*, 23.2 (Edited by H. Temporini & W. Haase, New York: de Gruyter, 1980).

HARLAND, P. A., 1996. 'Honours and Worship: Emperors, imperial cults and associations at Ephesus (first to third centuries)', *SR* 25.3: 319–34.

HARRISON, J. E., 1903. *Prolegomena to the Study of Greek Religion* (Cambridge: Cambridge University Press).

HARRISON, J. R., 1999. 'Paul, Eschatology and the Augustan Age of Grace', *TynBul* 50.1: 79–91.

HARVEY, A. E., 1976. *Jesus on Trial: A Study in the Fourth Gospel* (London: SPCK).
2002. Review of M. Asiedu-Peprah, *Johannine Sabbath Conflicts as Juridical Controversy*, *JTS* 53.1: 223–224.

HAWTHORN, J., 2000. *A Glossary of Contemporary Literary Theory* (London: Arnold, 4th edn).

HEAD, P. M., 2000. 'Some Recently Published NT Papyri From Oxyrhyncus: An Overview and Preliminary Assessment', *TynBul* 51.1: 1–16.

HEIL, J. P., 1981. *Jesus Walking on the Sea: Meaning and Gospel Functions of Matt 14:22–33, Mark 6:45–52 and John 6:15b–21* (AnBib 87; Rome: Biblical Institute Press).

HEILIGENTHAL, R., 1983. *Werke als Zeichen: Untersuchungen zur Bedeutung der menschlichen Taten im Früjudentum, Neuen Testament und Frühchristentum* (WUNT 2.9; Tübingen: Mohr Siebeck).

HELFMEYER, F. J., 1977. אות, in vol. 1 of *Theological Dictionary of the Old Testament* (eds. G.J. Botterweck & H. Ringgren; trans. J.T. Willis et al.; 11 vols.; Grand Rapids: Eerdmans, rev. edn): 167–88.

HENAUT, B. W., 1990. 'John 4:43–54 and the Ambivalent Narrator. A Response to Culpepper's Anatomy of the Fourth Gospel', *SR* 19.3: 287–304.

HENGEL, M., 1977. *Crucifixion: In the Ancient World and the Folly of the Message of the Cross* (London: SCM).

—, 1987. 'The Interpretation of the Wine Miracle at Cana: John 2: 1–11', in Hurst & Wright 1987: 83–112.

—, 1990. 'The Old Testament in the Fourth Gospel', *HBT* 12.1: 19–41.

—, 1995. *Studies in Early Christology* (Edinburgh: T&T Clark).

—, 1999. *Judaica, Hellenistica et Christiana: Kleine Schriften II* (WUNT 109: Tübingen: Mohr Siebeck).

HENRICHS, A., 1982. 'Changing Dionysiac Identities', in B.F. Meyer & E.P. Sanders (eds.) 1982: 137–160.

HIGGINS, A. J. B., 1962-3. 'The Sign of the Son of Man (Matt. XXIV. 30)', *NTS* 9: 380-2.

HILL, D., 1979. 'Jesus and Josephus' "messianic prophets"', in E. Best & R. McL. Wilson, *Text and Interpretation: Studies in the New Testament. Presented to Matthew Black* (Cambridge: Cambridge University Press): 143–54.

—, 1987. '"My Kingdom is Not of this World" (John 18.36)', *IBS* 9: 54–62.

HINDLEY, J. C., 1965. 'Witness in the Fourth Gospel', *SJT* 18: 319–36.

HOFBECK, S., 1970. *Semeion: Der Begriff des 'Zeichens' im Johannesevangelium unter Berücksichtigung seiner Vorgeschichte* (Münsterschwarzacher Studien 3; Münsterschwarzach: Vier-Türme-Verlag).

HOFIUS, O., 1976. 'Miracle, Wonder, Sign', in vol. 3 of *The New International Dictionary of New Testament Theology* (ed. C. Brown; Exeter; Paternoster): 620–43.

HOGAN, L. P., 1992. *Healing in the Second Tempel (sic) Period* (NTOA 21; Göttingen: Vandenhoeck & Ruprecht).

HOOKER, M. D., 1997. *The Signs of a Prophet: The Prophetic Actions of Jesus* (London: SCM).

HOPKINS, K., 1999. *A World Full of Gods: Pagans, Jews and Christians in the Roman Empire* (London: Weidenfeld & Nicholson, 1999).

HORSLEY, G. H. R., 1992. 'The Inscriptions of Ephesos and the New Testament', *NovT.* 34.2: 105–68.

HORSLEY, R.A., (ed.) 2004. *Paul and the Roman Imperial Order* (Harrisburg, PA.: Trinity International Press.

HOSKYNS, E. C., 1954. *The Fourth Gospel* (ed. F.N. Davey; 2 vols.; London: Faber & Faber).

HOUSTON, W. J., 1987. '"Today, in Your Very Hearing": Some Comments on the Christological Use of the Old Testament', in Hurst & Wright 1987: 37–47.

HOUTMAN, C., 1993, 1996, 2000, 2002. *Exodus* (HCOT; trans. J. Rebel & S. Woudstra; 4 vols.; Kampen: Kok Publishing House).

HURST, L. D. & N. T. WRIGHT (eds.), 1987. *The Glory of Christ in the New Testament: Studies in Christology in Memory of George Bradford Caird* (Oxford: Clarendon Press).

INCH, M., 1970. 'Apologetic Use of "sign" in the Fourth Gospel', *EQ* 42: 35–43.

INSTONE-BREWER, D., 2001. 'Jesus's Last Passover: the Synoptics and John', *ExpTim* 112/4: 122–3.

JACKSON, H. M., 1999. 'Ancient Self-Referential Conventions and their Implications for the Authorship and Integrity of the Gospel of John', *JTS* 50.1: 1–34.

JOHNS, L. L. & D. B. MILLER, 1994. 'The Signs as Witnesses in the Fourth Gospel: Reexamining the Evidence', *CBQ* 56.3: 519–35.

JONES, D. L., 1980. 'Christianity and the Roman Imperial Cult', *ANRW* II.23.2: 1023–54. Part 2, *Principat*, 23.2 (Edited by H. Temporini & W. Haase, New York: de Gruyter, 1980).

JONES, L. P., 1997. *The Symbol of Water in the Gospel of John* (JSNTSup 145; Sheffield: Sheffield Academic Press).

JUDGE, E. A., 1994. 'Judaism and the Rise of Christianity: A Roman Perspective', *TynBul* 45.2: 355–68.

JUST, F. N. W., 1997. 'From Tobit to Bartimaeus, From Qumran to Siloam: The Social Role of Blind People and Attitudes toward the Blind in New Testament Times' (PhD diss., Yale University).

KAHL, W., 1994. *New Testament Miracle Stories in their Religious-Historical Setting: A Religionsgechichtliche Comparison from a Structural Perspective* (FRLANT 163; Göttingen: Vandenhoek & Ruprecht).

KAMMLER, H-C., 1996. 'Die "Zeichen" des Auferstandenen. Überlegungen zur Exegese von Joh 20, 30+31', in O. Hofius & H-C Kammler (eds.) *Johannesstudien: Untersuchungen zur Theologie des vierten Evangeliums* (WUNT 2.88; Tübingen: Mohr Siebeck): 191–211.

KÄSEMANN, E., 1968. *The Testament of Jesus According to John 17* (trans. G. Krodel; NTL; London: SCM).

KEE, A., 1985. 'The Imperial Cult: the Unmasking of an Ideology' *SJRS* 6.2: 112–28.

KEE, H. C., 1982. 'Self-Definition in the Asclepius Cult', in Meyer & Sanders (eds.) 1982: 118–136.

—, 1986. *Medicine, Miracle & Magic in New Testament Times* (SNTSMS55; Cambridge: Cambridge University Press).

KERN, P. H., 1998. *Rhetoric and Galatians: Assessing an Approach to Paul's Epistles* (SNTSMS 101; Cambridge: Cambridge University Press).

KILEY, M., 1988. 'The Exegesis of God: Jesus' Signs in John 1–11', in D.J. Lull (ed.), *SBL Seminar Papers* (Atlanta: Scholars Press): 555–67.

KIM, S. S., 2001. 'The Relationship of the Seven Sign-Miracles of Jesus in the Fourth Gospel to the Old Testament' (PhD. diss., Dallas Theological Seminary).

KLAUCK, H-J., 2000. *The Religious Context of Early Christianity: A Guide to Graeco-Roman Religions* (trans. B. McNeil; Studies of the New Testament and its World; Edinburgh: T&T Clark).

KLAUSNER, J., 1956. *The Messianic Idea in Israel from Its Beginning to the Completion of the Mishnah* (trans. from the 3rd Hebrew edn by W.F. Stinespring; London: Allen & Unwin).

KNIBBE, D., 1978. 'Ephesos—Nicht nur die Stadt der Artemis', in Sahin et al. (eds.), *Studien zur Religion und Kultur Kleinasiens: Festschrift für Friedrich Karl Dörner zum 65. Geburtstag am 28. Februar 1976* (EPRO 66; 2 vols.; Leiden: Brill): 2. 489–503.

KNIERIM, R. P., 1968. 'The Messianic Concept in the First Book of Samuel', in F.T Trotter (ed.), *Jesus and the Historian: Written in Honor of Ernest Cadman Colwell* (Philadelphia: The Westminster Press): 20–51.

KOESTER, C. R., 1989. 'Hearing, Seeing and Believing in the Gospel of John', *Bib* 70.3: 327–348.

—, 1990. '"The Savior of the World" (John 4:42)', *JBL* 109.4: 665–80.

—, 1995. *Symbolism in the Fourth Gospel: Meaning, Mystery, Community* (Minneapolis: Fortress Press).

—, 1996. 'The Spectrum of Johannine Readers', in F.F. Segovia (ed.), *"What is John?": Readers and Readings of the Fourth Gospel* (SBLSymS 3; Atlanta: Scholars Press): 5–19.

KOESTER, H., 1985. 'The Divine Human Being', *HTR* 78.3–4: 243–52.

—, 1995. *Ephesos Metropolis of Asia: An Interdisciplinary Approach to its Archaeology, Religion, and Culture* (HTS 41; H. Koester (ed.); Valley Forge, Pa.: Trinity Press International).

KOSSEN, H. B., 1970. 'Who Were the Greeks of John xii 20?', in M.C. Rientsma et al., *Studies in John: Presented to Professor Dr. J.N. Sevenster on the Occasion of his Seventieth Birthday* (NovTSup; Leiden: Brill): 97–110.

KÖSTENBERGER, A. J., 1995. 'The Seventh Johannine Sign: A Study in John's Christology', *BBR* 5: 87–103.

—, 1998. *The Missions of Jesus & The Disciples According to the Fourth Gospel: With Implications for the Fourth Gospel's Purpose and the Mission of the Contemporary Church* (Grand Rapids: Eerdmans).

—, 1999. *Encountering John: The Gospel in Historical, Literary, and Theological Perspective* (EBS; Grand Rapids: Baker Books).

KOTZÉ, P. P. A., 1985. 'John and Reader's Response', *Neot* 19: 50–63.

KOVACS, J. L., 1995. '"Now Shall the Ruler of This World Be Driven Out": Jesus' Death as Cosmic Battle in John 12:20–36', *JBL* 114.2: 227–47.

KREITZER, L. J., 1996. *Striking New Images: Roman Imperial Coinage and the New Testament World* (JSNTSup 134; Sheffield: Sheffield Academic Press).

KRUGER, P. A., 1996: אוה, in vol. 1 of *The New International Dictionary of Old Testament Theology and Exegesis* (ed. Willem A. VanGemeren; 5 vols.; Carlisle: Paternoster, 1996): 331–33.

KUHN, K. G. et al., 1971.'Ισραήλ κ.τ.λ. in vol. 3 of *Theological Dictionary of the New Testament* (eds. G. Kittel & G. Friedrich; trans. G. Bromiley; 10 vols.; Grand Rapids: Eerdmans, 1964–1976): 356–91.

KYSAR, R., 1986. *John* (ACNT; Minneapolis: Augsburg).

—, 1993. *John: The Maverick Gospel* (Louisville, Ken.: Westminster/John Knox Press, rev. edn).

—, 1999. Review of P.N. Anderson, *Christology of the Fourth Gospel: Its Unity and Disunity in the Light of John 6*, in M.A. Sweeney (ed.), Review of Biblical Literature (Atlanta: SBL): 38–42.

LABAHN, M., 1999a. *Jesus als Lebensspender: Untersuchungen zu einer Geschichte der johanneischen Tradition anhand ihrer Wundergeschichten* (BZNW 98; Berlin: Walter de Gruyter).

—, 1999b. 'Between Tradition and Literary Art. The Use of the Miracle Tradition in the Fourth Gospel', *Bib* 80.2: 178–203.

—, 2000. 'Controversial Revelation in Deed and Word: The Feeding of the Five Thousand and Jesus' Crossing of the Sea as a 'Prelude' to the Johannine Bread of Life Discourse', *IBS* 22: 146–81.

LATTIMORE, R., 1934. 'Portents and Prophecies in Connection with the Emperor Vespasian', *CJ* 29.6: 441–9.

LEE, D. A., 1994. *The Symbolic Narratives of the Fourth Gospel: The Interplay of Form and Meaning* (JSNTSup 95; Sheffield: JSOT Press).

LIEBERT, E., 1984. 'That You May Believe: The Fourth Gospel and Structural Developmental Theory', *BTB* 14.2: 67–73.

LIEBESCHUETZ, J. H. W. G., 1979. *Continuity and Change in Roman Religion* (Oxford: Oxford University Press).

LIEU, J., 1999. 'Temple and Synagogue in John', *NTS* 45: 51–69.

LIGHTFOOT, R. H., 1956. *St. John's Gospel. A Commentary* (ed. C.F. Evans; Oxford: Oxford University Press).

LINCOLN, A. T., 1994. 'Trials, Plots and the Narrative of the Fourth Gospel', *JSNT* 56: 3–30.

—, 1998. ' "I Am the Resurrection and the Life": The Resurrection Message of the Fourth Gospel', in Longenecker 1998: 122–44.

—, 2000. *Truth on Trial: The Lawsuit Motif in John's Gospel* (Peabody, Massachusetts: Hendrickson).

LINDARS, B., 1972. *The Gospel of John* (NCB; London: Marshall, Morgan & Scott).

LINNEMANN, E., 1974. 'Die Hochzeit zu Kana und Dionysos', *NTS* 20: 408–18.

LIVINGSTONE, E. A. (ed.), 1980. *Studia Biblica 1978. II. Papers on the Gospels. Sixth International Congress on Biblical Studies Oxford 3-7 April 1978* (JSNTSup 2, Sheffield: JSOT Press).

LOADER, W., 1991. 'John 1:50–51 and the "Greater Things" of Johannine Christology' in C. Breytenbach & H. Paulsen (eds.), *Anfänge der Christologie: Festschrift für Ferdinand Hahn zum 65. Geburtstag* (Göttingen: Vandenhoek & Ruprecht): 255–74.

LOHSE, E., 1975. 'Miracles in the Fourth Gospel', in M.D. Hooker & C. Hickling (eds.), *What About the New Testament?: Essays in Honour of Christopher Evans* (London: SCM Press): 64–75.

LONGENECKER, R. (ed.), 1998. *Life in the Face of Death: The Resurrection Message of the New Testament* (McMaster New Testament Studies; Grand Rapids: Eerdmans).

LOWN, J. S., 1986. 'The Miraculous in the Greco-Roman Historians', *FF* 2.4: 36-42.

MACCORMACK, S., 1972. 'Change and Continuity in Late Antiquity: the ceremony of adventus', *Historia* 21: 721–52.

MACRAE, G., 1965. 'Miracles in the Antiquities of Josephus', in Moule 1965: 127–47.
MCCASLAND, S.V., 1932. 'Portents in Josephus and in the Gospels', *JBL* 51.4: 323–35.
—, 1939. 'The Asklepios Cult in Palestine', *JBL* 58.3: 221–27.
—, 1957. 'Signs and Wonders', *JBL* 76.2: 149–52.
MCGAUGHY, L. C., 1972. *Toward a Descriptive Analysis of EINAI as a Linking Verb in New Testament Greek* (SBLDS 6; Missoula, MT: SBL).
MACCINI, R. G., 1996. *Her Testimony is True. Women as Witnesses According to John* (JSNTSup 125; Sheffield: Sheffield Academic Press).
MADDEN, P. J., 1997. *Jesus' Walking on the Sea: An Investigation of the Origin of the Narrative Account* (BZNW 81: Berlin: Walter de Gruyter, 1997).
MAGIE, D., 1950: *Roman Rule in Asia Minor* (2 vols.; Princeton, N.J: Princeton University Press).
MALINA, B. R., 1992. 'Is There a Circum-Mediterranean Person? Looking for Stereotypes', *BTB* 22.2: 66–87.
MALINA B. R. & R. L. ROHRBAUGH, 1998. *Social-Science Commentary on the Gospel of John* (Minneapolis: Fortress Press).
MANETTI, G., 1993. *Theories of the Sign in Classical Antiquity* (trans. Caroline Richardson; Advances in Semiotics; Bloomington and Indianapolis: Indiana University Press).
MANSON, T. W., 1946–7. 'The Life of Jesus: A Survey of the Available Material (5) The Fourth Gospel', *BJRL* 30: 312–29.
MARCUS, J., 2000. *Mark 1–8: A New Translation with Introduction and Commentary* (AB 27; New York: Doubleday).
MARGUERAT, D. & Y. BOURQUIN, 1999. *How to Read Bible Stories: An Introduction to Narrative Criticism* (trans. John Bowden; London: SCM Press).
MARSHALL, I. H., 1978. *The Gospel of Luke. A Commentary on the Greek Text* (Exeter: The Paternoster Press).
MARTENS, E. A., 1996. םַע, in vol. 3 of *The New International Dictionary of Old Testament Theology and Exegesis* (ed. Willem A. VanGemeren; 5 vols.; Carlisle: Paternoster, 1996): 331–33.
MARTIN, W., 1986. *Recent Theories of Narrative* (Ithaca: Cornell University Press).
MARTYN, J. L., 1979. *History and Theology in the Fourth Gospel* (Nashville: Abingdon, rev. edn).
MEAD, A., 1985. 'The βασιλικός in John 4:46–53', *JSNT* 23: 69–72.
MEEKS, W., 1966. 'Galilee and Judea in the Fourth Gospel', *JBL* 85.2: 159–69.
—, 1967. *The Prophet King. Moses Traditions and the Johannine Christology* (NovTSup 14; Leiden: Brill).
MENKEN, M. J. J., 1987. 'Some Remarks on the Course of the Dialogue John 6, 25–34', *Bijdr* 48: 139–49.
—, 1993. '"The Christology of the Fourth Gospel: A Survey of Recent Research', in M.C. de Boer (ed.), *From Jesus to John: Essays on Jesus and New Testament Christology in Honour of Marinus de Jonge* (JSNTSup 84; Sheffield: Sheffield Academic Press): 292–320.
—, 1996. *Old Testament Quotations in the Fourth Gospel: Studies in Textual Form* (CBET 15; Kampen: Kok Pharos Publishing House).
MERENLAHTI, P. & RAIMO H., 1999. 'Reconceiving Narrative Criticism', in D. Rhoads & K. Syreeni (eds.), *Characterisation in the Gospel: Reconceiving Narrative Criticism* (JSNTSup 184; Sheffield: Sheffield Academic Press, 1999).
MEYER, B. F. & E. P. SANDERS (eds.), 1982. *Jewish and Christian Self-Definition: Volume Three: Self-Definition in the Graeco-Roman World* (London: SCM).
MEYER, H. A. W., 1874, 1878. *Critical and Exegetical Commentary on the New Testament: Part II, The Gospel of John* (trans. W.P. Dickson & F. Crombie; 2 vols.; Edinburgh: T&T Clark).

MICHAELS, J. R., 1989. *John* (NIBCNT; Peabody, Massachusetts: Hendrickson).

MINEAR, P. S., 1983. 'The Original Functions of John 21', *JBL* 102.1: 85–98.

—, 1984. *John: The Martyr's Gospel* (New York: The Pilgrim Press).

—, 1987. 'The Audience of the Fourth Evangelist', *Int* 31.4: 339–54.

MITCHELL, S., 1993. *Anatolia. Land, Men, and Gods in Asia Minor Volume I: The Celts in Anatolia and the Impact of Roman Rule* (Oxford: Clarendon Press).

MOLONEY, F. J., 1980. 'From Cana to Cana (John 2:1–4:54) and the Fourth Evangelist's Concept of Correct (and Incorrect) Faith', in Livingstone 1980: 185–213.

—, 1991. *Belief in the Word: Reading the Fourth Gospel: John 1–4* (Minneapolis: Fortress Press).

—, 1996. *Signs and Shadows: Reading John 5–12* (Minneapolis: Fortress Press).

—, 1999. *The Gospel of John* (SP 4; Minnesota: Collegeville).

—, 2002. Review of S. Hamid-Khani, *Revelation and Concealment of Christ. JTS* 53.2: 643–9.

MOMIGLIANO, A., 1986. 'How Roman Emperors Became Gods', *American Scholar* 55: 181–93.

MOORE, S., 1989. *Literary Criticism and the Gospels: The Theoretical Challenge* (New Haven: Yale University Press).

MORRIS, L., 1984. 'The Relation of the Signs and the Discourses in John', in W.C. Weinrich (ed.), *The New Testament Age. Essays in Honour of Bo Reicke. Vol. II* (2 vols.; Macon, Georgia: Mercer University Press): 363–72.

—, 1995. *The Gospel According to John* (NICNT; Grand Rapids: Eerdmans).

MOTYER, S., 1997a. *Your Father the Devil?: A New Approach to John and 'the Jews'* (Paternoster Biblical and Theological Monographs; Carlisle: Paternoster).

—, 1997b. 'Method in Fourth Gospel Studies: A Way Out of the Impasse?' *JSNT* 66: 27–44.

MOULE, C. F. D., 1965. *Miracles: Cambridge Studies in their Philosophy and History* (Cambridge: Cambridge University Press).

MOXNES, H., 1993. 'BTB Readers Guide: Honor and Shame', *BTB* 23.4: 168–76.

MURPHY-O'CONNOR, J., 1992. *The Holy Land: An Archaeological Guide from Earliest Times to 1700* (Oxford; Oxford University Press).

MUSSIES, G., 1988. 'Identification and Self-Identification of Gods in Classical and Hellenistic Times', in R. van den Broek et al. (eds.), *The Knowledge of God in the Graeco-Roman World* (EPRO 112; Leiden: Brill): 1–19.

NEIRYNCK, F., 1984. 'John 4.46–54. Signs Source and/or Synoptic Gospels', *ETL* 60.4: 367–75.

NEYREY, J. H., 1981. 'John III—A Debate Over Johannine Epistemology and Christology', *NovT* 23.2: 115–27.

—, 1987. 'Jesus the Judge: Forensic Process in John 8,21–59', *Bib* 68.4: 509–42.

—, 1995a. 'The Trials (Forensic) and Tribulations (Honor Challenges) of Jesus: John 7 in Social Science Perspective', *BTB* 26.3: 107–24.

—, 1995b. 'Despising the Shame of the Cross: Honor and Shame in the Johannine Passion Narrative', *Semeia* 68: 113–37.

NICOL, W., 1970. *The Sēmeia in the Fourth Gospel: Tradition and Redaction* (NovTSup 32; Leiden: Brill).

NOETZEL, H., 1960. *Christus und Dionysos: Bemerkungen zum religionsgeschichtlichen Hintergrund von Johannes 2,1–11* (Arbeiten zur Theologie 1; Stuttgart: Calwer Verlag).

NOLLAND, J., 1989. *Luke 1-9.20* (WBC 35a; Dallas: Word Books).

O'DAY, G. R., 1995. *The Gospel of John: Introduction, Commentary, and Reflections* (NIB IX; Nashville: Abingdon Press, 1994–2002).

—, 1997. 'John 6:15–21: Jesus Walking on the Water as Narrative Embodiment of Johannine Christology', in Culpepper 1997: 149–59.

O'ROURKE, J. J., 1999. 'Asides in the Gospel of John', in Orton 1999: 205–62.

OKURE, T., 1988. *The Johannine Approach to Mission: A Contextual Study of John 4:1–42* (WUNT 2.31; Tübingen: Mohr Siebeck).

OLSSON, B., 1974. *Structure and Meaning in the Fourth Gospel: A Text-Linguistic Analysis of John 2:1–11 and 4:1–42* (ConBNT 6; Lund: CWK Gleerup).

ORLIN, E. M., 1997. *Temples, Religion and Politics in the Roman Republic* (MnS 164; Leiden: Brill).

ORTON, D.E. (Compiler), 1999. *The Composition of John's Gospel. Selected Studies from Novum Testamentum* (Brill's Readers in Biblical Studies 2; Leiden: Brill).

ØSTENSTAD, G., 1998. *Patterns of Redemption in the Fourth Gospel: An Experiment in Structural Analysis* (Studies in the Bible and Early Christianity 38; Lampeter: The Edwin Mellen Press).

OSTER, R., 1990. 'Ephesus as a Religious Centre under the Principate', *ANRW* 18.3: 1661–1728. Part 2, *Principat*, 18.3 (Edited by H. Temporini & W. Haase, New York: de Gruyter, 1990).

PAINTER, J., 1986. 'John 9 and the Interpretation of the Fourth Gospel', *JSNT* 28: 31–61.

—, 1993. *The Quest for the Messiah: The History, Literature and Theology of the Johannine Community* (Edinburgh: T&T Clark, 2nd edn).

PARKER, P., 1962. 'John the Son of Zebedee and the Fourth Gospel', *JBL* 81.1: 35–43.

PATERSON, J. J., 1996. 'Wine', in S. Hornblower and A. Spawforth (eds.), *The Oxford Classical Dictionary* (Oxford: Oxford University Press, 3rd edn): 1622–3.

PERVO, R. I., 1994. 'PANTA KOINA: The Feeding Stories in the Light of Economic Data and Social Practice', in Bormann et al.: 163–94.

PETERSON, D. N., 2000. *The Origins of Mark: The Markan Community in Current Debate* (BIS 48; Leiden: Brill).

PFITZNER, V. C., 1977. 'The Coronation of the King', *CurTM* 4.1: 10–21.

PLUMER, E., 1997. 'The Absence of Exorcisms in the Fourth Gospel', *Bib* 78.3: 350–68.

PORTER, S. E., 1994. 'Can Traditional Exegesis Enlighten Literary Analysis of the Fourth Gospel? An Examination of the Old Testament Fulfilment Motif and the Passover Theme', in Evans & Stegner 1994: 396–28.

—, 1997. *Handbook of Classical Rhetoric in the Hellenistic Period: 330 B.C.—A.D. 400* (S. Porter (ed.); Leiden: Brill).

PRATT, M. L., 1977. *Toward a Speech Act Theory of Literary Discourse* (Bloomington: Indiana University Press).

PREISS, T., 1954. *Life In Christ* (trans. Harold Knight; SBT 13 London: SCM Press).

PRICE, S. R. F., 1984a *Rituals and Power: The Roman Imperial Cult in Asia Minor* (Cambridge: Cambridge University Press).

—, 1984b. 'Gods and Emperors: the Greek Language of the Roman Imperial Cult', *JHS* 104: 28–43.

—, 2000. 'The Place of Religion: Rome in the Early Empire', in A. K. Bowman et al. (eds.) *The Cambridge Ancient History Vol. X: The Augustan Empire, 43 B.C.–A.D.69* (Cambridge: Cambridge University Press, 2nd edn): 812–847.

PROPP, W. H. C., 1999. *Exodus 1–18: A New Translation with Introduction and Commentary* (AB 2; New York: Doubleday).

PRYOR, J., 1987. 'John 4:44 and the Patris of Jesus', *CBQ* 49.2: 254–63.

—, 1992. *John: Evangelist of the Covenant People: The Narrative and Themes of the Fourth Gospel* (Downers Grove: IVP).

PURCELL, N., 1995. 'Eating Fish. The Paradoxes of Seafood', in J. Wilkins et al. (eds.), *Food in Antiquity* (Exeter: University of Exeter Press): 132–49.

RABINOWITZ, P. J., 1977. 'Truth in Fiction: A Reexamination of Audiences', *Critical Inquiry* 4: 121–41.

—, 1989. 'Whirl Without End: Audience Orientated Criticism', in G.D. Atkins & L. Morrow (eds.), *Contemporary Literary Theory* (Massachusetts: University of Massachusetts Press): 81–100.

REINHARTZ, A., 1983. 'John 20: 30–31 and the Purpose of the Fourth Gospel' (PhD diss., McMaster University, Ontario).

—, 1992. *The Word in the World: The Cosmological Tale in the Fourth Gospel* (SBLMS 45; Atlanta: Scholars Press).

RENGSTORF, K. H., 1971. σημεῖον, κ.τ.λ. in vol. 7 of G. Kittel & G. Friedrich (eds.) *Theological Dictionary of the New Testament* (trans. G.W. Bromiley; 10 vols.; Grand Rapids: Eerdmans, 1964–1976): 7.200–69.

RENSBERGER, D., 1984. 'The Politics of John: The Trial of Jesus in the Fourth Gospel', *JBL* 103.3: 395–411.

—, 1989. *Overcoming the World: Politics and Community in the Gospel of John* (London: SPCK).

REMUS, H., 1982. 'Does Terminology Distinguish Early Christian From Pagan Miracles?', *JBL* 101.4: 531–551.

RESSEGUIE, J. L., 1982. 'John 9: A Literary–Critical Analysis', in K.R.R. Gros Louis (ed.), *Literary Interpretations of Biblical Narratives Vol. 2* (2 Vols.; Nashville; Abingdon): 295–303.

RICHARD, E. E., 1985. 'Expressions of Double Meaning and Their Function in the Gospel of John', *NTS* 31: 96–112.

RICOEUR, P., 1980. 'The Hermeneutics of Testimony', in P. Ricoeur, *Essays on Biblical Interpretation* (Philadelphia: Fortress Press, 1980): 119–54.

RIDDERBOS, H., 1997. *The Gospel According to John: A Theological Commentary* (trans. John Vriend; Grand Rapids: Eerdmans).

RIGA, P., 1963. 'Signs of Glory. The Use of "Semeion" in St. John's Gospel', *Int* 17: 402–424.

RIMMON-KENAN, S., 1983. *Narrative Fiction: Contemporary Poetics* (New Accents; London: Methuen).

ROBINSON, J. A. T., 1959–60. 'The Destination and Purpose of St John's Gospel', *NTS* 6: 117–131.

—, 1985. *The Priority of John* (ed. J.F. Coakley; London: SCM).

ROHDE, E., 1925. *Psyche: The Cult of Souls and Belief in Immortality among the Greeks* (London: Kegan Paul, Trench, Trubner & Co.).

RUNIA, D. T., 1986. *Philo of Alexandria and the Timaeus of Plato* (Philosophia Antiqua 44; Leiden: Brill).

SALIER, B., 1998. 'What's in a World? Κόσμος in the Prologue of John's Gospel', *RTR* 56.3: 105–117.

—, 1999. 'The World of John's Gospel: The Meaning and Function of κόσμος in the Gospel According to John' (MTh Diss., Australian College of Theology, Kensington, N.S.W.).

SANDMEL, S., 1962. 'Parallelomania', *JBL* 81.1: 1–13.

SARNA, N., 1987. *Exploring Exodus: The Heritage of Biblical Israel* (New York: Schocken Books).

—, 1991. *The JPS Torah Commentary: Exodus: The Traditional Hebrew text with the New JPS Translation* (JPS Torah Commentary; Philadephia: The Jewish Publication Society).

SCHERRER, S. J., 1984. 'Signs and Wonders in the Imperial Cult: A New Look at a Roman Religious Institution in the Light of Rev 13:13–15', *JBL* 103.4: 599–610.

SCHNACKENBURG, R., 1968, 1980, 1982. *The Gospel According to John* (trans. Kevin Smyth; 3 vols.; Kent: Burns & Oates).

SCHNELLE, U., 1992. *Antidocetic Christology in the Gospel of John: An Investigation of the Place of the Fourth Gospel in the Johannine School* (trans. L.M. Moloney; Minneapolis: Fortress Press).

SCHOLTISSEK, K., 1998. 'Johannine Studies: A Survey of Recent Research with Special Regard to German Contributions', *CurBS* 6: 227–59.

SCOTT, K., 1933. 'Statius' Adulation of Domitian', *American Journal of Philology* 54: 247–59.

—, 1975. *The Imperial Cult Under the Flavians* (Ancient Religion and Mythology; New York: Arno Press, repr. [orig. Stuttgart-Berlin: W. Kohlhammer, 1936]).

SCOTT, R. T., 1968. 'Religion and Philosophy in the Histories of Tacitus', *Papers and Monographs of the American Academy in Rome* 22: 53–70, 79–95.

SEGAL, A. F., 1981. 'Ruler of this World: Attitudes about Mediator Figures and the Importance of Sociology for Self-Definition', in E.P. Sanders et al. (eds.), *Jewish and Christian Self-Definition. Volume Two: Aspects of Judaism in the Graeco-Roman Period* (Philadelphia: Fortress Press, 1981): 245–268.

SHERWIN-WHITE, A. N., 1963. *Roman Society and Roman Law in the New Testament: The Sarum Lectures 1960-61* (Oxford: The Clarendon Press).

SIEGMAN, E. F., 1968. 'St. John's Use of Synoptic Material', *CBQ* 30.2: 182–98.

SIM, D. C., 2001. 'The Gospels for All Christians? A Response to Richard Bauckham', *JSNT* 84: 3–27.

SMALLEY, S., 1974. 'The Sign in John XXI', *NTS* 20: 275–88.

SMITH JR., D. M., 1975 'Johannine Christianity: Some Reflections on its Character and Delineation', *NTS* 21: 222–48.

SMITH, J. Z., 1974. 'Good News is No News: Aretalogy and Gospel', in Neusner, J. (ed.), *Christianity, Judaism and Other Greco-Roman Cults: Studies for Morton Smith at Sixty. Part I: New Testament* (SJLA 12; Leiden: Brill): 21–38.

SMITH, M., 1974. 'On The Wine God in Palestine (Gen 18; John 2 and Achilles Tatius'), in S. Lieberman (ed.), *Salo Wittmayer Baron Jubilee Volume On the Occasion of His Eightieth Birthday* (3 vols.; The American Academy for Jewish Research; New York: Columbia University Press): 2.815–29.

SMITH, R. H., 1962. 'Exodus Typology in the Fourth Gospel', *JBL* 81.4: 329–42.

SMITH, S. H., 1996. *A Lion With Wings: A Narrative–Critical Approach to Mark's Gospel* (The Biblical Seminar 38; Sheffield: Sheffield Academic Press).

SNAPE, H.C., 1954. 'The Fourth Gospel, Ephesus and Alexandria', *HTR* 47.1: 1–14.

SÖDING, T., 1996 'Die Macht der Wahrheit und das Reich der Freiheit: Zur johanneischen Deutung des Pilatus-Prozesses (Joh 18,28–19.16)', *ZTK* 93: 35–58.

SPROSTON, W. E., 1980. 'Satan in the Fourth Gospel', in Livingstone 1980: 307–11.

—, 1985. '"Is this not Jesus, the son of Joseph...?" (John 6:42). Johannine Christology as a Challenge to Faith', *JSNT* 24 (1985): 77–97.

STACEY, D., 1990. *Prophetic Drama in the Old Testament* (London: Epworth Press).

STALEY, J. L., 1988. *The Print's First Kiss: A Rhetorical Investigation of the Implied Reader in the Fourth Gospel* (SBLDS 82; Atlanta: Scholars Press).

—, 1995. *Reading With a Passion: Rhetoric, Autobiography, and the American West in the Gospel of John* (New York: Continuum).

STAMPS, D. L., 1997. 'The Johannine Writings', in Porter (ed.) 1997: 609–32.

STANTON G. N., 2002. *The Gospels and Jesus* (Oxford Bible Series; Oxford: Oxford University Press, 2nd edn).

STARK, R., 1992. 'Epidemics, Networks, and the Rise of Christianity', *Semeia* 56: 159–75.

—, 1996. *The Rise of Christianity: A Sociologist Reconsiders* (Princeton: Princeton University Press).

STAUFFER, E., 1955. *Christ and the Caesars: Historical Sketches* (London: SCM).

STIBBE, M. G. W., 1992. *John as Storyteller: Narrative Criticism and the Fourth Gospel* (SNTSMS 73; Cambridge: Cambridge University Press).

—, 1993. *John* (Readings: A New Biblical Commentary; Sheffield: JSOT Press).

TALBERT, C. H., 1975. 'The Concept of Immortals in Mediterranean Antiquity', *JBL* 94.3: 419–36.

—, 1978. 'Biographies of Philosophers and Rulers as Instruments of Religious Propaganda in Mediterranean Antiquity', *ANRW* 16.2:1619–51. Part 2, *Principat*, 16.2 (Edited by H. Temporini & W. Haase, New York: de Gruyter, 1978).

—, 1992. *Reading John: A Literary and Theological Commentary on the Fourth Gospel and the Johannine Epistles* (Reading the New Testament Series; London: SPCK).

TEMPLE, S., 1962. 'The Two Signs in the Fourth Gospel', *JBL* 81.2: 169–74.

TENNEY, M. C., 1975. 'Topics from the Gospel of John. Part II: The Meaning of the Signs', *BibSac* 132: 145–60.

THATCHER, T., 1994. 'A New Look at Asides in the Fourth Gospel', *BibSac* 151: 428–39.

THEISSEN, G., 1983. *The Miracle Stories of the Early Christian Tradition* (trans. F. McDonagh; John Riches (ed.); Philadelphia: Fortress Press).

—, 1999. *The Religion of the Earliest Churches. Creating a Symbolic World* (trans. J. Bowden; Minneapolis: Fortress Press).

THOMAS, J. C., 1995. '"Stop sinning lest something worse come upon you": The Man at the Pool in John 5', *JSNT* 59: 3–20.

THOMPSON, M. M., 1988. *The Incarnate Word: Perspectives on Jesus in the Fourth Gospel* (Peabody, MA: Hendrickson).

1991. 'Signs and Faith in the Fourth Gospel', *BBR* 1: 89–108.

TIEDE, D., 1984. 'Religious Propaganda and the Gospel Literature of the Early Christian Mission', *ANRW* 25.2: 1705–1729. Part 2, *Principat* 25.2 (Edited by H. Temporini & W. Haase, New York: de Gruyter, 1984).

TINH, T. T., 1982. 'Sarapis and Isis', in B.F. Meyer & E.P. Sanders (eds.) 1982: 101–117.

TOMSON, P. J., 2001. '"Jews" in the Gospel of John as Compared with the Palestinian Talmud, the Synoptics, and Some New Testament Apocrypha', in R. Bieringer et al. (eds.), *Anti–Judaism and the Fourth Gospel* (Louisville: Westminster John Knox Press, 2001): 176–212.

TOVEY, D., 1997. *Narrative Art and Act in the Fourth Gospel* (JSNTSup 151; Sheffield: Sheffield Academic Press).

TOYNBEE, J. M. C., 1971. *Death and Burial in the Roman World* (Aspects of Greek & Roman Life; London: Thames & Hudson).

TRIPOLITIS, A., 2002. *Religions of the Hellenistic-Roman Age* (Grand Rapids: Eerdmans).

TRITES, A. A., 1977. *The New Testament Concept of Witness* (Cambridge: Cambridge University Press).

TURNER, J. D, 1991. 'The History of Religions Background of John 10', in J. Beutler & R.T. Fortna (eds.) *The Shepherd Discourse of John 10: Studies by Members of the Johannine Writings Seminar* (SNTSMS 67; Cambridge: Cambridge University Press, 1991): 33–52.

TWELFTREE, G. H., 1999. *Jesus The Miracle Worker: A Historical and Theological Study* (Downers Grove: IVP).

TYLER, R. L., 1989. 'The Source and Function of Isaiah 6.9-10 in John 12.40' in J. Priest (ed), *Johannine Studies: Essays in Honor of Frank Pack* (Malibu, Calif: Pepperdine University Press, 1989): 205-220.

UNWIN, T., 1991. *Wine and the Vine: An Historical Geography of Viticulture and the Wine Trade* (London: Routledge).

VAN BELLE, G., 1994. *The Signs Source in the Fourth Gospel: Historical Survey and Critical Evaluation of the Semeia Hypothesis* (BETL 116; Leuven: Leuven University Press).

—, 1998. 'The Meaning of ΣΗΜΕΙΑ in John 20,30–31', *ETL* 74: 300–25.

VAN DEN HEEVER, G.A., 1992. 'Theological Metaphorics and the Metaphors of John's Gospel', *Neot* 26.1: 89–100.

—, 1998. 'Finding Data in Unexpected Places (Or: From Text Linguistics to Socio-Rhetoric). A Socio-Rhetorical reading of John's Gospel', in E.H. Lovering Jr. (ed.), *SBL 1998 Seminar Papers (Part 2)* (Atlanta: Scholars Press): 649–76.

VAN DER HORST, P., 1991. *Ancient Jewish Epitaphs: An Introductory Survey of a Millennium of Jewish Funerary Epigraphy* (300 BC– 700 CE) (CBET, Kampen: Kok Pharos Publishing House).

VAN DER WATT, J. G., 1995. 'The Composition of the Prologue of John's Gospel: The Historical Jesus Introducing Divine Grace', *WTJ* 57: 311–32.

—, 2000. *Family of the King: Dynamics of Metaphor in the Gospel according to John* (BIS 47; Leiden: Brill).

VANHOOZER, K. J., 1995. 'The Reader in New Testament Interpretation', in J.B. Green (ed.), *Hearing the New Testament: Strategies for Interpretation* (Grand Rapids: Eerdmans): 301–28.

VAN GRONINGEN, B. A., 1953. *In the Grip of the Past: Essay on an Aspect of Greek Thought* (Philosophia Antiqua 6; Leiden: Brill).

VAN IERSEL, B., 1998. *Mark: A Reader-Response Commentary* (JSNTSup 164; Sheffield: Sheffield Academic Press).

VAN TILBORG, S., 1989. 'The Gospel of John: Communicative Processes in a Narrative Text', *Neot* 23.1: 19–31.

—, 1996. *Reading John in Ephesus* (NovTSup 83; Leiden: Brill).

VAN UNNIK, W. C., 1959. 'The Purpose of John's Gospel', in K. Aland et al. (eds.) *Studia Evangelica I. Papers presented to the International Congress on "The Four Gospels in 1957" held at Christ Church, Oxford, 1957* (TU 73; Berlin: Akadamie-Verlag, 1959): 381–411.

VEYNE, P., 1990. *Bread and Circuses: Historical Sociology and Political Pluralism* (Abridged with an introduction by Oswyn Murray; trans. Brian Pearce; London: The Penguin Press).

VORSTER, W.S, 1989. 'The Reader in the Text: Narrative Material', *Semeia* 48: 21-39.

WAHLDE, U. C. VON, 1981. 'The Witnesses to Jesus in John 5:31–40 and Belief in the Fourth Gospel', *CBQ* 43.3: 385–404.

—, 1984. 'Literary Structure and Theological Argument in Three Discourses with the Jews in the Fourth Gospel', *JBL* 103.4: 575–84.

WALTERS, J., 1995. 'Egyptian Religions in Ephesos', in H. Koester (ed.) 1995: 281–310.

WARNER, M., 1990. 'The Fourth Gospel's Art of Rational Persuasion' in M. Warner (ed.) *The Bible as Rhetoric: Studies in Rational Persuasion and Credibility* (Warwick Studies in Philosophy and Literature; London: Routledge): 153–77.

WATSON, A., 1992. *The State, Law and Religion: Pagan Rome* (Athens, Ga: The University of Georgia Press).

WEBB, B., 1990. 'Zion in Transformation. A Literary Approach to Isaiah' in D.J.Clines et al. (eds), *The Bible In Three Dimensions* (Sheffield: Sheffield Academic Press): 65-84.

1996. *The Message of Isaiah: On Eagle's Wings* (BST; Leicester: IVP).

WEDDERBURN, A. J. M., 1987. *Baptism and Resurrection: Studies in Pauline Theology against Its Graeco-Roman Background* (WUNT 44; Tübingen: Mohr Siebeck).

WEEBER, K-W., 1993. *Die Weinkultur der Römer* (Zürich: Artemis & Winkler).

WELCK, C., 1994. *Erzählte Zeichen: Die Wundergeschichten des Johannesevangeliums literarisch untersucht. Mit einem Ausblick auf Joh 21* (WUNT 2.69; Tübingen: Mohr Siebeck).

WELLS, L., 1998. *The Greek Language of Healing from Homer to New Testament Times* (BZNW 83; Berlin: Walter de Gruyter).

WENGST, K., 1987. *Pax Romana and the Peace of Jesus Christ* (trans. John Bowden; London: SCM).

WENHAM, D., 1998. 'The Enigma of the Fourth Gospel: Another Look', in C. Rowland and C.H.T. Fletcher-Louis (eds.), *Understanding, Studying and Reading. New Testament Essays in Honour of John Ashton* (JSNTSup 153; Sheffield: Sheffield Academic Press): 102–28.

WESTCOTT, B. F., 1908. *The Gospel According to John: The Greek Text with Introduction and Notes* (2 vols.; London: John Murray).

WIEDEMANN, T., 1989. *Adults and Children in the Roman Empire* (London: Routledge, 1989).

WILKENS, W., 1969. *Zeichen und Werke: Ein Beitrag zur Theologie des 4. Evangeliums in Erzählungs-und Redestoff* (ATANT 55; Zürich: Zwingli).

WILKINS, J. M., 1993. 'Social Status and Fish in Greece and Rome', in G.V. Mars (ed.) *Food Culture and History* (London): 191–203.

WILLIAMS, C. H., 2000. *I am He: The Interpretation of 'Anî Hû' in Jewish and Early Christian Literature* (WUNT 2.113; Tübingen: Mohr Siebeck).

WINTER, B. W., 1994. 'Acts and Roman Religion. B. The Imperial Cult', in D.W.J. Gill & C. Gempf (eds.), *The Book of Acts in its Greco-Roman Setting. Vol. 2 of The Book of Acts in Its First Century Setting* (ed. B. W. Winter; Grand Rapids: Eerdmans, 1994): 93–103.

—, 1996. 'On Introducing Gods to Athens: An Alternative Reading of Acts 17:18-20', *TynBul* 47: 71–90.

WISTRAND, E., 1987. *Felicitas Imperatoria* (Göteborg: Acta Universitatis Gothoburgensis).

WITHERINGTON III, B., 1995. *John's Wisdom: A Commentary on the Fourth Gospel* (Louisville, Ken.: Westminster John Knox Press).

WRIGHT, N. T., 2000, 'A Fresh Perspective on Paul?', The T.W. Manson Memorial Lecture, presented at Westminster Abbey, October 26, 2000.

YOUNG, F. W., 1955. 'Study of the Relation of Isaiah to the Fourth Gospel', *ZNTW* 46.3-4: 215-223.

YOUNGER, F. W., 1966. *Gods, Men, and Wine* (London: The Wine and Food Society).

ZANKER, P., 1988. *The Power of Images in the Age of Augustus* (trans. A Shapiro; Jerome Lectures 16; Ann Arbor: University of Michigan Press).

ZELLER, D., 2001. 'New Testament Christology in its Hellenistic Reception', *NTS* 46: 312–33.

ZEVIT, Z., 1990. 'Three Ways to Look at the Ten Plagues. Were they Natural Disasters, a Demonstration of the Impotence of the Egyptian Gods or an Undoing of Creation?' *BRev* 6.3: 16–23, 42, 44.

ZIMMERLI, W., 1979, 1983. *Ezekiel. A Commentary on the Book of the Prophet Ezekiel, Chapters 1–24* (F.M. Cross et al. (eds.); trans. R.E. Clements; Hermeneia; 2 vols.; Philadelphia: Fortress Press).

Index of Authors

Anderson, P. N. 85, 88, 103, 113
Ashton, J. 148
Asiedu-Peprah, M. 48, 79, 81, 94, 96, 98
Aurenhammer 11, 67, 101

Bal, M. 62
Bammel, E. 92, 148
Barnett, P.W. 31, 32
Barr, J. 16
Barrett, C. K. 3, 11, 13, 18, 25, 46, 50, 51, 56,
    59, 74, 85, 108, 145, 150, 151
Barth, K. 13
Bauckham, R. 10, 51, 93, 143, 168
Beasley-Murray, G. R. 11, 85, 97, 126, 132,
    148
Becker, J. 53, 129
van Belle, G. 1, 2, 148, 149
Berlin, A. 62, 96
Betz, O. 40, 44, 67
Bevan, E. 133
Bittner, W. 3, 19, 20, 32, 54, 58, 81, 83, 88, 93,
    95, 122, 124, 128, 148, 177
Black II, C. C. 137
Blenkinsopp 124
Blomberg, C. L. 157
Bock, D.L. 42
Bolt, P. G. 6, 7, 42, 61, 73, 100, 115, 136, 169
Bonney, W. 53
Borgen, P. 85
Boring, E. 101
Brent, A. 166
Broer, I. 67
Brown, R. E. 3, 11, 12, 51, 55, 59, 85, 88, 98,
    108, 123, 124, 125, 148, 152, 158
Brownson, J. V.
Bultmann, R. 1, 2, 53, 67, 129, 148, 149, 155
Burkert, W. 102, 107, 137, 138
Burridge, R. A.
Buth, R. 149

Calvin, J. 84, 133
Carson, D. A. 11, 12, 52, 56, 127, 145, 148,
    149, 150, 153
Carter, W. 165

Carey, E. 27
Casey, M. 12
Cassidy, R. 164, 177
Charlier, J-P. 124
Chesnut, G. F. 166
Childs, B. S. 20
Clark, D. K. 3
Cole, A. 20
Collins, A.Y. 110
Collins, J. J. 94
Collins, M. S. 70
Collins, R. F. 50
Cotter, W. 101, 110
Cotterell, P. & M. Turner 4
Crapis, C. 37
Crook, J. A. 87
Crouch, F. L. 15
Culpepper, R. A. 3, 9, 12, 47, 126,
    127, 129, 131

Dahl, N. A. 47
Dahms, J. V. 159
Daly-Denton, M. 88
Davies, W. D. 101
Davies, W.D. & D.C. Allison 42
de Jonge, M. 89, 93, 151
Deissmann, A. 74
Derrett, J. D. M. 62, 159
Dodd, C. H. 13, 57, 64, 148
Dumbrell, W. J. 78
Duprez, A. 101
Durham, J. I. 21

Ebeling, G. 8
Eco, U. 6
Edwards, R. 10
Ehrenberg, V. & A.H.M. Jones 69,
    166, 167
Ensor, P. W. 91, 151
Esler, P.
Esser, A. 114
Evans, C. A. 94, 156

Fears, J. R. 166

Fee, G. D. 152
Fitzmyer, J. 94
Formesyn, R. 22, 28, 29, 30, 34
Fortna, R. T. 2
Freed, E. D. 18
Fretheim, T. E. 20
Frey, J. 12, 77, 124, 129, 134
Friebel, K. G. 24
Frier, B. W. 135, 136

Garland, R. 73, 114
Garnsey, P. 105
Gese, H. 51
Giblin, C. C. 58, 64
Gibson, J. 32, 41, 131
Glasson, T. F. 42, 55, 124
Goetchius, E. V. N. 153
Grant, F.C. 111
Gray, R. 30
Grayston, K. 67
Green, J.B. 42
Grigsby, B. 112
Gundry, R. 42

Haenchen, E. 55
Hagenow, G. 65, 70
Hanson, A. T. 3
Harrison, J. E. 138
Harvey, A. E. 47, 48, 78, 79, 87, 94, 155
Hawthorn, J. 7
Head, P. M. 47
Heever, G.A. van den 164, 177
Heil, J. P. 108
Heiligenthal, R. 89
Helfmeyer, F. J. 19
Henaut, B. W. 126, 152
Hengel, M. 11, 66, 67, 101, 163
Higgins, A. J. B. 42
Hill, D. 32
Hofbeck, S. 2, 3
Hopkins, K. 11
Hooker, M. D. 40, 41, 88, 89
Horsley, R.A. 12
van der Horst, P. 73
Hoskyns, E. C. 148
Houtman, C. 21, 22

Iersel, B. van 6, 7, 10
Instone-Brewer, D. 157

Jackson, H. M. 54, 153
Johns, L. L. & D. B. Miller 3, 4, 58, 177

Jones, H.L. 27
Just, F. N. W. 7, 89, 112, 114, 116

Kammler, H-C. 148
Kee, A. 165
Kern, P.H. 25
Kiley, M. 3
Klauck, H-J. 100, 166
Klausner, J. 93
Knibbe, D. 11, 107
Koester, C. R. 10, 53, 67, 69, 74, 111, 158, 164
Kossen, H. B. 122
Köstenberger, A. J. 3, 52, 145, 148
Kovacs, J. L. 123
Kuhn, K. G. 12
Kysar, R. 2

Labahn, M. 4, 5, 17, 55, 67, 74, 81, 84, 95, 98
Lattimore, R. 29, 73, 137
Lee, D. A. 114
Lewis & Reinhold   105
LiDonnici 116
Lightfoot, R. H. 86, 92
Lincoln, A. T. 17, 45, 47, 48, 89, 95, 120, 122, 147, 149, 150, 152, 153, 158, 159, 160, 163, 177
Linnemann, E. 67, 68
Loader, W. 63

MacCormack, S. 164
MacRae, G. 32
McCasland, S.V. 30, 101
McGaughy, L. C. 153
Magie, D. 70, 74
Malina B. R. & R. L. Rohrbaugh 62
Manetti, G. 37
Manson, T. W. 11
Marshall, I. H. 41
Martin, V. & Barns J.W.B. 152
Martyn, J. L. 88
Mead, A. 70
Meeks, W. 83, 87, 88
Menken, M. J. J. 18, 86, 126
Meyer, H. A. W. 107
Minear, P. S 148
Mitchell, S. 11, 165
Moloney, F. J. 8, 9, 10, 47, 51, 54, 56, 70, 97, 122
Moore, S. 6

Morris, L. 98, 148
Motyer, S. 9, 10, 11
Moxnes, H. 163
Murphy-O'Connor, J. 101

Naveh,J & S. Shaked 100
Neyrey, J. H. 54, 87, 164
Nicol, W. 53, 80, 148
Noetzel, H. 67
Nolland, J. 42

O'Day, G. R. 148
Okure, T. 153
Olsson, B. 50
Østenstad, G. 142
Oster, R. 11, 67, 70, 101

Pervo, R. I. 105
Porter, S. E. 86, 157
Preiss, T. 47, 48
Price, S. R. F. 12, 165
Propp, W. H. C. 20, 21
Pryor, J. 47, 56, 153
Purcell, N. 107

Rabinowitz, P. J. 9
Reinhartz, A. 13, 149
Rengstorf, K. H. 26, 27, 41, 42
Rensberger, D. 160
Resseguie, J. L. 114
Ricoeur, P. 147
Ridderbos, H. 50, 67, 108
Riga, P. 1
Rimmon-Kenan, S. 62
Robinson, J. A. T. 11, 12
Runia, D. T. 100

Salier, B. 13
Sarna, N. 21, 22
Scherrer, S. J. 168
Schnackenburg, R. 3, 53, 57, 82, 93, 124, 127, 133, 148
Schnelle, U. 149
Scott, K. 168
Scott, R. T. 29
Segal, A. F. 69
Sherk, R. K. 167

Sim, D. C. 10
Smith, M. 67
Smith, R. H. 3, 67
Smith, S. H. 61
Söding, T. 155
Stacey, D. 23, 24
Staley, J. L. 64
Stamps, D. L. 45
Stark, R. 11
Strack, Billerbeck 131
Stibbe, M. G.W. 67, 157

Thomas, J. C. 97
Thompson, M. M. 58, 76, 177
van Tilborg, S. 67, 107, 164, 165
Tinh, T. T. 111
Tomson, P. J. 12
Toynbee, J. M. C. 137
Trites, A. A. 47, 48

van Unnik, W.C. 11
Unwin, T. 65, 69

Vanhoozer, K. J. 5
Veyne, P. 105
Vorster 9

Wallace, D.B. 41, 53, 153
Walters, J. 111
Warner, M. 148
van der Watt, J.G. 13
Weeber, K-W. 65
Welck, C. 4, 60, 84, 95, 148
Wells, L. 101
Wengst, K. 154, 167
Wiedemann, T. 73
Wilkens, W. 52
Wilkins, J. M. 107
Winter, B. W. 11, 165
Witherington III, B. 12, 98

Young, F. W. 14
Younger, F. W. 65, 66, 67
Youtie, H.C. 35

Zevit Z. 22

Index of References

OLD TESTAMENT

Genesis

1.14	19
2.7	99, 162
4.15	19
9.12	19
9.15	21
15.1	109
17.11	19
26.24	109
27.28	66
44.23	58
46.3	109
49.10	88
49.11-2	66

Exodus

3.11	19,20
3.12	19,20, 40
4	21
4.1	21
4.5	21
4.8	21
4.9	21
4.1-9	19
4.7-8	19
4.11	116
4.22	21
4.30-31	20
4.31	19, 21
6.6	126
6.7	22
7.1-7	21
7.3	19, 22
7.5	22
7.9	19
8.18-9	22
8.22	22
9.14	22
9.16	22

10.2	22
11.9,10	19
12.12	22, 69, 157
12.22	157
12.46	157
13.9	19
14-15	109
31.13	19
34	51

Leviticus

19.14	115
26.26	115

Numbers

9.12	157
13.23	66
13.26	66
14.11	19, 21, 23, 57
14.22-24	23
15.5	66
15.7	66
17.3	19
19.12	58
21.4-9	23
21.6-9	55
21.8	19
21.8-9	124
21.9	19, 55, 75
24.17	88
26.10	19
33.4	22, 69

Deuteronomy

4.34-5	22, 23, 57
5.15	126
7.3	66
7.13	107
6.8	19
7.18-19	21

Deuteronomy (continued)

9.2-3	22
11.14	66, 107
13	23, 90
13.1-6	89
18	88, 93
18.15-22	83
19.15	81
19.15-21	61
27.18	115
28.28-9	115
28.39	66
28.65	115, 116
29.2-4	125
32.14	66
32.39	21, 99

Joshua

2.18	18
24.2-5	22

Judges

6.16-24	19
6.17	18
6.23	109
6.36-40	19

1 Samuel/1 Kingdoms (LXX)

2.34	20 (LXX), 40
4.10	19
5.1-5	22 LXX
6.4-6	22 LXX
10.1	18 LXX
10.1-16	19 LXX

2 Samuel

12.22-3	138

1 Kings/3 Kingdoms (LXX)

10.1-16	19 LXX
11.29-31	23 LXX
13.1-6	19 LXX
17.17-24	138
18.20-40	22 LXX
18.36-40	23 LXX
22.11	23 LXX

2 Kings/4 Kingdoms (LXX)

4.18-37	138
4.42-44	104
13.14-19	23 LXX
18.31	66 LXX
19.29	19 LXX, 40

2 Chronicles

32.24	19

Job

9.8	109
11.20	115, 116
17.5	115, 116
21.17	115, 116
21.29	20
33.4	99
38.16	109

Psalms

2.31	138
3.12	138
13.11	138
14.9-10	138
29.3	109
65.7	109
69.23	115, 116
77.32-57	23
85.8-9	23
88.10-12	138
104.15	66
134.5-13	22
146	94
146.8	117

Proverbs

3.10	66
13.9	115, 116
20.20	115, 116
24.19-20	115, 116
30.17	115

Ecclesiastes

11.10	58
12.15	58

Isaiah

5.26	24
6.10	126
7.10-17	19
8.18	41
11	93, 124, 159
11.1	124
11.2	93
11.2-4	124
11.3-4	124, 159
11.6-9	124
11.9	93
11.10	24, 42, 124
11.10-12	42, 124
11.10-16	124
11.12	19, 24, 124, 159, 161
13.2	19
16.10	66
19.1	69
20.1-4	23
20.3	41
24.7	66
25.6	66, 104, 105
26.9	138
26.19	93, 94
27.2-6	66
29.18	93, 94, 117
29.18-19	94
35.5	94, 99, 117
35.5-6	93
37.30	19, 20, 40
40-55	48
42	93, 117
42.1	47
42.6-7	116, 124
42.7	94, 117
43	159
43.1	109
43.1-5	109
43.9-10	159
43.10	48
43.11	159, 160
43.12	48
44.1-5	109
44.10	160
45.20	160
45.21	160
46.7	160
48.20-21	93
49.6	162
49.6-7	124
49.22	24, 42
51.10	109
53.1	126, 127
53.4	93
55	159
55.1	105
55.1-2	104
55.4	159
59.9-10	115
61	93
61.1	93, 94
62.10	24, 42
66	162
66.19	24, 42, 162

Jeremiah

10.2	18
13.1-11	23
28.7	66
28.12	19
28.27	19
31.12	66
51.29	24

Lamentations

3.1-2	115
3.6	115

Ezekiel

4-5	23
9.4-6	19
12.6	41
12.15	24
12.16	24
12.20	24
14.8	24
34.1-10	119
36	54
37.9	162

Daniel

4.1-3	22
6.25-8	22
12.2-3	138

Hosea

2.9	66

Hosea (continued)

2.22	66
14.7	66

Joel

1.9	66
2.19	66, 107
2.24	66
3.18	66

Amos

9.13-14	66

Micah

7.15	93

Zephaniah

1.17	115, 116

Zechariah

9.15-17	66
10.7	66
12.4	115, 116

APOCRYPHA

Tobit

5.10	115

Wisdom

5.11	36
5.12-13	20
19.13	36

Sir

36.3-6	
38.1-15	136
45.4-5	169

Ep Jer

37	117

2 Macc

5.21	110
6.13	20
7.9	138
7.14	138

3 Macc

3.24	36
6.32	20

NEW TESTAMENT

Matthew

12.39	40, 41
13.57	56
15.30	99
16.1	40
16.3	40
16.4	40, 41
21.14	99
24.3	39, 41
24.24	41, 57
24.30	42, 43
26.28	39

Mark

8.11	40
13.4	39, 41
13.22	41, 57

Luke

2.12	40
2.16	40
2.20	40
2.34	42, 43
11.16	40
11.20	40
11.29-32	41
14.21	99
21.7	39, 41
21.11	41
21.25	41

John

1-12	148, 150	2.5	59, 62
1.1	74, 113	2.6	64
1.1-5	13	2.9	62
1.1-11	125	2.10	62
1.1-13	13	2.11	46, 49, 50, 51, 52,
1.1-18	47, 78		53, 58, 59, 62, 75,
1.4	74		80, 83, 91, 130,
1.5	13, 53, 126		140, 149, 150
1.6-7	92	2.12	78
1.6-13	13	2.12-4.54	47
1.7	49	2.13	134
1.9-11	56	2.13-22	56
1.10	53, 126	2.17	51
1.10-11	77, 78	2.18	49, 51, 75, 81, 85
1.11	53, 56, 126	2.18-19	85, 150
1.11-13	46	2.18-22	142
1.12	51, 53, 143	2.19	86, 150
1.12-13	53, 127	2.19-22	52
1.14	50, 64, 75, 127, 143, 154	2.21	64
1.14-18	13	2.21	52
1.16	51, 92	2.21-2	52, 134
1.17	47, 60, 88	2.22	15
1.18	64, 69	2.23	49, 53, 55, 56, 59,
1.19	49		82, 83, 121, 149
1.19-34	47	2.23-25	52, 58
1.19-35	49	2.24	56
1.19-51	46, 47	2.24-25	53, 56
1.19-4.54	46, 47	2.25	54
1.21	83, 88	3.1	54
1.24-28	47	3.2	49
1.25	60	3.3	57
1.27	92	3.5	57, 127
1.29	46, 47, 63, 86, 29, 134, 157,	3.11	48, 54
	162	3.11-12	54
1.32-3	92	3.11-13	49
1.34	47, 92	3.12	59
1.35	46, 63	3.13	69
1.35-51	47	3.14	55, 75, 124
1.36	92	3.14-5	23
1.41	47	3.14-6	142
1.43	46, 63	3.15	60, 88
1.45	47, 56	3.16	47, 56, 129, 130,
1.45-51	46	147, 154	
1.46	56	3.16-21	69
1.49	47, 109, 153	3.18	81
1.50	63	3.19	49
2.1	46, 63	3.27	57
2.1-11	46, 49, 69, 118	3.27-30	49
2.3	62	3.31	54, 69
2.4	62, 64, 75	3.31-3	54
		3.31-4	54
		3.32	48

3.36	69	5.20	79, 80, 91
4.8	56	5.20-23	145
4.9	56	5.21	100, 132
4.14	57	5.21-24	98
4.15	159	5.21-30	80
4.19	83	5.24	91
4.22	14, 47, 118	5.25	134
4.25	47, 98	5.26	119
4.29	55	5.30-47	48
4.34	80	5.30-38	61
4.39	47, 49, 55, 164	5.31-47	80, 81
4.42	14, 47, 56, 71, 74, 76, 129	5.32	81
4.43-4	58	5.33-36	81
4.43-54	70, 72	5.36	79, 80, 81, 151
4.44	56, 58	5.36-37	89
4.45	59, 121	5.37	81
4.43-5	55	5.38	91
4.43-54	81	5.44	122, 126
4.46	46, 55, 58	5.46	122
4.46-54	47, 55, 149	5.47	88
4.47	55, 70, 71	6	87, 103, 106, 129, 132
4.48	49, 55, 57, 58, 59, 81	6.1-4	102
4.49	71	6.1-14	70
4.50	71, 81	6.1-15	85, 102, 103
4.51	71	6.2	79, 82, 83, 121
4.53	71	6.3	149
4.54	46, 49, 50, 59, 83, 149, 150	6.3-33	88
5	87, 111, 112, 132, 143, 144, 145, 146, 150	6.4	78, 86, 134
5-10	77, 117	6.5	102
5-12	150	6.6	103, 113
5.1	78, 96	6.7	103
5.1-11	87, 103	6.10	103
5.1-17	149	6.11	103
5.1-18	81, 96	6.14	78, 79, 82, 85, 87, 103, 121, 150
5.2	96	6.15	83
5.3	96	6.16	149
5.4	82, 99	6.16-21	107, 109
5.5	96	6.16-25	103
5.6	97, 103	6.18	108
5.7	96, 97, 99	6.19	108
5.9	97, 98	6.20	119
5.10	96	6.22-5	84, 108
5.11	97	6.24	84
5.13	96, 97	6.25	84
5.14	78, 81, 97	6.26	79, 81, 84, 85, 108
5.15	97	6.27	84, 104, 159
5.16-18	79	6.29	85, 152
5.18	90, 99	6.30	84, 85
5.19	57, 80	6.31	85
5.19-30	80	6.33	85, 104
5.19-47	78, 79		

6.35	57, 85, 86, 104, 119, 132	8.21	114
6.35-58	78	8.26	88, 159
6.36	85	8.28	55, 88, 142
6.37	58	8.28-9	89
6.39	104	8.31	53
6.40	85, 104, 119	8.31-2	119
6.44	104, 127	8.36	119
6.46	113	8.40	113
6.48	86, 104	8.41	89
6.51	86, 104, 119, 134, 142	8.44-5	126
6.53-4	132	8.47	127
6.53-6	132	8.48	90
6.53-8	85, 86, 104	8.51	58
6.54	104	8.52	58, 90
6.54-6	134	8.58	119
6.59	78	9	89, 111, 117
6.60-71	104	9.1-14	87
6.62	134	9.1-41	111
6.65	127	9.2	149
6.68	104, 119	9.4	112
6.70-71	109	9.5	112, 132
6.71	15	9.6-7	112
7	87, 95	9.8	112
7-8	90, 122	9.9	112
7.1	56	9.11	112
7.2	78	9.13	113
7.3	86, 87	9.14	113
7.12	122	9.15	113
7.13	126	9.16	79, 89, 90, 112,
7.14	78	113, 146, 150	
7.14-39	89	9.16-17	126, 128
7.16	88	9.18-22	113
7.20	90	9.24	113
7.21	80, 86, 87	9.25	113
7.21-2	87	9.29-30	159
7.23	80, 82, 87	9.30	90
7.27-8	159	9.31-3	113
7.30	64	9.32	90, 146
7.31	78, 79, 82, 83, 86, 87, 88, 93,	9.34	113
	121, 146, 153	9.37	114
7.37	119, 159	9.41	114
7.39	15, 164	10	91, 144, 157
7.40	78, 87, 88	10.5	58
7.41	87, 88	10.9	86
7.42	56	10.10	143, 157
7.47	122	10.11	86, 119
8	87, 89, 95	10.11-18	150
8.12	58, 86, 89, 112, 119, 132	10.14	119, 162
8.13	89	10.15-8	142
8.14	159	10.16	134
8.18	89	10.20	90
8.20	64	10.21	90

10.22	78, 90	11.47	120, 121, 134
10.22-5	153	11.47-54	77, 134
10.24	78, 90	11.48	122
10.25	128, 151	11.49-50	122
10.24-8	90	11.50	134
10.25	90	11.51-2	134
10.26	127	11.53	120
10.27	162	12	78, 120, 122, 124,
10.28	58, 157		148, 149, 150
10.32	90, 151	12.1-7	130
10.37	90, 91, 151	12.1-11	134
10.37-8	91, 128, 146, 153	12.2	134, 139
10.38	90, 91, 144	12.7	120, 134
10.39	92	12.9	122, 134, 159
10.39-40	92	12.11	122
10.40-42	77, 134	12.12-16	120
10.41	91, 114	12.16	15
10.42	79, 134	12.17-18	122
11	78, 129	12.18	120, 122, 150
11-12	120, 140	12.19	122
11.1	130	12.23	64, 142
11.1-44	129	12.23-4	120, 142
11.2	130	12.27	142
11.3	130	12.28	164
11.4	130, 131, 133, 140	12.30-2	120
11.5	130	12.31	157
11.8	131	12.31-2	142
11.13	131	12.31-3	140
11.15	131, 152	12.32	55, 120
11.16	131, 149	12.33	121
11.17	131	12.34	55
11.21	132	12.37	83, 121, 125, 126,
11.22	132		128, 146, 149
11.23	132	12.37-40	127
11.24-5	132	12.37-43	120, 125, 127
11.25	86	12.37-50	77
11.25-6	132	12.38	127
11.26	58	12.41	127
11.27	109, 129, 132, 153	12.42	126
11.33	133	12.43	126, 127
11.34	133	12.44-5	140
11.37	133	12.44-50	120, 127, 128,
11.38	133	140	
11.39	133	12.46	147
11.40	133, 140, 152	12.47	127, 128, 140,
11.43	127, 134	146	
11.44	134	12.47-8	128
11.45	55, 134	12.48	140
11.45-6	120, 121, 134	12.50	159
11.45-7	121	13-17	129, 143
11.45-53	120	13-21	142, 156
11.46	55, 121	13.1	125, 142, 143

13.1-3	78	18.33-38a	158
13.1-38	142	18.33-19.12	158
13.7-11	142	18.36-7	158
13.8	57	18.37	158
13.21	143	18.38	156, 159
13.23	143	18.39	159
13.35	147	19.1-3	160
13.38	58	19.1-5	159
14-16	142, 147	19.4	156
14.1-14	142	19.6	156
14.6	86, 154	19.7	159
14.10-11	151	19.9-11	158, 159
14.10-12	143, 144, 146	19.10	159
14.11	144	19.12	160
14.12	144, 147	19.14	157, 160
14.11-12	144, 147	19.15	160
14.13-14	142, 143	19.24	156
14.25	162	19.28	156
14.26	55, 142	19.29	157
14.27	142, 154, 162	19.31	157
14.29	152	19.33	157
15.1	86, 154	19.34	158
15.4	57	19.35	143, 145, 158
15.14-15	160	19.36	156
15.22-4	146, 147, 151	19.37	156, 157
15.23	146	20	163
15.24	143, 146, 169	20.1-2	161
15.26-7	49, 145, 162	20.2	161
15.26-16.15	142	20.3-10	161
15.27	142, 143, 147, 149, 154	20.9	161
16.4-15	143	20.11-18	161
16.5-11	162	20.14	162
16.8-11	49, 145	20.15	162
16.13	98, 142, 162	20.17	162
16.14	98	20.18	162
16.15	98	20.19	162
16.20-24	142	20.19-23	145, 162
16.33	142, 154, 162	20.20-31	149
17.4	80	20.21	154, 162
17.5	164	20.21-3	162
17.12	157	20.23	162
17.18	154	20.25	57, 162
17.20	145, 154	20.27	162
18	150, 155	20.29	153, 156, 163
18-20	155, 163	20.29-30	149
18.8	157	20.30	149
18.9	157	20.30-31	59, 83, 88, 89,
18.10-11	158		143, 147, 149,
18.11	58		151, 154, 155
18.20	78	20.31	153
18.23	156	21.19	125, 164
18.33	158	21.24	143, 145

John (continued)

| 21.4-5 | 155 |
| 21.25 | 55 |

Acts of the Apostles

1.3	36
2.22	40, 43
2.43	43
4.4	43
4.16	43
4.22	39
4.30	43
5.12	43
6.8	43
7.36	43
8.6	43
8.13	43
14.3	43
15.12	43
19.11	43

2 Corinthians

| 12.12 | 43 |

Galatians

| 6.11 | 36 |

2 Thessalonians

| 2.9 | 57 |
| 3.17 | 35, 40 |

Hebrews

| 2.4 | 40 |

1 John

2.22	153
4.15	153
5.1	153
5.5	153
5.21	153

Revelation

13.13	42
13.14	42
16.14	42
19.20	42

DEAD SEA SCROLLS

1QS
| 9.10-11 | 93 |

4QTest
| 5-8 | 93 |

4Q521 | 94 |

11Q13
| 1.18 | 94 |

RABBINIC WORKS

Gen Rab

| 71.6 | 115 |
| 100 | 131 |

Lev Rab

| 18.1 | 131 |

OTHER JEWISH AND
CHRISTIAN WORKS

Epistle of Barnabas

Barn

| 12.5-7 | 55 |

2 Baruch

| 29.5 | 66 |
| 29.5-8 | 105 |

John Chrysostom

Hom. Jo
| 38.2 | 98 |

Justin Martyr

Dial.
| 94.112 | 55 |

Sib Or
| 3.331 | 90 |
| 7.774-746 | 105 |

ANCIENT AUTHORS

Achilles Tatius

Leuc. Clit.
2.2	68
4.18.5	66
8.4.2	66

Aelian

Nat. an
| 4.34 | 114 |
| 10.45. | 114 |

Aelius Aristides

Eul
31-39	167
65	167
81	167
87	167
98	167
100	167
103	167

Herc.
| 40.12 | 101 |

Aelius Spartianus

Script. Hist. August.
| 9.32 | 116 |

Aeschlyus

Agamemnon
| 568-9 | 138 |
Eumenides
| 645-51 | 138 |

Anthology Graeca

Anth. Graec.
| 7.8 | 136 |
| 16.185 | 137 |

Appian

Bell. Civ.
2.5.36	28
2.16.116	28
2.36	30
4.1.4	28

Appollodorus

Bib.
1.4.2-3	110
2.7.7	138, 169
3.10.3	138

Apollonius Rhodius

Argon.
| 1.450-60 | 106 |
| 1.179-84 | 110 |

Apuleis

Metam.
2.29-30	139
8.12	115
11.6	138

Aretaeus

Cur. Acut.
1.1.28	65
2.3.10	65
2.3.12	65

Sign. Acut.
| 1.7 | 65 |

Sign. Diut.
| 1.7 | 65 |
| 1.7.2 | 100 |

Aristophanes

Plut.
| 410 | 101 |
| 653-80 | 99 |

Vesp.
| 122 | 101 |

Aristotle

An. Pr.
2.27   36

De an.
1.3.406b   138

Rhet.

1.2.15-18   36
1.9.33   89
2.25.8   36

Artemidorus

Oneir.

3.16   110

Athenaeus

Deipn.
1.2.36-7   65
1.2.37a-b   65
4.153b   106

Cassius Dio

Hist.
8.1-2   168
48.39.2   70
50.25.3-4   70
64.9.1   168
65.1.2-4   168
65.8.1   102
66.17   72

Cicero

Fin.
4.64   114

Inv.
1.43.81   38

Leg. man.
2.14.36   137

Rab. Perd.
9-17   163

Rep.
2.17   169

Sen.
10.33   73

Sest.
48.103   106

Tusc.
38-39   115

Verr.
2.5.168   163

Columella

Rust.
6.33.1   116

Demosthenes

Or.
19.58   39
19.61   39
21.35   39
36.12   39
42.24   39
54.9   39

Dio Chrysostom

Or.
1.33.2   26
3.30-31   110
4.61.1   26
6.3.1   26
11.29   110
11.85.1   28
11.98.4   28
15.30.1   26
31.35.8   26
32.17.4   26
32.31   106
33.50.8   26
36.16.2   26
38.18.1   28
63.1   26
66.26   106

Diodorus Siculus

Hist.
    1.25.2-7   101
    2.36.2   68, 107
    3.62-3   66
    3.66.2   68
    3.66.3   68
    33.15.1   163

Diogenes Laertius

Vita
    6.56   115
    7.27   106
    8.67   139
    9.43   106
    10.11   106
    10.131   106

Dionysius of Halicarnassus

Ant. Rom.
    1.59.4   27
    1.86.3   27
    2.5.1-5   28
    2.67.5   28
    2.68.2   27
    3.46.1   28
    3.47.4   28
    3.72.4   34
    4.6   28
    4.13.4   34
    4.80.2   28
    5.46.1   28
    7.46.4   34
    7.52.2   34
    8.56.1   27
    9.40.1   28
    9.41.3   28
    12.11.3   28

Dem.
    12.73   34

Is.
    15.22   34

Lys.
    19.8   34

Dioscurides

Mat. med.
    3.78   100

Epictetus

Diatr.
    1.20.12   117
    2.20.32   105, 107
    3.22.35   119
    4.7.26-7   72

Euripides

Alc.
    22   136
    419   135

Bacc.
    706-11   66

Hel.
    1285-7   138

Hipp.
    1473   136

Suppl.
    1109-13 136

Herodian
  Hist.
      4.1-11 166

Herodotus

Hist.
    3.62.3   138
    7.33-37   110

Hippocrates

Epid.

    1 Case 3   72
    1 Case 11 72
    3 Case 9   73

De arte
    3   136
    8   136

Hippocrates (continued)

Progn.

1	136
20	136
24	136
25	136

Morb. sacr.
| 4 | 136 |

Homer

Il.
2.243	119
2.254	119
7.86	26
13.26-30	110
21.56	138
23.326	26
23.326-8	26
23.843	26
24.551	138
24.756	138

Od.
3.236-9	136
8.192	26
8.192-8	26
8.195	26
9.108-11	105
11.218-9	138
11.218-22	100
20.111	26
24.329-332	26

Horace

Carm.
1.4.13	135
2.19	66
3.21.13-20	65

Josephus

A.J.
1.34	26
1.36	26
2.11	26, 31
2.13	26.
2.14	31

2.63	26
2.72	31
2.274	30, 31, 33
2.276	30, 31, 33
2.279-80	30
2.280	33
2.283	31
2.284-8	30
2.286	31
2.327	30
3.252	26
3.310	30
5.12	30
5.46	26
5.161	27
6.50	30
7.242	26
7.279	26
8.327	31
8.343	31
8.350	31
10.28	30
10.214	31
10.239	31
12.404	39
17.295	163
18.23	32
18.62	27
18.85-87	32
19.101	27
19.1	110
19.29	27
19.31	27
19.53	27
19.101	27
20.97-99	32
20.167-8	32
20.187	32

B.J.
1.23	168
1.106	72
1.656	72
2.118	32
2.253	163
2.258-60	32
2.261	32
2.390-1	168
3.401-4	168
4.263	168
4.622	168
5.368	168

B.J. (continued)

5.378	168
5.449-521	163
5.451	163
6.286	31
6.288-94	30, 31
6.291	31
6.295	31
6.296	31
6.315	31
7.438	32

Juvenal

Sat.

7.174	106
8.118	106
10.44-46	106
10.81	106

Livy

Ad Urb. Con.

22.13.19	163
34.45.7	114

Lucian

Hermot.

7	169

Peregr.

4	138, 169	
6	138, 169	30
	138, 169	
33	138, 169	
39	166	
44	72	

Salt.

45	138

Ver. hist.

1.7	67
2.11-13	105

Martial

Epig.

3.4.8-9	168
5.5	168

7.5.1-6	168
8.26	70
8.2.1-5	168
8.2.6-7	168
9.28.7-8	168
66.3-4	168

Menander

Frg.

924	110

Nonnus

Dion.

14.411-8	66

Pausanius

Descr.

2.26	68
2.26.5	138
2.27.2	101
2.27.4	138
4.10.6	115
4.12.10	116
10.32.12	101

Petronius

Satyr.

119.1-3	136

Philo

Aet.

2	33
23	35

Contempl.

85-89	33

Cher

58	115

Decal.

24	27
25	27
26	27
67-8	115

Det.
1	35
3	35
177	33
177.1	33

Ebr.
155-6	115

Fug.
123	115

Legat.
75-81	70
82-3	66
88	65,66
93-97	167
143-7	167
162	167
206	72
357	167

Migr.
68	*33*

Mos.
1.71	33
1.76	33
1.76-83	33
1.82	33
1.90	33
1.95	33
1.95-165	33
1.123-6	115
1.199	33
1.210	33
2.263	35

Opif.
49	27
58	33
125	72

Praem.
31	27

Prob.
39	35
89	35

Prov.
2.26	35

QG
3.2	33

Sacr.
80	27

Sobr.
4	115
45	72

Somn.
2.1	33

Spec.
1.90	35
2.189	33
3.160	163
4.138	33
4.202	115

Virt.
11.1	115

Philostratus

Vit. Apoll.
4.10	68, 72
4.45	139
6.10	

Pindar

Pyth.
3.47-56	101
3.50-52	138
4.61	110

Plato

Leg.
2672B	66

Rep
345C-E	119

Tim.
69D-84C	100
77C	100
88D	100

Plautus

Curc.
  1.1.61   101
  2.1.18-21 101

Pliny the Elder

Nat.
  2.16   72
  2.31.13   68
  2.231   68
  4.12.86   65
  4.14   65
  7.2.13   116
  7.12.51   114
  7.37.124 139
  7.51-2   138
  8.54.126 114
  8.62.151 114
  11.55.149 114
  11.113.272 114
  28.4.19   136
  28.7.36-39 116
  28.22.76 116
  29.1.3   138
  30.5   136
  36.107-8 163

Plutarch

Alex.
  14.8.2   29
  75.1.4   29

Ant.
  24.3   70

Arist.
  25.7.2   35

Cam.
  3.3.8   28
  35.5.12   28

Comp. Lys. Sull.
  1.3-4   35

Comp. Nic. Crass.
  3.5.6   35

Cons. ux.
  609E   73

Dem.
  8.3.3   35
  8.7.2   35

Fab.
  2.2.4   28

Fac.
  920B   136

Is. Os.
  373E   116

Lys.
  28.4   67

Nic
  23   28

Num.
  6.4.2   28

Per.
  6.2.7   28
  6.4.2   29

Publ.
  13.1.2   28
  13.3.2   28

Q.Conviv.
  6.671C-D 67

Rom.
  28.4   169
  28.7-8   169

Sera.
  564A-B   137
  565A-566A 137
  566A   100

Them.
  10.1.3-4 28

Tim.
  26.3.1   29

Virt. Prof.
76F	35
78B	35
82A	35
84A	35

Propertius

Eleg.
3.5.10-12	136

Quintilian

Inst.
4.9.8-11	38

Rhetorica ad Herrenium

Rhet. ad Her.
2.4.6-7	37
2.7.11	37
4.40.53	37

Seneca

Apol.
6	72

De Clem.
1.1.2	167
1.26.5	167

Ep.
4.5	135	
12.10		135

Herc. fur.
322-4		110

Oed.
949	115

Phoen.
179	115

Polyb.
7.4	167

Sextus Empiricus

Math.
1.34	115
1.261	138
11.238	115

Pyr.
3.264	115

Sophocles

Ant.
989	115

El.
138-9	138

Oed. tyr.
371	117
412	117
1367	115

Statius

Theb.
1.31	168

Silv.
3.4.20	168
4.2.14	168
4.3.134-5	168
5.1	168

Strabo

Geog.
1.1.6	26
1.1.18	34
1.4.1	26
2.1.17	26
3.1.9	26
4.6.1	34
5.4.3	34
8.3.30	34
8.4.1	34
8.6.22	34
12.3.27	34
14.1.44	99
14.2.5	105
17.1.48	26
17.1.53	34

Suetonius

Aug.
42   70
98.2   167

Cal.
4.3   136
19.2-3   110

Domit.
13.1-2   168

Jul.
76.1   165

Vesp.
5.2-6   168
7   102, 116

Tacitus

Agr.
31.2   135

Ann.
1.10.4   135
2.69   136
3.13   136
4.52   136
16.31   136

Hist.
1.3   168
1.10   168
2.73-81   168
4.3   168
4.81   29, 102, 117, 168
4.82   29
5.5   67

Thucydides

Hist.
2.47-52   72
2.51.6   72

Virgil

Aen.
5.101-2   106

5.1057-9   110
5.1081-85   110
6.791-4   166

Ecl.
4.5   166

Georg.
1.24-42   166

PAPYRI & INSCRIPTIONS

CE
1495.1-2   137

CIL
11.856   137
13.530   137

CLE
1.420   137

Ehrenberg & Jones (1976)
98   166
98.10   74
101.15-6   69

IG
14.2190   137

I. Priene
108.42   106
108.57   106
108.68   106
108.253-5   106

New Docs
I
2   111
2, 1.6   116
10 1.32   69
IV
114   73

VII
10   106

OGIS
655.2   166

P. Cair Zen

II 59192   35

PGM

XII. 278-283   139

P.Petaus
28   35

P. Oxy
115 1.9-10   135
1381 51-7   136
1453.11   166
1683   35
2996   35

Res Gest Div Aug
5.2   106
15.1-3   106
18.1   106

Sammelbuch
V 7574   35
V.8005   35

SEG
XIV 474   165

SIG
III.760   165

SIG
976   106
976.54-8   106

Index of Subjects

Alignment of reader (*see also* focalisation) 49,
        61, 114
– in Lazarus narrative 129, 134-5
– in death and resurrection narrative 156

Aristotle 36

Asclepius 101, 136

Audience
– authorial audience and 9-10, 14
– broadly conceived 11, 12
– communication strategy and 8-9
– educated by the Gospel 14
– as a focus of study 5-6
– Gospel audiences 10-11
– relationship with real reader 6, 9
– 'repertoire' of 7, 8
– shared cultural reality 11

Augustus
– and Imperial ideology 74, 165-6

Background of the Gospel 8
– and foreground 8

Belief
– content of 152
– purpose of the Gospel and 152-3
– signs and 14, 21, 51, 53, 58, 71, 91, 117, 122,
        126, 152, 154, 175
– movement to 98

Beloved Disciple
– function of 143
– witness to resurrection 161

Benefactions 69-70
– Emperors and 70, 106
– food and 105-6
– public banquets 106

Blindness
– as punishment 115
– death and 115
– in the ancient world 114-5
– cures of 116
– healed by emperors 116
– symbolic meaning of 114, 117
– Yahweh and healing of 116
– weakness and 115

Cana 49

Crucifixion
– ancient accounts of 163
– transformed understanding of 164

Death
– children and 73
– help from 136
– in Lazarus narrative 131
– in the ancient world 135-6

Death of Jesus
– anticipated 52
– blood and water and 158
– hour of glory and 64, 123, 150
– narrative understanding of 142
– and resurrection as a sign 55, 75,
        85, 123-4, 142-3, 150-1, 170,
        173

Demeter 105
– Eleusian mysteries and 107, 137

Dionysus
– cult of 137
– imperial connections 70
– compared to Jesus 69, 76
– in Johannine studies 66-7
– legends concerning 67-8
– popularity of 67
– wine and 66

Disease (*see also* Illness)
– in the ancient world 11, 17

Disciples 109, 149
– audience of signs 154
– κόσμος and 147, 154
– response to signs 51, 109
– sending of 162
– appointed witnesses 142, 147

Domitian
– imperial ideology and 168

Ephesus 10-11

Elijah 104

Elisha 104

Eschatological expectations 47, 132

Faith; see Belief

Feeding of 5000 102-104

Fever 72-74

Focalisation (*see also* alignment)
   61-2, 98, 108, 156

Food
– abundance of as messianic sign 104
– benefactions and105-6
– as a feature of utopian literature 105
– provision of 105
– scarcity and 105

Forensic motif (*see also* signs, forensic use of)
– associated with σημεῖον references
   17, 60, 75, 91, 94, 117-8, 126, 128, 172
– disciples and 143
– death of Jesus and141, 155
– in John's Gospel 48-51, 77-9, 113
– in Isaiah 48
– rhetorical function 95, 128
– words, works and 147

Gathering of God's people 124

Glory 23
– and crucifixion 164
– 'the hour' and 64, 123, 150, 164

– in the first sign 50, 63
– κόσμος and 127
– of God in Isaiah 127
– signs and130, 140

Greater works 80, 144-5

Healing
– blindness 112
– Emperors and101-2, 116
– sign of the kingdom 99

Healing sanctuaries 99, 101-2

Hour, the 64, 123
– glory and 123, 164
– σημεῖον and 122-3

'I am' saying 108-9, 111, 119

Illness
– death and 100, 130
– lameness 99-100
– sin and 97, 111
– various words for 99

Imperial Cult 12
– ideology of 165
– implicitly critiqued 74, 165
– prevalence of 165

Implied reader (*see also* Audience)
   6

Isaiah
– blindness in 117
– Gospel's content and 14, 125
– σημεῖον references 24, 42, 93,
   124-6
– Messiah in 93-4, 124, 159
– quoted in the Gospel 126
– sees God's glory 127

Isis 111, 119
Jesus
– ability to heal 71, 74, 97, 117
– aggressively performing signs
   103, 113
– anger 132-3
– benefactor 69, 106-7, 117
– death of (see Death of Jesus)
– glory and identity of 50-1

Jesus (continued)
– greater than Dionysus 69, 76
– homeland of 56
– Roman emperors and (see Roman
Emperors)
– judge 80, 98
– king 157-61, 164
– lamb 92, 157, 161, 164
– lifegiver 17, 71, 74, 81, 97, 103-4, 117, 134,
    139, 151, 157-8, 168, 172, 175, 178
– a prophetic figure 83, 122
– 'the Prophet like Moses' 83, 88
– Messiah 88-90, 117-8, 153
– resurrection of (see Resurrection)
– saviour of the world 74
– shepherd 157, 161, 164
– signs and identity of 17, 51, 86 111, 117, 119,
    128, 133, 140
– supernatural knowledge of 96, 130
– supremacy of 69, 111, 119, 123
– uniqueness of 69, 119
– words of 59

John the Baptist
– signs and 91-2
– witness to Jesus 91

Josephus and signs
– general references 26
– "religious uses' 30
– Moses and 31-2

Judgement 98
– Messiah as Judge 124, 159
– Positive and negative aspects 80-1
– signs and 22, 80-1, 146
– Passover as judgement 157

Κόσμος 13, 14, 47
– signs and 146, 154
– trial of 147

Kingdom of God 54

Kingship
– death in the Gospel and 164
– portrayal of Jesus and 157-61
– as testifying to truth 159

Lameness, ancient physiology of 100

Lazarus 120
– raising of as a sign 121

Life 98
– after death in ancient world 137-8
– imperial ideology and 166
– resurrection and 132
– life expectancy in ancient world
    135

Literary Study
– of the Fourth Gospel 3-5

Magicians 136

Messiah
– signs and 42, 86-8, 90, 93-4, 124-
    5, 152-3
– Jesus as 47, 89, 117, 124, 151,
    153, 157
– in Isaiah 93-4, 124

Moses 42, 75, 85, 104
– relationship to Jesus 47
– signs in Egypt 20-21

Mystery Cults 137

Narrative Criticism 4, 5
– and linear reading 15

Nicodemus
– Jesus and 54

Orphism 137-8

OT Scriptures
– as Gospel background 3, 14

Paraclete 49

Paralysis
– ancient physiology of 100
– connoting death 100

Passover 78, 104, 134, 157

Philo and signs
– general references 26
– religious references 33
– Moses and 33

Physicians 136

Pilate 156
– Jesus' trial before 158-60
– κόσμος and 159

Predestination 127-8

Prologue
– cosmological story in 13

Proof 34-5
– strong proof 36
– accumulative proof 36-39, 94-5, 172, 175

Prophets and signs 23, 42

Purpose of the Gospel 147-54
– signs and 148-9

Reader-to-text analysis 16-17, 62, 171

Repertoire of audience 7, 8

Resurrections
– impossibility of 138

Resurrection of Jesus
– anticipated 52
– as a sign (see also death of Jesus) 75
– narrative of 161-3
– creation, Israel and 162
– contrasted with contemporary views 169

Rhetorical impact
– how achieved 16-17, 173-4

Roman Emperors
– as 'saviours' 74
– associated with Dionysus 70
– contrasted with Jesus 74, 164-8, 173
– death and 135-6
(*See also* Augustus, Domitian, Vespasian, Imperial Cult)

Sabbath
– Jesus and 97-9

Septuagint
– Use of σημεῖον in 18

Sea walking
– ancient gods and heroes and 109-110
– as divine manifestation 109
– as a Johannine sign 84, 108
– kings and emperors and 110
– dreams of 110
– narrative of 107-9

Seeing
– life and 114
– signs and 55-9, 84, 121, 163, 175
– vocabulary of in the resurrection accounts 162

Sign Prophets 31-2

Signs
– accessible through testimony 72
– ancient interpretation of 28-9
– ancient evaluation of 29
– in ancient literature 34-38
– belief and; see Belief
– criteria for defining 51-2, 150
– death of Jesus and 122 (*see also* Death of Jesus)
– eschatological signs in the synoptics 41
– failure of 121-2, 125
– forensic use 20, 91, 128, 140
– glory and 50-51
– Jesus' identity and 17, 51, 75, 89, 95, 140, 154, 169, 172 (*see also* Jesus: signs and identity of)
– judgement and 22
– knowledge of God and 60
– metaphorical usage 24
– narratives and Gospel structure 139-40
– narratives; features of 76
– numbering of 59
– as omens or portents 28, 61, 95
– ongoing role 147
– plurality of 60, 75, 83, 90, 94-5, 121, 148, 155, 170
– polemical function 17, 22, 68-9, 76, 90, 102, 107, 111, 140, 164-8
– polemical function in Old Testament 22
– purpose of the Gospel and 147-54
– reader identification and 14-5

Signs (continued)
– referent of 148
– requesting   52
– as a signal 19, 24, 26
– and sonship 21
– symbolic interpretation of 86, 114
– as visible phenomena 19
– and works; see Works
– and Yahweh 19

Signs Source 1
– criticism of 2

Signs and wonders 21, 23, 39-40
– positively viewed 57

Son of Man
– the cross and 63
– lifted up 55, 123
– sign of 42

Temple Cleansing 51
– not a σημεῖον 51-2

Text-to-reader analysis 16, 61, 171

Vespasian 101
      – as a healer 101-2, 116
      – Augustan imperial ideology
      and 167-8

Wine
      – connotations of 65-66
      – Dionysus and 66-7
      – Mediterranean diet and 64-5
– varieties 65

Witness 48
– Beloved disciple as 143
– disciples as 147, 149-50, 154, 162
– Jesus as 159
– signs as 61, 81, 87, 94
– to resurrection 161

Words and works of Jesus 146, 151

Works 79
– signs and 79-81, 85, 90, 144-6
– testimony of the Father and 81

Wissenschaftliche Untersuchungen zum Neuen Testament

Alphabetical Index of the First and Second Series

Ådna, Jostein: Jesu Stellung zum Tempel. 2000. *Volume II/119.*

Ådna, Jostein and *Kvalbein, Hans* (Ed.): The Mission of the Early Church to Jews and Gentiles. 2000. *Volume 127.*

Alkier, Stefan: Wunder und Wirklichkeit in den Briefen des Apostels Paulus. 2001. *Volume 134.*

Anderson, Paul N.: The Christology of the Fourth Gospel. 1996. *Volume II/78.*

Appold, Mark L.: The Oneness Motif in the Fourth Gospel. 1976. *Volume II/1.*

Arnold, Clinton E.: The Colossian Syncretism. 1995. *Volume II/77.*

Ascough, Richard S.: Paul's Macedonian Associations. 2003. *Volume II/161.*

Asiedu-Peprah, Martin: Johannine Sabbath Conflicts As Juridical Controversy. 2001. *Volume II/132.*

Avemarie, Friedrich: Die Tauferzählungen der Apostelgeschichte. 2002. *Volume 139.*

Avemarie, Friedrich and *Hermann Lichtenberger* (Ed.): Auferstehung – Ressurection. 2001. *Volume 135.*

Avemarie, Friedrich and *Hermann Lichtenberger* (Ed.): Bund und Tora. 1996. *Volume 92.*

Baarlink, Heinrich: Verkündigtes Heil. 2004. *Volume 168.*

Bachmann, Michael: Sünder oder Übertreter. 1992. *Volume 59.*

Back, Frances: Verwandlung durch Offenbarung bei Paulus. 2002. *Volume II/153.*

Baker, William R.: Personal Speech-Ethics in the Epistle of James. 1995. *Volume II/68.*

Bakke, Odd Magne: 'Concord and Peace'. 2001. *Volume II/143.*

Balla, Peter: Challenges to New Testament Theology. 1997. *Volume II/95.*

– The Child-Parent Relationship in the New Testament and its Environment. 2003. *Volume 155.*

Bammel, Ernst: Judaica. Volume I 1986. *Volume 37.*

– Volume II 1997. *Volume 91.*

Bash, Anthony: Ambassadors for Christ. 1997. *Volume II/92.*

Bauernfeind, Otto: Kommentar und Studien zur Apostelgeschichte. 1980. *Volume 22.*

Baum, Armin Daniel: Pseudepigraphie und literarische Fälschung im frühen Christentum. 2001. *Volume II/138.*

Bayer, Hans Friedrich: Jesus' Predictions of Vindication and Resurrection. 1986. *Volume II/20.*

Becker, Michael: Wunder und Wundertäter im früh-rabbinischen Judentum. 2002. *Volume II/144.*

Bell, Richard H.: Provoked to Jealousy. 1994. *Volume II/63.*

– No One Seeks for God. 1998. *Volume 106.*

Bennema, Cornelis: The Power of Saving Wisdom. 2002. *Volume II/148.*

Bergman, Jan: see *Kieffer, René*

Bergmeier, Roland: Das Gesetz im Römerbrief und andere Studien zum Neuen Testament. 2000. *Volume 121.*

Betz, Otto: Jesus, der Messias Israels. 1987. *Volume 42.*

– Jesus, der Herr der Kirche. 1990. *Volume 52.*

Beyschlag, Karlmann: Simon Magus und die christliche Gnosis. 1974. *Volume 16.*

Bittner, Wolfgang J.: Jesu Zeichen im Johannesevangelium. 1987. *Volume II/26.*

Bjerkelund, Carl J.: Tauta Egeneto. 1987. *Volume 40.*

Blackburn, Barry Lee: Theios Anēr and the Markan Miracle Traditions. 1991. *Volume II/40.*

Bock, Darrell L.: Blasphemy and Exaltation in Judaism and the Final Examination of Jesus. 1998. *Volume II/106.*

Bockmuehl, Markus N.A.: Revelation and Mystery in Ancient Judaism and Pauline Christianity. 1990. *Volume II/36.*

Bøe, Sverre: Gog and Magog. 2001. *Volume II/135.*

Böhlig, Alexander: Gnosis und Synkretismus. Teil 1 1989. *Volume 47* – Teil 2 1989. *Volume 48.*

Böhm, Martina: Samarien und die Samaritai bei Lukas. 1999. *Volume II/111.*

Böttrich, Christfried: Weltweisheit – Menschheitsethik – Urkult. 1992. *Volume II/50.*

Bolyki, János: Jesu Tischgemeinschaften. 1997. *Volume II/96.*

Bosman, Philip: Conscience in Philo and Paul. 2003. *Volume II/166.*

Bovon, François: Studies in Early Christianity.
2003. *Volume 161.*
Brocke, Christoph vom: Thessaloniki – Stadt
des Kassander und Gemeinde des Paulus.
2001. *Volume II/125.*
Brunson, Andrew: Psalm 118 in the Gospel of
John. 2003. *Volume II/158.*
Büchli, Jörg: Der Poimandres – ein paganisier-
tes Evangelium. 1987. *Volume II/27.*
Bühner, Jan A.: Der Gesandte und sein Weg im
4. Evangelium. 1977. *Volume II/2.*
Burchard, Christoph: Untersuchungen zu
Joseph und Aseneth. 1965. *Volume 8.*
– Studien zur Theologie, Sprache und Umwelt
des Neuen Testaments. Ed. von D. Sänger.
1998. *Volume 107.*
Burnett, Richard: Karl Barth's Theological
Exegesis. 2001. *Volume II/145.*
Byron, John: Slavery Metaphors in Early
Judaism and Pauline Christianity. 2003.
Volume II/162.
Byrskog, Samuel: Story as History – History as
Story. 2000. *Volume 123.*
Cancik, Hubert (Ed.): Markus-Philologie. 1984.
Volume 33.
Capes, David B.: Old Testament Yaweh Texts in
Paul's Christology. 1992. *Volume II/47.*
Caragounis, Chrys C.: The Development of
Greek and the New Testament. 2004.
Volume 167.
– The Son of Man. 1986. *Volume 38.*
– see *Fridrichsen, Anton.*
Carleton Paget, James: The Epistle of Barnabas.
1994. *Volume II/64.*
*Carson, D.A., O'Brien, Peter T. and Mark
Seifrid* (Ed.): Justification and Variegated
Nomism: A Fresh Appraisal of Paul and
Second Temple Judaism. Volume 1: The
Complexities of Second Temple Judaism.
Volume II/140.
Ciampa, Roy E.: The Presence and Function of
Scripture in Galatians 1 and 2. 1998.
Volume II/102.
Classen, Carl Joachim: Rhetorical Criticsm of
the New Testament. 2000. *Volume 128.*
Colpe, Carsten: Iranier – Aramäer – Hebräer –
Hellenen. 2003. *Volume 154.*
Crump, David: Jesus the Intercessor. 1992.
Volume II/49.
Dahl, Nils Alstrup: Studies in Ephesians. 2000.
Volume 131.
Deines, Roland: Jüdische Steingefäße und phari-
säische Frömmigkeit. 1993. *Volume II/52.*
– Die Pharisäer. 1997. *Volume 101.*
– / *Niebuhr, Karl-Wilhelm (Hrsg.):* Philo und
das Neue Testament. 2004. *Volume 172.*

Dettwiler, Andreas and *Jean Zumstein (Ed.):*
Kreuzestheologie im Neuen Testament.
2002. *Volume 151.*
Dickson, John P.: Mission-Commitment in
Ancient Judaism and in the Pauline
Communities. 2003. *Volume II/159.*
Dietzfelbinger, Christian: Der Abschied des
Kommenden. 1997. *Volume 95.*
Dobbeler, Axel von: Glaube als Teilhabe. 1987.
Volume II/22.
Du Toit, David S.: Theios Anthropos. 1997.
Volume II/91
Dunn , James D.G. (Ed.): Jews and Christians.
1992. *Volume 66.*
– Paul and the Mosaic Law. 1996. *Volume 89.*
Dunn, James D.G., Hans Klein, Ulrich Luz and
Vasile Mihoc (Ed.)*:* Auslegung der Bibel in
orthodoxer und westlicher Perspektive. 2000.
Volume 130.
Ebel, Eva: Die Attraktivität früher christlicher
Gemeinden. 2004. *Volume II/178.*
Ebertz, Michael N.: Das Charisma des Gekreu-
zigten. 1987. *Volume 45.*
Eckstein, Hans-Joachim: Der Begriff Syneidesis
bei Paulus. 1983. *Volume II/10.*
– Verheißung und Gesetz. 1996. *Volume 86.*
Ego, Beate: Im Himmel wie auf Erden. 1989.
Volume II/34
Ego, Beate and *Lange, Armin* with *Pilhofer, Peter
(Ed.):* Gemeinde ohne Tempel – Community
without Temple. 1999. *Volume 118.*
Eisen, Ute E.: see *Paulsen, Henning.*
Ellis, E. Earle: Prophecy and Hermeneutic in
Early Christianity. 1978. *Volume 18.*
– The Old Testament in Early Christianity.
1991. *Volume 54.*
Endo, Masanobu: Creation and Christology.
2002. *Volume 149.*
Ennulat, Andreas: Die 'Minor Agreements'.
1994. *Volume II/62.*
Ensor, Peter W.: Jesus and His 'Works'. 1996.
Volume II/85.
Eskola, Timo: Messiah and the Throne. 2001.
Volume II/142.
– Theodicy and Predestination in Pauline
Soteriology. 1998. *Volume II/100.*
Fatehi, Mehrdad: The Spirit's Relation to the
Risen Lord in Paul. 2000. *Volume II/128.*
Feldmeier, Reinhard: Die Krisis des Gottessoh-
nes. 1987. *Volume II/21.*
– Die Christen als Fremde. 1992. *Volume 64.*
Feldmeier, Reinhard and *Ulrich Heckel* (Ed.):
Die Heiden. 1994. *Volume 70.*
Fletcher-Louis, Crispin H.T.: Luke-Acts:
Angels, Christology and Soteriology. 1997.
Volume II/94.

Förster, Niclas: Marcus Magus. 1999.
Volume 114.

Forbes, Christopher Brian: Prophecy and
Inspired Speech in Early Christianity and its
Hellenistic Environment. 1995. *Volume II/75.*

Fornberg, Tord: see *Fridrichsen, Anton.*

Fossum, Jarl E.: The Name of God and the
Angel of the Lord. 1985. *Volume 36.*

Foster, Paul: Community, Law and Mission in
Matthew's Gospel. *Volume II/177.*

Fotopoulos, John: Food Offered to Idols in
Roman Corinth. 2003. *Volume II/151.*

Frenschkowski, Marco: Offenbarung und
Epiphanie. Volume 1 1995. *Volume II/79 –*
Volume 2 1997. *Volume II/80.*

Frey, Jörg: Eugen Drewermann und die
biblische Exegese. 1995. *Volume II/71.*
– Die johanneische Eschatologie. Volume I.
1997. *Volume 96.* – Volume II. 1998.
Volume 110.
– Volume III. 2000. *Volume 117.*

Freyne, Sean: Galilee and Gospel. 2000.
Volume 125.

Fridrichsen, Anton: Exegetical Writings. Edited
by C.C. Caragounis and T. Fornberg. 1994.
Volume 76.

Garlington, Don B.: 'The Obedience of Faith'.
1991. *Volume II/38.*
– Faith, Obedience, and Perseverance. 1994.
Volume 79.

Garnet, Paul: Salvation and Atonement in the
Qumran Scrolls. 1977. *Volume II/3.*

Gese, Michael: Das Vermächtnis des Apostels.
1997. *Volume II/99.*

Gheorghita, Radu: The Role of the Septuagint
in Hebrews. 2003. *Volume II/160.*

Gräbe, Petrus J.: The Power of God in Paul's
Letters. 2000. *Volume II/123.*

Gräßer, Erich: Der Alte Bund im Neuen. 1985.
Volume 35.
– Forschungen zur Apostelgeschichte. 2001.
Volume 137.

Green, Joel B.: The Death of Jesus. 1988.
Volume II/33.

Gregory, Andrew: The Reception of Luke and
Acts in the Period before Irenaeus. 2003.
Volume II/169.

Gundry Volf, Judith M.: Paul and Perseverance.
1990. *Volume II/37.*

Hafemann, Scott J.: Suffering and the Spirit.
1986. *Volume II/19.*
– Paul, Moses, and the History of Israel. 1995.
Volume 81.

Hahn, Johannes (Ed.): Zerstörungen des
Jerusalemer Tempels. 2002. *Volume 147.*

Hannah, Darrel D.: Michael and Christ. 1999.
Volume II/109.

Hamid-Khani, Saeed: Relevation and Concealment of Christ. 2000. *Volume II/120.*

Harrison; James R.: Paul's Language of Grace
in Its Graeco-Roman Context. 2003.
Volume II/172.

Hartman, Lars: Text-Centered New Testament
Studies. Ed. von D. Hellholm. 1997.
Volume 102.

Hartog, Paul: Polycarp and the New Testament.
2001. *Volume II/134.*

Heckel, Theo K.: Der Innere Mensch. 1993.
Volume II/53.
– Vom Evangelium des Markus zum viergestal-
tigen Evangelium. 1999. *Volume 120.*

Heckel, Ulrich: Kraft in Schwachheit. 1993.
Volume II/56.
– Der Segen im Neuen Testament. 2002.
Volume 150.
– see *Feldmeier, Reinhard.*
– see *Hengel, Martin.*

Heiligenthal, Roman: Werke als Zeichen. 1983.
Volume II/9.

Hellholm, D.: see *Hartman, Lars.*

Hemer, Colin J.: The Book of Acts in the Setting
of Hellenistic History. 1989. *Volume 49.*

Hengel, Martin: Judentum und Hellenismus.
1969, ³1988. *Volume 10.*
– Die johanneische Frage. 1993. *Volume 67.*
– Judaica et Hellenistica.
Kleine Schriften I. 1996. *Volume 90.*
– Judaica, Hellenistica et Christiana.
Kleine Schriften II. 1999. *Volume 109.*
– Paulus und Jakobus.
Kleine Schriften III. 2002. *Volume 141.*

Hengel, Martin and *Ulrich Heckel* (Ed.): Paulus
und das antike Judentum. 1991. *Volume 58.*

Hengel, Martin and *Hermut Löhr* (Ed.):
Schriftauslegung im antiken Judentum und
im Urchristentum. 1994. *Volume 73.*

Hengel, Martin and *Anna Maria Schwemer:*
Paulus zwischen Damaskus und Antiochien.
1998. *Volume 108.*
– Der messianische Anspruch Jesu und die
Anfänge der Christologie. 2001. *Volume 138.*

Hengel, Martin and *Anna Maria Schwemer*
(Ed.): Königsherrschaft Gottes und himm-
lischer Kult. 1991. *Volume 55.*
– Die Septuaginta. 1994. *Volume 72.*

Hengel, Martin; Siegfried Mittmann and *Anna
Maria Schwemer* (Ed.): La Cité de Dieu /
Die Stadt Gottes. 2000. *Volume 129.*

Herrenbrück, Fritz: Jesus und die Zöllner. 1990.
Volume II/41.

Herzer, Jens: Paulus oder Petrus? 1998. *Volume 103.*

Hoegen-Rohls, Christina: Der nachösterliche Johannes. 1996. *Volume II/84.*

Hofius, Otfried: Katapausis. 1970. *Volume 11.*

– Der Vorhang vor dem Thron Gottes. 1972. *Volume 14.*

– Der Christushymnus Philipper 2,6-11. 1976, ²1991. *Volume 17.*

– Paulusstudien. 1989, ²1994. *Volume 51.*

– Neutestamentliche Studien. 2000. *Volume 132.*

– Paulusstudien II. 2002. *Volume 143.*

Hofius, Otfried and *Hans-Christian Kammler:* Johannesstudien. 1996. *Volume 88.*

Holtz, Traugott: Geschichte und Theologie des Urchristentums. 1991. *Volume 57.*

Hommel, Hildebrecht: Sebasmata. Volume 1 1983. *Volume 31* – Volume 2 1984. *Volume 32.*

Hvalvik, Reidar: The Struggle for Scripture and Covenant. 1996. *Volume II/82.*

Johns, Loren L.: The Lamb Christology of the Apocalypse of John. 2003. *Volume II/167.*

Joubert, Stephan: Paul as Benefactor. 2000. *Volume II/124.*

Jungbauer, Harry: „Ehre Vater und Mutter". 2002. *Volume II/146.*

Kähler, Christoph: Jesu Gleichnisse als Poesie und Therapie. 1995. *Volume 78.*

Kamlah, Ehrhard: Die Form der katalogischen Paränese im Neuen Testament. 1964. *Volume 7.*

Kammler, Hans-Christian: Christologie und Eschatologie. 2000. *Volume 126.*

– Kreuz und Weisheit. 2003. *Volume 159.*

– see *Hofius, Otfried.*

Kelhoffer, James A.: Miracle and Mission. 1999. *Volume II/112.*

Kieffer, René and *Jan Bergman (Ed.):* La Main de Dieu / Die Hand Gottes. 1997. *Volume 94.*

Kim, Seyoon: The Origin of Paul's Gospel. 1981, ²1984. *Volume II/4.*

– "The 'Son of Man'" as the Son of God. 1983. *Volume 30.*

Klauck, Hans-Josef: Religion und Gesellschaft im frühen Christentum. 2003. *Volume 152.*

Klein, Hans: see *Dunn, James D.G.*.

Kleinknecht, Karl Th.: Der leidende Gerechtfertigte. 1984, ²1988. *Volume II/13.*

Klinghardt, Matthias: Gesetz und Volk Gottes. 1988. *Volume II/32.*

Koch, Michael: Drachenkampf und Sonnenfrau. 2004. *Volume II/184.*

Koch, Stefan: Rechtliche Regelung von Konflikten im frühen Christentum. 2004. *Volume II/174.*

Köhler, Wolf-Dietrich: Rezeption des Matthäusevangeliums in der Zeit vor Irenäus. 1987. *Volume II/24.*

Köhn, Andreas: Der Neutestamentler Ernst Lohmeyer. 2004. *Band II/180.*

Kooten, George H. van: Cosmic Christology in Paul and the Pauline School. 2003. *Volume II/171.*

Korn, Manfred: Die Geschichte Jesu in veränderter Zeit. 1993. *Volume II/51.*

Koskenniemi, Erkki: Apollonios von Tyana in der neutestamentlichen Exegese. 1994. *Volume II/61.*

Kraus, Thomas J.: Sprache, Stil und historischer Ort des zweiten Petrusbriefes. 2001. *Volume II/136.*

Kraus, Wolfgang: Das Volk Gottes. 1996. *Volume 85.*

– and *Karl-Wilhelm Niebuhr (Ed.):* Frühjudentum und Neues Testament im Horizont Biblischer Theologie. 2003. *Volume 162.*

– see *Walter, Nikolaus.*

Kreplin, Matthias: Das Selbstverständnis Jesu. 2001. *Volume II/141.*

Kuhn, Karl G.: Achtzehngebet und Vaterunser und der Reim. 1950. *Volume 1.*

Kvalbein, Hans: see *Ådna, Jostein.*

Kwon, Yon-Gyong: Eschatology in Galatians. 2004. *Volume II/183.*

Laansma, Jon: I Will Give You Rest. 1997. *Volume II/98.*

Labahn, Michael: Offenbarung in Zeichen und Wort. 2000. *Volume II/117.*

Lambers-Petry, Doris: see *Tomson, Peter J.*

Lange, Armin: see *Ego, Beate.*

Lampe, Peter: Die stadtrömischen Christen in den ersten beiden Jahrhunderten. 1987, ²1989. *Volume II/18.*

Landmesser, Christof: Wahrheit als Grundbegriff neutestamentlicher Wissenschaft. 1999. *Volume 113.*

– Jüngerberufung und Zuwendung zu Gott. 2000. *Volume 133.*

Lau, Andrew: Manifest in Flesh. 1996. *Volume II/86.*

Lawrence, Louise: An Ethnography of the Gospel of Matthew. 2003. *Volume II/165.*

Lee, Pilchan: The New Jerusalem in the Book of Relevation. 2000. *Volume II/129.*

Lichtenberger, Hermann: see *Avemarie, Friedrich.*

Lichtenberger, Hermann: Das Ich Adams und das Ich der Menschheit. 2004. *Volume 164.*

Lierman, John: The New Testament Moses. 2004. *Volume II/173.*

Lieu, Samuel N.C.: Manichaeism in the Later Roman Empire and Medieval China. ²1992. *Volume 63.*

Loader, William R.G.: Jesus' Attitude Towards the Law. 1997. *Volume II/97.*

Löhr, Gebhard: Verherrlichung Gottes durch Philosophie. 1997. *Volume 97.*

Löhr, Hermut: Studien zum frühchristlichen und frühjüdischen Gebet. 2003. *Volume160.*

– *:* see *Hengel, Martin.*

Löhr, Winrich Alfried: Basilides und seine Schule. 1995. *Volume 83.*

Luomanen, Petri: Entering the Kingdom of Heaven. 1998. *Volume II/101.*

Luz, Ulrich: see *Dunn, James D.G.*

Mackay, Ian D.: John's Raltionship with Mark. 2004. *Volume II/182.*

Maier, Gerhard: Mensch und freier Wille. 1971. *Volume 12.*

– Die Johannesoffenbarung und die Kirche. 1981. *Volume 25.*

Markschies, Christoph: Valentinus Gnosticus? 1992. *Volume 65.*

Marshall, Peter: Enmity in Corinth: Social Conventions in Paul's Relations with the Corinthians. 1987. *Volume II/23.*

Mayer, Annemarie: Sprache der Einheit im Epheserbrief und in der Ökumene. 2002. *Volume II/150.*

McDonough, Sean M.: YHWH at Patmos: Rev. 1:4 in its Hellenistic and Early Jewish Setting. 1999. *Volume II/107.*

McGlynn, Moyna: Divine Judgement and Divine Benevolence in the Book of Wisdom. 2001. *Volume II/139.*

Meade, David G.: Pseudonymity and Canon. 1986. *Volume 39.*

Meadors, Edward P.: Jesus the Messianic Herald of Salvation. 1995. *Volume II/72.*

Meißner, Stefan: Die Heimholung des Ketzers. 1996. *Volume II/87.*

Mell, Ulrich: Die „anderen" Winzer. 1994. *Volume 77.*

Mengel, Berthold: Studien zum Philipperbrief. 1982. *Volume II/8.*

Merkel, Helmut: Die Widersprüche zwischen den Evangelien. 1971. *Volume 13.*

Merklein, Helmut: Studien zu Jesus und Paulus. Volume 1 1987. *Volume 43.* – Volume 2 1998. *Volume 105.*

Metzdorf, Christina: Die Tempelaktion Jesu. 2003. *Volume II/168.*

Metzler, Karin: Der griechische Begriff des Verzeihens. 1991. *Volume II/44.*

Metzner, Rainer: Die Rezeption des Matthäusevangeliums im 1. Petrusbrief. 1995. *Volume II/74.*

– Das Verständnis der Sünde im Johannesevangelium. 2000. *Volume 122.*

Mihoc, Vasile: see *Dunn, James D.G..*

Mineshige, Kiyoshi: Besitzverzicht und Almosen bei Lukas. 2003. *Volume II/163.*

Mittmann, Siegfried: see *Hengel, Martin.*

Mittmann-Richert, Ulrike: Magnifikat und Benediktus. *1996. Volume II/90.*

Mußner, Franz: Jesus von Nazareth im Umfeld Israels und der Urkirche. Ed. von M. Theobald. 1998. *Volume 111.*

Niebuhr, Karl-Wilhelm: Gesetz und Paränese. 1987. *Volume II/28.*

– Heidenapostel aus Israel. 1992. *Volume 62.*

– see *Deines, Roland*

– see *Kraus, Wolfgang*

Nielsen, Anders E.: "Until it is Fullfilled". 2000. *Volume II/126.*

Nissen, Andreas: Gott und der Nächste im antiken Judentum. 1974. *Volume 15.*

Noack, Christian: Gottesbewußtsein. 2000. *Volume II/116.*

Noormann, Rolf: Irenäus als Paulusinterpret. 1994. *Volume II/66.*

Novakovic, Lidija: Messiah, the Healer of the Sick. 2003. *Volume II/170.*

Obermann, Andreas: Die christologische Erfüllung der Schrift im Johannesevangelium. 1996. *Volume II/83.*

Öhler, Markus: Barnabas. 2003. *Volume 156.*

Okure, Teresa: The Johannine Approach to Mission. 1988. *Volume II/31.*

Onuki, Takashi: Heil und Erlösung. 2004. *Volume 165.*

Oropeza, B. J.: Paul and Apostasy. 2000. *Volume II/115.*

Ostmeyer, Karl-Heinrich: Taufe und Typos. 2000. *Volume II/118.*

Paulsen, Henning: Studien zur Literatur und Geschichte des frühen Christentums. Ed. von Ute E. Eisen. 1997. *Volume 99.*

Pao, David W.: Acts and the Isaianic New Exodus. 2000. *Volume II/130.*

Park, Eung Chun: The Mission Discourse in Matthew's Interpretation. 1995. *Volume II/81.*

Park, Joseph S.: Conceptions of Afterlife in Jewish Insriptions. 2000. *Volume II/121.*

Pate, C. Marvin: The Reverse of the Curse. 2000. *Volume II/114.*

Peres, Imre: Griechische Grabinschriften und neutestamentliche Eschatologie. 2003. *Volume 157.*

Philonenko, Marc (Ed.): Le Trône de Dieu. 1993. *Volume 69.*

Pilhofer, Peter: Presbyteron Kreitton. 1990. *Volume II/39.*

– Philippi. Volume 1 1995. *Volume 87.* – Volume 2 2000. *Volume 119.*

– Die frühen Christen und ihre Welt. 2002. *Volume 145.*

– see *Ego, Beate.*

Plümacher, Eckhard: Geschichte und Geschichten. Aufsätze zur Apostelgeschichte und zu den Johannesakten. Herausgegeben von Jens Schröter und Ralph Brucker. 2004. *Volume 170.*

Pöhlmann, Wolfgang: Der Verlorene Sohn und das Haus. 1993. *Volume 68.*

Pokorný, Petr and *Josef B. Souček:* Bibelauslegung als Theologie. 1997. *Volume 100.*

Pokorný, Petr and *Jan Roskovec* (Ed.): Philosophical Hermeneutics and Biblical Exegesis. 2002. *Volume 153.*

Porter, Stanley E.: The Paul of Acts. 1999. *Volume 115.*

Prieur, Alexander: Die Verkündigung der Gottesherrschaft. 1996. *Volume II/89.*

Probst, Hermann: Paulus und der Brief. 1991. *Volume II/45.*

Räisänen, Heikki: Paul and the Law. 1983, ²1987. *Volume 29.*

Rehkopf, Friedrich: Die lukanische Sonderquelle. 1959. *Volume 5.*

Rein, Matthias: Die Heilung des Blindgeborenen (Joh 9). 1995. *Volume II/73.*

Reinmuth, Eckart: Pseudo-Philo und Lukas. 1994. *Volume 74.*

Reiser, Marius: Syntax und Stil des Markusevangeliums. 1984. *Volume II/11.*

Richards, E. Randolph: The Secretary in the Letters of Paul. 1991. *Volume II/42.*

Riesner, Rainer: Jesus als Lehrer. 1981, ³1988. *Volume II/7.*

– Die Frühzeit des Apostels Paulus. 1994. *Volume 71.*

Rissi, Mathias: Die Theologie des Hebräerbriefs. 1987. *Volume 41.*

Roskovec, Jan: see *Pokorný, Petr.*

Röhser, Günter: Metaphorik und Personifikation der Sünde. 1987. *Volume II/25.*

Rose, Christian: Die Wolke der Zeugen. 1994. *Volume II/60.*

Rothschild, Clare K.: Luke Acts and the Rhetoric of History. 2004. *Volume II/175.*

Rüegger, Hans-Ulrich: Verstehen, was Markus erzählt. 2002. *Volume II/155.*

Rüger, Hans Peter: Die Weisheitsschrift aus der Kairoer Geniza. 1991. *Volume 53.*

Sänger, Dieter: Antikes Judentum und die Mysterien. 1980. *Volume II/5.*

– Die Verkündigung des Gekreuzigten und Israel. 1994. *Volume 75.*

– see *Burchard, Christoph*

Salier, Willis Hedley: The Rhetorical Impact of the Sēmeia in the Gospel of John. 2004. *Volume II/186.*

Salzmann, Jorg Christian: Lehren und Ermahnen. 1994. *Volume II/59.*

Sandnes, Karl Olav: Paul – One of the Prophets? 1991. *Volume II/43.*

Sato, Migaku: Q und Prophetie. 1988. *Volume II/29.*

Schäfer, Ruth: Paulus bis zum Apostelkonzil. 2004. *Volume II/179.*

Schaper, Joachim: Eschatology in the Greek Psalter. 1995. *Volume II/76.*

Schimanowski, Gottfried: Die himmlische Liturgie in der Apokalypse des Johannes. 2002. *Volume II/154.*

– Weisheit und Messias. 1985. *Volume II/17.*

Schlichting, Günter: Ein jüdisches Leben Jesu. 1982. *Volume 24.*

Schnabel, Eckhard J.: Law and Wisdom from Ben Sira to Paul. 1985. *Volume II/16.*

Schutter, William L.: Hermeneutic and Composition in I Peter. 1989. *Volume II/30.*

Schwartz, Daniel R.: Studies in the Jewish Background of Christianity. 1992. *Volume 60.*

Schwemer, Anna Maria: see *Hengel, Martin*

Scott, James M.: Adoption as Sons of God. 1992. *Volume II/48.*

– Paul and the Nations. 1995. *Volume 84.*

Shum, Shiu-Lun: Paul's Use of Isaiah in Romans. 2002. *Volume II/156.*

Siegert, Folker: Drei hellenistisch-jüdische Predigten. Teil I 1980. *Volume 20* – Teil II 1992. *Volume 61.*

– Nag-Hammadi-Register. 1982. *Volume 26.*

– Argumentation bei Paulus. 1985. *Volume 34.*

– Philon von Alexandrien. 1988. *Volume 46.*

Simon, Marcel: Le christianisme antique et son contexte religieux I/II. 1981. *Volume 23.*

Snodgrass, Klyne: The Parable of the Wicked Tenants. 1983. *Volume 27.*

Söding, Thomas: Das Wort vom Kreuz. 1997. *Volume 93.*

– see *Thüsing, Wilhelm.*

Sommer, Urs: Die Passionsgeschichte des Markusevangeliums. 1993. *Volume II/58.*

Souček, Josef B.: see *Pokorný, Petr.*

Spangenberg, Volker: Herrlichkeit des Neuen Bundes. 1993. *Volume II/55.*

Spanje, T.E. van: Inconsistency in Paul? 1999.
Volume II/110.
Speyer, Wolfgang: Frühes Christentum im
antiken Strahlungsfeld. Volume I: 1989.
Volume 50.
– Volume II: 1999. *Volume 116.*
Stadelmann, Helge: Ben Sira als Schriftgelehr-
ter. 1980. *Volume II/6.*
Stenschke, Christoph W.: Luke's Portrait of
Gentiles Prior to Their Coming to Faith.
Volume II/108.
Sterck-Degueldre, Jean-Pierre: Eine Frau
namens Lydia. 2004. *Volume II/176.*
Stettler, Christian: Der Kolosserhymnus. 2000.
Volume II/131.
Stettler, Hanna: Die Christologie der Pastoral-
briefe. 1998. *Volume II/105.*
Stökl Ben Ezra, Daniel: The Impact of
Yom Kippur on Early Christianity. 2003.
Volume 163.
Strobel, August: Die Stunde der Wahrheit. 1980.
Volume 21.
Stroumsa, Guy G.: Barbarian Philosophy. 1999.
Volume 112.
Stuckenbruck, Loren T.: Angel Veneration and
Christology. 1995. *Volume II/70.*
Stuhlmacher, Peter (Ed.): Das Evangelium und
die Evangelien. 1983. *Volume 28.*
– Biblische Theologie und Evangelium. 2002.
Volume 146.
Sung, Chong-Hyon: Vergebung der Sünden.
1993. *Volume II/57.*
Tajra, Harry W.: The Trial of St. Paul. 1989.
Volume II/35.
– The Martyrdom of St.Paul. 1994.
Volume II/67.
Theißen, Gerd: Studien zur Soziologie des
Urchristentums. 1979, ³1989. *Volume 19.*
Theobald, Michael: Studien zum Römerbrief.
2001. *Volume 136.*
Theobald, Michael: see *Mußner, Franz.*
Thornton, Claus-Jürgen: Der Zeuge des
Zeugen. 1991. *Volume 56.*
Thüsing, Wilhelm: Studien zur neutestamentli-
chen Theologie. Ed. von Thomas Söding.
1995. *Volume 82.*
Thurén, Lauri: Derhethorizing Paul. 2000.
Volume 124.
Tomson, Peter J. and *Doris Lambers-Petry*
(Ed.): The Image of the Judaeo-Christians in
Ancient Jewish and Christian Literature.
2003. *Volume 158.*

Trebilco, Paul: The Early Christians in Ephesus
from Paul to Ignatius. 2004. *Volume 166.*
Treloar, Geoffrey R.: Lightfoot the Historian.
1998. *Volume II/103.*
Tsuji, Manabu: Glaube zwischen Vollkommen-
heit und Verweltlichung. 1997. *Volume II/93*
Twelftree, Graham H.: Jesus the Exorcist. 1993.
Volume II/54.
Urban, Christina: Das Menschenbild nach dem
Johannesevangelium. 2001. *Volume II/137.*
Visotzky, Burton L.: Fathers of the World. 1995.
Volume 80.
Vollenweider, Samuel: Horizonte neutestamentli-
cher Christologie. 2002. *Volume 144.*
Vos, Johan S.: Die Kunst der Argumentation bei
Paulus. 2002. *Volume 149.*
Wagener, Ulrike: Die Ordnung des „Hauses
Gottes". 1994. *Volume II/65.*
Walker, Donald D.: Paul's Offer of Leniency
(2 Cor 10:1). 2002. *Volume II/152.*
Walter, Nikolaus: Praeparatio Evangelica. Ed.
von Wolfgang Kraus und Florian Wilk.
1997. *Volume 98.*
Wander, Bernd: Gottesfürchtige und Sympathi-
santen. 1998. *Volume 104.*
Watts, Rikki: Isaiah's New Exodus and Mark.
1997. *Volume II/88.*
Wedderburn, A.J.M.: Baptism and Resurrection.
1987. *Volume 44.*
Wegner, Uwe: Der Hauptmann von Kafarnaum.
1985. *Volume II/14.*
Weissenrieder, Annette: Images of Illness in the
Gospel of Luke. 2003. Volume II/164.
Welck, Christian: Erzählte ‚Zeichen'. 1994.
Volume II/69.
Wiarda, Timothy: Peter in the Gospels . 2000.
Volume II/127.
Wilk, Florian: see *Walter, Nikolaus.*
Williams, Catrin H.: I am He. 2000.
Volume II/113.
Wilson, Walter T.: Love without Pretense. 1991.
Volume II/46.
Wischmeyer, Oda: Von Ben Sira zu Paulus.
2004. *Volume 178.*
Wisdom, Jeffrey: Blessing for the Nations and
the Curse of the Law. 2001. *Volume II/133.*
Wucherpfennig, Ansgar: Heracleon Philologus.
2002. *Volume 142.*
Yeung, Maureen: Faith in Jesus and Paul. 2002.
Volume II/147.

*For a complete catalogue please write to the publisher
Mohr Siebeck • P.O. Box 2030 • D–72010 Tübingen/Germany
Up-to-date information on the internet at www.mohr.de*